Advanced Rese:
Applied Psychol.gy

MW01196660

This is the first comprehensive guide to the range of research methods available to applied psychologists. Ideally suited to students and researchers alike, and covering both quantitative and qualitative techniques, the book takes readers on a journey from research design to final reporting.

The book is divided into four sections, with chapters written by leading international researchers working in a range of applied settings:

- Getting Started
- Data Collection
- Data Analysis
- Research Dissemination

With coverage of sampling and ethical issues, and chapters on everything from experimental and quasi-experimental designs to longitudinal data collection and focus groups, the book provides a concise overview not only of the options available for applied research but also of how to make sense of the data produced. It includes chapters on organisational interventions and the use of digital technologies and concludes with chapters on how to publish your research, whether it's a thesis, journal article or organisational report.

This is a must-have book for anyone conducting psychological research in an applied setting.

Paula Brough is Professor of Organisational Psychology in the School of Applied Psychology, Griffith University, Australia. Paula conducts research in organisational psychology with a specific focus on occupational health psychology. Paula's primary research areas include: occupational stress, employee health and well-being, work-life balance and the psychosocial work environment. Paula assesses how work environments can be improved via job redesign, supportive leadership practices and enhanced equity to improve employee health, work commitment and productivity. Paula is an editorial board member of the *Journal of Organisational Behavior, Work and Stress* and the *International Journal of Stress Management*.

Advanced Research Methods for Applied Psychology

Design, Analysis and Reporting

Edited by
Paula Brough

Routledge
Taylor & Francis Group

LONDON AND NEW YORK

First published 2019
by Routledge
2 Park Square, Milton Park, Abingdon, Oxon OX14 4RN

and by Routledge
711 Third Avenue, New York, NY 10017

Routledge is an imprint of the Taylor & Francis Group, an informa business

British Library Cataloguing-in-Publication Data
A catalogue record for this book is available from the British Library

Library of Congress Cataloging-in-Publication Data
Names: Brough, Paula, editor.
Title: Advanced research methods for applied psychology: design, analysis and reporting / edited by Paula Brough.
Description: Abingdon, Oxon; New York, NY: Routledge, [2018] | Includes bibliographical references and index.
Identifiers: LCCN 2018013223 | ISBN 9781138698895 (hb : alk. paper) | ISBN 9781138698901 (pb : alk. paper) | ISBN 9781315517971 (eb)
Subjects: LCSH: Psychology, Applied—Methodology.
Classification: LCC BF636 .A33 2018 | DDC 158.072/1—dc23
LC record available at https://lccn.loc.gov/2018013223

ISBN: 978-1-138-69889-5 (hbk)
ISBN: 978-1-138-69890-1 (pbk)
ISBN: 978-1-315-51797-1 (ebk)

Typeset in Bembo
by Apex CoVantage, LLC

For Doug and Sylvester, with thanks for all the life, love and laughter.

Contents

Contributors

Gary Allen *Griffith University, Australia*

Amanda Biggs *Griffith University, Australia*

Duygu Biricik Gulseren *Saint Mary's University, Canada*

Candice Bowman *Griffith University, Australia*

Paula Brough *Griffith University, Australia*

Jennifer Brown *Mannheim Centre for Criminology, London School of Economics, UK*

Dorey S. Chaffee *Colorado State University, USA*

Rachel Davies *Griffith University, Australia*

Christian Dormann *University of Mainz, Germany*

Patrick D. Dunlop *University of Western Australia, Australia*

Erin M. Eatough *Baruch College & The Graduate Center, CUNY, USA*

Roberta Fida *University of East Anglia, UK, and Sapienza University of Rome, Italy*

Gwenith G. Fisher *Colorado State University, USA*

Toni Fowlie *University of Waikato, New Zealand*

David Gough *University College London, UK*

Bradley E. Gray *Baruch College & The Graduate Center, CUNY, USA*

Christina Guthier *University of Mainz, Germany*

Amy Hawkes *Griffith University, Australia*

Joel M. Hektner *North Dakota State University, USA*

Joshua L. Howard *University of Western Australia, Australia*

Liz Jones *Griffith University, Australia*

E. Kevin Kelloway *Saint Mary's University, Canada*

Craig McGarty *Western Sydney University, Australia*

Olav Muurlink *Central Queensland University, Australia*

Kimberly A. Neuendorf *Cleveland State University, USA*

Stefano Occhipinti *Griffith University, Australia*

Michael O'Driscoll *University of Waikato, New Zealand*

John O'Gorman *Griffith University, Australia*

Seamus O'Reilly *Cork University Business School, Ireland*

Michelle Richardson *University College London, UK*

Andrew Robertson *TRA, New Zealand*

Maree Roche *University of Waikato, New Zealand*

Alan Sloane *Cork University Business School, Ireland*

David Shum *Griffith University, Australia*

Chris G. Sibley *University of Auckland, New Zealand*

Caley Tapp *Griffith University, Australia*

Carlo Tramontano *Coventry University, UK*

Danielle R. Wald *Baruch College & The Graduate Center, CUNY, USA*

Zoe C. Walter *University of Queensland, Australia*

Stephen A. Woods *University of Surrey, UK*

Yanyun Yang *Florida State University, USA*

William H. Yeaton *Florida State University, USA*

Michael J. Zyphur *The University of Melbourne, Australia*

1 Introduction to *Advanced Research Methods for Applied Psychologists*

Paula Brough

Introduction

The necessity for this book primarily arose from the long-term recognition that many post-graduates do not seem to be suitably equipped to consider the multiple nuances involved in conducting high quality psychological research. In addition, their available pathways to suitably educate themselves about research designs, research methods, data cleaning, statistical analyses, academic writing, and so on were multiple and somewhat convoluted. What was needed was a 'one-stop shop' discussing current research dilemmas to inform and assist them in their research training. An informed collection of current research methods and analyses issues providing a broad overview of the most relevant research topics for thesis students and other researchers in this field was considered to be of the most value, with clear directions also provided to explore more detailed discussions about each topic.

The aim of this book, therefore, is to assist (novice) researchers to understand how topics such as research design, data collection techniques, missing data analysis, and research outputs, for example, are all inter-related and that each should be duly considered when starting a research project. The 'siloing' of such key research topics (e.g., 'research design', 'statistical analysis', 'research publication') is acknowledged to be necessary for a suitable depth of detail. However, this compartmentalisation also contains the risk that researchers, even at the post-graduate level, may overlook the broad context and may not fully consider all the essential factors required to produce high quality research. Importantly, this book is intended to provide a direct bridge between pertinent academic research in research methods and the conducting of a research thesis within the applied psychology field. This book therefore fills a widely acknowledged gap concerning the difficulties interpreting the enormous field of research method literature, including recent developments, by junior researchers.

The increasing volume of postgraduate researchers in psychology and related fields is indicative of several key drivers, namely: a growth in intrinsic interest to conduct psychological research; recognition of the value of a postgraduate qualification for career development; and arguably the strongest driver (within Australia at least), the increased requirement for psychologists to complete a postgraduate qualification containing a research thesis component for professional psychology registration purposes. Hence the motivations of postgraduates to undertake their research project are mixed, to say the least. At the same time, most university academics are experiencing significant work-intensification processes. Academic time spent in teaching, research, and supervision work tasks are subject to increased monitoring and being reduced into specific allocations of work hours (e.g., a formal allocation of 18 hours per year to supervise a psychology master's student in their thesis research), while annual academic outputs in both the research and teaching components are subject to increasing (and often unrealistic) pressures. The resulting time available for the supervision of theses research students is therefore becoming increasingly compressed. Therefore, this book is intended to be of direct value to both (increasingly busy) academic supervisors and their theses students as a useful reference point for the most relevant issues concerned with the conducting of postgraduate thesis research.

This book provides pertinent reviews of 24 key and current topics relevant to researchers within applied psychology and related fields. This book discusses the entire research process and is divided into four sections for clarity:

1   Section 1: *Getting started.* This first section focuses on the initial research planning and design stages and consists of four chapters discussing the design of impactful research (Chapter 2); research sampling techniques (Chapter 3); research ethics and legal issues (Chapter 4); and instrumentation (Chapter 5).

2   Section 2: *Data collection.* This section provides a review of 10 of the most common methods of data collection. The chapters discuss the most relevant issues concerning systematic reviews and meta-analyses (Chapter 6); the use of archival data (Chapter 7); an overview of qualitative research methods (Chapter 8); interviews, focus groups and the Delphi technique (Chapter 9); experimental and quasi-experimental research designs (Chapter 10); surveys and web research (Chapter 11); assessing cognitive processes (Chapter 12); longitudinal data collection (Chapter 13); diary studies, event sampling, and smart phone 'apps' (Chapter 14); and the design of organisational interventions (Chapter 15).

3   Section 3: *The nitty gritty: data analysis.* This collection of eight chapters discusses what to do with data once it is collected. These chapters focus on the different methods of treating missing data (Chapter 16); preparing data for analysis (Chapter 17); content analysis and thematic analysis (Chapter 18); conducting 'real' statistical analyses (Chapter 19); using mediation test and confidence intervals with bootstrapping (Chapter 20); the use of structural equation modelling (Chapter 21); multilevel modelling (Chapter 22); and finally data assessments via social network analysis (Chapter 23).

4   Section 4: *Research dissemination.* The final section consists of two chapters which discuss the two main methods to write up and disseminate

thesis research, namely, a discussion of how to publish research (Chapter 24), and finally, the key considerations in writing up research for theses and organisational reports (Chapter 25).

I am extremely grateful to the esteemed group of experts featured in this collection, who each provided thoughtful discussions about these 24 pertinent topics impacting applied psychological research and related fields. I am appreciative of my invitations answered from all over the world with enthusiasm from key leaders in their fields. This has provided the book with a strong international perspective, which was my goal, for none of these research issues are limited to any one specific geographical context. I also aimed to ensure representation of the chapter authors from all fractions of applied psychology (e.g., clinical, organisational, social, occupational health, developmental, forensic, and cognitive) and a variety of related fields (e.g., business, law, management, mathematics, and computer science).

I believe this book has achieved my aims of providing an initial 'one-stop shop' for those at the early stages of conducting applied psychological research. All researchers regardless of their level of experience are certainly encouraged to produce high quality research which offers a meaningful contribution to the advancement of applied psychological knowledge. I hope this book directly assists you to achieve this research quality within your own project, and also conveys to you the excitement and enthusiasm for research and its multiple processes, which I and all the chapter authors readily expressed.

With my very best wishes for your research adventures!

Professor Paula Brough

Section 1

Getting Started

This first section of this book focuses on the initial research planning and design stages. The four chapters here will furnish you with valuable information about what research is all about and will hopefully help you to answer your own basic question of *why* you are doing all of this. These chapters remind you about the value of **designing your research** so that it can actually have an impact (Chapter 2) and of how to decide upon your **research sample** and how to recruit (and retain) your research participants (Chapter 3). Chapter 4 provides essential information about how to conduct **ethical research**, and Chapter 5 discusses how to choose and/or design **research measures** for inclusion in your study.

2 Designing impactful research

Paula Brough and Amy Hawkes

Introduction: ensuring research has impact

The necessity of spending sufficient time designing a research project cannot be emphasised enough. In practice, research projects are often influenced by time, resources, or sampling constraints, and these are, of course, the key 'research limitations' commonly listed in both published research articles and research theses. It is unfortunate that producing research which has relatively little impact (other than for the researcher themselves) is quite easy to accomplish. We acknowledge that a student's experience of research training gained via the production of a research thesis is a viable outcome in itself. However, we also recognise that student research projects can often produce minimal other impact (i.e., for an organisation and/or for scholarly knowledge), and this is often a consequence of an inadequate project design. Appropriately designing a research project to produce useful insights and actual advances in knowledge requires time and thoughtful consideration. Allowing for insufficient time to thoroughly design a project is a common mistake made at all levels of research. In this chapter we discuss five of the basic features of applied psychological research which are essential to consider in the appropriate design of research and which maximise the opportunities of research achieving an actual external impact.

The applied scientific method

The training in how to conduct impactful research is a continuous developmental process that is improved with direct experience and with the value of hindsight. However, good research is also directly informed by the existing scholarly evidence and the critical consideration of key research principles, namely those of the *scientific method*. As researchers we are taught the basic principles of conducting *good science*, which in sum consists of the planned inclusion of 'reliable and valid measures, sufficient and generalisable samples, theoretical sophistication, and research design that promotes causal generalisations' (Sinclair, Wang, & Tetrick, 2013, p. 397). Additionally, as *applied researchers*, appropriate considerations must also be given to the implications of the research for society, organisations, and/or other end users. Pertinent discussions of the evolution of the scientific method for applied psychology research are plentiful and are recommended for further reading (e.g., Gurung et al., 2016; Hubbard, 2016). These discussions also include notable critiques of pertinent research issues, such as the recognition of common weaknesses (e.g., bias, replicability), avoiding arbitrary choices of analyses (e.g., Ioannidis et al., 2014), and an understanding of *conceptual* and *terminological diversity*, which is the use of multiple names within the literature for the same essential ideas (Sinclair et al., 2013). The components of the applied scientific method identified can be considered as a useful guide to planning and designing research projects. We discuss these five research principles in more detail here and strongly encourage researchers to confirm that their projects do adequately address each one of these principles.

The inclusion of reliable and valid measures

It is rare for a psychological construct to be assessed by just one specific measure. Instead, multiple measures commonly exist within the literature purporting to assess any single construct. For example, even a construct as specific as psychological burnout is typically assessed by one of three instruments: the *Maslach Burnout Inventory* (MBI) (Maslach, Jackson, & Leiter, 1981), the *Copenhagen Burnout Inventory* (CBI) (Kristensen, Borritz, Villadsen, & Christensen, 2005), and the *Oldenburg Burnout Inventory* (OLBI) (Halbesleben & Demerouti, 2005). However, a very commonly assessed construct such as job satisfaction is measured by a multitude of different instruments, some of which assess job satisfaction within specific occupations such as human services (Spector, 1985) and nursing (Mueller & McCloskey, 1990; Stamps & Piedmonte, 1986). Other job satisfaction measures are targeted more generally across workers from multiple occupations (e.g., Brayfield & Rothe, 1951; Lambert, Hogan, & Barton, 2001; Seashore, Lawler, Mirvis, & Cammann, 1982; Warr, Cook, & Wall, 1979), while other 'measures' of job satisfaction are devised of just one item; for a pertinent review of these single item assessments, see, for example, Wanous, Reichers, and Hudy (1997).

The diligent researcher is therefore recommended to amass the multiple measures of *each* research construct from the literature and review each measure for appropriate levels of validity and reliability (as well as other characteristics such as relevance to the research sample, etc.). These two psychometric characteristics for each measure should be described within the thesis (both as reported within the literature and as produced by the researcher's project), thereby clearly demonstrating evidence for the suitability of each individual measure included in the research. With such an array of published measures to choose from, the inclusion of an instrument with *inadequate* psychometric characteristics (e.g., a scale reliability coefficient of below .70) is difficult to justify within a research thesis and is indicative of an inadequate level of research skills and/or comprehension. It is, therefore, surprising and very unfortunate how often measures described by inadequate psychometric characteristics are actually included in post-graduate research projects. A more detailed discussion about the selection of appropriate research measures is provided in Chapter 5: 'Instrumentation'.

The inclusion of sufficient and generalisable research samples

Often applied psychological research is restricted by the access to an appropriate research sample. The inclusion of a relatively easy to access ('convenient') undergraduate student research sample is often utilised within pilot studies testing new methods or measures. However, the majority of applied research requires the inclusion of specific 'real life' samples such as full-time workers, school children, or clinical health populations. Certainly the ability to publish applied research may be restricted for studies wholly reliant on student research samples; for pertinent discussions, see, for example, Dipboye and Flanagan (1979) and Gordon, Slade, and Schmitt (1986). This restriction is primarily due to the relevance of the research, that is, the degree to which a student sample can adequately represent a 'real life' sample, or the degree to which the research results can be *generalised* to a 'real life' sample.

The development of electronic survey administrations has increased the scope for including large samples within research investigations. The time and costs associated with hard-copy pen and paper survey administrations are no longer considered to be limitations for the design of electronic-based survey-based research. Instead, for example, researchers often have the capacity to sample *all* workers with access to a computer employed by an organisation, as opposed to sampling only a small proportion of workers with hard-copy surveys. The development of computer modelling for data analysis (e.g., structural equation modelling, or SEM) has also increased the need for large numbers of survey *respondents*, which in turn has also resulted in large samples of workers being *invited* to participate in research investigations (taking into account participant non-response and attrition). The inclusion of large research samples in research investigations is accompanied by a number of strengths and weaknesses which require consideration, and these are discussed in more detail in Chapter 3 in this book: 'Research sampling', as well as elsewhere (e.g., Sarpy, Rabito, & Goldstein, 2013). Two key advantages of large research samples, for example, are of course that concerns about statistical power and the representativeness of the respondents are greatly reduced. However, questions about the representativeness of the research respondents to workers external to a specifically sampled organisation or employment sector, or even a specific country or geographical region, are now increasingly being raised (e.g., Brough et al., 2013) and hence require appropriate consideration in the research design stage.

The inclusion of evidence of theoretical sophistication

As noted earlier, it is paramount that a research investigation is designed on the premise that it is able to contribute to current scholarly discussions of the research topic. This requires demonstration by the researcher that they are aware of these current discussions *and* also aware of the wider older research which informs these discussions. Failure to conduct a thorough literature review can produce instances of 'reinventing the wheel', simple replications of existing research, or the omission of key theoretical approaches and/or research constructs. Research which purports to introduce 'new' measures or constructs should especially take care to ensure the genuine novelty of these constructs and should appropriately demonstrate that the new measure/construct is not simply re-badging existing tools/variables, as is more broadly described by *conceptual or terminological diversity*, noted previously.

The issue of theoretical sophistication also includes consideration being given to the *advancement* of scholarly knowledge by actually building on existing research findings and recommendations. One pertinent example of where research recommendations are often ignored – and the research field consequentially suffers from stagnation – is the continued popularity of designing and conducting cross-sectional research investigations for the study of concepts which are well established as a *process* rather than a state, such as the stress and coping process, for example. Despite repeated calls for stress and coping research to incorporate longitudinal research designs (Biggs, Brough, & Drummond, 2017; Brough, O'Driscoll, Kalliath, Cooper, & Poelmans, 2009; Taris & Kompier, 2014; Zapf, Dormann, & Frese, 1996), the vast majority of investigations in this field still adopt cross-sectional research methods. This, of course, is primarily because cross-sectional research is easier, cheaper, and quicker to conduct and analyse compared to research based on longitudinal designs, but consequently does little to advance our knowledge of the process of stress and coping (see also Brough, Drummond, & Biggs, 2018). Thus, due consideration must be given to both the specific topic being investigated *and* its appropriate method of assessment in order to adequately address the issue of theoretical sophistication.

The inclusion of research designs that promotes causal generalisations

A common mistake when writing the hypotheses and results of a cross-sectional research investigation is to describe the associations between the research variables using language which implies a *causal* relationship, i.e., *X predicts Y* or *X causes Y*. Even though a research investigation may have been designed based upon an independent variable 'having an impact' upon a dependent variable, and we may test this 'impact' with multiple regression analyses, which (somewhat confusingly) describes independent variables as 'predictor' variables, if this investigation is cross-sectional, then it is unable to demonstrate any causality. Cross-sectional research designs only inform us of 'associations' or 'relationships' which exist between the variables, and this is the correct terminology to adopt in the write-up of this research. Longitudinal research designs which assess how a variable impacts upon a second variable over time do provide a test of causality, although this is dependent upon a 'suitable' time lag occurring; see Chapter 13. 'Longitudinal Data Collection', for a detailed discussion of this point.

As we noted earlier, the inclusion of a research design which does test causality remains in the minority within applied psychological research. This is despite repeated reviews promoting the need for this research and calling for researchers to conduct more investigations based upon longitudinal or quasi-experimental research designs, for example (e.g., Brough & Biggs, 2015; Brough & O'Driscoll, 2010; Taris & Kompier, 2014; Zapf et al., 1996). Both experimental and quasi-experimental research designs in the field of applied psychology are discussed in detail in Chapter 10 of this book. While we acknowledge the increased difficulties associated with conducting research investigations based upon longitudinal or quasi-experimental research designs, these difficulties alone should not actively hinder their use.

The inclusion of research implications for the end users

One of the primary aims of applied psychological research is to provide information and/or an outcome for the end user, be that a client, an organisation, a research participant, or such like. Research articles and theses commonly provide this evidence in a section headed 'practical implications of the research', in addition to a section discussing the 'theoretical implications'. It is important that the practical implications or outcomes of the research are duly considered in the initial research design stage, and it is surprising how often this consideration is lacking. So it is important to actually consider and specifically describe how an employee self-report survey, for example, will actually improve the working conditions for the respondents and will improve the social and/or financial outcomes for the sampled organisation. Such considerations are doubly important for research, including an intervention or training components. This process of *research evaluation* should be considered during the research design process and formally built into the research project, but it is surprising how often this evaluation process is not considered in sufficient detail.

In their recent chapter discussing the research evaluation process, Brough, Campbell, and Biggs (2016) emphasised the importance of identifying exactly why a research intervention succeeds or fails and how any success can best be objectively assessed. Thus, the purposeful design and adoption of *evidence-based practices* is a core characteristic of applied research, and this certainly includes a formal research evaluation process. Brough et al. (2016) described a basic model of the research evaluation process, consisting of four key characteristics:

1   **A formal needs assessment**. To ascertain that the intervention is actually required for the specific research participants and to identify the specific behaviours or procedures requiring change.
2   **The intervention**. Appropriately designed to achieve the identified changes and including a consideration of how both organisational (macro) and individual (micro) processes may impact on the intervention success (see also Biggs & Brough, 2015; Brough & Biggs, 2015).

3   **Improvement of performance**. Demonstrating via objective evidence that the intervention actually did improve the goals specified in the needs assessment. Careful consideration of the appropriate length of time required to show evidence of any improvement is required.

4   **Feedback process**. Feedback about the impact and difficulties experienced during the intervention stage is necessary for organisational learning and development and to ensure the validity and efficacy of any future delivery of the intervention programme. This simple research evaluation process is illustrated in Figure 2.1:

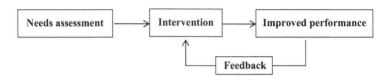

Figure 2.1 A basic research evaluation process

Source: From (Brough et al., 2016), cited with permission

Conclusion

In this chapter we have focused on the intrinsic principles which govern good psychological research, focusing specifically on the five key characteristics of the applied scientific method. Due to space restraints we have not addressed the more basic research components such as types of research variables (e.g., independent and dependent variables), associations between these variables (e.g., direct, indirect, moderating, and reciprocal relationships), and the development of research hypotheses and research models. This information is of course, also essential in the research design process and does require appropriate consideration (see, for example: Badia & Runyon, 1982; Becker, 2005; Creswell, 2013; Goodwin, 2009; Marks & Yardley, 2004; Sommer & Sommer, 1991; Spector & Meier, 2014). We discussed how the five key characteristics of the applied scientific method should each be duly considered by researchers in the design of research which aims to have an external impact. These five characteristics consist of the inclusion of reliable and valid measures; the inclusion of sufficient and generalisable research samples; the inclusion of evidence of theoretical sophistication; the inclusion of research designs that promotes causal generalisations; and the inclusion of research implications for the end users. In the discussion of the research implications for the end users we also described the four basic components of the research evaluation process and urged researchers to ensure this process is directly addressed by their research projects. In sum, this chapter suggests that by directly considering each one of these five methodological characteristics, a researcher will take the correct steps to ensure their research project is appropriately designed and actually does have some form of external impact.

References

Badia, P., & Runyon, R. P. (1982). *Fundamentals of behavioral research*. London, UK: Random House.

Becker, T. E. (2005). Potential problems in the statistical control of variables in organizational research: A qualitative analysis with recommendations. *Organizational Research Methods*, *8*(3), 274–289.

Biggs, A., & Brough, P. (2015). Explaining intervention success and failure: What works, when, and why? In M. Karanika-Murray & C. Biron (Eds.), *Derailed organizational stress and well-being interventions: Confessions of failure and solutions for success* (pp. 237–244). London, UK: Springer.

Biggs, A., Brough, P., & Drummond, S. (2017). Lazarus and Folkman's psychological stress and coping theory. In C. L. Cooper & J. Quick. (Eds.), *The Wiley handbook of stress and health: A guide to research and practice*. (pp. 351–364). London, UK: John Wiley & Sons.

Brayfield, A. H., & Rothe, H. F. (1951). An index of job satisfaction. *Journal of Applied Psychology*, *35*(5), 307–311.

Brough, P., & Biggs, A. (2015). The highs and lows of occupational stress intervention research: Lessons learnt from collaborations with high-risk industries. In M. Karanika-Murray & C. Biron (Eds.), *Derailed organizational stress and well-being interventions: Confessions of failure and solutions for success* (pp. 263–270). London, UK: Springer.

Brough, P., Campbell, J., & Biggs, A. (2016). Evaluation. In P. Brough, J. Campbell, & A. Biggs (Eds.), *Improving criminal justice workplaces: Translating theory and research into evidence-based practice* (pp. 79–92). London, UK: Routledge.

Brough, P., Drummond, S., & Biggs, A. (2018). Job support, coping and control: Assessment of simultaneous impacts within the occupational stress process. *Journal of Occupational Health Psychology*, *23*(2), 188–197. http://dx.doi.org/10.1037/ocp0000074

Brough, P., & O'Driscoll, M. (2010). Organizational interventions for balancing work and home demands: An overview. *Work & Stress*, *24*, 280–297. doi:10.1080/02678373.2010.50680

Brough, P., O'Driscoll, M., Kalliath, T., Cooper, C. L., & Poelmans, S. (2009). *Workplace psychological health: Current research and practice*. Cheltenham, UK: Edward Elgar.

Brough, P., Timms, C., Siu, O. L., Kalliath, T., O'Driscoll, M., Sit, C., . . . Lu, C. Q. (2013). Validation of the job demands-resources model in cross-national samples: Cross-sectional and longitudinal predictions of psychological strain and work engagement. *Human Relations*, *66*, 1311–1335. doi:10.1177/0018726712472915

Creswell, J. W. (2013). *Research design: Qualitative, quantitative, and mixed methods approaches*. London, UK: Sage.

Dipboye, R. L., & Flanagan, M. F. (1979). Research settings in industrial and organizational psychology: Are findings in the field more generalizable than in the laboratory? *American Psychologist*, *34*(2), 141–150.

Goodwin, C. J. (2009). *Research in psychology: Methods and design*. London, UK: John Wiley & Sons.

Gordon, M. E., Slade, L. A., & Schmitt, N. (1986). The "science of the sophomore" revisited: From conjecture to empiricism. *Academy of Management Review*, *11*(1), 191–207.

Gurung, R. A., Hackathorn, J., Enns, C., Frantz, S., Cacioppo, J. T., Loop, T., & Freeman, J. E. (2016). Strengthening introductory psychology: A new model for teaching the introductory course. *American Psychologist*, *71*(2), 112–124.

Halbesleben, J. R. B., & Demerouti, E. (2005). The construct validity of an alternative measure of burnout: Investigating the English translation of the Oldenburg Burnout Inventory. *Work & Stress*, *19*(3), 208–220.

Hubbard, R. (Ed.). (2016). *Corrupt research: The case for reconceptualizing empirical management and social science.* Los Angeles, CA: Sage.

Ioannidis, J. P. A., Greenland, S., Hlatky, M. A., Khoury, M. J., Macleod, M. R., Moher, D., . . . Tibshirani, R. (2014). Increasing value and reducing waste in research design, conduct, and analysis. *The Lancet, 383*(9912), 166–175.

Kristensen, T. S., Borritz, M., Villadsen, E., & Christensen, K. B. (2005). The Copenhagen Burnout Inventory: A new tool for the assessment of burnout. *Work & Stress, 19*(3), 192–207.

Lambert, E. G., Hogan, N. L., & Barton, S. M. (2001). The impact of job satisfaction on turn-over intent: A test of a structural measurement model using a national sample of workers. *The Social Science Journal, 38*(2), 233–250.

Marks, D. F., & Yardley, L. (2004). *Research methods for clinical and health psychology.* London, UK: Sage.

Maslach, C., Jackson, S. E., & Leiter, M. P. (1981). *Maslach Burnout Inventory: MBI.* Palo Alto, CA: Consulting Psychologists Press.

Mueller, C. W., & McCloskey, J. C. (1990). Nurses' job satisfaction: A proposed measure. *Nursing Research, 39,* 113–117.

Sarpy, S. A., Rabito, F., & Goldstein, N. (2013). Sampling in occupational health psychology. In R. R. Sinclair, M. Wang, & L. E. Tetrick (Eds.), *Research methods in occupational health psychology* (pp. 229–247). New York, NY: Routledge.

Seashore, S., Lawler, E., Mirvis, P., & Cammann, C. (1982). *Observing and measuring organizational change: A guide to field practice.* New York, NY: Wiley.

Sinclair, R. R., Wang, M., & Tetrick, L. E. (2013). Looking toward the future of OHP research. In R. R. Sinclair, M. Wang, & L. E. Tetrick (Eds.), *Research methods in occupational health psychology: Measurement, design and data analysis* (pp. 395–414). New York, NY: Routledge.

Sommer, B., & Sommer, R. (1991). *A practical guide to behavioral research: Tools and techniques.* Oxford: Oxford University Press.

Spector, P. E. (1985). Measurement of human service staff satisfaction: Development of the job satisfaction survey. *American Journal of Community Psychology, 13*(6), 693–713.

Spector, P. E., & Meier, L. L. (2014). Methodologies for the study of organizational behavior processes: How to find your keys in the dark. *Journal of Organizational Behavior, 35*(8), 1109–1119.

Stamps, P. L., & Piedmonte, E. B. (1986). *Nurses and work satisfaction: An index for measurement.* Ann Arbor, MI: Health Administration Press.

Taris, T. W., & Kompier, M. A. J. (2014). Cause and effect: Optimizing the designs of longitudinal studies in occupational health psychology. *Work & Stress, 28*(1), 1–8.

Wanous, J. P., Reichers, A. E., & Hudy, M. J. (1997). Overall job satisfaction: How good are single-item measures? *Journal of Applied Psychology, 82*(2), 247–252.

Warr, P., Cook, J., & Wall, T. (1979). Scales for the measurement of some work attitudes and aspects of psychological well-being. *Journal of Occupational Psychology, 52*(2), 129–148.

Zapf, D., Dormann, C., & Frese, M. (1996). Longitudinal studies in organizational stress research: A review of the literature with reference to methodological issues. *Journal of Occupational Health Psychology, 1,* 145–169.

3   Research sampling

A pragmatic approach

Andrew Robertson and Chris G. Sibley

Research sampling: a pragmatic approach

Imagine you're a dog. Now imagine that you spend a lot of your time trying to guess where your family members go when they leave you at home and drive away in the car each workday morning. You're a highly intelligent dog, and so you base your guesses on your own experiences of being in the car. Based on these experiences, you know that the options for where your family drive to each morning without you are (a) the beach, (b) the dog park, (c) or the vets. You think this last one is unlikely as they only drive there with you once or twice a year.[1] Of course our hypothetical dog will never be able to reliably estimate where its family drive to during the day without it. First because, well, it's a dog; but more importantly because the dog's sample of car trips is not random. The sample is in fact very seriously biased. By contrast, if the dog is only interested in trying to guess where it is being taken when it gets taken in the car itself, then its previous experience should work quite well for guessing where it is likely to go. In the first case the dog is not drawing a sample that is representative of the target population about which it wants to make guesses (where its family drive to without it). In the second case the dog's sample frame reliably represents the target population about which it wants to make guesses (where its family drive to with it also in the car).

The basic concept of taking a sample that is representative of the population about which you want to make inferences is as critical to scientific research as it is to hypothetical dogs left alone at home. Sampling can also get complex very quickly, and there are a large number of ways that you can design your sampling strategy or analyse your data to help increase the reliability and predictive validity of your estimates. In the first half of the chapter we describe the core concepts of sampling, including different types of samples, considerations about response rate, margin of error, sample weighting, and adjustment. In the second half of the chapter we outline practical recommendations and present a series of hypothetical case studies for how researchers might go about designing a sample in a variety of complex organisational and research contexts, including examples from common types of research based on our experience in industry. We also discuss factors to consider if you are on a limited budget and relying on sampling from undergraduate students or Mturk (if this is the case, then a lot of the other technical details in this chapter about sample design are redundant).

Core concepts relating to sampling

Types of samples

For the purpose of this chapter we've divided sampling into two broad categories – *probability* and *non-probability*. When researchers discuss 'scientific sampling', they're usually talking about probability sampling, which is also called *random sampling*. However, it can be costly, time consuming, and often impractical to collect a purely random sample. Alternative approaches are often used.

Probability sampling

You're using probability sampling when each person sampled has a known probability of random selection, or if it's possible to calculate a person's chance of selection. If you can't do this, you're using non-probability sampling.

Simple random sampling (a pure probability sample)

The simple random sample is the building block for all scientific sampling. In a survey that employs simple random sampling, each respondent has an *equal* chance to be included. Let's say you randomly select 300 employees in an organisation with a total workforce of 2,000 and ask them to complete a questionnaire. Let's assume that in this hypothetical sample, the response rate is 100%, because the 300 employees were 'compelled' by their CEO to take part. This is a pure simple random sample, because every one of the 2,000 employees has a known and equal chance to be included. A summary of this sample design is presented in Figure 3.1.

In reality, it's nearly impossible to collect a purely random sample. There are two reasons for this:

1   *Non-response error (and response bias).* Some people will not respond to a request to complete a survey. In fact, some *types* of people, such as young males, are less likely to respond than others. People opting not to participate contribute to *non-response error*. If the people that do take part are *meaningfully* different from those who refuse, this creates *response bias*.
2   *Non-coverage error.* It can be difficult to invite everyone in a target population to take part. For example, if you carry out a telephone survey of all adults living in a country, you will be systematically excluding people who do not have a landline. This is a type of non-coverage. This problem occurs with many different types of sampling, because very rarely do researchers have access to every individual in the target population.

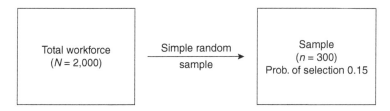

Figure 3.1 Example of a simple random sample

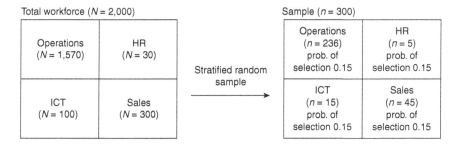

Figure 3.2 Example of a stratified sample

Stratified sampling

Stratified probability sampling can help to reduce the impact of survey error. If a researcher knows in advance that response rates will be lower or higher for certain groups, they can stratify their sample by known characteristics in advance and target a specific number of respondents in each stratum. A simple example might be departmental group, where two departments within an organisation are less likely to complete a survey than two other departments. If you know in advance the department within which each employee works, you can stratify the target population and target a specific number of employees within each of four strata. To achieve the desired number of completed surveys within each stratum, we may need to send out additional reminders or use other strategies to maximise response (e.g., incentives) within a specific stratum. A summary of this sample design is presented in Figure 3.2. This approach is still a probability sample, as long as you are *randomly selecting* the employees within each stratum and each respondent has a known chance of being selected.

Disproportionate stratified sampling

Continuing with this example, you might also apply a different selection probability to each stratum. That is, you might randomly select a higher number of employees from departments where you anticipate a lower response and vice versa (see Tables 3.4 and 3.5, where we provide this information for key factors in the New Zealand context). This is known as disproportionate stratified

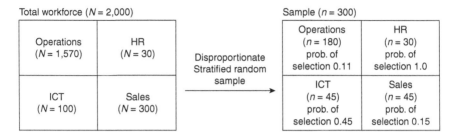

Figure 3.3 Example of a disproportionate stratified sample

probability sampling. You can also use this approach to over-select a particular group of respondents. Let's say you're interested to know the views of ICT and HR staff, but based on your *proportionate* sampling scheme, you'll only receive 20 completed questionnaires from these departments in total. In this situation you may want to disproportionately over-select staff in these departments and under-select staff in larger departments. A summary of this sample design is presented in Figure 3.3. In this example we're attempting to survey all HR staff, and we're over-selecting ICT staff by almost half. Sales staff are still sampled proportionately, and operations staff are under-sampled. This approach can still be considered a probability sample. Each employee has a known chance of random selection.

You would be correct if you argued this sampling scheme is delivering an unrepresentative sample of employees at the organization; however, this can be corrected for at the weighting stage (we discuss this later). And again, it can often be worth it if you want to make inferences about small subgroups in the population.

Cluster sampling

Sometimes it's impractical to attempt to gather a pure random sample. Take national door-to-door surveys as an example. Although it would be possible to randomly select 1,000 individual households in a country, it would be unfeasible to send an interviewer to each randomly selected household. The travel costs for each interviewer would blow any survey budget. In these circumstances a more practical approach would be to stratify the country's geography in some way (e.g., high density urban, semi-urban, provincial, and rural), randomly select areas within each stratum, and then carry out a 'cluster' of interviews within each randomly selected area. This is still probability sampling because you're able to calculate the probability of the area and person being selected. The problem with cluster sampling is people within a cluster can be more similar to each other than they are to people in other areas (e.g., similar ethnic identity or socio-economic status), which leads to an unrepresentative sample. You can reduce the impact of this on your survey estimates by selecting a larger number of areas and using a smaller cluster size (i.e., six interviews rather than 10 interviews per cluster), but of course this all adds to the cost.

The importance of response rates

If you've read this far you probably appreciate that response rates are important in survey sampling. *Response rates are important.* A high response rate is an indication your sample is a good reflection of the population it was taken from and is not skewed toward or away from any particular type of person. However, the response rate is not the only indicator of sample quality. It is easily possible to encounter situations where a higher response rate may potentially produce a poorer quality sample. For example, the Department of Conservation in New Zealand measured visitation to recreation areas in three different ways over eight years. Initially, questions were placed in a *telephone 'omnibus' survey*, with a range of other questions from other clients. When being invited to take part, respondents had no knowledge of the content of the survey. The survey then moved to a *customised telephone* approach. Under the customised approach, potential respondents were randomly selected and were sent a pre-notification letter explaining what the survey was about and that an interviewer may call. Some interviews were carried out using an online panel, but no pre-notification letter was sent. This method increased the response rate over the omnibus approach. Finally, the survey moved to a *sequential mixed-method* approach, where people were selected at random from the electoral roll and sent an invitation via post to complete an online survey. Those who didn't complete the online survey within a given timeframe were then sent a paper-based self-completion questionnaire. This method delivered the highest response rate, but under this approach potential respondents find out more about the topic of the survey, and in many cases may even see all the questions, before deciding whether to take part.

The risk with giving people a lot of information about a survey is that those who are more involved or interested in the topic (and hence also more likely to have visited recreation sites) are more likely to take part. Figure 3.4 shows the approximate response rates for each approach and reported recreation area visitation over time. You can decide yourself which results are more plausible, but in our opinion the data suggest that the visitation figure may be correlated with the amount of pre-interview information given to respondents.

Response rates are declining in many surveys around the globe. Table 3.1 shows the declining response rate reported by Pew Research from 1997 (36%) to 2012 (only 9%). However, while Pew reports some quite dramatic declines in response rate, their analyses indicate that samples with a low response rate can still provide reliable information about the population when designed well and when using sensible sample weights (Pew Research Centre, 2012). The take-home message is *not* that response rates aren't important. It's that they should not be seen as the *main driver* of sample quality. Minimising response bias is much more crucial for producing reliable population estimates. We could probably increase the response rate for every survey by making the topic sound exciting and interesting, but we wouldn't be making the research more robust.

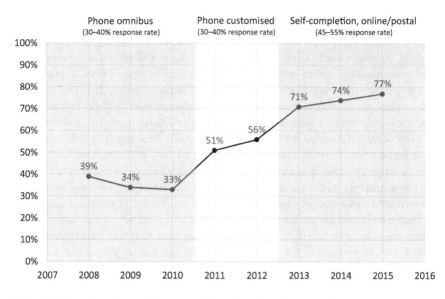

Figure 3.4 Sample estimate of the proportion of people who reported visiting a Department of Conservation recreation area in the past 12 months

Source: Department of Conservation Annual Survey, 2017

Table 3.1 Response rates reported by the Pew Research Center for typical household telephone surveys they conducted between 1997–2012

	1997%	2000%	2003%	2006%	2009%	2012%
Contact rate	90	77	79	73	72	62
Cooperation rate	43	40	34	31	21	14
Response rate	36	28	25	21	15	9

Note: Contact rate defined as percent of households in which an adult was reached. Cooperation rate defined as percent of households that yielded an interview. Response rate defined as percent of households sampled that yielded an interview. Rates were calculated following the American Association for Public Opinion Research standards. Source: data reported in report from Pew Research Centre (2012) assessing the representativeness of public opinion surveys

Weighting and adjustment

As mentioned earlier, a sample can never be truly representative, due to different types of sampling error (i.e., non-coverage and non-response error). To mitigate this, researchers will often 'weight' their data. They'll also do this when they've employed a disproportionate sample scheme, like in the sample above to illustrate disproportionate stratified probability sample. In the example in

Figure 3.3, we would need to calculate 'cell weights' for each cell in the table and assign that weight to each respondent based on which cell they're in. Each member of the operations team would receive a weight of 1.3, the HR team 0.2, the ICT team 0.3, and the sales team 1.0 (we sampled the sales team in the correct proportion, so their responses are not up- or down-weighted). Once you've calculated the weight for each respondent, common data analysis packages will allow you to easily apply it when you're analysing your data. For more information about sample weights, see Groves, Fowler, Couper, Lepkowski, Singer, and Tourangean (2004).

Sampling error

Sampling theory provides a method for determining the degree to which a result based on a random sample may differ to the 'true result' (if a census were taken). Let's say a poll of 1,000 people found that 50% supported interest being charged on student loans, and 50% opposed it. Using Equation 3.1, we could say this result, based on a random sample of 1,000 people, has a margin of error of around +/−3.1 percentage points at the 95% confidence level. In the formula p is the proportion ($p = .5$), and n is the sample size.

$$\text{(Equation 3.1)} \quad \textit{Margin of Errror} = 1.96 \sqrt{\frac{p(1-p)}{n}}$$

This means, if you were to re-run the survey 100 times, taking a random sample each time, in 95 of those times your survey estimate for percentage support/oppose would fall somewhere between 46.9% and 53.1%. So we can say that we are 95% confident that the 'true score' lies somewhere between these two values. You can see in Figure 3.5 that the margin of error decreases with larger sample sizes, and as percentages move away from 50%. That is, for a given sample size, a poll result of 10% or 90% will have a lower margin of error than a poll result of 50%.

If your population is small and known (i.e., the total number of people working in a company, as opposed to the total number of people living in a country), then you should instead use Equation 3.2. This version includes what is often referred to as the 'finite population correction' (N is the total population size).

$$\text{(Equation 3.2)} \quad \textit{Margin of Errror} = 1.96 \sqrt{\frac{p(1-p)}{n}} \sqrt{\frac{N-n}{N-1}}$$

You can also calculate confidence intervals for means as well as percentages. Equation 3.3 is the standard formula for estimating a 95% confidence interval for the sample mean. As with the margin of error for a proportion, if you were

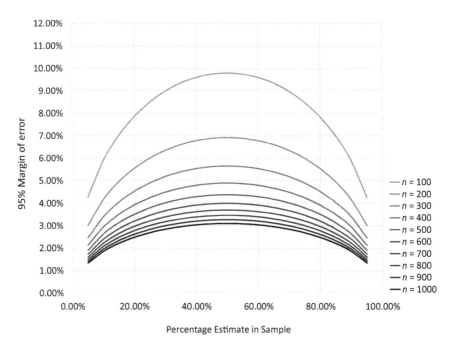

Figure 3.5 95% margin of error as a function of sample size and percentage estimate in sample

to rerun this survey 100 times, taking a random sample each time, in 95 of those times your survey estimate would fall somewhere within this interval.

$$(\text{Equation 3.3}) \quad 95\% \: Confidence \: Interval \: = \text{Mean} \pm 1.96 \frac{SD}{\sqrt{n}}$$

Design effects

When you weight your data to adjust for sampling error or a disproportionate sampling scheme, you introduce a 'design effect'. A design effect increases your margin of error. Design effects are calculated based on the degree of weighting required to adjust your sample to match the known population characteristics. The higher the design effect, the higher the margin of error. Essentially, weighting has a similar impact to reducing your sample size. You'll sometimes hear researchers refer to the 'effective sample size', which is smaller than their actual sample size. This effective sample size is the size of the sample after accounting for the design effect.

Common non-probability samples

Probability sampling can be expensive. Probability samples typically involve several steps to increase the representativeness of the survey by contacting the smallest number of people possible to achieve the target completion rate. This involves time and money.

Quota sampling

One alternative and more cost-effective approach to a probability sample is quota sampling, which was developed by the market research industry. Under this approach, researchers set targets, or quota, based on certain demographic characteristics of the population, such as age, gender, or region. The job of the researcher thus changes from trying to maximise the survey response rate to trying to achieve a specific target quota. Once a target is achieved, all other respondents in that specific group are screened out and not interviewed.

Although this approach is often less expensive, there are some potential cons. These are:

1   Because you don't know in advance who is going to be screened out, there is no way to calculate the probability of selection or margin of error. Sampling theory doesn't apply.
2   This approach assumes that the people screened out of a quota are similar to the people who were interviewed. This may not be the case, as people screened out are those contacted later in the field work period, and people who are harder to reach may differ in many ways – for example being more likely to be shift workers, those with multiple jobs, or those who are generally less likely to be home during the initial contact attempt.

Having said this, sometimes it is simply not possible or practical to conduct a probability survey. This includes situations where your target population is a very small proportion of the overall population (such as people who have bought a car in the last six months relative to all car owners) or where a very low response rate is inevitable (such a people who work as manual labourers and who have the lowest response rate in the New Zealand Attitudes and Values Study; see Table 3.5). In these situations, quota sampling is a pragmatic approach.

Undergraduate students

The most widely employed ad hoc samples are undergraduate psychology students. For instance, from 1990–2005, 87.7% of the articles on prejudice published in the *Journal of Personality and Social Psychology* relied on student samples (Henry, 2008). This is widely agreed to be the leading journal in social psychology. Other top journals show a similar preference for under-graduate samples over this same time period, with 93.8% of the articles on prejudice in *Personality and Social Psychology Bulletin* and 98.1% of articles on prejudice in the *Journal of Experimental Social Psychology* using student samples (Henry, 2008). On the one hand, it seems that as a field, we know an awful lot about the psychology of undergraduate university students in WEIRD (Western, educated, industrialised, rich, and democratic) nations but possibly not quite so much about other populations (Henrich, Heine, & Norenzayan, 2010; Sears, 1986). On the other hand, the extent to which sampling undergraduates is problematic depends upon whether or not they adequately represent the population of interest for a given research question. Aside from the obvious benefits of these students being a relatively cheap (or free) and relatively captive audience, Dasgupta and Hunsinger (2008) provided an excellent summary of the costs and benefits of focusing on undergraduate samples in the study of prejudice and stereotyping. In our view, these same pros and cons apply to the science of industrial and organi-sational psychology,\ and applied psychology generally. We reproduce their list in Table 3.2.

Based on Henry's (2008) numbers, you could be forgiven for assuming that it is easily possible to have a successful career in psychology or organi-sational science and publish in top journals in the field by focusing solely on the study of undergraduate students. However, this assumption might not be as valid now was it was in 1990–2005. As the incoming editor of the *Journal of Personality and Social Psychology*, Kitayama (2017, p. 359) signalled his con-cern about the focus on undergraduate samples, and particularly those from North American and Western European universities. In his opening edito-rial for the journal, he stated, for example, that: "As Editor, I will weigh the inclusiveness of subject populations more seriously. Ultimately, I believe that this intentional expansion of the subject base – not only in size but also in diversity – in our science is the best step toward addressing the challenges we face today".

Table 3.2 Costs and benefits of using undergraduate student samples

Cons of using student samples
- Restricted range in student samples is an obstacle to theory development
- Students lack particular psychological characteristics that are important to theory development
- Some relevant workplace or other applied contexts cannot be captured in academic environments

Pros of using student samples
- Academic environments may contain theoretically interesting variables.
- Students possess theoretically interesting characteristics.
- Student samples provide an efficient means to develop theories before testing their generalisability in broader samples.

Source: Dasgupta & Hunsinger, 2008, p. 90–95

Facebook and social media

With the advent of social media platforms such as Facebook and Twitter there are new ways to approach and solicit responses from large numbers of people. The most obvious of these is to use social media for snowball sampling by posting a link promoting an online questionnaire and encouraging Facebook friends and friends of friends, Twitter followers, etc., to complete it. Another obvious way to collect data via Facebook is by paying for targeted advertising. For example, you could pay to create an advertisement linking to an online questionnaire that appears on the news feeds of people who match specific demographics, such as gender or region. Facebook also allows advertisers to upload hashed (one-way unique encrypted) databases of names and contact details that may then be matched to a similarly hashed version of Facebook's own user database. When the contact details, name, email, etc., match with the details of existing Facebook profiles, then those people can then be sent a targeted advertisement. We caution researchers using this approach to carefully consider the ethics of uploading a database (even a hashed one) of contact details from their sample frame for external matching.

There are also some less obvious and clever ways in which social media can be used to sample specific and often hard to reach populations in certain cases. In an innovative study, Bhutta (2012), for example, used Facebook to collect a sample of about 4,000 baptised Catholics – and did so with little-to-no budget. Bhutta (2012) outlined the following steps taken to achieve this:

1   Create a new Facebook group to recruit potential participants who match the target population. Include a description asking group members to forward the invitation and invite others who fit the target criteria to also join. In Bhutta's (2012) case the target population were baptised Catholics, and the group was called 'Please Help Me Find Baptized Roman Catholics!'
2   On the group page, provide evidence legitimising the group and explaining its purpose. For example, Bhutta (2012) included a list of anticipated questions they planned to ask, a discussion and link to research justifying non-probability sampling, links to the university website, and a list of responses to commonly asked queries posted on the page.
3   Contact the administrators of other similar groups on Facebook and ask them to advertise the group on their pages. In Bhutta's (2012) case, this was other Catholic groups.
4   Bhutta (2012) then also sent a mass message to all of her Facebook friends encouraging them to join the group if they were eligible and to pass the message on to their friends. Depending on the focus of your research, you might, however, consider skipping this step if the target population does not have a high level of overlap with your social network on Facebook.
5   Close the group before it exceeds the size at which the administrator is no longer able to send mass messages to all group members. Consider starting a second group for overflow. At the time which Bhutta (2012) collected

their sample, Facebook imposed a limit of 5,000 members for the mass message function to work.

6   Send a mass message to all group members inviting them to complete the online questionnaire.

We suspect that this method of data collection may work well if the target population shares some sort of common identity or social interest. It is also important to note that a key aspect of recruitment relies on providing details about the topic of study and who you are trying to recruit, so as to encourage people to join the group. The sample will thus tend to be biased toward people who are interested in the research topic. That said, this remains an innovative and cost-effective method of data collection that could be useful when these caveats are not of concern.

Amazon's Mechanical Turk

Amazon's Mechanical Turk (or Mturk) provides another low-cost and easy option for data collection (see Buhrmester, Kwang, & Gosling, 2011; Woo, Keith, & Thornton, 2015). Mturk is an online crowdsourcing platform in which researchers can pay people to complete online questionnaires, experiments, etc. You could argue that the most compelling argument in favour of Mturk is that at least it is not an undergraduate sample. However, many of the same concerns about the limited focus on a small segment of the population and the inability to generalise to other populations remain. The research literature in organisational psychology is experiencing a rapid increase in the use of Mturk samples (Keith, Tay, & Harms, 2017). However, very few articles in leading organisational psychology journals published from 2012–2015 relied solely on Mturk samples; most articles including an Mturk sample are multi-study papers that also conceptually replicate or extend upon the effect of interest in another (non-Mturk) sample. If you opt to collect an Mturk sample (perhaps as a low-cost initial test-of-concept), then it is sensible to supplement this with another sample drawn from the population of interest collected using a more

Table 3.3 Reporting checklist for Mturk samples

Worker characteristics	• Sample size
	• Average age
	• Gender (e.g., %Male)
	• Education
	• Percentage from US
	• Racial/ethnic makeup
	• First language
	• Employment status (full-time, part-time, unemployed)
Qualifications	• Nature of qualifications
Prescreens	• Nature of prescreen
	• Implementation of prescreen
	• % Excluded based on prescreen

	• Number of participants agreeing to participate in main study
Self-selection	• Bounce rate (when possible)
	• Completion rate (when possible)
Compensation	• Base payment
	• Bonuses
	• Average task time
Research design	• Nature of research design
	• Materials used
	• Manipulations
	• Number of participants in each condition (experimental design)
	• Attrition rates/attrition rates per condition (experimental design)/attrition rates between waves of data collection (time-separated design)
	• Time between waves of data collection (time-separated design)
Attention checks	• Nature of attention checks
	• Number of participants removed from final analysis

Source: Reproduced from Keith et al. 2017, Table 5

well-defined sampling design – assuming of course that the population of interest in your research is not Mturk workers per se.

For those who opt to use Mturk samples for their research, Keith et al. (2017) provided an excellent discussion of design issues when using Mturk (such as pre-screening, compensation, and attention checks). Keith et al. also provided a reporting checklist for research using Mturk samples, and we echo their recommendation that this checklist be followed when reporting Mturk research (see Table 3.3).

Hypothetical case studies

In this section we integrate the content on sampling theory already covered and describe a series of hypothetical case studies outlining how you could go about designing a sample in a variety of complex organisational and research contexts. These examples are drawn from our own experiences working in industry, running political polls, and managing a large-scale national probability longitudinal panel study, the *New Zealand Attitudes and Values Study*. These case studies cover a wide range of different types of challenging sample designs and contexts that we have experienced in the last decade of work in the area and should provide a useful frame of reference for those who are starting out in the organisational science or polling industries.

Case study one: estimating the cost of tax compliance among small and medium businesses

Summary of scenario

A government agency wants to estimate the administrative costs that small and medium businesses incur when meeting their annual tax obligations. They decide to survey 1,000 businesses and ask a range of questions designed to measure the number of hours and other costs involved. They know a sample of 1,000 is common in surveys and has a margin of error of $+/-3.1$ percentage points at the 95% confidence level.

Some of the key challenges of this scenario

1   Upwards of 80% of all businesses are very small or sole-traders (e.g., build-ers, contractors). A simple random sample cannot be used, because we need to obtain robust estimates for small *and* medium-sized businesses.
2   It's necessary to under-select small businesses and over-select medium sized businesses so we can gain robust estimates for both groups. However, given the population proportions (i.e., 80% small vs. 20% medium), the degree of weighting required would be extreme. This will have a large *design effect* and would increase the overall margin of error for the survey estimates, making them less reliable. If you carry out an even number of interviews with small and large businesses (500 of each), after weighting the data your sample of 1,000 would have an *effective* sample size of around 735.
3.   Response rates are notoriously low among businesses, so efforts are needed to maximise them as much as possible. Because this research will be carried out using public money, it would be inappropriate to offer an incentive such as a prize draw.

Outline of how sampling could be approached

Dealing with the design effect is straightforward in this scenario. If you boost your total sample to around 1,400 and instead survey 700 businesses in each group, your effective sample size will now be larger (around 1,030), and this will give the government agency the level of sampling error they're willing to accept. Dealing with the low response rate is more difficult. Maximising the response rate could involve a range of strategies. Firstly, you could mail a survey pre-notification letter from the government agency, signed by the CEO or gov-ernment minister. This would increase the legitimacy of the research. A short time after sending the questionnaire, reminder activity would need to begin. In the scenario, this might include a reminder postcard to non-respondents, a second reminder with a new copy of the questionnaire (in case the first was lost or discarded), and then potentially reminder telephone calls. An advantage of reminder telephone calls is that in addition to giving businesses another reminder, you can also ascertain the reasons for non-response.

Case study two: estimating public support for local government amalgamation

Summary of scenario

A government agency needs to estimate public support for amalgamating several local councils. This is a politically charged topic, as people are often passionate about the needs of their local area. A telephone survey was commissioned to gain a robust measure of support and to understand the key issues at play for residents.

Some of the key challenges of this scenario

1   A substantial proportion of the local population identify with a specific ethnic minority group that are less likely to have a home telephone.
2   The views of the ethnic minority group are important. It's also well known that the ethnic minority group represents a substantial portion of the population, and they are less likely to have a home telephone. While it would be possible to capture their views through the telephone survey (and up-weight their results), it is possible that those with a telephone differ from those without a telephone.

Outline of how sampling could be approached

In this situation a good approach could be to carry out a combined telephone and door-to-door survey. The telephone survey could use a standard approach where local telephone numbers are stratified by area and randomly generated (stratified random sampling). The door-to-door survey could randomly select areas and interview a cluster of 10 people living in each area who identify with the ethnic minority group in question (cluster sampling). In this scenario, it would be a good idea to ensure that the chance of selecting an area is in proportion to number of people from the ethnic minority group who live in the area. Doing this ensures your door-to-door survey is going to increase the number of responses from those in the ethnic minority group.

Case study three: randomly selecting passengers at a border crossing

Summary of scenario

A border protection agency needs to estimate its rate of success at preventing risk items from crossing the border. Passengers can go through six different levels of biosecurity screening, from no screening (just walking the border) through to full inspection of them and all their belongings.

Some key challenges to sampling in this scenario

1   Border protection staff are trained to risk profile and target certain types of passengers for certain types of risk goods. This is a problem for sampling because if a staff member is targeting people for the purposes of estimating the rate of success at detecting risk items, their selection is non-random. Assuming their targeting is more accurate than chance, this will result in an overestimation of the proportion of people detected with at-risk items.

2   Passengers can pass through a number of different screening points at the border. Critical to the approach is the need to sample passengers once they have passed through the last possible screening point (i.e., have 'made it through all screening'). This is the only way to estimate the effectiveness of screening points.

3   Some screening procedures have a higher frequency of passengers passing through them than others. For example, more people might walk straight through with no screening than those who are targeted for full and exhaustive inspection.

Outline of how sampling could be approached

A specific team of border staff should be recruited and trained to use random selection and not to target people based on any sort of risk profile or their own stereotypes. Selection procedures need to be standardised across each screening point. Critically, selection needs to take place after the passenger has passed through all screening points and there is no other possibility for the passenger to be targeted by standard screening operations (e.g., no possibility of being targeted by sniffer dogs next to the exit). The selection procedure would also need to include details about where those carrying out selection should stand (e.g., how far behind all screening points), what to do when a group of passengers (e.g., a family) is passing through at the same time, and what to say to passengers who are selected (e.g., 'you have been selected for additional screening, this is random'). Finally, to estimate the success of each type of screening, passengers passing through low-frequency screening points (e.g., full check) need to be oversampled relative to passengers passing through high-frequency screening points (e.g., walking straight through).

Case study four: the New Zealand Attitudes and Values Study

If you have the funding to support it, then nothing beats conducting your own large-scale national probability sample.[2] The benefits of a large-scale simple random sample of a nation's population (or adult population) are numerous. For example, you will by default generate a random sample of people of all different occupations, all different levels of education, different types of employment status, level of socio-economic status, and so forth. The *New Zealand Attitudes and Values Study* (NZAVS) is one such study.

The initial wave of the NZAVS drew a random sample of 25,000 people from the New Zealand Electoral Roll in 2009.[3] The sample frame thus represented registered voters aged over 18 in New Zealand. People have to be publicly listed on the electoral roll, barring case-by-case concerns about privacy. The roll is available for scientific and health research and includes postal information, occupation, names, and a DOB range (but not email or phone numbers). The electoral commission estimate that the electoral roll contains about

89% of eligible voters. Because the sample was random, everyone listed on the roll had an equal chance of being selected, and the roll overlaps closely with the target population of interest (adult permanent residents of New Zealand).

The NZAVS contacted the 25,000 selected people by posting them an information sheet and a pen-and-paper questionnaire. One thing to note is that the information sheet clearly explained how participants were selected from the electoral roll and that this information was available for research purposes. The study also offered a grocery voucher prize draw of $1,000 vouchers in total. One common option for this type of design would be to also include a pre-notification letter (letting people know they have been selected and to expect the questionnaire in the mail) and one or more reminders for people who do not respond. The NZAVS did not employ pre-notifications or follow-ups for the initial sample, but if the funding is available, then this is something to consider, as it can increase the response rate.

The response rate to the 2009 initial NZAVS postal sample was 16.2%.[4] Tables 3.4 and 3.5 provide a breakdown of the response rate for different sample characteristics that were also available in the electoral roll. As can be seen, people with different demographics (e.g., age, occupation, SES) are not equally likely to respond. This is important to know because it indicates that the likelihood that someone responded to the NZAVS questionnaire differed depending on their demographic characteristics, such as their SES or occupation. This in turn could bias the sample. For example, women were far more likely to respond than men, and this can be broadly seen from the different response rates based on title/prefix, with those listed as 'Mr' having a response rate of 13.4% and those listed as 'Miss', 'Mrs' or 'Ms' having response rates of 15.7%, 18.8%

Table 3.4 Differential rates of response for age and regional deprivation in a random postal survey

	Response rate	*Total N*
Age categories		
Age 18–25	16.1%	1,152
Age 26–35	11.6%	3,924
Age 36–45	14.6%	4,610
Age 46–55	16.3%	5,179
Age 56–65	19.5%	4,194
Age 66 and over	18.3%	5,941
Total	16.2%	25,000
Regional Deprivation		
1 – lowest deprivation	19.5%	2,654
2	18.0%	2,646
3	16.7%	2,454
4	17.0%	2,336

(*Continued*)

Table 3.4 (Continued)

	Response rate	Total N
5	17.6%	2,347
6	16.8%	2,361
7	16.3%	2,206
8	14.4%	2,182
9	13.0%	2,089
10 – highest deprivation	12.1%	2,006
Residual/missing	15.2%	1,719
Total	16.2%	25,000

Note: These data are based on the first random postal sample from the *New Zealand Attitudes and Values Study* collected in 2009. The sample frame was 25,000 registered voters in New Zealand, randomly selected from the New Zealand electoral roll.

Table 3.5 Differential rates of response for title/prefix and occupation in a random postal survey

	Response rate	Total N
Title		
Dr	23.1%	121
Miss	15.7%	3,319
Mr	13.4%	10,051
Mrs	18.8%	6,028
Ms	20.7%	1,778
Residual/missing	18.0%	3,703
Total	16.2%	25,000
Occupation		
Managers	18.3%	2,703
Professionals	23.9%	3,975
Technicians and trades workers	14.6%	1,908
Community and personal service workers	17.3%	949
Clerical and administrative workers	21.1%	1,452
Sales workers	16.6%	950
Machinery operators and drivers	13.6%	619
Labourers	12.8%	1,229
Residual/uncoded	13.1%	11,215
Total	16.2%	25,000

Note: These data are based on the first random postal sample from the *New Zealand Attitudes and Values Study* collected in 2009. The sample frame was 25,000 registered voters in New Zealand, randomly selected from the New Zealand electoral roll.

and 20.7%, respectively. Often, these types of biases are determined after the fact based on comparison with census information or other known properties of the population, and the post-stratification sample weights are estimated to correct for such biases. Different response rates for different ethnic groups are one form of sampling bias that is often corrected for after the fact.

The information provided in Tables 3.4 and 3.5 may be valuable to researchers who have access to large sample frames such as an electoral roll, which may often include similar demographic characteristics. In such a case, you could use the information we have provided to estimate the expected response rate for those of a particular occupation, age group, etc., in advance of data collection. Looking at Table 3.5, if, for example, you had access to a sample frame with information about occupation, then you might opt to oversample machinery operators and drivers and labourers because you know from the NZAVS that they are less likely to respond to postal questionnaires relative to professionals and clerical and administrative workers. The information we provide about the differential response rates for age groups, those living in less or more deprived regions, and those with different titles/prefixes (as a proxy for gender) could all be useful for this purpose.

Conclusion

Once you know a little bit about sampling theory it is easy to pick holes in sample designs and describe why no design is perfect. No sample design is perfect. In our view, the job of a good survey researcher is not to design the perfect sample (hence, *survey* researcher, not *census* researcher), it is to understand why you can't; to identify sources of error in your sampling design, whatever they may be; and to put strategies in place that mitigate these sources of error where possible – all on a limited budget. There are many decisions involved in deciding upon and designing a sampling strategy. Here is a list of some of the common decisions you should consider (with the caveat that things can, of course, get far more complex than any simple list of bullet points can do justice to).

A brief decision guide for sample design

1 *Define the population you want to study.* This could be adults in your country, or people with a particular occupation, or people who are likely to vote in an upcoming election, or people with a specific health condition, etc.
2 *Define your sample frame and determine sources of non-coverage.* This could be landline telephone numbers, the electoral roll (if you are lucky enough to have access), people walking past a particular corner on a street, a list of email addresses of employees, people who respond to an advertisement, etc. Try to use a sample frame that has a high level of overlap with your target population and hence minimises the extent of under-coverage (i.e., minimises the extent to which your sample frame does not reliably overlap with your target population).
3 *Consider sources of response bias.* These could be based on differences in response rates for a particular group (such as younger men) or some people being more willing than others to respond to your survey because of the specific topic (sometimes it can be better to make the topic sound boring, rather than exciting, especially if your target population includes

people who may not be interested or enthusiastic about the topic you are studying).

4   *Decide on how you are going to measure responses.* Make a decision about whether you will use a self-report pen-and-paper questionnaire, use interviewers who read out the questions, use an online questionnaire, have research assistants observe and code behaviour, or collect your measures in some other way.

5   *Decide on whether to measure your focal question of interest as a categorical, count, or continuous variable.* Is your key question asking about supporting one thing versus another or voting for one party versus another (a categorical measure), or is your focal question better suited to being measured as a count variable (the number of times something happened) or as a continuous variable, such as the relative strength of agreement with a series of attitude statements.

6   *Decide on how wide a margin of error you are willing to accept.* Make a decision about how accurate you want your estimate to be. This is a little more tricky, as it can depend on what percentage level of support you observe for a categorical (yes/no) survey question or on the standard deviation of your responses for a continuous (disagree to agree Likert-style) question. For example, do you need to be confident that the estimate based on your sample data is within 2% of the population, 3% of the population value, 5% of the population value, etc.? A general rule of thumb for a poll is that you should collect about 1,000 people, which gives a margin of error of about 3%.

7   *Estimate your expected response rate.* Make an informed guess about your likely response rate. Try to base this on information about response rates of other similar studies, using similar sampling strategies and similar types of questions (and that take about the same amount of time to complete).

8   *Calculate how many people you need to sample.* This calculation should be based on at least two things. First, how wide a margin of error you are willing to accept, and second, your expected response rate. For example, if you want your sample to have a 3% margin of error, then you need to collect responses from about 1,000 people. If you expect your response rate to be about 15%, then to collect responses from 1,000 people you would need to sample about 7,000 people (that would give you 1,050 responses at a response rate of 15%). This gets more complex if you need to also account for design effects.

9   *Calculate how many people you need to sample (Part II).* If your research involves conducting statistical analyses beyond simple percentage estimates, such as multiple regression, structural equation modelling, or ANOVA, then you should also conduct power analyses to determine how large a sample size you need in order to reliably detect the effect you are predicting, given that it actually exists. In this case, you must determine your sample size in advance. Estimating required sample size for power analysis can get quite complex and depends on a lot of factors. Faul, Erdfelder, Lang, and Bucher (2007) and Muthén and Muthén (2002) provide excellent guides on how to conduct power analyses for different types of statistical models.

Notes

1 One of us (CS), can't help but wonder if this is actually so far away from the truth about what his dog does spend time doing when left alone during the workday.
2 This is a fairly large 'if'. Often compromises will have to be made when designing the sampling strategy for smaller-scale research projects. In such cases, existing data from large-scale national probability samples can be invaluable both for validating your own more focused sample frame, or if you can get access to an existing national probability dataset, then using that data and perhaps collecting a supplementary sample with a more in-depth and focused set of measures of the specific population of interest (such as people with a particular type of occupation).
3 The NZAVS also included two other samples of 10,000 and 5,500 people at time one which were conducted separately and also employed various other sample designs to refresh the sample during subsequent waves. Here, we describe only the initial 25,000 random sample.
4 One thing to note in passing is that subsequent random samples conducted as part of the NZAVS and following the same procedure have shown a steadily decreasing response rate, with the latest response rate to a 2017 random sample being 9%.

Recommended further reading

Groves, R. M., Fowler, F. J., Couper, M. P., Lepkowski, J. M., Singer, E., & Tourangean, R. (2004). *Survey methodology*. London, UK: John Wiley & Sons.

References

Bhutta, C. B. (2012). Not by the book: Facebook as a sampling frame. *Sociological Methods and Research, 41*, 57–88.

Buhrmester, M., Kwang, T., & Gosling, S. D. (2011). Amazon's Mechanical Turk: A new source of inexpensive, yet high-quality, data? *Perspectives in Psychological Science, 6*, 3–5.

Dasgupta, N., & Hunsinger, M. (2008). The opposite of a great truth is also true: When do student samples help versus hurt the scientific study of prejudice? *Psychological Inquiry, 19*, 90–98.

Department of Conservation Annual Survey of New Zealanders. (2017). Retrieved from www.doc.govt.nz/about-us/our-role/managing-conservation/recreation-management/visitor-statistics-and-research/survey-of-new-zealanders/

Faul, F., Erdfelder, E., Lang, A. G., & Bucher, A. (2007). G★Power 3: A flexible statistical power analysis program for the social, behavioral, and biomedical sciences. *Behavior Research Methods, 39*, 175–191. https://doi.org/10.3758/BF03193146

Groves, R. M., Fowler, F. J., Couper, M. P., Lepkowski, J. M., Singer, E., & Tourangean, R. (2004). *Survey methodology*. London, UK: John Wiley & Son.

Henrich, J., Heine, S. J., & Norenzayan, A. (2010). Most people are not WEIRD. *Nature, 466*(7302), 29.

Henry, P. J. (2008). College sophomores in the laboratory redux: Influences of a narrow data base on social psychology's view of the nature of prejudice. *Psychological Inquiry, 19*, 49–71.

Keith, M. G., Tay, L., & Harms, P. D. (2017). Systems perspective of Amazon Mechanical Turk for organizational research: Review and recommendations. *Frontiers in Psychology, 8*, 1359. doi:10.3389/fpsyg.2017.01359

Kitayama, S. (2017). Editorial, journal of personality and social psychology: Attitudes and social cognition. *Journal of Personality and Social Psychology, 112*, 357–360.

Muthén, L. K., & Muthén, B. (2002). How to use a Monte Carlo study to decide on sample size and determine power. *Structural Equation Modeling, 4*, 599–620.

Pew Research Centre (2012). *Assessing the representativeness of public opinion surveys* (Technical Report). Retrieved from www.people-press.org/2012/05/15/assessing-the-representative ness-of-public-opinion-surveys/

Sears, D. O. 1986. College sophomores in the laboratory: Influences of a narrow data base on social psychology's view of human nature. *Journal of Personality and Social Psychology, 51*, 515–530.

Woo, S. E., Keith, M., & Thornton, M. A. (2015). Amazon Mechanical Turk for industrial and organizational psychology: Advantages, challenges, and practical recommendations. *Journal of Industrial and Organizational Psychology, 8*, 171–179.

4 Research ethics for human research and legal issues

Gary Allen and Olav Muurlink

Ethical practice

It is relatively easier to understand ethical practice in terms of what it is *not*. It is widely agreed that researchers who engage in fabricating or falsifying data or results or engage in plagiarism fall into the category of what Martinson, Anderson, and De Vries (2005) famously referred to as 'scientists behaving badly' (p. 737). Extreme cases have been reported in the media, with a recent example including *Scientific Medicine's* 'Research Leader of the Year 2005', Woo-Suk Hwang exposed as technically a 'good' scientist who had committed a host of frauds in stem cell and cloning laboratories that were exposed by a combination of internal peer review and investigations by the media (Saunders & Savulescu, 2008). These extreme cases tend to suggest misbehaviour is rare, and good behaviour is the norm. However, a 2009 meta-analysis of studies (Fanelli, 2009) assessing falsifying/fabricating practices suggests that at least 2% of scientists admit to this practice (assuming also then that some scientists falsify and/or fabricate work without admitting to it). However, over a third of scientists admit to straying into the grey area of questionable research practices (QRPs), which includes misrepresentation, inaccuracy, and bias (Steneck, 2006). Again, the figure probably underestimates the real extent of QRPs, with the prevalence figures relying on the accuracy and honesty of scientists' self-reflection. Cases of QRPs that appear in peer-reviewed papers appear to be sharply increasing, although whether this is evidence of an increase in fraud or a greater willingness of journals to police integrity is unsure (Steen, 2011), but pressure to publish is likely to play a role. One of the oft-cited cases of misconduct is a physicist who published at the rate of almost a paper a week until his work was discredited (Service, 2003).

Formal ethics approval processes are becoming a prerequisite of human research in many jurisdictions, but the rise of the ethics committee does not necessarily correspond with a rise in ethical practice. The question 'Have you done ethics yet?' is commonly posed to research students and researchers not in the spirit of 'Have you understood the ethics implications of your study yet?' but instead refers to the bureaucratic process. Whether or not a compliance/enforcement model – and the associated adversarial tone to interactions that can develop between researchers, ethics reviewers, and research office staff – is counterproductive has not been the subject of formal research. Evidence from studies on compliance and enforcement approaches to learning in general suggest that intrinsic incentives to assist 'scientists to behave themselves' are likely to be more effective (Kohn, 2006). This chapter does not discuss what a research institution can do to adopt the more constructive resourcing reflective practice approach, but suggested reading on this matter can be found at the end of this chapter.

Similarly, a more constructive approach to the design of ethical research projects in psychology may well involve careful reflection *before* a formal research ethics review is prepared. Similarly, the ethical researcher understands that responsibilities don't end with the moment a project receives formal ethics approval. Real ongoing responsibility continues through the data collection, analysis, and the production of research outputs. The pressure to commence a project is perhaps understandable, but this is countered by increasing public scrutiny on the previously sheltered world of research.

This chapter utilises a component approach to the design of a project. Not every project will necessarily have all the components described here; they may occur in a different order, and they may be more iterative – such as in participant-directed action research. It is not our intention to imply this is the *only* way to appropriately design psychology, but in a sense, action research offers one of the more ethically nuanced approaches.

Reasons for conducting research

Ethics committees are increasingly being asked to judge not just whether a project carries significant ethical risk but whether the benefits of the project justify that risk. The 'publish or perish' dictum is not a reason that these committees acknowledge. It isn't generally acceptable to conduct psychology research purely on a whim or for the sake of idle curiosity – especially if there is a risk of harm or significant burden upon others. Thus, it is essential to have – and be able to articulate – a clear sense of why the research is being conducted. Will the project make a likely contribution to academic, scientific, clinical, or other knowledge or practice? For some research designs there may be a hypothesis or theory to explore, but that isn't essential for research to be ethically sound.

Building a rationale for conducting a particular project is in this sense not dissimilar to building a case for accepting a research article for publication: pertinent questions should be addressed, such as: 'Is the research project founded on a body of previously published work?' and conversely, 'Does this project extend previously published work?' When writing ethics applications or research articles for submission to good journals, rejections come from not being able to answer these questions in the affirmative *and demonstrate* that this is the case. Having said that, one well-cited author in the field suggests that 85% of medical research studies (including clinical trials, where ethical scrutiny is high) 'are not useful' (Ioannidis, 2016, p. 1). Ionnadis also describes the features that makes research 'useful', and these include linking the research to an identifiable problem and context; identifying an 'information gain', ensuring the context where the research applies has some pragmatic 'real life' as opposed to idealised value; and ensuring the research demonstrates value for money, feasibility, and transparency.

There is also an additional consideration less commonly seen in applications that come before ethics review panels. Panels that handle many applications may fail to recognise the less visible costs of *not* conducting a particular study. This occurs, for example, in cases where there is risk, but the risk plausibly includes risks of *not* conducting the project. Research projects with designs that were common in the 1960s and 1970s would generally be difficult, but not impossible, to replicate today. It would be interesting to see how an ethics panel would review Milgram's early 1960s research that saw participants deceived into thinking they had used electric shocks to 'train' humans to the point of cardiac arrest! However, in 2009, Burger (2009) successfully replicated Milgram's obedience-to-authority studies. The study was considered ethically sound after recommendations from the institution's ethical review board. The recommended changes to the experiment included making 150 volts (rather than 450 volts) the top of the 'shock' range and screening out participants who previously had been diagnosed with a psychiatric disorder or who were taking medications for emotional difficulties.

This view – that research needs to say something new in order to be worth doing and publishing – needs to be contrasted with the ethical question of the consequences of repressing replication studies. Bornstein (1990), remarked that in the social sciences replication studies were 'difficult to publish . . . and present some special methodological and interpretative problems for researchers' (p. 72). Yet, in Google Scholar, a 2017 search for the exact phrase 'failure to replicate' or similar phrases yields tens of thousands of results, demonstrating the value of replication studies as a form of exacting peer review. For researchers proposing a replication study, the pertinent issue is clearly justifying the need for a replication.

In reality, the vast majority of published research observes a tension between being novel and being based on tried and true methods. Being aware of and drawing upon previous studies not only increases the likelihood a planned project will be successful, safe, and respectful, it is more likely to be considered favourably by a research ethics review body. Grounding new projects in existing research also helps ensure that risks are minimised, managed, or mitigated to a level that is close to established norms. Similar to the value in acknowledging the overlap between a current research project and the body of work that came before it, the key here is being *transparent*. Failure to disclose even on minor matters can become major ethical issues, and even relatively serious errors can be forgiven if acknowledged in a transparent manner. It is important to consider, for example, whether the researchers have any potential conflicts of interest with regard to their proposed project. The presence of such conflicts probably won't automatically compromise a project, but a failure to disclose or otherwise appropriately manage a conflict could do so. Consequently, researchers are urged to err on the side of caution when considering if they have potentially perceived conflicts of interest.

Expertise and capacity issues

Doctoral-level training doesn't automatically qualify one to conduct research, and even when researchers, in their enthusiasm to explore and publish, fail to reflect on their suitability for a project – in terms of accreditation, experience, and expertise – then ethics committees certainly do. Complex projects may well require a team to cover the range of skills, but in addition to possessing the technical competence to complete a project, research leaders are also required to have the cultural and social skills required to navigate cultural protocols, beliefs, and traditions. Clearly articulating, in advance, the roles different team members will play and aligning those roles to their demonstrable skills are essential in ensuring this element of ethical practice is 'right'. Equally, it is important to map out whether individuals will require professional development and supervision. By clearly identifying a research team's expertise and roles within the proposed project, it is then easier to identify if a team needs to be expanded to bring in further expertise, and also the implications when a researcher leaves the project team. This kind of preparation is optimal for achieving both research and ethical goals. However, most national human research ethics standards merely require research ethics review bodies to consider the expertise of researchers to safely and successfully conduct a proposed project. Discussing research with the First Nations in Canada, Schnarch (2004), for example, argued that 'appropriate' expertise extends all the way to the language used in creating materials for research and for final results reporting.

Another form of 'resources' with ethical implications is the financial wherewithal and the issue of suitable facilities/equipment to complete the study. Superficially, this may appear to be more a research governance than ethical matter. It may not normally be the role of a research ethics committee to review the budget for a project, but the ethical question is to ask whether it is fair for research participants to ask them to give up their time, be exposed to risk, or otherwise accept the burdens of participation if a project is going to be closed down early because of insufficient funds? As the risks inherent in a project increase and as the perceived benefits of the project decrease, this question becomes more pressing. Such considerations may be especially acute if it could leave harms unaddressed (e.g., participants being exposed to a stimulus intended to elicit stress with the follow-up strategy intended to extinguish the negative feelings). Should a project proceed and find itself foundering due to lack of funds, researchers need to consider whether it is possible to salvage data and achieve some of the planned outcomes. Reporting the failure to complete, is increasingly a requirements of ethical review panels, but beyond the statutory requirements, research leaders need also to consider reporting the implications to participants.

Data and design

One of the advantages of the increasing formality and stringency of ethics review processes is that it encourages researchers to work through the processes of the research project before it is taken into the field or the laboratory. This is particularly important when considering how data will be generated, collected, retrieved, or accessed to achieve the project's stated objectives. Increasingly, in an era of cloud-based storage of data, questions are being asked about data security – especially regarding research *conducted* online (Nosek, Banaji, & Greenwald, 2002; and also see the discussions in Chapter 11 in this book about web-based research).

The diversity of research designs and methodologies means discussing the research challenges inherent in designs is too extensive to address within this chapter. Each research design has its own ethical peculiarities, challenges, strengths, and weaknesses. For example, an online survey that doesn't collect personally identified information might seem ideal for collecting frank accounts about attitudes on a sensitive and contentious topic, but it might also exclude some important voices (e.g., someone whose disability and living circumstances might make the completion of the survey unrealistic) and might create unfortunate and stressful problems for researchers (e.g., being unable to act if a participant uses the survey to indicate an intention to self-harm). When researchers are also participants, or participants are co-researchers (within action research or co-design approaches, for example) this makes it relatively difficult to control and predict ethical risks and requires experienced researchers to navigate all the implications. Increasingly, ethics committees like to see evidence that the processes have been thought through, looking favourably on 'run sheets' showing how interviewers will conduct focus groups, for example, or instructions or protocols issued to research assistants. These steps may feel premature or onerous at the ethics application stage, but they are methodologically good practices for research that might otherwise be only loosely planned.

Participants

Most principle-based national human research ethics frameworks include *respect* as a core ethical principle, extolling the imperative that participants be respected as human beings rather than merely a means to an end. The Helsinki Declaration, for example, states that 'while the primary purpose of . . . research is to generate new knowledge, this goal can never take precedence over the rights and interests of individual research subjects' (WMA, 2014, paragraph 8). This principle is relevant for both primary and secondary data (for example, see Chapter 7 in this book discussing the use of archival data). For research based on secondary data, the human focus and the associated rights and interests are reduced but not eliminated. Ethical considerations are still relevant. While consent may have been given for one particular purpose, it may not have been given for the purpose determined by the secondary data researcher.

When participants are to be directly involved in a project, it is important to consider how they will be initially contacted and formally recruited, whether they will be subject to any screening, and whether these strategies could expose them to risk (in some cases the fact someone was approached about participating in a project could be cause for embarrassment or even physical harm). For example, in domestic violence cases, extreme caution is urged in cases where participants may still be at risk of violence, in case the mere involvement in research may pose a risk. Typical of the approaches taken to mitigate this is a study by Coker, Follingstad, Garcia and Bush (2017), who followed extreme caution in telephone interviews with their study participants consisting of women who had experienced intimate partner violence while undergoing treatment for cancer. Interviewers asked the female participants if they were alone or if someone might listen in on the call, and if women did not feel safe to complete the interview, the interview would be rescheduled. Even when it proceeded, the interviewers provided a safe word or phrase that could be used to end the call immediately and without suspicion. Other studies take place in safe zones where participants are physically removed from any threat.

Screening can be a risk-mitigation strategy, but again, consideration needs to be given as to the relevant expertise and suitability of the screener, how the process is documented, and in some cases, what potential participants are told – including those eliminated by the screening. These are not only key considerations for good design and practice of psychology, but these are also matters that will be of interest to research ethics review bodies and can help build positive relations with participants.

Building positive relations with participants has important ethical implications. Particularly in vulnerable or important minority populations that may need to be studied again in future, a researcher has an obligation not to 'burn bridges' for future researchers. Some minorities have characteristics – such as genetic rarity – that make them of high value to the research community, but they can develop 'research fatigue' (Clark, 2008), and researchers should be particularly alert to creating a good research experience in such cases. Another common feature in national frameworks is discussions about the vulnerability of whole categories of persons whose welfare needs to be safeguarded from any maleficence by researchers. The response to this (perception of) vulnerability is not always straightforward. Does your research design or materials effectively compound that vulnerability and disempower the target population by reinforcing negative messages? The risk that researchers are a source of actual harm to vulnerable groups needs to be acknowledged. Finally, Rosenthal (1994) usefully suggested that researchers should think of participants as a 'granting agency', or in more current terms a 'donor' or 'in-kind' support to a project, rather than as mere experimental 'fodder'. Shifting the mindset of researchers in this direction improves the chances of a project being respectful and ethical at the same time.

Consent

In the previous section, the challenges of dealing with vulnerable populations was discussed, including instances of when vulnerability and consent interact.

The researcher can take a cautious approach and eliminate vulnerable samples, or those who may lack the capacity to make full informed consent, but is the generalisability of the study then limited to the non-vulnerable? Does the fact a cohort of participants have an intellectual impairment mean they can never make an informed decision about participating? In longitudinal studies, does consent obtained at Time 1 also apply to Time 2?

Contemporary standards in ethics require that consent needs to be *explicitly* obtained. To illustrate current standards, a recent large-scale study by Facebook, where researchers defended themselves against a consent issue by talking about the fine print embedded in Facebook's terms of use, caused a furor. The case demonstrates that one cannot ethically 'get around' consent through a purely legal approach. Even extending consent in the opposite direction can have its pitfalls. The long quasi-legal package that has become the default approach to consent of many researchers is not the optimal way to facilitate informed and voluntary consent. Unless potential participants have legal qualifications, these forms merely offer the appearance of informed consent and may result in participants being confused rather than informed. Finally, over-informing participants of study intent can contravene the scientific merit of the study, rendering its completion a waste of participants' time. Psychologists are particular aware of the risks of disclosing to participants too much about what they expect to find in case expectancy effects impact the participants' responses (Price, Finniss, & Benedetti, 2008). Finally, *hyper-claiming* or over-claiming (telling granting agencies, ethics committees, or participants that the research will achieve ends it is in fact unlikely to achieve) is a particularly unwise and unethical approach. Over-claiming can undermine the whole notion of 'informed' consent.

Outputs and after

There is a reasonable contention that research is not truly complete until the results have been widely disseminated; this is especially true if public funds have supported the research. Equally, modern academe can be fairly criticised for an obsession with publication that results in researchers slicing data into increasing thin servings to maximise output and to behave in ways that conform to 'existing practices, paradigms, and approaches' (Bouchikhi & Kimberly, 2001, p. 79) rather than genuinely seeking the advancement of knowledge.

Physicist Jeffrey Scargle's famous paper on publication bias (1999) noted that in the social sciences a 'study is [too often considered] worthwhile only if it reaches a statistically significant positive conclusion' (p. 92). This is a subset of a broader ethical issue: most university research is publicly funded, and increasingly the funders are demanding that results are published in open-access journals (Suber, 2012) despite residual prejudices against such journals. While making data available through open data sites is the next step in observing the spirit in which funding is made available to researchers, as we noted earlier, providing future researchers access to what amounts to secondary data has ethical implications. On the positive side it might reduce the burden on highly researched populations, while on the negative, issues of privacy and extended consent and stringent requirements for de-identifying data come into play.

We've discussed earlier the prejudice against pure replication studies and the associated favouring of studies that confirm hypotheses (Greenwald, 1975). These are problems that can be ethically overcome by researchers summarising results and including them in research reports favoured in open publication sites such as Researchgate or simply on university sites – or more controversially in journals such as the *Journal of Articles in Support of the Null Hypothesis*. These approaches improve science by allowing the inclusion of otherwise unpublished studies that collectively may better represent reality (Scargle, 2000).

Conclusion

As influential psychologist Robert Rosenthal persuasively argues, 'bad science makes for bad ethics' (1994, p. 128), and this chapter has suggested that the oft-maligned ethics review process can in fact be perceived positively. The question of the quality of the research design of a study may again seem to be outside the remit of an institutional ethics review panel, but rather than taking an adversarial or defensive view of the recommendations of a panel, feedback from ethics panels can be used to hone designs. They are, in a sense, an additional layer of peer review which includes members of the laity.

Further reading

The U.S. Office of Human Protections maintains an excellent compilation of international human research ethics arrangements (which is updated annually): www.hhs.gov/ohrp/ sites/default/files/international-compilation-of-human-research-standards-2017.pdf

References

Bouchikhi, H., & Kimberly, J. R. (2001). 'It's difficult to innovate': The death of the tenured professor and the birth of the knowledge entrepreneur. *Human Relations, 54*(1), 77–84.

Bornstein, R. F. (1990). Publication politics, experimenter bias and the replication process in social science research. *Journal of Social Behavior and Personality, 5*(4), 71–81.

Burger, J. M. (2009). Replicating milgram: Would people still obey today? *American Psychologist, 64*(1), 1–11.

Clark, T. (2008). "We're over-researched here!" Exploring accounts of research fatigue within qualitative research engagements. *Sociology, 42*(5), 953–970.

Coker, A. L., Follingstad, D. R., Garcia, L. S., & Bush, H. M. (2017). Intimate partner violence and women's cancer quality of life. *Cancer Causes & Control, 28*(1), 23–39.

Emanuel, E. J., Grady, C. C., Crouch, R. A., Lie, R. K., Miller, F. G., & Wendler, D. D. (2008). *The Oxford textbook of clinical research ethics.* Oxford: Oxford University Press.

Fanelli, D. (2009). How many scientists fabricate and falsify research? A systematic review and meta-analysis of survey data. *PloS one, 4*(5), e5738.

Greenwald, A. G. (1975). Consequences of prejudice against the null hypothesis. *Psychological Bulletin, 82*(1), 1–20.

Ioannidis, J. P. (2016). Why most clinical research is not useful. *PLoS Medicine, 13*(6), e1002049.

Kohn, A. (2006). *Beyond discipline: From compliance to community*. Alexandria, VA: Association for Supervision and Development.

Martinson, B. C., Anderson, M. S., & De Vries, R. (2005). Scientists behaving badly. *Nature, 435*(7043), 737–738.

Nosek, B. A., Banaji, M. R., & Greenwald, A. G. (2002). E-research: Ethics, security, design, and control in psychological research on the Internet. *Journal of Social Issues, 58*(1), 161–176.

Price, D. D., Finniss, D. G., & Benedetti, F. (2008). A comprehensive review of the placebo effect: Recent advances and current thought. *Annual Review of Psychology, 59*, 565–590.

Rosenthal, R. (1994). Science and ethics in conducting, analyzing, and reporting psychological research. *Psychological Science, 5*(3), 127–134.

Saunders, R., & Savulescu, J. (2008). Research ethics and lessons from Hwanggate: What can we learn from the Korean cloning fraud? *Journal of Medical Ethics, 34*(3), 214–221.

Scargle, J. D. (2000). Publication bias: The "file-drawer" problem in scientific inference. *Journal of Scientific Exploration, 14*(1), 91–106.

Schnarch, B. (2004). Ownership, control, access, and possession (OCAP) or self-determination applied to research: A critical analysis of contemporary first nations research and some options for first nations communities. *International Journal of Indigenous Health, 1*(1), 80–95.

Service, R. F. (2003). Scientific misconduct: More of Bell Labs physicist's papers retracted. *Science, 299*(5603), 31.

Steen, R. G. (2011). Retractions in the scientific literature: Is the incidence of research fraud increasing? *Journal of Medical Ethics, 37*(4), 249–253.

Steneck, N. H. (2006). Fostering integrity in research: Definitions, current knowledge, and future directions. *Science & Engineering Ethics, 12*(1), 53–74.

Suber, P. (2012). Ensuring open access for publicly funded research. *British Medical Journal, 345*, e5184.

WMA. (2014). *World Medical Association Declaration of Helsinki: Ethical principles for medical research involving human subjects*. Retrieved from www.wma.net/policies-post/wma-declaration-of-helsinki-ethical-principles-for-medical-research-involving-human-subjects/

5   Instrumentation

Stephen A. Woods

The importance of measurement in applied psychology

Are you a scientist? The default answer for applied psychologists is of course, 'yes'. Yet how do you know? In the absence of common physical markers of being a scientist, it might be argued that perhaps values play a key part; presumably you think scientifically and value evidence, logic, critical reason, and research in forming conclusions? Knowing and following the 'scientific method' for research and problem solving would also be a good indicator of a person's status as a scientist. Nevertheless, I am certain these propositions can be (in fact, are, and will continue to be) debated philosophically.

Actually, much about what it means to be a scientist in our everyday thinking is subjective perception. So, at the outset of this chapter, I intend to make a bold claim and establish an axiom of science: careful measurement. Regardless of the phenomena being studied, in pursuit of understanding, all scientists must *measure* those phenomena carefully in order to draw reliable and replicable conclusions.

Operationalizing research: deciding what to measure

In all forms of measurement in research in applied psychology, it is necessary to take decisions about *what* to measure and *how* to measure. It is critical to separate the two parts. Research questions and theory dictate the *what*, which in turn determines the *how*. In following a rational–empirical model of research, the task of the researcher is to translate research problems into answerable questions and then to use theory to present a rational proposal about the answer to the question and an explanation about why the answer is expected. This is the starting point of assembling research instrumentation: i.e., theory testing.

Whetten (1989) sets out the features of sound theory. For the purposes of measurement, it is critical that the individual components and factors of the theory are identifiable and their pattern of relationships specified. These factors form the measurement targets in the research. Operationalizing the factors involves defining them in such a way that permits straightforward measurement, and in practice, the degree of effort required for this step varies dependent on the nature of the factors.

For example, in a theoretical explanation of the relations of personality and job performance in customer service, we would likely draw on past research (e.g. meta-analyses; Barrick & Mount, 1991) that report such associations. In almost all of these studies, the Big Five personality factors (extraversion, agreeableness, conscientiousness, emotional stability, and openness) form the basis of measurement of personality traits. These five trait areas are well evidenced in personality structure research (e.g. Woods & Anderson, 2016; John & Srivastava, 1999; McCrae & Costa, 1997) but also are measured frequently. In this case, our theorizing could justifiably discuss how performance behaviour in service jobs aligns to the traits of the Big Five. In this case, the factors within the theory are defined operationally from the outset (i.e., our research will involve measuring the Big Five).

An alternative situation would be to propose a general theoretical relationship. For example, we could propose that workers with higher well-being are more productive (see Woods, 2008), because their positive affect and sense of attachment to their employer leads them to be more motivated to work hard. Here there are three main factors to operationalize: well-being, performance, and motivation. Well-being could be defined as job satisfaction and organizational commitment (Meyer & Allen, 1991). Performance could be operationalized in a number of ways but would depend greatly on the jobs that participants do. If they all worked in sales, then we might look at objective productivity indices. However, if they worked in a variety of different roles, then we might operationalize performance as general task proficiency or organizational citizenship behaviour (i.e., being a helpful, proactive colleague; Williams & Anderson, 1991). Motivation might be operationalized in different ways, such as drive for performance, sense of meaningfulness, goal orientation, extrinsic and intrinsic motivation, or positive affect. Past theory and research would help us decide the most appropriate.

A final form of research situation would be one in which there is little past theory and research that clearly points to ways of operationalizing the research. For example, a human resource manager may be interested to evaluate whether staff training in stress management has led people to feel more in control of their perceptions of stress and ability to cope with demands. Here, the need is to measure the outcome of the training. In such a situation, the literature might help provide a general grounding in the nature of stress perceptions and coping ability, but the specific nature of the organization, job, and training being evaluated will also influence the operationalization of the outcome variables and how they are measured. In short, some new measurement instrument is probably needed (discussed further later).

This example also illustrates the intersection of measurement and research design: it should be clear that a pre- and post-measurement design is optimal to examine change after the training, and ideally an experimental design in which a control group is also measured would make the research most robust (see Chapter 10 for further information). Common research design problems that are relevant for instrumentation include avoidance of common method bias

(Podsakoff, MacKenzie, Lee, & Podsakoff, 2003) and appropriate positioning of measurements in longitudinal designs (Ployhart & Vandenberg, 2010).

Measurement scales and their basic properties

The remainder of this chapter is focused on the application of quantitative measurement scales. Many of the principles around using measurement scales in research also apply to other quantitative measurement techniques (such as behavioural observation). For clarity, a scale is a set of survey items designed to measure a focal *construct*. In Box 5.1, there are presented a number of short scales published in the literature. Respectively they measure job satisfaction, task performance, and extraversion from the Big Five. It should be clear from reading the items in the scale that each one is focused on a specific construct and that the items share a high degree of consistency.

In the classical model of testing, this consistency represents the common core of the items. The classical model explains that theoretically, each item measures a part of the construct. To measure the construct perfectly, a researcher would need to use a hypothetical 'universe' of possible items to measure the construct (Kline, 1999). In practice, scales are typically 12 items or fewer, and so measurement of constructs is imperfect and subject to a degree of error. In research studies, testing the accuracy of a measure involves estimating or quantifying the amount of error through analyses of reliability.

Box 5.1   Examples of published measures

A job satisfaction scale

This set of items deals with various aspects of your job. Indicate how satisfied or dissatisfied you feel with each of these features of your present job.

Indicate how satisfied or dissatisfied you are by using this scale:

1   = Highly Dissatisfied
2   = Somewhat Dissatisfied
3   = Neutral
4   = Somewhat Satisfied
5   = Highly Satisfied

Items Satisfaction level

1   The physical work conditions.
2   The freedom to choose your own method of working.
3   Your fellow workers.

4   The recognition you get for good work.
5   Your immediate boss.
6   The amount of responsibility you are given.
7   Your rate of pay.
8   Your opportunity to use your abilities.
9   Industrial relations between management and workers in your firm.
10   Your chance of promotion.

To score this scale, simply add up the responses to each item, and divide by 10 (i.e. the number of items).

Adapted from: Warr, P., Cook, J., & Wall, T. (1979). Scales for the measurement of some work attitudes and aspects of psychological well-being. *Journal of Occupational Psychology*, *52*, 129–148.

Measuring task performance

Use the following items to rate the performance of a colleague, subordinate, or supervisor. Use the rating scale below:
   This person:

1   Adequately completes assigned duties.

   Almost Never   1   2   3   4   5   Almost Always

2   Fulfils responsibilities specified in the job description.

   Almost Never   1   2   3   4   5   Almost Always

3   Performs tasks that are expected of him/her.

   Almost Never   1   2   3   4   5   Almost Always

4   Meets formal performance requirements of the job.

   Almost Never   1   2   3   4   5   Almost Always

5   Engages in activities that will directly affect his/her performance evaluation.

   Almost Never   1   2   3   4   5   Almost Always

6   Neglects aspects of the job he/she is obligated to perform.

   Almost Never   1   2   3   4   5   Almost Always

7   Fails to perform essential duties.

   Almost Never   1   2   3   4   5   Almost Always

Williams, L. J. & Anderson, S. E. (1991). Job satisfaction and organizational commitment as predictors of organizational citizenship and in-role behaviours. *Journal of Management*, *17*, 601–617

Measuring Conscientiousness from the Big Five

To what extent do you perceive the following to be an accurate description of you?

1   = Highly inaccurate
2   = Somewhat inaccurate
3   = Neutral
4   =Somewhat accurate
5   =Highly accurate

In general, I. . .

1   Am always prepared
2   Follow a schedule
3   Pay attention to details
4   Like order
5   Get chores done right away
6   Am exacting in my work
7   Leave my belongings around.
8   Make a mess of things.
9   Often forget to put things back in their proper place.
10 Shirk my duties.

International Personality Item Pool. (2001). *A scientific collaboratory for the development of advanced measures of personality traits and other individual differences*. Retrieved March 25, 2001, from Oregon Research Institute website: http://ipip.ori.org.

Reliability

The reliability of a test is evident in two properties: (1) the extent to which the test produces scores that are stable over time and (2) the extent to which the items on a test are consistent.

Stability over time

The first and most straightforward way to measure test reliability is to examine whether the scores obtained are stable over time (test-retest reliability). The viability of this technique depends on the construct being measured and the extent to which, theoretically, it is assumed to be stable over a given time interval. An assumption of trait theories of personality is that the attributes themselves are reasonably stable in the short term (although it is now accepted that traits do develop over longer periods; see Woods, Lievens, De Fruyt, & Wille, 2013 for a review). Scores of people at two time points may be correlated to see the degree of stability, with high positive correlations (above 0.7, and ideally above 0.8) indicating that the scores are generally stable.

Internal consistency

Internal consistency analyses test the theoretical assumption that the items on the test all tap into the construct of interest. Computation of Cronbach's alpha or coefficient alpha is derived based on the correlations of each individual item with the overall score obtained from the measure (item-total correlations). These reliabilities are reported in journal articles as indicants of the adequacy of the measurements used in research studies. Values above 0.7 are desirable for internal consistency reliability. Coefficient alpha is a versatile analytic technique that is simultaneously valuable for evaluating the reliability scales and guiding their design and construction.

Validity

Alongside measurement reliability, validity is the second basic, yet crucial property of measurement scales (Clark & Watson, 1995). *Measurement validity* concerns the extent to which a scale measures the construct that it claims to measure. *Criterion validity* is the extent to which a scale is associated with a relevant range of criteria.

Face validity is concerned with the way that the test looks to the people who are completing it. It is a qualitative judgement about whether the scale items appear relevant for their purpose. Content validity is a similarly qualitative appraisal of the test validity but made by subject-matter experts rather than the test-takers. This is an important step in scale construction (see later in this chapter).

Construct validity is the closest form of validity to the general conceptualisation of measurement validity (that the test measures what it claims to measure). Unlike other forms of validity, showing that a test has construct validity does not involve a single method or technique, but rather a range of statistical analyses are performed in order to establish an evidence base for the validity of the test. Such analyses will usually include evaluation of convergent and divergent validity, analyses of the factor or dimensional structure of the test, and correlations of test scores with other relevant indicators. In situations where a new measure is designed for a research study, testing its construct validity is an important step.

Finally, **criterion validity** is concerned with showing that a measure predicts criteria in a theoretically and conceptually meaningful way. In applied psychology, particularly, the purpose of measuring a psychological construct is usually to predict some outcome or criterion of interest. In scale design, it is therefore helpful to show that the measure is associated with relevant criteria so that in novel hypothesis testing, null results may be interpreted more reliably (i.e., because null results using the measure stand in contrast to past observed criterion effects, ruling out the possibility that the scale simply does not predict criteria).

Deciding between published measures or new measures

At the point that variables in research have been operationalized, applied psychologists need next to decide on whether to use an existing published measure or design something new. Earlier we explored the theoretical perspectives in research studies that point researchers to a decision. However, theoretical concerns must be combined with practical concerns to reach a decision. In this section, four factors are identified that would help researchers determine the most appropriate decision for their study.

Construct definition

The first factor draws on issues raised in operationalizing theory. Operationalization will naturally point a researcher to either an established set of defined constructs (e.g., personality dimensions; well-being components) or more novel, less well-defined constructs. Where constructs are well-defined within the research literature, it is reasonable to assume that those constructs have been effectively measured to enable the accumulation of research evidence. In such cases, it is advisable to use established measures, since the research is likely seeking to either contribute to or apply findings in the accumulated literature. Divergence from established measurement methods would hinder achievement of either aim. In cases where constructs are poorly defined, new scale development is in order.

Research context

The context of the research is also a determinant of measurement strategy. For example, in work and organizational psychology, the organizational and job context of participants could have some impact on measurement needs. For example, performance measures that include innovative work behaviour may be ineffective where jobs afford little opportunity for innovation. Scale modification or construction could be needed. *Cultural context* is another good example of an external factor affecting our decision about measurement approach. Measures could have been designed and validated in a particular culture, for example, and the transferability of those measures to new cultures is therefore worthy of consideration. There could be items that are inappropriate or irrelevant in the cultural context of the research (e.g., items concerning alcohol use on a health-behaviour measure would be inappropriate in cultures where participants are mainly from an Islamic background). More fundamentally, measures may need to be translated into a different language, which could influence the properties (reliability and validity) of the measure. Here, some scale development work is also necessary.

Practicality

Practical demands are a major influence on choices about measurement in applied psychology. Most research is carried out as fieldwork, and consequently there are limits on what can be achieved with data collection with participants which affect how measurement is approached. Scale length, for example, is an important consideration. It is unlikely that participants will devote long periods of time to complete surveys, and even if they do, the quality of data collected decreases as people become demotivated to read items and respond carefully. So a careful evaluation of the length and necessity of scale items is required.

In many cases, the literature presents a variety of different scale lengths for measuring similar constructs. For example, job satisfaction can be measured with the items listed earlier, or alternatively with a single item (e.g., Nagy, 2002). The Big Five can be measured using 240 items of the NEO PIR (40–50 minutes administration time; Costa & McCrae, 1992), 44 items in the Big Five Inventory (5 minutes administration time; John, Donahue, & Kentle, 1991), or even five single items (1–2 minutes administration time; Woods & Hampson, 2005). There is clearly a length-bandwidth trade-off to consider. The more items included in a scale, the broader the assessment of the construct under scrutiny.

Where the literature does not offer a suitable short measure for research, it is possible to construct a new measure by validating a reduced set of items from an existing full scale or writing new items. A final word on scale-item wordings is relevant here; scale length is not solely a function of the number of items it contains but also their content. Complex wording in items should be avoided wherever possible because it adds significantly to administration time and, importantly, detracts from measurement validity and quality (Clark & Watson, 1995).

Scale age

Good scales, published in the literature, are generally well-used in research. This is because when a scale becomes an accepted method of measuring a construct, it is more straightforward for new studies to contribute to the research conversation if they also apply that scale. Scales can be used for many decades in this way. It is worth considering, however, if scales are necessarily effective because they have longevity. Research moves on, and it is good measurement practice for scales and items to be refreshed and improved over time. Critical review of published measures is therefore required to understand if they remain representative of the state of the art.

Scale development

The purpose of this chapter is not to provide a guide to scale development; for that, there are excellent, proven methodologies (see Hinkin, 1995; 1998). In this section, however, some key issues and steps in the scale development process are highlighted.

Inductive or deductive

The purpose of scale development will determine largely if a deductive or inductive approach is needed (see Burisch, 1984). If the scale is completely new (i.e., little is known about the optimal operational definition), then an inductive approach is necessary, which means that the construct needs to be elaborated, explored, and sampled very widely in an initial selection of items. If the scale is developed for reasons of scale reduction or refinement, then a deductive approach is more appropriate because it is likely that the general nature of the construct is well understood and defined in past research. Item writing can be more deliberately targeted at specific aspects of the construct to make the scale design straightforward and direct.

Item writing and refinement

Drawing together some key points raised in the chapter so far, it should be apparent that scale effectiveness is a function of the items within it. Clarity in the expression of each item is important, avoiding multiple components within single items, and keeping syntactic logic simple for easy reading. Positively and negatively keyed items are generally desirable where constructs are truly bipolar (e.g., personality dimensions where positive and negative poles of a dimension mean different things, such as introversion vs. extraversion). However, note that in very short scales including both positively and negatively keyed items may add unnecessary complexity and detract from the scale reliability. Refinement of items is a matter of content validity, and Hinkin (1995) outlined practical steps for working with subject experts to include and exclude items from the initial item set prior to data collection. Insight at this stage can have a big impact on the quality of the scale.

Sampling and piloting

New measures should be piloted and validated prior to being included in research studies. The piloting process involves collecting data on the full pool of scale items and any other scales needed for benchmarking or criterion validation to enable validation analyses to be carried out. Data should be collected from a representative sample of participants, large enough to divide into 2/3 and 1/3 sub-samples, leaving sufficient numbers of participants in each sample for appropriate structural analyses.

In practice, researchers may find that an extensive scale development pilot is unnecessary for their work. A judgement must be made about the extent to which a measure is pivotal to the research and its integration with other litera- ture. For example, for research on the Big Five, it would be essential to show that any new scale for measuring the factors was wholly equivalent to existing measures. However, in the earlier example of the evaluation of training, the outcome measures would serve as general indicators of training effects. Their equivalence to other published research measures is probably less critical. In this case, the properties of the measures can more justifiably be evaluated '*in situ*', i.e., within the main research study itself based on the sample participants, provided there are sufficient numbers.

Structural analyses

The main emphasis of analyses of new scales is to establish structural validity of the measure. There are three main techniques that are applied sequentially: exploratory factor analysis, coefficient alpha analysis, and confirmatory factor analysis (Anderson & Gerbing, 1988). *Exploratory factor analyses* (see Goldberg & Velicer, 2006 for a guide and Ford, MacCallum, & Tait, 1986 for a critique) are conducted to determine the underlying factorial structure of the items in the scale. In simple scale design, a single factor model is sought, showing that all items represent the focal construct. Items that load weakly on a single factor or cross load onto other factors are removed from the scale (Reise, Waller, & Comrey, 2000). *Alpha testing* next provides a diagnostic of the reliability of the scale and the extent to which each item is consistent with the scale as a whole. Structural validity is improved by removing items that reduce reliability of the scale, thereby improving consistency. Finally, the resultant item configuration of the scale post-analyses is tested in an independent sample through *confirmatory factor analysis* (CFA). CFA is a methodology that tests the fit of data to a pre- specified structure, providing a number of fit indices for interpretation. There are extensive guides to CFA in the literature (e.g., see Floyd and Widaman, 1995, in respect of scale design). Practically, the need to run both exploratory and confirmatory analyses in separate samples is addressed through the 2/3 and 1/3 splitting of the research sample.

Convergent and discriminant validity

The principle of convergent and discriminant validity is that scales (and their items) should be shown to converge and diverge from constructs in sensible ways (Campbell & Fiske, 1959). How it is established depends on the construct being measured and the purpose of the scale construction. Establishing *conver- gent validity* where a short scale is being constructed, for example, involves cor- relating the new scale with the longer alternative (i.e., benchmarking against the validated scale). For more novel scales, convergence of items can be exam- ined by examining item correlations with factor scores derived from the whole scale. *Discriminant validity* is equally important to examine. The utility of any measure is, in part, a function of the extent to which it represents constructs that would otherwise be unmeasured in a study or in the literature as a whole. Correlations between new scales and their items with measures of other constructs permit scale independence to be examined, referred to as discriminant validity. This serves two purposes. One is to show that items do not converge with unrelated constructs. So where a measure of conscientiousness has been designed, it would be expected that the items and the scale are uncorrelated or less strongly correlated with scales measuring the other Big Five dimensions. The second purpose is to show that a new construct is genuinely unique from constructs that exist already in the literature. For example, for theoretical testing, it could be important to show that a mediating variable is genuinely distinct from an outcome variable (i.e., that the scales used to measure each one are truly representative of different constructs). An example was reported in the study of Woods and Sofat (2013), who used discriminant validity analyses to distinguish measures of psychological meaningfulness and work engagement used in their study.

Processes for specific scale design needs

The general principles of scale design and structural analyses can be applied in a wide array of settings and to address the majority of situations where scale development is needed. However, the literature on scale development is huge, and there are plenty of specific techniques that may be applied depending on the research need. For example, in the construction of performance measures, a recent development is the ProMES technique (Pritchard, 1995). This technique reflects the contextualized and applied nature of performance measurement, providing prescriptive techniques for seeking and testing information from job holders and other stakeholders in the research. In personality scale design, specific recommendations can be found for item writing (e.g., Burisch, 1984), and also for structural analyses using CFA (Hopwood & Donnellan, 2010). CFA in personality measures, for example, is made more complex because of the multi-factorial nature of most personality constructs and items (see Woods & Anderson, 2016).

Techniques for translation also vary based on the objective of the scale design. There are multiple methods of translating survey items (e.g., Maneesri-wongul & Dixon, 2004), which vary in their complexity and application. Commonly applied is a method in which items are translated and back-translated to determine the scale content retention. However, the applications of this method are commonly misunderstood. Firstly, the method is most well suited to the study of cross-cultural differences, where scale equivalence is essential (Hui & Triandis, 1985). Second, the method does not guarantee quality translation; in fact, an accurate back-translation can indicate that the item content is retained but may result in poorly written items in the new language that do not accurately represent native written communication. Where cross-cultural equivalence is less important (e.g., when research is designed to be applied only in a specific culture), a bilingual and committee approach could be preferable in which a bilingual speaker provides an initial translation, which is then circulated among a committee to check the expression and content of the translations for authenticity and appropriateness. The message that comes through clearly from the literature on scale design is that while there are general principles of designing instrumentation in applied psychology research, there is no one 'best way' for all situations. Careful consideration of both the research purpose and context are required.

Summary

In this chapter, issues of instrumentation – the selection, construction and application of measurement techniques – have been discussed and explored. If one accepts that an axiom of science is careful measurement and that applied psychologists are scientist practitioners, then it should be clear that measurement in research is a key standard upon which the scientific status of psychology is (and should be) judged. Recognizing this, the literature on measurement in applied psychology is rich and diverse. This chapter has presented some of the key issues and areas that researchers need to think about in study design. These begin with operationalizing theory to decide *what* to measure. Once defined, strategies for measurement can be decided upon. A key decision is whether to use published measures vs. designing new measures, and a number of factors have been considered that help guide that decision. Whether designing new scales or using existing scales, measurement methodology from a variety of applied psychological and behavioural scientific literatures help ensure that measurement is reliable and valid. Care in the application of these methods is a foundation of effective applied psychological research.

References

Anderson, J. C., & Gerbing, D. W. (1988). Structural equation modeling in practice: A review and recommended two-step approach. *Psychological Bulletin, 103*(3), 411–423.

Barrick, M. R., & Mount, M. K. (1991). The big five personality dimensions and job performance: A meta-analysis. *Personnel Psychology, 44*, 1–26.

Burisch, M. (1984). Approaches to personality inventory construction: A comparison of merits. *American Psychologist, 3*, 214–227.

Campbell, D. T., & Fiske, D. W. (1959). Convergent and discriminant validation by the multitrait-multimethod matrix. *Psychological bulletin, 56*(2), 81.

Clark, L. A., & Watson, D. (1995). Constructing validity: Basic issues in objective scale development. *Psychological Assessment, 7*(3), 309–319.

Costa, P. T., & McCrae, R. R. (1992). *Revised NEO Personality Inventory (NEO-Pi-R) and NEO Five-Factor Inventory (NEO-FFI) professional manual*. Odessa, FL: Psychological Assessment Resources.

Floyd, F. J., & Widaman, K. F. (1995). Factor analysis in the development and refinement of clinical assessment instruments. *Psychological Assessment, 7*(3), 286–299.

Ford, J. K., MacCallum, R. C., & Tait, M. (1986). The application of exploratory factor analysis in applied psychology: A critical review and analysis. *Personnel Psychology, 39*(2), 291–314.

Goldberg, L. R., & Velicer, W. F. (2006). Principles of exploratory factor analysis. *Differentiating Normal and Abnormal Personality, 2,* 209–337.

Hinkin, T. R. (1995). A review of scale development practices in the study of organizations. *Journal of Management, 21*(5), 967–988.

Hinkin, T. R. (1998). A brief tutorial on the development of measures for use in survey questionnaires. *Organizational Research Methods, 1*(1), 104–121.

Hopwood, C. J., & Donnellan, M. B. (2010). How should the internal structure of personality inventories be evaluated? *Personality and Social Psychology Review, 14*(3), 332–346.

Hui, C. H., & Triandis, H. C. (1985). Measurement in cross-cultural psychology a review and comparison of strategies. *Journal of Cross-Cultural Psychology, 16*(2), 131–152.

John, O. P., Donahue, E. M., & Kentle, R. L. (1991). *The "Big Five" Inventory – Versions 4a and 54.* Berkeley, CA: Institute of Personality and Social Research, University of California.

John, O. P., & Srivastava, S. (1999). The Big Five trait taxonomy: History, measurement, and theoretical perspectives. In L. A. Pervin & O. P. John (Eds.), *Handbook of personality theory and research* (pp. 139–153). New York, NY: Guilford Press.

Kline, P. (1999). *The handbook of psychological testing.* London, UK: Routledge.

Maneesriwongul, W., & Dixon, J. K. (2004). Instrument translation process: A methods review. *Journal of Advanced Nursing, 48*(2), 175–186.

McCrae, R. R., & Costa Jr, P. T. (1997). Personality trait structure as a human universal. *The American Psychologist, 52*(5), 509–516.

Meyer, J. P. & Allen, N. J. (1991). A three-component conceptualization of organizational commitment. *Human Resource Management Review, 1,* 61–89.

Nagy, M. S. (2002). Using a single-item approach to measure facet job satisfaction. *Journal of Occupational and Organizational Psychology, 75*(1), 77–86.

Ployhart, R. E., & Vandenberg, R. J. (2010). Longitudinal research: The theory, design, and analysis of change. *Journal of Management, 36*(1), 94–120.

Podsakoff, P. M., MacKenzie, S. B., Lee, J. Y., & Podsakoff, N. P. (2003). Common method biases in behavioral research: A critical review of the literature and recommended remedies. *Journal of Applied Psychology, 88*(5), 879–903.

Pritchard, R. D. (1995). *Productivity measurement and improvement: Organizational case studies.* Westport, CT: Greenwood Publishing Group.

Reise, S. P., Waller, N. G., & Comrey, A. L. (2000). Factor analysis and scale revision. *Psychological Assessment, 12*(3), 287–297.

Warr, P., Cook, J., & Wall, T. (1979). Scales for the measurement of some work attitudes and aspects of psychological well-being. *Journal of Occupational Psychology, 52,* 129–148.

Whetten, D. A. (1989). What constitutes a theoretical contribution? *Academy of Management Review, 14* (4), 490–495.

Williams, L. J., & Anderson, S. E. (1991). Job satisfaction and organizational commitment as predictors of organizational citizenship and in-role behaviours. *Journal of Management, 17,* 601–617.

Woods, S. A. (2008). Performance measures: The elusive relationship between job performance and job satisfaction. In S. Cartwright & C. L. Cooper (Eds.), *The Oxford handbook of personnel psychology.* Oxford: Oxford University Press.

Woods, S. A., & Anderson, N. R. (2016). Toward a periodic table of personality: Mapping personality scales between the five-factor model and the circumplex model. *Journal of Applied Psychology, 101*(4), 582.

Woods, S. A., & Hampson, S. E. (2005). Measuring the big five with single items using a bipolar response scale. *European Journal of Personality, 19*, 373–390.

Woods, S. A., Lievens, F., De Fruyt, F., & Wille, B. (2013). Personality across working life: The longitudinal and reciprocal influences of personality on work. *Journal of Organizational Behavior, 34*, S7–25.

Woods, S. A., & Sofat, J. A. (2013). Personality and engagement at work: The mediating role of psychological meaningfulness. *Journal of Applied Social Psychology, 43*, 2203–2210.

Section 2

Data collection

This second section of this book provides you with a useful discussion of the 10 key methods which you may choose to use to collect your research data. The chapter authors discuss the most relevant information about each method, including the principal advantages and disadvantages, and also provide you with key references for further more detailed reading about each method. These chapters inform you not so much of the *how* of each method but instead the *why* you might choose to base your study on a specific method or method*s*.

Chapter 6 discusses the recent increase in popularity of **systematic reviews** and clearly demonstrates that conducting a systematic review is not necessarily an 'easier' method of data collection. Chapter 7 describes the inclusion of **archival data** and provides useful insights for working with (usually) someone else's dataset. Chapter 8 provides a useful overview of the most commonly used **qualitative methods** within applied psychology research, while Chapter 9 discusses three of the most frequently used qualitative methods in more detail: **interviews, focus groups and the Delphi technique**. Chapter 10 provides a detailed discussion of **experimental and quasi-experimental research methods** and suggests how including two or more of these methods can be useful. Chapter 11 discusses the increasing use of self-report surveys within psychology research, including **web-based surveys**. Methods of collecting data to assess **cognitive processes** are described in Chapter 12, while Chapter 13 provides a useful commentary on **longitudinal data collection** methods, including a discussion of current best practice. Chapter 14 focuses on **diary studies, event sampling and smart phones 'apps'**, including the recent popularity of **experience sampling methods**. Finally, Chapter 15 provides a discussion of the key issues involved in collecting data via conducting **organisational interventions**.

6   Systematic reviews

David Gough and Michelle Richardson

Knowing what we know from research

The aim of systematic reviews is to bring together what we know from research. If research may help inform any personal or policy or practice decisions, then there needs to be a way to clarify what is known from that research. Similarly, before undertaking any new research, it is sensible to know what is already known from pre-existing studies.

Research can be understood as critical systematic enquiry for public use (Stenhouse, 1981). Primary research engages with the world to create theory and empirical data to understand that world. Systematic reviews ask the same questions and use similar research paradigms and methods as primary research. The difference is that the data for the reviews are the findings of the primary studies. The research samples of reviews are pre-existing primary studies. Reviews are thus very similar to primary research but at a higher secondary or 'meta'-level of analysis. Umbrella reviews (reviews of reviews) that bring together and synthesize the findings of pre-existing reviews are then a tertiary form of meta-level of analysis.

There are two main components of the logic of systematic reviews. The first is that we need to know what we know from research (and how we know it). The second is that bringing together and clarifying that knowledge is itself a form of research and needs to be undertaken according to the agreed principles of research. In particular, the research methods need to be rigorous within the accepted standards and principles of the research paradigm being applied, and these methods need to be explicitly reported and thus accountable. Primary research is expected to be systematic because it is research. Research reviews should also be systematic. Systematic reviews are thus 'reviews of existing research using explicit, accountable rigorous research methods' (Gough, Oliver, & Thomas, 2017, p 5). The term 'systematic' only needs to be applied because, traditionally, reviews have not been always very explicit about their methods.

Reviews of research can enable those who are not professional researchers (such as policy makers, professional practitioners, users of services and others) to access the known evidence base and thus to be able to more easily participate in debates dependent on research evidence (Gough & Elbourne, 2002). Non-academic user participation in reviews may also lead to different types of review questions and clarify what future research would most help such user needs. Reviews can thus have a wide role in increasing policy, practice and public participation in research.

Approaches to systematic reviews and synthesis

The logic of systematic reviews applies to all research questions, all types of research questions and to all paradigms and methods of research. Reviews are likely to reflect the paradigms and methods used by primary research addressing similar questions in two ways. First, a review on a particular question is likely to include primary studies that have examined that question. Second, the method of reviewing is likely to reflect the assumptions and approaches of that type of primary research. An important distinction between approaches to research analysis (in both primary research and in reviews) is between the degree to which a study aggregates or configures data (Gough, Thomas, & Oliver, 2012; Sandelowski, Voils, & Leeman, 2012).

Aggregative approaches to synthesis

Aggregation is commonly used to test hypotheses through collecting empirical data. Primary research testing, for example, the hypothesis that a certain action has a particular effect, may use experimentally controlled evaluations. A review asking the same research question would be likely to include such experimental studies and to use a review method reflecting the same research approach (an *a priori* approach that aggregates data).

Such systematic reviews aiming to assess the impact of interventions typically seek effect size data from each study and then use statistical meta-analysis to produce an overall effect size. Experimental approaches are used to control for confounding variables, and reviewers are concerned to avoid bias from lack of proper randomization and various forms of selection bias. At the systematic review level, there may be concern about heterogeneity of the intervention, the samples and the contexts across studies that may undermine the statistical assumptions of the analysis. Heterogeneity can be explored through *a priori* hypothesis (theory) testing subgroup analysis or post hoc (theory developing) configuration of statistical associations. Theory development is important for understanding the causal processes (theory of change) and considering the transferability and generalizability of research findings to new contexts (Kneale, Thomas, & Harris, 2015).

Configuring approaches to synthesis

Configuring is commonly used to organize ideas, concepts and theories. Primary research asking how to conceptualize the processes occurring in some phenomena may, for example, use small scale qualitative methods such as ethnography. A review asking the same research question would be likely to include such ethnographic or similar small scale qualitative studies and to use a review method reflecting the same research approach (an iterative approach that configures conceptual data).

Conceptual reviews such as meta ethnography and thematic syntheses may use 'bottom up' approaches identifying conceptual themes in the reports of individual studies and then arranging (configuring) these to build up meta-level concepts. Other approaches may use more 'top down' approaches through the use of some initial conceptual frame, as in framework synthesis (Carroll, Booth, Leaviss, & Rick, 2013).

Reviews concerned with configuring concepts are less likely to be concerned with issues such as selection bias. They are more concerned that the data collection and reporting is true to the meaning and context from where it was drawn and the interpretations of the primary researchers whose studies are being reviewed. They are interested in heterogeneity and its meaning.

Dimensions of difference in reviews

Figure 6.1 summarizes some of the ways that predominantly aggregative and predominantly configuring reviews may differ. Many reviews may lie somewhere between these extremes on all or some of the dimensions. One example is the previously mentioned use of post hoc exploration (configuration) of how independent and dependent variables relate to each other in a predominantly aggregative statistical meta-analysis. Another example is framework synthesis using some *a priori* concepts in a predominantly configuring review.

Reviews may also use mixed methods. This can be through reviewing together a sample of studies using different methods or through a review having sub-questions (applied in parallel or sequentially) that each apply different types

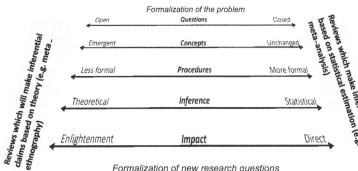

Figure 6.1 Dimensions of differences in approaches to systematic reviews

(Figure 3.11 in Gough and Thomas, 2017, p. 69)

of reviews methods and include different types of primary studies. An example is a review by the EPPI-Centre on weight management programmes (Sutcliffe et al., 2016). The first sub-question sought successful weight loss methods and mechanisms as perceived by those who had used or delivered weight management programmes. The second sub-question assessed the effectiveness of the perceived effective features from experimental studies. Case studies were then undertaken with local services to explore the nature of current weight management provision and to consider the implications of the review findings for future service provision (Sutcliffe et al., 2016).

Another example of a multi-stage review is a review that first configures the nature and structure of a mid-level theory that naming and shaming reduces anti-social behaviour and that then aggregates data to examine whether there is evidence that the causal processes proposed by the theory occur in practice (Pawson, 2010). The realist approach is interesting, as it used an iterative explorative approach to aggregation compared to the more aggregative *a priori* approach used by some other theory-driven complex reviews.

There are also many other dimensions of difference between reviews (Gough et al., 2012, Gough, & Thomas, 2017). One example is the breadth and depth of review questions and the amount of work done by a review. A review may have a broad or narrow question and may address it with a rather shallow or in a very detailed way. So, whatever resources are available to undertake a review, then, there are choices to be made in how these are used to construct the breadth and depth of a research question. As time and resources are often limited, some advocate rapid reviews. These tend to be both narrow and shallow in order to reduce the scope of the review. Alternatively, they may reduce the rigour with which the review is undertaken. Either way, the usefulness of the review may be reduced. In contrast, mixed-methods reviews are likely to be addressing broader review questions in more depth and so be more complex reviews.

Review questions and identifying studies

The first stage in a review is determining the research question that the review wishes to answer. This review question needs to be 'unpacked' to clarify any implicit assumptions and the question's 'conceptual framework'. Without clarity about the question being asked, it is difficult to operationalize the process of review necessary to answer that question. In some cases, though, there may be some iteration and development of the question as the review proceeds (just as in some primary research).

Inclusion criteria

Inclusion criteria define what pre-existing studies will be used to answer the review question. These may include the topic addressed, the research methods used by the primary studies and any date and language restrictions. In iterative reviews, the inclusion criteria may evolve during the process of the review in light of the number of studies retrieved and the research priorities. In order to assist with the specification of inclusion criteria, a number of acronyms have been developed. PICO, for example, refers to 'population, intervention, comparison and outcomes', which are common components in research to test the impact of an intervention. SPIDER refers to 'sample, phenomenon of interest, design, evaluation and research type' as common components of exploratory evaluative research questions (Cooke, Smith, & Booth, 2012).

Search strategy

The search strategy is the plan to identify the studies defined by the inclusion criteria. The strategy will specify where and how to search. This may include detailed plans for searching specified electronic bibliographic databases, hand searching of chapters in books, searching of particular websites and general web searching. For some review questions, relevant studies may be most likely found in particular bibliographic databases. For other questions, studies may be most likely found as reports on government or other organizational websites. Formally published papers[1] may be seen to have the advantage of being peer reviewed, but this may not be a very strict or fit for purpose (for the review) form of appraisal and the review itself should check the quality of all included studies. Also, a search restricted to bibliographic databases may miss crucial studies. Collaboration with an information specialist who understands the conceptual complexities of reviewing can be invaluable.

The search of subject specific websites may identify relevant research reports (Stansfield, Dickson, & Bangpan, 2016). General web searching can also be a very productive or useful as a check of the effectiveness of the main search strategy. This may be better achieved through a general Internet search than through Google Scholar, which is similar to a bibliographic database of journal publications.

Another check is to see if all the studies known prior to the search are identified by the search. The reference lists of already known studies can also be a source of studies. Both of these methods are useful but can be dangerous as the main methods of searching, as they may lead you to only find studies similar to the ones that you already know.

The broader the search, the more sensitive it will likely to be in finding studies that meet the criteria. The more sensitive the search, however, the less specific it is and the more non-relevant studies will be identified. A more specific search may be more efficient, but it may miss some relevant studies. Searches for review questions that come from an *a priori* research aggregative paradigm are likely to be as exhaustive as possible in order to minimize risk of bias in aggregation (Brunton, Stansfield, Caird, & Thomas, 2017). Searches for configurative reviews asking open questions may also be best achieved through an exhaustive strategy, though this might not always be the case. In some reviews you may only need on example of each type of study. In that situation, a purposeful strategy may be adopted until saturation for a particular issue or concept is achieved (Booth, 2016).

Screening

The process for checking that studies identified by the search strategy meet the inclusion criteria is called screening. This may be a two-stage process when searching bibliographic databases with study abstracts. The abstracts identified by the search can be checked in order to make a preliminary screening decision. If the abstract suggests that the study is a possible 'include' (i.e., meets the inclusion criteria), the full paper is sought, and then a final decision on inclusion can be made. The process of screening can be explicitly reported using a flow diagram such as in the PRISMA reporting guidelines (Moher, Alessandro Liberati, Tetzlaff J, Altman DG, & the PRISMA Group, 2009).

Coding and managing information about studies

The studies included in a review are the samples for the review. Data are required from each study in order to:

- Manage each study through the review process;
- To describe (map) the research field as defined by the inclusion criteria;
- Appraise quality and relevance of the studies; and
- Identify and synthesize the findings of the studies.

The way that data are coded and collected from studies varies considerably across reviews. In a statistical meta-analysis measuring the effect of an intervention, the statistical effect sizes may be collected and synthesized. In some cases, such statistical synthesis is not appropriate, and other data may be collected to allow some form of narrative analysis. Some reviews have more iterative coding of qualitative data with thematic coding of the text in primary study reports, as, for example, in meta ethnographic reviews (Melendez-Torres, Grant, & Bonell, 2015). If a review has multiple sub-questions with sequential or parallel stages, then there are likely to be multiple inclusion criteria and multiple types of studies, each of which may require different forms of coding (Kneale et. al., 2015).

Systematic maps

The description of all of the individual studies included in the review can be combined to provide a 'map' of the research field (as defined by the inclusion criteria)[2] (Gough & Thomas, 2017; Peersman, 1996). All reviews describe the included studies in some way, but this varies in extent. A systematic map can be understood as a systematic description and analysis of the research field defined by a review question (Gough & Thomas, 2017).

The nature of the map will depend upon its purpose and focus and the data that has been coded from each study. In the EPPI-Centre, we often map the research field on about 15 forms of data. Some of these codes may be generic to all reviews, some may be specific to reviews on particular questions or issues or topics and some may be review specific. Maps do not normally include study findings which will not have been quality and relevance appraised.

Maps detail what has been studied in a research field and how it has been studied and can also show gaps in what has been studied. As the map is defined by the review question and its inclusion criteria, this research field may cut across traditional academic or practice disciplines. One example of a map is research on personal development planning (PDP or self-regulation of learning). This showed that at that time, research in the USA mostly examined the effects of PDP using controlled experimental evaluations, whereas in the UK the studies were mostly descriptive natural experiments of process and effect (Gough, Kiwan, Sutcliffe, Simpson, & Houghton, 2003).

Maps can be products in their own right, and sometimes a review may not proceed past this stage to synthesis of research findings. If the review does proceed to synthesis, then the map can assist in several ways. First, the map can inform how the synthesis is undertaken. In some cases, information from the map may suggest that it is not helpful or practicable to synthesize all of the studies, and a decision can be made to narrow the review question and to synthesize only a subset of the included studies. Knowing that the map can be narrowed for synthesis allows reviewers to include a broader range of studies in the map to provide a context for interpreting the synthesis. It can also allow a broad initial question creating a broad map followed by a number of separate syntheses based on sub-questions with narrower inclusion criteria. Second, the map can provide information describing the research field to provide a context for undertaking and interpreting the findings of the synthesized studies.

Automating reviews

Reviews involve considerable human input, and thus time and money. Automation is being introduced into the review process to make the processes more efficient, more linked up and possibly more accurate. One area where automation can assist is in searching and screening of studies. As already mentioned, it can be difficult to search for particular methods of research. If software can be taught to distinguish between examples of papers reporting different methods, then this can be used to make searches more sensitive (Marshall, Noel-Storr, Kuiper, Thomas, & Wallace, in press; Stansfield, O'Mara-Eves, and Thomas, 2017). Similarly, studies identified by a search can be screened by reviewers, and the text mining software can then 'learn' the nature of the included studies and order the yet-to-be-screened studies in terms of the likelihood of inclusion. This makes the screening process by reviewers more efficient, and in some cases it may also be possible to stop screening when the remaining unscreened studies are unlikely to include any relevant studies (O'Mara-Eves, Thomas, McNaught, Miwa, & Ananiadou, 2015). Automation can also be used to constantly search for new studies that might meet a review's inclusion criteria and allow timely updating of reviews as 'living reviews' (Thomas et al., 2017).

Appraising justifiable evidence claims

Research produces findings (evidence claims) that aim to answer the research question. In terms of a systematic review, the appraisal of the evidence claims are based on three main issues: (a) how the review was conducted; (b) the individual studies used by the review; and (c) the nature of the total evidence identified (Gough, 2016; Liabo, Gough, & Harden, 2017). These are discussed in turn.

Appraising methods of review

Reporting tools and guidelines exist that state what issues are important about how a review is conducted, and these tools can be used to appraise the standards of reported reviews. Appraisal of the review includes the appropriateness of the method, appropriateness of the focus of the review and the quality of the execution of the review. Reviews can be challenging, and so good quality reviews will have skilled reviewers piloting and development of the stages of work and double parallel coding of some stages of the review (such as, for example, screening and data coding). Reviewer skills include the methods of reviewing and academic, practice and user knowledge and perspectives on what is being studied.

The PRISMA statement (Moher et al., 2009) is a reporting guideline for methods of systematic review with a 27-item checklist and a flow diagram of studies identified in a review. The statement was originally designed for evaluating statistical meta-analysis reviews of the impact of interventions. It has been extended for other types of reviews including network meta-analysis and for reporting protocols and abstracts equity issues (Welch et al., 2016). MOOSE is a reporting guideline for observational studies (Stroup, Berlin et al., 2008) and RAMESES is for realist synthesis (Wong, Greenhalgh, Westhorp, Buckingham, & Pawson, 2013).

There are also tools for evaluating completed reviews such as AMSTAR (Shea et al., 2017). The updated tool has 16 items for appraising *a priori* hypothesis testing reviews of health care interventions. The appraisal items are concerned primarily with different types of potential bias. Another tool is ROBIS, which covers a wider range of review methods such as intervention, diagnosis, prognosis and actiology reviews (Whiting, Savović, Higgins, Caldwell, Reeves, Shea, Davies, Kleijnen, Churchil & the ROBIS Group, 2016). There are fewer appraisal tools for more iterative reviews although there is a planned extension of PRISMA for meta-ethnography called eMERGe (France et al., 2015).

Appraising evidence included in a review

The appraisal of included studies is a standard stage in the process of undertaking many types of review and is one of the reasons for coding information from the included studies.

The reporting and appraisal tools already discussed often include items on included studies, but there are many other tools for only appraising included studies. Many tools are concerned with bias in appraising *a priori* aggregative studies (Katrak, Bialocerkowski, Massy-Westropp, Kumar, Grimmer, 2004), whilst others appraise more iterative qualitative configuring studies (for example, Spencer, Ritchie, Lewis, & Dillon, 2003), and some appraise mixed methods studies (Heyvaert, Hannes, Maes, & Onghena, 2013).

Appraising the nature of the total evidence identified

Tools like GRADE examine both the included studies (as in the previous section) and the totality of evidence. GRADE is used to appraise the evidence for predominantly aggregative reviews on the impact of health interventions (Guyatt et al., 2008). GRADE assesses the evidence. GRADE-CERQual assesses the quality of findings of primarily configuring conceptual syntheses (Lewin et al., 2015). With the exception of GRADE, the tools for appraising evidence included in a review mostly focus on the quality of execution of studies of particular research designs rather than on the relevance of method and focus to the research question. An exception is realist synthesis, where Pawson (2006) argued that an individual study may be of poor quality and yet may contribute 'good' evidence for the review question.

Interpreting and using evidence from systematic reviews

Evidence claims can inform policy, practice and personal decision making. The evidence claims of reviews are based on all of the relevant evidence, and so the claims should be broader than those of individual studies. Other factors beyond research are obviously important in decision making. There have been attempts to help formalize some of these other factors. Part of the GRADE tool (and associated Evidence to Decision frameworks) examine factors such as the cost, feasibility and acceptability of health treatments (that a review shows to be effective; Alonso-Coello et al., 2016). Other approaches such as that by NICE[3] in England include stakeholder driven deliberative processes to synthesize and interpret research and other evidence within a framework of social values in order to develop guidance for practice in health and social care (Gough et al., 2014).

Interpreting and applying research evidence involves social values and judgement, but so does the whole research process. Different individuals and groups may have different ideas about how the world is constructed and conceptualized and what is important to study and how. Primary research and systematic reviews of that research provide explicit rigorous methods of making justifiable evidence claims within the constraints of particular perspectives, values and priorities. Reviews alone, though, do not overcome the problem that research seems to have little impact on decision making, and so we need to progress research on research use (Gough, Stewart, & Tripney, 2017). Involving the potential users of the research in the review process may make it more likely that the review reflects their perspectives, values and priorities and thus be of more relevance and potential use to them.

Conclusion

This chapter has considered the use of rigorous and explicit methods to systematically review existing literature in order to generate a more comprehensive understanding of research pertaining to a research question than is possible from individual studies alone. The chapter explores the diversity in approaches to reviewing that reflect the variation in types of research questions and research methods in the social, behavioural and medical sciences. The usefulness of a review will depend on the quality and suitability of the review methods in relation to the question asked, the sufficiency of the evidence produced and its relevance to the users' needs. Review methods therefore need to be rigorous and reported explicitly so that each review can be evaluated using appropriate quality assurance. Emerging information technologies such as text mining are particularly *promising* for assisting with screening in *systematic reviews*. Recommendations that arise from systematic reviews should be based not only on the best evidence about what works but also what people consider to be most appropriate and feasible. The challenge of how to get the policy and practice world to engage with the best evidence is not unique to systematic reviews, but it is a very important one. The attempts to formalize and institutionalize some aspects of these processes could make some of these priorities and values more overt and thus more open to societal debate and decision making.

Notes

1 Not formally published literature can be referred to as grey or gray literature, though the term is not so important as: (a) modes of disseminating research changes and (b) reliance on the reviews' quality appraisal methods.
2 Systematic mapping is sometimes referred to as scoping, but the term scoping is also sometimes used to mean a quick non-systematic review – maybe prior to a systematic review.
3 National Institute for Health and Care Excellence.

References

Alonso-Coello, P., Schunemann, H. J., Moberg, J., Brignardello-Petersen, R., Akl, E. A., Davoli, M., . . . GRADE Working Group. (2016). GRADE Evidence to Decision (EtD) frameworks: A systematic and transparent approach to making well informed healthcare choices. 1: Introduction. *BMJ, 353*, i2016.

Booth, A. (2016). Searching for qualitative research for inclusion in systematic reviews: A structured methodological review. *Systematic Reviews, 5*, 74.

Brunton, V. J., Stansfield, C., Caird, J., & Thomas, J. (2017). Finding relevant studies. In D. Gough, S. Oliver, J. Thomas (Eds.), *An introduction to systematic reviews* (2nd ed.). London, UK: Sage.

Carroll, C., Booth, A., Leaviss, J., & Rick, J. (2013). "Best fit" framework synthesis: Refining the method. *BMC medical research methodology, BMC Medical Research Methodology, 13*(1), 37.

Cooke, A., Smith, D., Booth, A. (2012). Beyond PICO: The SPIDER tool for qualitative evidence synthesis. *Qualitative Health Research, 22*(10), 1435–1443.

France, E., Ring, N., Noyes, J., Maxwell, M., Duncan, E., Turley Uny, I. (2015). Protocol-developing meta-ethnography reporting guidelines (eMERGe). *BMC Medical Research Methodology, 15*, 103.

Gough, D. A. (2016). *Evidence standards: A dimensions of difference framework for justifiable evidence claim (with special reference to systematic reviews).* London, UK: EPPI-Centre, University College London.

Gough, D., & Elbourne, D. (2002). Systematic research synthesis to inform policy, practice and democratic debate. *Social Policy and Society, 1*, 1–12.

Gough, D., Kenny, C., Vigurs, C., Stansfield, C., Rosen, R., & Taylor, T. (2014). *Social values related to the development of health and care guidance.* Report of the Research Support Unit for the National Institute for Health and Care Excellence. London, UK: EPPI-Centre, Social Science Research Unit, Institute of Education, University of London. https://eppi.ioe.ac.uk/cms/Publications/Systematicreviews/NICESocialValues/tabid/3698/Default.aspx

Gough, D. A., Kiwan, D., Sutcliffe, K., Simpson, D., & Houghton, N. (2003). A systematic map and synthesis review of the effectiveness of personal development planning for improving student learning. In *Research evidence in education library.* London, UK: EPPI-Centre, Social Science Research Unit, Institute of Education, University of London.

Gough, D., Oliver, S., & Thomas, J. (2017). Introducing systematic reviews. In D. Gough, S. Oliver, J. Thomas (Eds.), *Introduction to systematic reviews* (2nd ed.). London, UK: Sage.

Gough, D., Stewart, R., & Tripney, J. (2017). Using research findings. In D. Gough, S. Oliver, & J. Thomas (Eds.), *Introduction to systematic reviews* (2nd ed.). London, UK: Sage.

Gough, D., & Thomas, J. (2017). Commonality and diversity in reviews. In D. Gough, S. Oliver, & J. Thomas (Eds.), *Introduction to systematic reviews* (2nd ed.). London, UK: Sage.

Gough D, Thomas, J., & Oliver S. (2012). Clarifying differences between review designs and methods. *Systematic Reviews, 1*, 28.

Guyatt, G. H., Oxman, A. D., Kunz, R., Falck-Ytter, Y., Vist, G. E., Liberati, A., & Schunemann, H. J., & GRADE Working Group et al. (2008). Going from evidence to recommendations. *British Medical Journal, 336*, 1049–1051.

Heyvaert, M., Hannes, K., Maes, B., & Onghena, P. (2013). Critical appraisal of mixed methods studies. *Journal of Mixed Methods Research, 7*(4), 302–327.

Katrak, P., Bialocerkowski, A. E., Massy-Westropp, N., Kumar, S., Grimmer, K. A. (2004). A systematic review of the content of critical appraisal tools. *BMC Medical Research Methodology, 4*, 22.

Kneale, D., Thomas, J., Harris, K. (2015). Developing and optimising the use of logic models in systematic reviews: Exploring practice and good practice in the use of programme theory in reviews. *PLoS One, 10*(11).

Lewin, S., Glenton, C., Munthe-Kaas, H., Carlsen, B., Colvin, C. J., Gülmezoglu, M., Noyes, J., Booth, A., Garside, R., & Rashidian, A. (2015). Using qualitative evidence in decision making for health and social interventions: An approach to assess confidence in findings from qualitative evidence syntheses (GRADE-CERQual). *PLoS Med, 12*(10).

Liabo, K., Gough, D., Harden, A. (2017). Developing justifiable evidence claims. In D. Gough, S. Oliver, & J. Thomas (Eds), *Introduction to systematic reviews* (2nd ed.). London, UK: Sage.

Marshall, I. J., Noel-Storr, A. H., Kuiper, J., Thomas, J., & Wallace, B. C. (in press). Machine learning for identifying randomized controlled trials: An evaluation and practitioner's guide. *Research Synthesis Methods.*

Melendez-Torres, G. J., Grant, S., & Bonell, C. (2015). A systematic review and critical appraisal of qualitative metasynthetic practice in public health to develop a taxonomy of operations of reciprocal translation. *Methods of Research Synthesis, 6*, 357–371.

Moher, D., Alessandro Liberati., Tetzlaff, J., Altman, D. G., & the PRISMA Group. (2009). Preferred reporting items for (SR) and meta-analyses: The PRISMA statement. *Ann Intern Med 358*:264–269.

O'Mara-Eves, A., Thomas, J., McNaught, J., Miwa, M., & Ananiadou, S. (2015). Using text mining for study identification in systematic reviews: A systematic review of current approaches. *Systematic Reviews, 4*(1), 5.

Pawson, R. (2006). Digging for nuggets: How 'bad' research can yield 'good' evidence. *International Journal of Social Research Methodology, 9*(2), 127–142.

Pawson, R. (2010). Evidence and policy and naming and shaming. *Policy Studies, 23*(3), 2002.

Peersman, G. (1996). *A descriptive mapping of health promotion studies in young people* (EPPI Research Report). London, UK: EPPI-Centre, Social Science Research Unit, Institute of Education, University of London.

Sandelowski, M., Voils, C. I., Leeman, J., Crandell, J. L. (2012). Mapping the mixed methods-mixed research synthesis terrain. *Journal of Mixed Methods Research, 6*(4), 317–331.

Shea, B. J., Reeves, B. C., Wells, G., Thuku, M., Hamel, C., Moran, J., Moher, D., Tugwell, P., Welch, V., Kristjansson, E., & Henry, D. A. (2017). AMSTAR 2: A critical appraisal tool for systematic reviews that include randomised or non-randomised studies of healthcare interventions, or both. *BMJ, 358*, j4008.

Spencer, L., Ritchie, J., Lewis, J., Dillon, L. (2003). *Quality in qualitative evaluation: A framework for assessing research evidence.* London, UK: Cabinet Office. Retrieved from www.gov.uk/government/publications/government-social-research-framework-for-assessing-research-evidence

Stansfield, C., Dickson, K., & Bangpan, M. (2016). Exploring issues in the conduct of website searching and other online sources for systematic reviews: How can we be systematic? *Systematic Reviews. 5*(1), 191.

Stansfield, C., O'Mara-Eves, A., Thomas, J. (2017). Text mining for search term development in systematic reviewing: A discussion of some methods and challenges. *Res Synth Methods*, 1–11. Retrieved from http://doi.wiley.com/10.1002/jrsm.1250

Stenhouse, L. (1981). What counts as research. *British Journal of Educational Studies. 29*(2), 103–114.

Stroup, D. F., Berlin, J. A., Morton, S. C., Olkin, I., Williamson, G. D., Rennie, D., Moher, D., Becker, B. J., Sipe, T. A., & Thacker, S. B. (2000). Meta-analysis of observational studies in epidemiology: A proposal for reporting. Meta-analysis of observational Studies in Epidemiology (MOOSE) group. *JAMA, 358*, 2008–2012.

Sutcliffe, K., Richardson, M., Rees, R., Burchett, H., Melendez-Torres, G. J., Stansfield, C., & Thomas, J. (2016). *What are the critical features of successful Tier 2 weight management programmes for adults? A systematic review to identify the programme characteristics, and combinations of characteristics, that are associated with successful weight loss.* London, UK: EPPI-Centre, Social Science Research Unit, UCL Institute of Education, University College London. https://eppi.ioe.ac.uk/cms/Publications/Systematicreviews/Weightmanagementreview/tabid/3675/Default.aspx

Thomas, J., Noel-Storr, A., Marshall, I., Wallace, B., McDonald, S., Mavergames, C., ... Living Systematic Review Network. (2017). Living systematic reviews: 2. Combining human and machine effort. *Journal of Clinical Epidemiology*. Retrieved from www.sciencedirect.com/science/article/pii/S0895435617306042

Welch, V., Petticrew, M., Petkovic, J., Moher, D., Waters, E., White, H., Tugwell., & the PRISMA Bellagio Equity Group. (2016). Extending the PRISMA statement to equity-focused systematic reviews (PRISMA-E 2012): Explanation and elaboration. *Journal of Clinical Epidemiology, 70*, 68–89.

Whiting, P., Savović, J., Higgins, J. P. T., Caldwell, D. M., Reeves, B. C., Shea, B., Davies, P., Kleijnen, J., Churchil, R., & ROBIS Group. (2016). ROBIS: A new tool to assess risk of bias in systematic reviews was developed. *Journal of Clinical Epidemiology*, *69*, 225–234.

Wong, G., Greenhalgh, T., Westhorp, G., Buckingham, J., Pawson, R. (2013). RAMESES publication standards: Realist syntheses. *BMC Medicine*, *11*, 21.

7 Research using archival data

Gwenith G. Fisher and Dorey S. Chaffee

Introduction

Archival data are existing data, such as survey responses, records, texts or other information, that are examined for any purpose other than the purpose(s) for which the data were originally collected (Fisher & Barnes-Farrell, 2013; Shultz, Hoffman, & Reiter-Palmon, 2005). Archival data are typically used for secondary data analysis in one of two ways. First, data may be reexamined for the same purpose that was under consideration when data were initially collected. Second, data may be examined for a purpose that is distinct from its original purpose, thereby deriving novel information from the dataset to address questions that are unrelated to the reasons the data were collected. Therefore, in a research investigation, archival data can be the focal source of data (e.g., responses to an employee climate survey) or be a supplement to another primary data source (e.g., data from human resources records or the Occupational Information Network (O★NET) linked to data from a primary data source, such as a survey).

Types of archival data

Archival data encompass any existing data that are utilized for a purpose other than the focal purpose for which the data were initially collected. Although not exhaustive, Singleton and Straits (2005) provided a useful taxonomy to classify types and sources of archival data. In the following section we review the four types of archival data that might be considered most relevant to applied psychology researchers. These include social science data archives; public documents, datasets, or official records; private documents or records; and mass media.

Social science data archives

Typically, social science data archives can be differentiated from other types of archival data based on the purpose for which the data were originally collected. Social science data archives are data originally collected for research purposes and are often made publically available to the research community in an effort to facilitate research. For example, many publicly available data archives are the result of large investments made by government agencies, such as the U.S. National Institutes of Health, that increasingly require researchers whose work is funded by these agencies to share the data they have collected in order to maximize the use of a particular dataset in order to inform public policy. Many of these datasets have been developed with the express purpose of establishing a data resource that can be used by researchers from different fields of study to address numerous questions. Because data collection and maintenance can be expensive and labour intensive, these datasets typically share several common characteristics. Specifically, they are often intentionally designed to include measures that will be of broad interest and of lasting value, utilize sophisticated population sampling techniques, are subject to rigorous testing and evaluation of the study content and data quality, often provide a support for distributing the data to the research community and include a research plan to disseminate research findings. Many of these purpose-built research archives may be of interest to applied psychology researchers. We discuss three of these types of these data archives here: large-scale surveys, public social science archives and private datasets.

Large-scale surveys

Numerous datasets from large-scale surveys exist for public use. A few examples include the National Health Interview Survey (NHIS), the General Social Survey (GSS), the Study of Midlife Development in the U.S. (MIDUS), the National Study of the Changing Workforce (NSCW) and the Survey of Health, Ageing, and Retirement in Europe (SHARE). Increasingly these large-scale survey datasets are being designed to include variables and measures that are used in other large-scale national surveys, which facilitates cross-national comparison research. Additionally, the Eurobarometer and the International Social Survey Program (ISSP) are examples of multi-nation collaborations, and these are growing in number.

Public social science data archives

Another form of publicly available data are archives, which include collections of many different types of studies. Two large examples of such archives in the U.S. include the Inter-University Consortium for Political and Social Research (ICPSR), which is part of the Institute for Social Research at the University of Michigan and the Roper Center at the University of Connecticut. ICPSR data collections span a wide variety of topics (e.g., economic behaviour and attitudes, organizational behaviour, social institutions and behaviour), include national and international collections (e.g., Eurobarometer Survey Series, Midlife Development in the United States Series), contain datasets collected by private organizations (e.g., American Association of Retired Persons; AARP), and provide numerous series datasets that are updated continuously (e.g., Research and Development (RAND) Aging Studies in the Developing World Series, the General Social Surveys). Further, the ICPSR website provides an array of excellent resources to help students utilize the data archives. However, it is important to note that although data archives are publicly available, some cost may be involved in obtaining access to these data.

Private datasets

Compared to the aforementioned publicly available datasets, private datasets differ in that they are not available for public use. Private datasets refer to existing data that were previously collected for research or evaluative purposes, including a researcher's own data collected from a prior study or data collected by outside researchers or agencies. One example of a private dataset is the U.S. Navy career development dataset. Access to and utilization of private datasets for secondary analysis research is contingent on the data owner's willingness to share a private resource, and therefore a starting point to obtain access to the private dataset is to contact the owner of the data (e.g., lead researcher, agency). Clear communication of the value of the research questions to be addressed and the development of a trusting relationship with the data owner(s) are often key to obtaining access to private datasets.

Public documents, datasets or official records

There are many sources of publicly available data in the form of public documents, datasets and official records that are available on individuals and organizations and may be of particular interest to applied psychology researchers. Examples include the U.S. Census Bureau data (which collects data at the individual level as well as employer data via the U.S. Census Bureau Business Register database), the U.S. Bureau of Labor Statistics (which conducts a number of surveys such as Census of Fatal Occupational Injuries and the Current Population Survey) and a number of other official records such as birth certificates or death information (e.g., the National Death Index), and O★NET. Developed by the U.S. Department of Labor, O★NET serves as a primary source of occupational information in the U.S. because it contains several hundred variables with detailed information about specific occupations, including detailed characteristics of work and workers such as worker characteristics, worker requirements, experience requirements, job requirements, workforce characteristics and occupation-specific labour market information. One benefit of using public documents, datasets or official records is that they are most always free.

Private documents or records

Compared to data from social science archives and other public documents or private research datasets, a distinguishing feature of archival data from private documents and records is that these data were not necessarily collected for research purposes. Instead, these documents and records are typically collected about individuals for other reasons. Examples of these data include human resources or other organizational records, such as company records of workplace injuries and illness, and individuals' medical records, school records, financial statements and credit history, among others. Although certain data are publicly available (e.g., some records collected by government agencies), other data are truly private and protected by specific privacy laws and regulations (e.g., medical records). Thus, to obtain access to these data, special permission is often required.

Mass media

Over the last decade, the utilization of data for secondary analysis that were collected via mass media has grown exponentially. The advancement of technology and wide-spread use of the Internet has increased not only the number of mass media sources but also access to these data. These data include a wide range of sources including newspapers, magazines, television, movies and sources on the Internet, including blogs and videos (e.g., YouTube) as well as social media (e.g., LinkedIn, Facebook, Twitter).

The use of archival data within the applied psychology field

The use of archival data for research in applied psychology continues to increase. This trend may reflect challenges associated with collecting primary data from certain sources (e.g., organizational samples), advancements in information technology that are collecting greater quantities of data and facilitate data storage and access, and requirements from grant funding agencies that primary data collected as part of a funded research project be made available to others in the research community. In the following sections we discuss some of the advantages to using existing data as well as some of the inherent challenges. We then provide best practice recommendations for conducting research in psychology using existing data and secondary analysis.

Opportunities and advantages to using archival data

There are several advantages to using archival data, especially in applied psychology research. These include available data, data with specific research designs and methodology, large sample size, data representative of population or subpopulation, broader scope of variables, objective rather than subjective data, and data suitable for student research projects.

Available data

Perhaps the most obvious advantage to using archival data is that the data are readily available. Having data available can circumvent primary data collection, which is often a time-consuming and expensive step in the research process.

There are numerous sources of existing data that can be obtained at no cost to the data user. Similarly, existing data can be excellent for pilot testing ideas before investing the time and resources necessary for primary data collection. However, as discussed later, using data collected by others may come with costs and consequences and is not always less time-consuming and cost effective than primary data collection. Nonetheless, thoughtful use of existing data can be an efficient way to move research projects along more quickly.

Data with specific research designs or methodology

In addition to already existing data, another advantage to using archival data is the opportunity to access datasets based on a particular research design or methodology that is especially challenging to implement. For example, access to longitudinal data is one of the most obvious advantages to using existing data in applied psychology research. These data can include repeated or multiple observations among participants over time. In addition, many datasets are advantageous to researchers because they may have a large sample size and/or sample from a broader geographical area than what a researcher could feasibly collect on his or her own.

Population/subpopulation representative

In recent years there has been growing emphasis on sampling techniques in psychology research in order to increase the generalizability of research results (Bergman & Jean, 2016; Fisher & Sandell, 2015). Researchers can use archival datasets to obtain representative data on a variety of specific populations. For example, the Health and Retirement Study, which is a U.S. national probability sample of adults age 51 or older, is an excellent source for researchers with interests in studying older adults. Archival datasets are useful because they can also contain information on specific subpopulations (e.g., a particular gender, race/ethnic group or occupational sector) and hard-to-reach subpopulations that may be difficult to obtain in primary data collection (e.g., pregnant workers who were laid-off or terminated from their job). Many large datasets have purposefully incorporated systematic oversampling of some low-frequency populations, while other archival datasets have been collected with a specific purpose or population in mind (e.g., survivors of prostate cancer who are currently employed).

Broader scope of variables

As previously mentioned, large archival datasets often include a broad scope of variables with data on a variety of topics that span across disciplines. Thus, archival datasets can offer a unique advantage by way of facilitating interdisciplinary and cross-disciplinary research and providing researchers an opportunity to address boundary-spanning questions that would be difficult to study otherwise.

Objective rather than subjective data

Archival datasets frequently include or are linked to objective data such as a company's administrative data (e.g., sickness absences, work accidents), biomarkers, physical performance measures and other forms of data that may be difficult to obtain as part of a primary data collection. Objective data may also help avoid or mitigate the drawbacks of using subjective data (e.g., self-report measures). For example, when combined with subjective data, objective data can help avoid issues with self-report bias and minimize or alleviate concerns of common method bias and other types of measurement error. However, even objective data are subject to a variety of errors, some of which are discussed in the 'Challenges' section.

Suitable for student research projects

One of the benefits of archival data is that they may be very useful for student research projects. Archival data can provide students with available data so that they do not need to collect data themselves, which can be very time consuming. Students can also develop important skills, such as how to identify, retrieve, merge and manage large-scale datasets.

Challenges and disadvantages to using archival data

Large, complex databases

Many archival datasets often consist of large, complex databases that are designed and prepared by someone other than the data user. As such, archival datasets may be difficult to navigate and are often not user friendly in terms of how easy it is to acquire and set up the data. Data documentation may lack clarity. Some datasets may require special software to convert the dataset to a usable data file. Often the extent to which a researcher can readily assemble and utilize an archival dataset is a function of the quality and extent of documentation provided with the dataset. Although datasets vary in terms of documentation, ideally a dataset should be accompanied by a codebook that details the variables used in the study, including measurement properties and sources, in addition to a description of the methodology used in data collection. Archival data may require data users to invest extra time to become familiar with the data and to set up the data for analysis. Thus, using archival data often involves more work on the front end of a research project. Large and complex datasets require strong data management skills to be able to merge and assemble data files, construct variables, and recode values assigned to variables. We strongly encourage archival data users to budget sufficient time for data management prior to beginning actual data analysis.

Complex sample survey designs and need for sample weights

Many archival datasets, in particular large-scale population-based surveys, use complex sample survey designs (e.g., probability sampling, clustering and stratification) that require data users to apply sample weights or other variables in order to properly account for survey design features during data analysis. Sample weights are used to adjust sample design characteristics so that statistical computation of point and variance estimates accurately represent the population. Complex sampling techniques are especially useful for generalizing to an entire population of interest. However, they can increase the complexity of data analysis. In some cases, special software may be needed because some statistical software packages are more capable of handling complex sample survey design features than others.

Lack of desirable measurement properties

A primary drawback to using archival data involves whether and how variables of interest are measured. Because archival data are sometimes collected independent of the research questions being addressed, oftentimes measures of interest may be missing or less than optimal for measuring certain constructs. For example, as previously mentioned, many large-scale survey datasets are designed to cover a broader scope of variables and obtain information on a variety of topics. As a result, constructs are often measured with only a few items, or in some cases, a single item, which limits the researcher's ability to evaluate the quality of the measure. Further, when variables of interest are omitted from the dataset, researchers often resort to proxy measures for their variables of interest. Although research-constructed variables and measures with poor or unknown psychometric quality may be subject to criticism, using such data may still be useful for research when the strengths of the research design outweigh the limitations (e.g., sampling methodology, longitudinal design). Nonetheless, careful consideration of measures available in the dataset is warranted to determine whether or not the dataset is suitable for the researcher's purposes.

Missing data

Many archival datasets, in particular longitudinal datasets, contain missing values. Data collected by someone else can make it more difficult to ascertain the reason(s) why data are missing. It is important for researchers to invest time in understanding patterns of missing data because, similar to the aforementioned measurement issues, patterns of missing data may also influence the usability of the data for the researcher's purposes. To determine whether or not the dataset is suitable for the researcher's intended purposes, an initial examination of the distributions of all variables of interest and missing data patterns is strongly recommended. If using a dataset with missing data, it is important to apply the most appropriate statistical methods to treat missing data. See also Chapter 16 for a detailed discussion of missing data.

Objective rather than subjective measures

Objective data are frequently included in archival datasets and offer many advantages over subjective data such as reducing (or eliminating) certain types of measurement error that are associated with self-report and common method bias. However, objective measures are not error free, and in many cases objective data may be of poorer quality than certain kinds of subjective data. The quality of objective data is highly contingent on the methods used to collect and record the data. For example, data in the form of administrative records may be tainted by errors introduced during data entry by a clerk entering an incorrect code in health care records, or errors may be introduced when the data were collected by an equipment malfunction (e.g., a laboratory machine not calibrated correctly). In addition, it is often difficult to obtain reliability estimates for objective sources of data. Finally, the dataset may contain objective measures on a topic that may be more appropriately assessed via self-report. Taken together, it is critical to examine the measurement properties of all variables of interest in the dataset and carefully consider the strengths and limitations of each data source when determining the suitability of the dataset to answer the research question.

Old data

Another potential drawback to using archival datasets is the data may have been collected a long time ago. A primary concern is that old data may no longer be relevant and/or generalizable to the current phenomenon under investigation, although the degree to which old data may be an issue is largely dependent on the topic and question under investigation. When examining the suitability of an archival data source, we encourage researchers to consider the relevance and generalizability concerns associated with the use of older datasets. Many archival datasets are part of ongoing data collection efforts and are often an opportune source to investigate how phenomena change over time.

Too much data

Archival data are often from rich datasets containing numerous variables across a broad array of topics. Given the broad array of possibilities, having a rich dataset can be overwhelming. One challenge associated with having too much data is that researchers run the risk of approaching the dataset in an unfocused way and have greater difficulty narrowing the scope of the study to a reasonable analysis. To counteract this challenge, research questions should be specified *a priori*, and then data obtained from an appropriate existing source to analyze the question. That is not to say that all research using archival data should be deductive or that research questions can't be formulated *after* identifying a particular dataset. However, it's inappropriate to use existing datasets for fishing expeditions or primarily drive the research agenda.

Ethical issues

One important consideration in the use of archival data is that data users need to consider ethical issues involved in using the data. For example, is the proposed use of the archival data in line with the manner in which the data were collected? Were data collected in a manner consistent with ethical guidelines in one's own field of study?

Lack of suitability for student research projects

Previously we mentioned that one advantage of archival data is that they may be suitable for student research projects. However, archival data may not be suitable because the size and complexity of the dataset may not lend itself well to use by students. Additionally, students may lack the data management or other skills to effectively use the dataset. Preparing data for analysis may be incredibly time-consuming and, in some ways, more challenging than designing and collecting one's own data.

Conclusion and recommendations

Archival data has both advantages and disadvantages. We conclude by providing a series of recommendations to anyone who may be considering the use of archival data for a research project:

1   Identify and focus research questions before looking for datasets.
2   Assess the appropriateness of the dataset to answer the research question.
3   Learn about key aspects of the dataset (e.g., survey design, sampling, how constructs are operationalized, what variables are available, etc.).
4   Budget a sufficient amount of time for data management such as data acquisition, merging, data file formatting, analyses of psychometric properties, etc.
5   Investigate/address ethical and/or Institutional Review Board (IRB) issues early on.
6   Network with others who have used the same data source.

References

Bergman, M. E., & Jean, V. A. (2016). Where have all the "workers" gone? A critical analysis of the unrepresentativeness of our samples relative to the labor market in the industrial – organizational psychology literature. *Industrial and Organizational Psychology, 9*(1), 84–113.

Fisher, G. G., & Barnes-Farrell, J. L. (2013). Use of archival data in OHP research. In R. R. Sinclair, M. Wang, & L. E. Tetrick (Eds.), *Research methods in occupational health psychology: State of the art in measurement, design, and data analysis* (pp. 290–322). New York, NY: Routledge.

Fisher, G. G., & Sandell, K. (2015). Sampling in industrial – organizational psychology research: Now what? *Industrial and Organizational Psychology, 8*(2), 232–237.

Shultz, K. S., Hoffman, C. C., & Reiter-Palmon, R. (2005). Using archival data for I-O research: Advantages, pitfalls, sources, and examples. *The Industrial-Organizational Psychologist, 42* (3), 31–37.

Singleton, R. A., & Straits, B. C. (2005). *Approaches to social research* (4th ed.). New York, NY: Oxford University Press.

8 Overview of qualitative methods

Olav Muurlink

Introduction

The view of research methods in psychology depends not just on where you sit but when. If you sat, for example, on the shores of the new science in the United States in the 1970s, you would see experimental methods as far as the eye could see, whereas if you took in the sights of European psychology 50 years before, the work of Jung and Freud and their celebrated studies of non-random samples of $N = 1$ would have dominated the view. As psychology matures, it is beginning to expand its toolbox, adding to the kit rather than abandoning tools as it progresses. In this chapter, we examine some the qualitative tools, and more generally, the qualitative approach. This approach has been used to tackle the same problems that 'traditional' experimental or other quantitative methods allow us to tackle, but in some cases it offers an angle to tackle research problems that are *qualitatively* different to 'traditional' research questions. For the conventionally trained psychology researcher, qualitative research methods can be shrouded in translucent jargon, something this chapter will avoid.

Histories of qualitative research in social science tend to place the first formal roots of the approach in the fifteenth-century histories of voyages by Europeans to the 'New World' (Vidich & Lyman, 1994), but here the viewer/researcher was placed in very much the same position as the modern quantitative researcher: detached from the topic, observing an entity that could be explained without reference to the prejudices/philosophy of the observer. There is something *qualitatively* different about where the modern qualitative researcher sits in relation to the research project. The assumption shared by most qualitative researchers is that researchers are 'socially situated', not at an artificial remove from the research project. So qualitative research theory makes it clearer than its quantitative counterpart that there is a connection between philosophies on the one hand, and methodology and methods on the other. The qualitative researcher will rarely begin to assemble a research project without first thinking of their place in relation to the project.

In the late nineteenth century, German philosopher Wilhelm Dilthey, himself an empiricist who dabbled in psychology, began to lay bare the epistemological assumptions that went into research. He usefully distinguished explanatory psychology (where the researcher's epistemology subjugates the researched) from descriptive psychology, where the researcher attempts to understand the world of the researched from the "structural nexus of consciousness" (Dilthey, 1977). Dilthey's work, which came to influence early twentieth-century sociology more than psychology, remained *positivist*, that is, knowledge could be gained on the basis of sensory experience (you *can* believe your eyes) which is interpreted through reason and logic, as opposed to *interpretivist*, an influential and relatively new view of social science that sees the focus shift off the object of investigation to the investigator and how ideas, concepts and even language shape 'reality' (Weber, 2004). That change began to take hold in the 1960s.

However, while qualitative research has carved out a substantial place in the social sciences in general, within mainstream academic psychology it is fair to say it has only carved out a substantial *niche*. There *are* nevertheless many extraordinarily influential examples of qualitative research inside mainstream psychology. For example, note the emergence of Maslow's hierarchy of needs (Maslow built his work on cases of what he called "exemplary people", what in today's terms would be called case studies; [Maslow, Frager, Fadiman, McReynolds, & Cox, 1970]) and Kohlberg's use of storytelling techniques in semi-structured interviews to build his stage theory of moral development (Kohlberg, 1984).

In this chapter I will discuss some of the better-known qualitative approaches relatively briefly, and while their ontological complexity makes it difficult to do each justice in brief form, one can controversially argue that these approaches are still powerful if mishandled or handled superficially.

Ethnography

Ethnography is the systematic study of people and cultures, where researchers (or what Agar calls "professional strangers"; [1996]) immerse themselves in the context of the subjects, aiming to understand the subjective point of view of those observed as well as the mechanisms of social behaviour. It's still empirical, but it acknowledges that context can transform meaning and that things operate in systems. The ethnographer is "both researcher and research instrument" (McFarland, 2014, p. 97). The techniques of the autoethnographer, once armed with a research question, having conducted a literature review and gained entrance to the target community usually, like Mars, involves *participant observation* (to remove distance between the researcher and the researched) which is recorded in field notes and the collection of other data, including artefacts (defined as anything created by humans which offers insight into them, or their culture), so as to avoid memory biases, and henceforth to analysis and interpretation.

Understanding the connection between elements of the system is the work of ethnography. The term *critical* ethnography simply puts more emphasis on the theory, and has been described as an 'appropriation' of conventional ethnography "to transform it into a project concerned with bringing about human emancipation" (Hammersley, 2013, p. 96). From a researcher's (as opposed to activist's) perspective, the focus is on revealing the power relations at work in research and in the subject of research. Ethnographers used to be trained by doing ethnography – and Gerald Mars' *Cheats at Work* (1983), looking at workplace crime, was an example of the method: Mars got out of his office, abandoned any concept of a 'laboratory', and took up jobs working behind bars and in factories, winning the trust of the people he wrote about. However, now ethnography has changed, with less reference to immersion, less sensitivity to subjective values. "Whereas the classical approach was one of spending considerable time in the field, learning the nuances and 'deep meanings' of the system, we now find 'hit and run' forays into the field being termed 'ethnography'", as critic Ray Rist suggests, giving rise to "blitzkrieg ethnography" (Rist, 1980).

Autoethnography is perhaps even more troubled, with the author/researcher moved centre stage. Inevitably, autoethnography offers highly personalised accounts (Sparkes, 2002) and reduces the opportunity for validation of method or findings and, inevitability, almost any pretence to generalisability. This needs to be distinguished from William Wundt's work on introspection in the nineteenth century, involving structured recording of thoughts and sensation by subjects themselves, where the aim is establishing objective and replicable relationships.

Phenomenology

Phenomenology and ethnography are not so far removed from each other. Again, it is an openly *interpretative* approach to research. Phenomenological analysis is designed to explore the participant's view of the topic that the researcher has chosen, looking for what Conrad aptly calls the "insider's perspective" (1987). So taking a phenomenological approach to health psychology, for example, doesn't deny that bodies and bodily processes including illness exist but embraces the fact that two patients diagnosed with the same illness may come to experience that illness very differently due to their different *sense-making* – the interpretative process by which individuals assign meanings to things that have happened to them. Phenomenology may start with raw data such as an interview, working from a single case with the researcher reading the interview repeatedly before marking themes and apparently significant elements, looking for potential connections between them. A single case, if sufficiently rich, can be written up as a case study in its own right or can be used as a preliminary template to analyse other cases, with the researcher moving back and forth between the cases as new insights emerge. This can become cumbersome with a large dataset of participants, with Smith, Flowers, Osborn, and Yardley (1997) suggesting that in these cases, a more cursory examination of a larger number of transcripts allows an early settling on a number of shared themes, followed by more detailed coding in a second stage.

Phenomenology tends to be closely focused on searching for patterns and connections between themes, as well as points of disconnect or tensions – involving the *exceptional case*, for example. In quantitative psychology, the exceptional case is commonly discarded as an outlier, but exceptional cases can be considered within qualitative approaches, illuminating the limits of standard classifications and suggesting new (however rare) relationships between variables (Ermakoff, 2014). Oliver Sacks' work (1987) is an easy illustration of the value of such outliers in understanding normative behaviour.

Discourse analysis

Discourse analysis can be distinguished from phenomenology in that it shares a commitment to the importance of language, but discourse analysis is less ambitious in its attempts to 'get at' the underlying cognitive structure of the subject. So, while Potter and Wetherell (1987) might regard words as behaviour in their own right, phenomenology is aimed at revealing underlying cognitive structure and what the subject feels and thinks about the subject, assuming a reality that can be unwrapped using words. The difference between discourse analysis and phenomenology is not crisp. Discourse analysis is a general term that covers a number of approaches that regard language, or more broadly signs or symbols (analysis of which encompasses the field of *semiotics*), as phenomena worth detaching from the producers of signs or symbols and examining on their own. Its proponents include French philosophers such as Michel Foucault, whose *Archaeology of Knowledge* (1972) explored knowledge through how it was expressed, although Foucault saw expression in signs and symbols beyond language – including the structure of buildings, for example, in his gamut. Foucault may have done himself a disservice by expressing his ideas in a language that readers struggled to decode, and the influence of Foucault (who drew psychology into many of his better-known texts) on discourse analysis, if anything, has increased since the 1970s. However, stripping some of the philosophical and literary theory away from discourse analysis reveals a set of techniques that analyses syntactic structure, gestures, diction phonetics and linguistic style and assumes that exact choices of expression reveal some deeper truth about the individual, much in the manner of Freud's psychoanalysis. Even though he regarded words as "predestined to ambiguity" (Freud, 1901, p. 294), Freud time and again focuses on the exact words of a patient in drawing his conclusions. It is worth noting that Freud regarded psychoanalysis not so much as a theory but as a new scientific research *method*.

Narrative research

Narrative research is commonly distinguished from discourse analysis even though it is commonly defined as any study that uses or analyses "narrative materials" (which includes literary works, but also field notes by an anthropologist for example, or personal letters; [Lieblich, Tuval-Mashiach, & Zilber, 1998]). The key distinction appears to be the focus on more or less coherent *stories*, although those stories can be 'small' and specific or 'big' stories, which may be about historical events, for example. This focus on stories is considered well-advised considering the power of story over the construction of everyday life. This key concept is by no means easy to pin down, with Bruner (1986) arguing that it involves a unique sequence of events or mental events that can be real or imaginary, that connect to forge links between the exceptional and the ordinary or perhaps, to use the language from methodology, to generalise from the individual case. The evidence from outside qualitative research accumulated by cognitive psychologists suggests that humans struggle to consider discrete events as being truly independent from each other (Ladouceur, Paquet, & Dubé, 1996), instead ascribing connection and causation even when the events are 'purely' random. Unlike grounded theory or phenomenological analysis, there are no how-to guides to teach the newcomer 'a' method of doing narrative analysis, and there are few, if any, rules (Squire et al., 2014). Like other approaches canvassed here, narrative research does not assume a single absolute version of human reality, or indeed one correct reading of that reality. Narrative research asks the same difficult questions that other approaches ask; for example, "are narratives shaped by the audiences to whom they are delivered?" (Squire et al., 2014, p. 6).

Grounded theory

Grounded theory emerged as a term in sociological theory-making in the 1950s, with Karl Lewin using the term in a text on management research in 1951, but the term exploded into the scholarly literature in the 1980s after a volume by Glaser and Strauss marked its arrival in 1967 (Glaser, Strauss, & Strutzel, 1968) before peaking before the turn of the century. While the approach can be systematic, its popularity lies in its flexibility, and this flexibility partly can be traced to a battle between Glaser, who continued to evangelise for grounded theory in its original form ("all is data" [2007]), and Strauss, whose approach permitted theory that had emerged early (for example with a first interview) to be developed by purposive sampling of further interviewees. Putting aside this argument, at its simplest, grounded theory involves the constructing of theory through the analysis of data – a process not unique to qualitative research. While the archetype of quantitative research might be theory first, data collection second, the cyclical nature of science (modifications as a result of failures of theory that Karl Popper regarded as central to the nature of good science [Popper, 1959]) means that at certain points in time, even traditional quantitative research may resemble the essence of grounded theory.

The process of *doing* grounded theory often starts with the analysis (or even the collection) of data, with data being tagged with codes and sorted into categories, but it can be regarded as distinct to other qualitative approaches in that some authors encourage leaping into data collection and analysis *without* having done a preliminary literature review and *without* recording and transcribing (for example) interviews, although these 'purer' versions of grounded theory are far from universally accepted (Charmaz, 2014). Theory developed through grounded theory processes has the advantage of being *parsimonious*, in that the researcher doesn't have to sift through existing theory to retrofit onto data; *innovative*, because it generally generates new theory; and *valid*, because it is sourced in in data. Grounded theory and phenomenology are particularly susceptible to being mistaken for each other, focusing as they both do on the "richness of human experience . . . the subject's own frame of reference and . . . flexible data collection procedures" (Baker, Wuest, & Stern, 1992, p. 1355). Phenomenology, more than grounded theory (unless one takes the purist approach) relies on the experience of the subject, without the benefit of previous research, whereas grounded theory may well regard previous research (emerging from a literature review, for example) as mere data from which theory might emerge. Grounded theory is also less concerned about generalisability, instead focused on the degree of fit between the theory and the data and the degree to which it explains what has, and is, happening, in the group represented by the data (Glaser et al., 1968).

Action research

Action research is also known as 'participatory action research'. While the method is regarded as new, like much of qualitative research it has shared roots with other methods. German-American social psychologist Kurt Lewin is regarded as the founder of action research as a relatively distinct form of study. In the first paper he published on the method, he described it usefully as "a spiral of steps, each of which is composed of a circle of planning, action and fact-finding about the result of the action" (Lewin, 1946, p. 206). In action research, then, the idea of the researcher being separate to the research is openly regarded as a fiction. Rather than just being considered compromised or coloured by bias, the researcher is seen as being an active agent in the research process and the research context.

Lewin's influence made it acceptable for research to be regarded as a collaboration between stakeholders and the social scientists investigating them. Lewin's spiral recognised that theory could drive research and practice, but that *doing things* with the 'subject' of one's research was a shortcut to theory. Action research also asks "what really is the purpose of social research" (McTaggart, 2002, p. 1) and answers it by saying 'change': researchers not only change the reality they observe but also *should* seek to change it. One of the shortcomings of action research is the issue of generalisability. Are results derived from local conditions and a particular researcher apt to apply to larger contexts and different researchers? Validity, however, is less of a problem with action research than other forms of research, being the ultimate in applied science (Brydon-Miller, Greenwood, & Maguire, 2003).

Historical research

Historical research can be defined as being a process of systematically examining past events, aimed at clarifying a concept, a place, a time or social phenomena. In terms of *method*, it is an umbrella term that can include qualitative and quantitative methods. Historical research almost inevitably ends up drawing from archival data, although it can rely, like other qualitative approaches, on contemporaneous interviews. Historical researchers treat archival data as 'witnesses' or 'evidence', and from the perspective of some of the other forms of qualitative research discussed in this chapter, historical research can at times exhibit a naïve attitudes towards 'facts' (the 'history as a repository of facts' fallacy [Rowlinson, 2005]). The sheer scale of history can also pose an obstacle to a historical research project. For example, one of the giants of modern social psychology, Roy Baumeister, conducted an analysis of the emergence of the modern idea of 'selfhood' (1987) using two types of what he called 'evidence': historical data and literature (including especially fiction). The problem with defining evidence so broadly, particularly when dealing with such a large topic, is that the amount of data *cannot* be systematically analysed in a reasonable time period, and the result can 'degenerate' into a literature review. Data collection is (often) not regarded as a neutral process, with the researcher's position again impacting how materials are chosen and understood. "No archival sources are neutral" (Ginzburg, 2013), because the authors of the original data may have had their eye on history – even beyond the limits of their own subjectivity. One curiosity of historical research is that it regards as primary data material that would otherwise be commonly considered secondary data. Here, primary sources of historical research data might include first-person accounts of events, as well as music and photographs, while secondary sources are regarded as those who did not experience events first-hand, even when they collected claim to be directly connected (e.g., as eyewitnesses) to events (Lundy, 2012). The process of historical research involves, in relatively traditional fashion, identifying a research topic/problem/aim or question first, then collecting, evaluating, synthesising and reporting on data.

Case study research

Case study research, in common with most of the methods discussed here, involves inducting theory from data, but it is generally understood as a method focused on plotting the boundaries of a project rather than specifying too exactly what happens within those boundaries. What makes 'case study' approaches different to the other approaches is that it explicitly focused on building understanding of the dynamics between variables present in a single setting, although it can then generalise from the particular case. So the case study will focus on a single identifiable event, a single project, company or industry. The method is flexible enough to incorporate multiple levels of analysis in a single study (Yin, 1984; e.g., industry and specific organisation) and even encompass mixed methods, with survey data being combined with interview transcripts. The case study can be aimed at describing a phenomenon or testing or generating theory.

An influential example of case study research in psychology is Yuille and Cutshall's (1986) study of a fatal shooting incident in Vancouver, conducted in cooperation with the Royal Canadian Mounted Police. Thirteen of 21 eyewitnesses to the shooting agreed to participate in a research interview four to five months after the incident, with semi-structured interviews mimicking police protocols taking place – with the addition of two misleading questions. The case study was well-designed, thorough and very high in validity, leading to questioning of the generalisability of laboratory studies showing that eyewitness testimony was highly vulnerable to leading questions and deterioration of memory. While this study showed the value of a single case in disconfirming what had been regarded as a general phenomenon, case study approaches are often quite vulnerable to selection biases.

Organisations that are prepared to cooperate with researchers are arguably not typical organisations, and some researchers go to lengths to ensure that sampling processes in selecting cases mimic the processes in 'standard' quantitative approaches (e.g. Muurlink, Wilkinson, Peetz, & Townsend, 2012).

Conclusion

There is a family resemblance between the different forms of qualitative research, and a critical analysis of the 'different' forms reveals large areas of overlap. Attempts at policing these boundaries can have the side-effect of dissuading newcomers from qualitative research approaches altogether. Qualitative methods in psychology have a long and rich history sometimes overlooked in a modern psychology school. As a means of generating ideas and gaining insight into the lived experience of the traditional psychology 'subject', qualitative research deserves a place in every researcher's toolbox. While some qualitative techniques can be trained in a prescriptive and step-by-step manner, perhaps the single greatest strength of qualitative research is its flexibility, with an agile researcher with ability in clinical work perhaps best equipped to take advantage.

Further reading

Qualitative Psychology is a new APA journal that explains its purpose as being a home for qualitative researchers and theoreticians who are determined to explain the "lived or narrated experience in its natural setting" in a "way that attempts to persuade others of the sensibleness of the sense they make". It's a place where both theory, techniques and examples of qualitative research have a home. Good overviews of qualitative research methods with a less specific psychology focus are published by imprints such as Sage, Wiley and others, with new editions out almost annually.

References

Agar, M. H. (1996). *The professional stranger: An informal introduction to ethnography.* New York, NY: Academic Press.

Baker, C., Wuest, J., & Stern, P. N. (1992). Method slurring: The grounded theory/phenomenology example. *Journal of Advanced Nursing, 17*(11), 1355–1360.

Baumeister, R. F. (1987). How the self became a problem: A psychological review of historical research. *Journal of Personality and Social Psychology, 52*(1), 163.

Bruner, J. (1986). *Actual minds, possible worlds.* Cambridge, MA: Harvard University Press.

Brydon-Miller, M., Greenwood, D., & Maguire, P. (2003). Why action research? *Action Research, 1*(1), 9–28.

Charmaz, K. (2014). *Constructing grounded theory.* Thousand Oaks, CA: Sage.

Conrad, P. (1987). *The experience of illness: Recent and new directions.* London: Tavistock.

Dilthey, W. (1977). Ideas concerning a descriptive and analytic psychology (1894). *Descriptive psychology and historical understanding* (pp. 21–120). London, UK: Springer.

Ermakoff, I. (2014). Exceptional cases: Epistemic contributions and normative expectations. *European Journal of Sociology, 55*(2), 223–243.

Foucault, M. (1972). *The archaeology of knowledge.* London: Tavistock Publications.

Freud, S. (1901). *The psychopathology of everyday life.* Harmondsworth: Penguin Books Ltd.

Ginzburg, C. (2013). *Clues, myths, and the historical method.* Baltimore, MD: Jophn Hopkins University Press.

Glaser, B., Strauss, A., & Strutzel, E. (1968). *The discovery of grounded theory: Strategies for qualitative research. Nursing Research, 17*(4), 364–365.

Hammersley, M. (2013). *What's wrong with ethnography?.* London, UK: Routledge.

Kohlberg, L. (1984). *The psychology of moral development: The nature and validity of moral stages.* San Francisco, CA: Harper & Row.

Ladouceur, R., Paquet, C., & Dubé, D. (1996). Erroneous perceptions in generating sequences of random events1. *Journal of Applied Social Psychology, 26*(24), 2157–2166.

Lewin, K. (1946). Action research and minority problems. *Journal of Social Issues, 2*(4), 34–46.

Lieblich, A., Tuval-Mashiach, R., & Zilber, T. (1998). *Narrative research: Reading, analysis, and interpretation* (Vol. 47). Thousand Oaks, CA: Sage.

Lundy, K. S. (2012). Historical research. In P. L. Munhall (Ed.), *Nursing research* (pp. 381–398). Sudbury, MA. Jones & Bartlett Learning.

Mars, G. (1983). *Cheats at work: An anthropology of workplace crime.* London: Unwin Paperbacks.

Maslow, A. H., Frager, R., Fadiman, J., McReynolds, C., & Cox, R. (1970). *Motivation and personality* (Vol. 2). New York, NY: Harper & Row.

McFarland, D. M. (2014). How to do ethnography. *Nursing Research Using Ethnography: Qualitative Designs and Methods in Nursing, 95.*

McTaggart, R. (2002). Chapter 1: Action research scholar: The role of the scholar in action research. *Counterpoints, 183,* 1–16.

Muurlink, O. T., Wilkinson, A., Peetz, D., & Townsend, K. (2012). Managerial autism: Threat – rigidity and rigidity's threat. *British Journal of Management, 23* (Supplement S1), S74–S87.

Popper, K. (1959). *The logic of scientific discovery.* New York, NY: Basic Books.

Potter, J., & Wetherell, M. (1987). *Discourse and social psychology: Beyond attitudes and behaviour.* Thousand Oaks, CA: Sage.

Rist, R. C. (1980). Blitzkrieg ethnography: On the transformation of a method into a movement. *Educational Researcher, 9*(2), 8–10.

Rowlinson, M. (2005). *Historical research methods. Research in organizations: Foundations and methods of inquiry* (pp. 295–312). San Francisco, CA: Berett-Kohler Publishers.

Sacks, O. (1987). *The man who mistook his wife for a hat.* New York, NY: Harper Perennial.

Smith, J. A., Flowers, P., Osborn, M., & Yardley, L. (1997). Interpretative phenomenological analysis and the psychology of health and illness. *Material Discourses of Health and Illness,* 68–91.

Sparkes, A. C. (2002). Autoethnography: Self-indulgence or something more. *Ethnographically Speaking: Autoethnography, Literature, and Aesthetics,* 209–232.

Squire, C., Andrews, M., Davis, M., Esin, C., Harrison, B., Hydén, L.-C., & Hydén, M. (2014). *What is narrative research?* London: Bloomsbury Publishing.

Vidich, A. J., & Lyman, S. M. (1994). Qualitative methods: Their history in sociology and anthropology. *Handbook of Qualitative Research*, *2*, 37–84.

Weber, R. (2004). Editor's comments: The rhetoric of positivism versus interpretivism: A personal view. *MIS Quarterly*, iii–xii.

Yin, R. (1984). *Case study research*. Beverly Hills, CA: Sage Publications.

Yuille, J. C., & Cutshall, J. L. (1986). A case study of eyewitness memory of a crime. *Journal of Applied Psychology*, *71*(2), 291.

9 Interviews, focus groups, and Delphi techniques

Jennifer Brown

Introduction

Most applied psychologists are employed in four main areas: clinical, educational and occupational psychology and government service, e.g., as prison psychologists (Hartley & Branthwaite, 2000). Whether practitioner and/or researcher, much of what they do involves exploring people's experiences and behaviour. Nearly 80 years ago, the American psychologist Gordon Allport expressed the view that if you want to know something about people's activities, the best way of finding out is to ask them. The three methods described in this chapter offer distinct ways of doing this.

Interviews broadly defined are an "interaction in which two or more people are brought together into direct contact for at least one party to learn something from the other" (Brenner, Brown, & Canter, 1985). A focus group is a facilitated group discussion that is "focused" on a particular topic (Millward, 2000). The Delphi technique structures a group communication process by bringing together a panel of experts to formulate a prediction or set of priorities (Dalkey, 1967). By and large, the topics of interest addressed by these methods can be characterised as "real world" problems (see Robson & McCarten, 2016, for a comprehensive guide when preparing for and conducting applied research).

The chapter that follows will briefly outline the history, indicate strengths and weaknesses, show how to conduct, and offer some dos and don'ts of these three methods. These are intended as guidance, so just following these tips does not necessarily mean the research design, application of the method or conclusions drawn from the analysed data are sound. The requirements for the robustness of the findings (i.e., the demands of reliability and validity) may depend on the purpose of the study and the audience to whom the results are disseminated (peer reviewers are likely to be more demanding than a client or research sponsor).

Some preliminary pointers may be helpful before reading the chapter:

- There is a vast accumulated literature on these methods, and a chapter such as this can only provide a skeleton outline, so other indicative resources will be provided within and at the end of the chapter.

- Your choice of a method must be appropriate to the underlying assumptions of your epistemological approach (very broadly, a positivist position, in which knowledge is thought to be more objective and factual, or constructionist, in which knowledge is thought to be more subjective and gained through interaction with an informant).
- The chosen method should permit collection of appropriate data that answers the research question(s).
- The method must meet the needs for the capability and competence of the targeted respondent population.
- It is important to be mindful of how the data generated by these methods are to be analysed (the subject of Section 3 of this book) as part of the decision to opt for one or other or a combination of methods.
- Such methods are often employed to address sensitive or pressing topics and may recruit potentially vulnerable groups which impinge on ethical and possibly legal issues (see Chapter 4 for a discussion of these).
- Allow sufficient time; become aware of the skills required and other resources (e.g., equipment, rooms, etc.) needed that accompany method of choice.

Origins

Reliance on oral methods to derive knowledge goes back to the fifth century and Herodotus' *History*. In modern times one of the first general social science methods textbooks to include a treatise on the research interview was Odum and Jocher (1926, as cited in Platt, 2012) and was very much in the fact-finding tradition of social enquiry. By the mid-1950s, influenced by counselling and communication theory, the unstructured interview evolved and a tension materialised between the accuracy and precision provided by a uniform administration and asking invariant questions and the experiential non-directive approach typified by Carl Rogers (Platt, 2012). The further move away from the experimental tradition in the 1960s and '70s saw the emergence of social constructionism and the idea that people generate their own meanings of their experience through the giving of "accounts" (see Harré and Secord, 1972). This converged with the development of qualitative analytic methods such as grounded theory, discourse analysis, conversational analysis, interpretative phenomenological analysis and narrative analysis (see Chapter 8 in this collection and also Howitt, 2011). There are different forms of interviews which Gray (2009) characterises as *structured* (often used to collect data to accompany quantitative analysis); *semi-structured* (to allow probing of views and opinions); *non-directive* (a free-form exploration of issues); *focussed* (which tends to limit responses to a known situation or experience); and *informal conversation interviews* (relying on spontaneous generation of questions during the interview).

A "deceptively" simple method, the invention of focus groups in social science research is usually credited to Robert Merton in the 1940s, although probably was in use some 20 years prior to this (Wilkinson, 2004). The main use of focus groups prior to the late 1970s was mostly as a market research tool. But during the 1980s, this method was adopted by health researchers in areas such as family planning, preventative health interventions and sexual health, particularly in relation to HIV/AIDS (Wilkinson, 2004). By the 1990s the method had spread across a wider range of disciplines (such as education, communication and media studies, and feminist research). More recently, community-based participative consultations use this method as a way to garner expertise from the lived experiences of locals as well as technical experts across a variety of topics salient to particular localities (Daley et al., 2010).

The Delphi method owes its name to the Delphic Oracle, which was consulted to provide authoritative predictions about some major undertaking by the Ancient Greeks (Kennedy, 2004). In its modern manifestation, the RAND Corporation developed this technique initially as a way to forecast the Soviet Union's ballistic missile policy to allow the U.S. military to calculate the number of atomic bombs it would need for its defence (Dalkey, 1967). Classified as a "subjective-intuitive method", Delphi is often employed when there is limited time and some urgency in requiring a steer to solve a pressing, complex problem (Rowell et al., 2015). Basically, the technique is aimed at soliciting expert opinion to generate ideas and then establish a measure of agreement over preferred solutions. Widely applied, Delphi has been particularly used in medical and nursing research, community projects, education and management, and government policy application (see Linstone & Turoff, 1975, for an exposition and examples of this method).

Interviews

Fundamentally, an interview is a conversation in which questions may be posed by the researcher in a structured, semi-structured or unstructured format to gain first-hand insights into some topic. Employment of interviews hail from a mixture of positivist and non-positivist epistemological positioning to a social constructionist viewpoint of knowledge (Gray, 2009). They can be used as the sole data-gathering instrument; may be a pilot used as a precursor to designing a questionnaire or to explore or test hypotheses; or be an adjunct to a questionnaire survey, fleshing out richer meanings to closed-ended questions (Rowley, 2012). Choosing a particular type of interview depends on the purpose of the study and the objectives of the research. Kinds of interview vary in terms of the degree to which:

- the interview schedule specifies the questions (ranging from a strictly followed invariant defining and ordering of questions to an aide memoire of themes to be addressed);
- there is a balance of open and closed questions;
- they are interviewer- or respondent-led; and
- they yield a balance of quantitative and qualitative data.

Table 9.1 Summary advantages and disadvantages of the research interview

Advantages	Disadvantages
Flexible	Can generate volumes of "messy" data which are difficult to analyse
Can incorporate other data elicitation processes (such as psychometric test or rating scales)	Not so amenable to statistical generalisation
Rich, in-depth data	Time consuming to set up and conduct as well as lengthy periods spent on analysis
More manageable sample size	Potential for interviewer bias
Respondents potentially more receptive and informative	Dependent on the skill of the interviewer and capacities and cooperation of the respondent
Permits responsivity to social cues (i.e., non-verbal communication)	

The above table summarises the pros and cons of interviewing. Overall, interview data provides rich and elaborated details of the experiences of the research participant. Analysis through can be time consuming and labour intensive, although computer aided qualitative analyses such as N-Vivo can greatly assist. The next table (9.2) lists some basic tips when conducting an interview.

A research interview can be used at virtually any stage of a research enquiry and on any topic. Recruiting respondents is often by some form of *purposive sampling*, or, if a particularly elusive groups of informants, the *snowball method* may be used. This is where a respondent suggests another contact who may be willing to participate in the research (see Chapter 3 in this collection and Atkinson and Flint, 2001 for a briefing about the technique).

Some general principles for conducting interviews include:

- pre-preparing the introduction (the explanation for the interview sets the context, tone and style and will influence the conduct of the interview and the type of material elicited);
- establishing the ground rules for your informant that describe the purpose of the research and the conditions pertaining to the conducting of the interview (e.g., the person can stop at any time and withdraw, signing of an informed consent and reassurances about confidentiality and explaining the use the data will be put to);
- testing the comprehensibility and logical sequencing of questions through a pilot;
- knowing how to establish rapport with the interviewee;
- having good listening skills;
- checking that any equipment to record the interview is in good working order;
- making additional preparations if the interview informant is likely to be vulnerable or potentially difficult;

Table 9.2 List of dos and don'ts when conducting interviews

Dos	Don'ts
Adjust the interview schedule in the light of feedback from the pilot	Introduce assumptions before asking a question
Be thoroughly familiar with the schedule before starting interviews proper	Use non-verbal cues to imply the respondent is giving the "right" answers
Use probes if insufficient detail is obtained from initial answer	Use complicated phrasing or jargon words
Provide non-directive non-verbal encouragement	Use leading questions
Use straightforward ordinary language in asking questions	Use general "catch-all questions" (e.g., tell me everything you know about [the topic of the research])
Take tissues and be prepared for any distress experienced by informant	Change roles (e.g., adopt counsellor mode)

- being aware of and taking avoiding measures for any possible sources of interviewer bias (e.g. taking a liking or dislike to a particular informant);
- as a rule of thumb, recruiting a minimum of 12 informants; and
- assigning at least three hours to manually transcribe one hour of interview recording.

Often interviews are conducted face to face. Increasingly, telephone interviewing provides an economical alternative, but these are not really suitable for sensitive topics or more intensive inquiries. Ideally, interviews should have a natural rhythm and a manageable pace.

Any interview material is reliant on the informant being able (and willing) to provide the information asked of them. Breakwell (2012) suggests that there is no evidence to suppose that data gathered through an interview is any less reliable or valid than that collected by other means. She nevertheless proposes a number of strategies that can help eliminate researcher bias effects such as providing training prior to the conducting of the interviews, using electric recoding rather than note-taking and adopting some form of inter-rater reliability when establishing themes or coding for analysing data.

Focus groups

Not tied to any particular theoretical position, the overall objective of focus groups is to get close to the participants' understanding of and perspectives on particular issues rather than generating generalisable data (Millward, 2000). Focus groups can be employed as the main data-gathering method, used as a ground-clearing pilot to elicit key issues (often as a precursor to a quantitative survey) or used as a qualitative supplement to a quantitative survey (Barbour, 2005). The data obtained from a focus group comprise some appreciation of group processes, i.e., the dynamics through which people interact, express and develop their views and the content of views expressed. Thus the recording of evidence might include observations of non-verbal behaviour (such as fidgeting or facial reactions) and noting para-linguistic features, such as interruptions, overlapping speech and tone of voice (Wilkinson, 2016). In addition, the verbatim content of the discussion forms the corpus of material to be content analysed. Means to record evidence may be by note-taking, audio and/or audio-visual recordings.

Randomised sampling is not really necessary for focus groups, as it is usually a target group that is wanted. Some form of systematic strategy should be employed when making up a focus group and consideration given to screening criteria, e.g., if the discussion was about rape, may it be better to have single-sex or mixed groups? Sessions probably should last up to one hour but no longer than two hours. Questions may relate to experiences or behaviour, opinions or values, feelings, knowledge, background and demographics (Rosenthal, 2016). Tables 9.3 and 9.4 provide a listing of the main advantages and potential hazards of focus groups, together with some advice when conducting focus groups.

Key requirements in running focus groups as a means of data collection include:

- having a facilitator with basic interviewing skills, some knowledge of group dynamics and preferably some experience of running group discussions including people management skills in order to manage difficult, particularly talkative or shy participants;
- preparing well to identify broad parameters of the study, timescale available, number of groups necessary, types of participants and how to recruit them, how to record the data;

Table 9.3 Summary of the main advantages and disadvantages of focus groups

Advantages	Disadvantages
Can tackle sensitive topics	Can be hijacked by dominant participant
Good for potentially vulnerable or hard-to-reach respondents	Dependent on the skills of the facilitator
May encourage participation of individuals otherwise reluctant to talk one to one	Can be chaotic and unwieldy
Give "voice" to ordinary people involved in controversial issues	Allows individuals "to hide" by remaining unengaged
Provide ongoing feedback monitoring some intervention	Data can be unstructured and voluminous, not readily amenable to summary analysis
Probes underlying attitudes and beliefs	Not suitable for accessing individual's narratives (as difficult to extricate from the flow of the group discussion)
Examines issues more holistically	Not good for measuring attitudes
Generates rich data through group dynamics	Do not supply data amenable to statistical generalisation
Allows observation of process	May be driven by the needs of the client not prepared to invest time and money in validating results
Flexible in terms of location, timing and sampling	

Table 9.4 List of dos and don'ts when running a focus group

Dos	Don'ts
Pilot process	Have groups too big/too small
Plan thoroughly	Include participants of different status
Provide directions to venue	Become overly engaged in a particular participant's contribution
Steer with suitable probes	Answer specific questions generated by group participants
Encourage all to participate	Switch role (i.e., fall into counselling rather than group facilitator mode)
Anticipate how to handle distressed/ dominant/silent participants	Allow participants to either dominate or "hide"
Have a contingency plan if you need to terminate session	
Over recruit	
Allow for between 6–10 participants	
Identify key roles (moderator, note taker)	
Have tissues, name labels, pens	

- well-developed focus group schedule of questions that will engage participants, uses appropriate terminology, is sufficiently open-ended to allow diverse views to be expressed, flows logically;
- inclusion of other materials such as vignettes, card sorts, pictures and video clips to vary and stimulate discussion;
- pre-writing introduction and ending scripts;
- practicing before running the actual group to ensure the equipment, schedule, timings all work;
- finding an appropriate comfortable and accessible venue; and
- supplying suitable refreshments.

At their best, focus groups which are welcoming and non-judgmental can be a powerful means to elicit rich and meaningful data (Côté-Arsenault & Morrison-Beedy, 2005). Poorly designed or ill-executed focus group session can be disastrous and impoverish a research study (Barbour, 2005). Kidd and Parshall (2000) note that because focus groups evolved outside the mainstream tradition of qualitative research there were no concomitant developments in validity and reliability standards for the data. They provide a helpful discussion of how to enhance the explanatory power of the data.

Focus groups are helpful in identifying the thinking, perceptions and impressions of a particular group and are especially good when eliciting views of interest groups who may be difficult to access. Well run, they can yield a great deal of informative data but which are not readily generalisable.

Delphi technique

As the Delphi technique involves both qualitative and quantitative elements, it crosses the methodological divide. The aim of the Delphi method is quite often to generate policy solutions under conditions of uncertainty and pressurised time horizons and where there may be a lack of clarity. Table 9.5 provides a brief summary of the usefulness and possible pitfalls of the Delphi technique. As such, they may be of particular benefit to practitioners. Delphi has, for example, been used to assess the views of expert providers of services and compared them with users as expert recipients (Kennedy, 2004). However, the Delphi method is generally viewed as an exploratory technique or as a platform for future research and represents a step in knowledge building.

There are four essential features:

- A moderator (researcher) selects participating experts who remain anonymous to each other so that each may freely express their opinion.
- Information is reviewed and refined over a number of "rounds" by the moderator.
- The moderator provides controlled feedback of the collective view.
- There is statistical collation of results.

Given that knowledgeable participants are specially chosen for their expertise, some form of purposive sampling is usually adopted; thus inclusion criteria are required. This may involve recruiting an expert with a minority or divergent view in order to explore the full range of opinions. A panel of experts (unknown to each other) is thus created to participate across two or more questionnaire rounds. Data generated usually comprise open-ended material in which relevant issues are identified in the first round. The moderator collates these and constructs a questionnaire survey to allow for some further

Table 9.5 Summary of advantages and disadvantages of the Delphi technique

Advantages	Disadvantages
Flexible in terms of subject matter and locale of participants (as is conducted remotely)	High levels of commitment and resilience are required, as rounds can be onerous and drop out can be quite high
Pinpoints areas of agreement and disagreement in an existing knowledge area	Generalisation is limited (another panel may come to a different view) or the same panel may come to a different conclusion at a different point in time
Economical, as avoids travel costs etc.	Outcomes are only as good as the quality of the expertise of panellists
Provides inbuilt feedback	
Minimises bias from dominant personalities	Anonymity may limit agreement to participate as individuals may want personal recognition for their contribution
Anonymity encourages honest responses	Moderator may not run rounds effectively
Provides levels of agreement in areas where there is often an absence of empirical evidence	Original problem formulation may be either too vague or over specified that compromises expert's individual opinions
Is a quick and efficient method	Limited research establishing the efficacy of implementation of Delphi conclusions in the field

consideration by panellists in a second round. This is usually in the form of a numerical rating scale of importance, or agreement on some policy position or proposed intervention or evaluation. Here it is important to observe principles of good survey design (see Chapter 11) and avoid ambiguous or repetitive items (Iqbal & Pipon-Young, 2009). A further evaluative round comprises feedback of panellists' scores on the preceding questionnaire items, and they are asked to reconsider these in the light of this feedback and indicate whether they wish to change their responses. Basic descriptive statistics are calculated (e.g., percentages, means, standard deviations) to establish the panellists' consensus.

Key requirements in running a Delphi study are:

- having both qualitative analytic skills to collate idea generated in round one and quantitative skills in questionnaire construction and statistical analysis for subsequent rounds;
- providing a clear problem specification;
- establishing clarity of purpose, to establish diversity of opinions on a topic or generating a consensus (divergent views may be an important outcome);
- deciding on the number of rounds required and timeframe for their execution;
- careful selection of panellists through specified inclusion (and exclusion) criteria.
- choice between 10–20 panellists (but no more than 50); larger panels tend to provide more stable results; and
- give panellists about two weeks to respond.

Delphi methods have been increasingly included in the armoury of techniques for evidence-based practice (Jorm, 2015). However, production of a report or even publication of results is insufficient to guarantee implementation. In planning a Delphi study, it is often helpful to include questions about implementation as one of the questions for the experts to consider. Table 9.6 list the key considerations when undertaking a Delphi consultation.

Table 9.6 List of dos and don'ts when conducting a Delphi panel

Dos	*Don'ts*
Have a clear objective	Choose panellists who are simply knowledgeable; rather, use the most qualified individuals
Provide rapid turnaround of feedback	Choose panellists with variable levels of knowledge
Encourage reassessment of initial standpoint in the light of subsequently expressed views by panellists	Use too few panellists
Use a minimum of three iterations – open-ended, collated questionnaire and final evaluation rounds	Send feedback distorting the panellists aggregated views trying to "mould" opinion
Where disagreement, ask panellist to expand their reasoning for their opinion	
Electronic communication most efficient	

Delphi techniques tend not to employ conventional scientific criteria of reliability and validity (Powell, 2003). Instead, "goodness of fit" criteria may be used, such as the explicitness of the inclusion criteria for choosing experts. Face validity can be present in terms of the coherence, usefulness and applicability of recommendations. Additionally or alternatively, comparison of two expert panels considering the same topic may be undertaken.

Conclusion

Choosing the most appropriate method is an integral part of the research process. Sometimes less experienced researchers may think qualitative methods such as interviewing are easier and quicker than conducting a quantitative survey, as there are fewer participants to recruit and use of statistical analyses is minimised. Actually, designing an interview schedule, focus group protocol or specifying the problem in a Delphi round is exacting and requires considerable skill. Analysing qualitative data is time consuming and often involves subtle and nuanced interpretations. The best advice is to choose the method that most adequately fits the needs of the potential respondents and best serves to answer the research question.

Further reading

The compendium of data collection and analytic methods in the edited collection by Glynis Breakwell and colleagues (2012) is an excellent starter text for a good overview. David Silverman's (2016) edited book on qualitative methods has comprehensive coverage and includes details of interviewing and focus group methodologies. The *Sage Handbook of Interview Research* edited by Gubrium and others (2001) is a more focussed text with specific chapters providing helpful guidance on conducting and analysing data gathered by means of interviews and focus groups. Whilst directed at nurses and health professionals, Keeney, McKenna, and Hasson (2010) provide an accessible description, critique and "how to" do Delphi based studies.

References

Atkinson, R., & Flint, J. (2001). Accessing hidden and hard-to-reach populations: Snowball research strategies. *Social Research Update, 33*(1), 1–4. Retrieved from http://sru.soc.surrey.ac.uk/

Barbour, R. S. (2005). Making sense of focus groups. *Medical Education, 39*(7), 742–750. doi:10.1111/j.1365–2929.2005.02200.x

Breakwell, G., Smith, J., & Wright, D. (Eds.). (2012). *Research methods in psychology* (4th edition). London, UK: Sage.

Brenner, M., Brown, J., & Canter, D. (1985). Introduction. In M. Brenner, J. Brown., & D. Canter (Eds.), *The research interview: Uses and approaches* (pp. 1–8). London, UK: Academic Press.

Côté-Arsenault, D., & Morrison-Beedy, D. (2005). Maintaining your focus in focus groups: Avoiding common mistakes. *Research in Nursing & Health, 28*(2), 172–179. doi:10.1002/nur.20063

Daley, C. M., James, A. S., Ulrey, E., Joseph, S., Talawyma, A., Choi, W. S.,. . .& Coe, M. K. (2010). Using focus groups in community-based participatory research: Challenges and resolutions. *Qualitative Health Research, 20*(5), 697–706. doi:10.1177/1049732310361468

Dalkey, N. (1967). *Delphi*. Santa Monica, CA: RAND Corporation. Retrieved from www.rand.org/pubs/papers/

Gray, D. (2009). *Doing research in the real world* (2nd edition). Los Angeles, CA: Sage.

Gubrium, J., Holstein, J., Marvasti, A., & McKinney, K. (Eds.). (2001). *The sage handbook of interviewing research: The complexity of the craft* (2nd edition). Los Angeles, CA: Sage.

Harré, R., & Secord, P. F. (1972). *The explanation of social behaviour*. Oxford, UK: John Wiley & Son.

Hartley, J., & Branthwaite, A. (2000). *The applied psychologist*. Buckingham, UK: Open University Press.

Howitt, D. (2011). Using qualitative methods to research offender and forensic patients. In K. Sheldon, J. Davies, & K. Howells (Eds.), *Research in practice for forensic professionals* (pp. 132–158). Abingdon, UK: Routledge.

Iqbal, S., & Pipon-Young, L. (2009, July). The Delphi method. *The Psychologist, 22*, 598–601. Retrieved from https://thepsychologist.bps.org.uk/

Jorm, A. F. (2015). Using the Delphi expert consensus method in mental health research. *Australian and New Zealand Journal of Psychiatry, 49*(10), 887–897. doi:10.1177/0004867415600891

Keeney, S., McKenna, H., & Hasson, F. (2010). *The Delphi technique in nursing and health research*. Oxford, UK: Wiley.

Kennedy, H. P. (2004). Enhancing Delphi research: Methods and results. *Journal of Advanced Nursing, 45*(5), 504–511. doi:10.1046/j.1365–2648.2003.02933.x

Kidd, P. S., & Parshall, M. B. (2000). Getting the focus and the group: Enhancing analytical rigor in focus group research. *Qualitative Health Research, 10*(3), 293–308. doi:10.1177/104973200129118453

Linstone, H. A., & Turoff, M. (Eds.). (1975). *The Delphi method: Techniques and applications* (Vol. 29). Reading, MA: Addison-Wesley.

Millward, L. (2000). Focus groups. In G. Breakwell, S. Hammond, & C. Fife-Schaw. (Eds.), *Research methods in psychology* (2nd ed., pp. 274–292). London, UK: Sage.

Platt, J. (2012). The history of the interview. In J. Gubrium, J. Holstein, A. Marvasti, & K. McKinney (Eds.), *The Sage handbook of interviewing research: The complexity of the craft* (2nd edition). Los Angeles, CA: Sage.

Powell, C. (2003). The Delphi technique: Myths and realities. *Journal of Advanced Nursing, 41*(4), 376–382. doi:10.1046/j.1365–2648.2003.02537.x

Robson, C., & McCarten, K. (2016). *Real world research; A resource for users of social science research methods in applied settings*. Chichester, UK: John Wiley & Sons.

Rosenthal, M. (2016). Qualitative research methods: Why, when, and how to conduct interviews and focus groups in pharmacy research. *Currents in Pharmacy Teaching and Learning, 8*(4), 509–516. doi:10.1016/j.cptl.2016.03.021

Rowell, L. L., Polush, E. Y., Riel, M., & Bruewer, A. (2015). Action researchers' perspectives about the distinguishing characteristics of action research: A Delphi and learning circles mixed-methods study. *Educational Action Research, 23*(2), 243–270. doi:10.1080/09650792.2014.990987

Rowley, J. (2012). Conducting research interviews. *Management Research Review, 35*(3/4), 260–271. doi:10.1108/01409171211210154

Silverman, D. (Ed.). (2016). *Qualitative research.* Los Angeles, CA: Sage.

Wilkinson, S. (2004). Focus groups. In G. Breakwell. (Ed.), *Doing social psychology research* (pp. 344–376). Oxford, UK: BPS/Blackwells.

Wilkinson, S. (2016). Analysing focus group data. In D. Silverman (Ed.), *Qualitative research: Theory, method and practice* (4th edition., pp. 83–100). London, UK: Sage.

10 Experimental and quasi-experimental designs

Verities & Balderdash[1]: designating designs to discern the difference

William H. Yeaton

Acknowledgements: The author wishes to thank Justin Mason, Brian Moss, Carla Paredes-Drouet, Jason Richie, and Yanyun Yang for their thoughtful comments on earlier drafts.

In the last decade, three researchers (Elizabeth Levy Paluck, Susan Murphy, and Esther Duflo) have received the prestigious MacArthur fellowship for their imaginative program of research. In each instance, rigorous randomized studies were a fundamental part of their methodology, which addressed *how* we assess solutions to difficult problems. In stark contrast, over the last half-century, perhaps the most famous and influential studies in psychology (Milgram's laboratory work with compliance, Zimbardo's Stanford Prisoner's study, and Rosenhan's indictment of psychology's inability to discern mental illness) lacked formal control groups, used mostly descriptive statistics, and included small samples.

While these MacArthur fellows each implemented experiments, the three incredibly impactful psychology studies used non-rigorous study designs. In no instance were quasi-experimental designs utilized. Why not? Perhaps most readers judged topics chosen for quasi-experiments to be insufficiently provocative or ignored their inherent advantages (Frieden, 2017) (e.g., more timely evidence, larger samples, and longer-term follow-ups in quasi-experiments).

Characterizing research designs and an annotated bibliography

A primary aim of this chapter is to enhance the utilization and credibility of quasi-experiments and to provide readers with a more expansive menu of design options.[2]

Unfortunately, it seems impossible to provide anything resembling an adequate "how to" for viable experiments and quasi-experiments in the span of a single chapter. As a partial remedy for readers unfamiliar with particular designs, Table 10.1 (at the end of this chapter) includes a brief description of characterizing elements of designs discussed here along with Xs and Os diagrams.

The bald question: Why designs? The short answer: to maximize inferential quality. And, to play the expert card, Don Rubin noted, "Design trumps analysis" (2008). High-quality designs provide a sound counterfactual (Fisher, 1935; Morgan & Winship, 2008) against which to compare results in the intervention group. Such counterfactuals allow us to reduce the number of threats for each validity type, the primary aim of the contemporary methods "bible" (SCC: Shadish, Cook, & Campbell, 2002, along with Shadish & Cook, 2009, an update to the 2002 testament). While design decisions may have an impact on construct, external, and statistical conclusion validity, my focus will be on internal validity (casual inference). (To be clear, my sense of cause is consistent with the three principles noted in SCC: (1) cause precedes effect; (2) cause and effect are correlated; (3) rival explanations of the causal relationship are implausible.)

Bill Trochim's Social Research Methods website and his accompanying textbook (Trochim, Donnelley, & Arora, 2016) represent wonderful resources for familiarizing readers with both designs and validity threats. In yet greater detail, SCC articulates the many validity threats and their relevance to different designs. While a thorough discussion of validity threats is beyond this chapter's scope, many consider SCC as required reading to develop a deep understanding of relationships between designs and validity threats.

Criteria for choosing among possible research designs (including rule-outs)

The primary working principle in the choice of a research design is straightforward: use the inferentially strongest design. First consider *all* (seriously!) possible design choices. Then, from among the feasible designs, implement the one eliminating the greatest number of validity threats. Better still, choose a design that eliminates validity threats other studies have not. If your design controls selection bias while few or no other published studies have adequately done so, your research will make a substantial contribution to knowledge. Certainly, there remain many substantive areas that lack experiments or fail to include well-controlled quasi-experiments. (But beware, there are likely good reasons why rigorous studies do not yet exist.)

Here, I provide a set of decision considerations (including advantages and disadvantages) for each design. These considerations are not exhaustive; other determinants exist; the named considerations represent some of the most salient dimensions. For each design, if a consideration rules out its use, it will be designated by "RO". Fortunately, RO considerations are generally not redundant, as the elimination of one design possibility does not simultaneously eliminate others. RO conditions also represent proxy measures of each design's flexibility. To the degree that RO conditions commonly exist, the design is not easily implementable.

Randomized studies (RCTs, experiments) RO

Typically, researchers must have authority to conduct randomization and to gather informed consent from participants. Big advantage: compared to inferential statistics in quasi-experiments, RCTs offer easy-*er* statistical analysis options (e.g., ANOVA, *t*-test, chi-square). "Up front" costs are higher for RCTs, but later, inferential qualifications and data analysis issues are reduced.

SMART designs (sequential multiple allocation research trials) RO

SMART designs have the same rule-out restrictions as RCTs but require that participants remain available for extended periods – at least two rounds of research. Attrition (differential dropout rate) can rear its ugly head in each stage. With multiple stages, intervention adherence is doubly challenging. Blinding and diffusion are further complicated by sequential approaches.

RD (regression discontinuity) RO

Pretest and post-test measures must be available for the control group as well as the intervention group. Lack of consistent adherence to the cut-point (substantial crossovers from intervention to control group or vice versa) represents a second rule-out condition. Researchers must be skilled in statistical modelling to correctly ascertain the pattern of assignment (pretest) and post-test scores (e.g., linear, quadratic, cubic). Contemporary standards encourage researchers to utilize both parametric and non-parametric discontinuity estimates (Kratochwill, Hitchcock, Horner, Levin, Odom, Rindskopf, & Shadish, 2010). In a fortunate set of circumstances, a large discontinuity may partially compensate for study weakness.

CITS (controlled interrupted time series) RO

Should the intervention diffuse to the control group, inferential quality will be substantially reduced. Baseline differences in trend between intervention and control groups (selection by maturation) will greatly compromise the value of the counterfactual, though statistical modelling can compensate (e.g., St. Clair, 2014). While skills in longitudinal data analysis are required, many important interventions can be evaluated when retrospective data are available.

NECG (non-equivalent control group) design RO

Identification of important covariates (those that correlate highly with dependent variables or predict self-selection into intervention and control groups) is critical in producing unbiased estimates of effect. Knowledge of relevant statistical modelling and data analytic procedures are paramount with NECG. Currently, data analysts will almost certainly choose from ANCOVA or various versions of propensity score matching procedures (Shadish, 2013).

Interrupted time series (ITS) RO

Gradual implementation of or incomplete adherence to the intervention can destroy inferential quality (then, effects do not immediately occur and "other", non-intervention attributions will be made). This rule-out criterion also applies to CITS. The longitudinal nature of the design increases its ability to detect change and to rule out threats (e.g., maturation, testing, and regression). In Chapter 6, SCC discuss classic examples of ITS.

Regression point displacement (RPD) RO

If researchers choose the intervention unit to "game" the contrast to the regression line of control units (i.e., maximize displacement by picking particularly motivated or comparatively advantaged participants), the quality of causal inference is seriously periled. In Germany, Kowalski, Yeaton, Kuhr, and Pfaff (2016) evaluated the effectiveness of performance feedback given to staff in breast cancer care hospitals. Each control hospital had also previously participated in a best practices workshop, but staff in those hospitals did not receive subsequent performance feedback. Hospital-level data provided the unit of analysis, and pretests and post-tests were systematically collected. We corroborated RPD estimates and validated RPD with estimates from a strong quasi-experiment, CITS. By utilizing more than one intervention group, we minimized chances that a single, randomly chosen intervention unit was the initially best- or worst-performing hospital.

Note: RPD uses an atypical counterfactual, the regression line established by the pretest and post-test of each of multiple control group units. RPD probes for a statistically significant, vertical displacement created by the pretest and post-test of the intervention group. RPD is not a mini-RCT; pretest equivalence is *not* the aim of random choice of the intervention group.

Common Cause (CC) RO

The design's short history argues against the formulation of RO standards based on empirical evidence, though the design's logic is based on a long-standing philosophical tenet (similarity) of J.S. Mill. If the intervention produces a consistent pattern of increase or decrease across multiple study units (when rival explanations or theories of change within units remain constant), causal inference is enhanced.

Since there is typically a single pretest and a single post-test for each of the design's intervention units (one OXO), internal validity threats germane to each unit should be addressed. Thus, researchers must be wary of the full lineup of potential suspects: history, maturation, testing, regression, instrumentation, and differential attrition. Enhanced causal inference occurs when the duration between intervention and pretest and between intervention and post-test is both short and equal (minimizes instrumentation and maturation); treatment is delivered at different times to different units (minimizes history and maturation); measures are not taken from "tests", in the education sense (minimizes testing); and interventions are not systematically delivered to units when scores are atypically low or high (minimizes regression). Attrition will be reduced when study conditions discourage dropouts (short durations from intervention to pretest and post-test, and incentives are provided to remain in study). Use of multiple OXOs may mean that internal validity threats are not consistently present (but not always absent).

Use more than one design for each research question

When one imagines experiments and quasi-experiments, it is virtually automatic to make a decision *between* two designs; choose an experiment or a quasi-experiment. But a third option exists; choose more than one design for the same research question. Intentionally, multiple designs enhance casual inference by applying different analyses, causal estimates, and study samples. Unfortunately, facility with multiple designs, best learned in graduate school, is rare.

Suggestions to combine designs have existed for several decades (Yeaton, unpublished). For example, Boruch (1975) urged researchers to couple designs of varying quality or to implement them in tandem. As a method of validating a quasi-experiment, to gauge the degree of potential bias, many contemporary researchers combine both an experiment and a quasi-experiment. There is now a rich literature using so-called within-study comparisons (WSC) to empirically validate three of the most important quasi-experiments (NECG; Cook, Shadish, & Wong, 2008; RD; Shadish, Galindo et al. 2011; and CITS; St.Clair et al. 2014). However, that validation process is not the essential aim of the multiple-design approach encouraged here.

Instead, the primary purpose of including more than one design follows from the scientific tradition that probes of capital-T truth are best achieved via replication (e.g., Open science collaboration, 2015). This replicative process may take the form of conducting both an experiment and a quasi-experiment or two quasi-experiments, to answer the same research question, in the same publication. The idea is to provide multiple estimates but, again, not to use one estimate to establish the degree of correctness of another. Rather, the fundamental goal is to establish a set of corroborating results that mirror the critical multiplist approach (e.g., Shadish, 1993), allowing one to legitimately claim benefit.

The multiple-design approach does not require additional samples. One could also utilize the same sample within the context of different designs. Wing and Cook (2013) artificially created an RD design from an RCT by eliminating half the treatment and half the control group scores and validated RD estimates at different cut-points. Kowalski et al. (2016) created an RPD design from a CITS design by using the average pretest and post-test scores in the intervention group (the first or last pretest or post-test could also have been used).

My current research interests reflect this embedded design approach. In the first of three such studies (Moss, Yeaton, & Lloyd, 2014), an experiment and a quasi-experiment were combined to yield multiple estimates of benefit in developmental education (a cut-point was established from an early freshman year pretest in mathematics). The experiment, owing to small sample size,

lacked statistical power, while the RD had thousands of participants. We anticipated that some RD students would cross over from the developmental group
to the control group. Given administrative rules for course attendance, such
migration was not feasible in the experiment. Differential attrition loomed as
a larger threat in the experiment than the quasi-experiment. Different analytic
approaches were used in the two designs (e.g., *t*-test for the RCT, both parametric and non-parametric regressions in the RD). Across designs, statistically
significant, consistently positive effects of similar size argued for an achievement
advantage for developmental education students – precisely the promise of the
embedded design approach.

A second education study focused on academic probation but combined
three designs: RE, RD, and RPD (Yeaton & Moss, 2018). In the RD, students
with grade point averages in the range 1.00–1.99 received a strongly worded
warning letter delivered by certified mail. Controls, with GPAs 2.0+, received
no intervention. In the RCT, a random sample of *D* students was randomly
allocated to receive either the certified letter or the standard email warning. In
the RPD, for a *random sample* of *D* students, those from a random choice of one
of 10 "groups" (1.00–1.09, 1.10–1.19. . . 1.90–1.99) were randomly *allocated* to
receive the certified letter (remaining nine groups acted as control units). With
three designs (here, the RCT was also used to validate the seldom-used RPD),
despite different analytic procedures, though different validity threats loomed in
different designs, we found consistent effects favouring warning letters.

In the third instance (Kowalski, Yeaton, Kuhr, & Pfaff, 2016), results from a
strong quasi-experiment (CITS) were combined with those of the inferentially
weaker RPD not only to establish corroborating evidence of effect across designs
but also to validate the RPD. Detailed feedback was given to clinical staff from
intervention hospitals after participation in a best practices workshop. Breast
cancer patients subsequently expressed greater satisfaction than no-treatment
controls, though neither design produced statistically significant results. However, by virtue of the preponderance of consistent, positive evidence from both
embedded designs, our claim of benefit was substantially enhanced.

Use single-case and between-groups designs for each research question

Another seldom-used research strategy combines within-group ("single-case
design"; SCD) and between-groups studies, within the same publication. For
example, after a baseline period, reversal designs (symbolically, ABAB) introduce
an intervention, remove it, and then reestablish it. Multiple baseline designs
introduce the intervention in one "leg" (often a group), then stagger introduction in other legs. One examines the functional relationship of dependent
variable change in the presence and absence of intervention, both within- and
between-groups.

Experiments and quasi-experiments most often utilize between-groups
comparisons of averages. I know of no publication in which single-case

relationships between independent and dependent variables were first established in the context of a small set of participants over an extended number of trials (days, sessions, etc.) and then followed by a large, between-groups study design to further substantiate the intervention. (The interested reader is referred to Kratochwill et al., 2010 and to books by Jon Bailey & Burch 2002 and Alan Kazdin 2011) for expert discussion of SCD methods.)

The notion of a pilot study is well ingrained in science. But why are evaluations of between-groups studies that first implement scientifically sound SCDs as pilots virtually unknown? I argue that few researchers have requisite skills with both design types. Few graduate students take courses that adequately cover both kinds of inquiry. The two methods communities seldom read each other's publications. Group designs require superior knowledge of statistics, while SCDs typically lack inferential statistics. Largely due to the efforts of Will Shadish and Larry Hedges (e.g., Shadish, 2014), appropriate statistical techniques for SCDs have been recently developed. Once again, there is a long tradition of either-or but not both.

In the reminder of the chapter, I expand upon two themes: (1) design choice can be facilitated by examining the same or similar research questions in another discipline; (2) there are easily accessible settings in which students can conduct experiments and quasi-experiments. These settings provide an opportunity to implement many different research designs possibilities. I finish with a description of the ways in which design considerations help to ameliorate many of the most common problems one faces while conducting high-quality research.

Thinking in templates to facilitate design choice

By now, the theme is apparent: design matters, and it matters a lot. Weak designs can both over- or underestimate intervention effects, as evidenced by many meta-analyses (e.g., Ioannides et al., 2001). Shadish et al. (2008) used the best possible evidence, two-stage randomization, to demonstrate that results in observational and randomized studies can vary by 9–25% for unadjusted vocabulary and mathematics outcomes.

One way to think about design choice examines a particular research question but, loosely, considers that same question as it appears in slightly different forms in distinctly different disciplines. (Campbell, 1969, also makes a strong argument for reading outside one's own disciple.) Think of teaching as drug delivery, regard memory rehabilitation as yoga posture practice, or consider gene alteration as cognitive restructuring. In the first case, to create a large menu of ways to assess teaching interventions, do not (first) read the education literature. Explore the range of designs used to evaluate drug delivery and examine their attendant research questions (note the kinds of analyses and measures used, along with their limiting conditions).

To further flesh out template thinking, imagine you wish to study the impact *on teachers* of teaching within inner-city schools (or impact on those who counsel prisoners). I claim that you would gain mightily by using a rich template of the deleterious impacts of caregiving on caregivers. (I realize that care does not equal teaching but bear with my conceptual "stretch".) You identify a published caregiver RCT (e.g., Schulz et al., 2003) but cannot immediately see how inner-city school teachers, like caregivers, could realistically be randomized to give or not give care. You imagine a study in which the most burdened caregivers received assistance and thereby consider an RD study of the most burdened inner-city teachers. You find an NECG report in which caregivers and non-caregivers were compared for subsequent mental health issues (and realize that inner-city and suburban teachers could analogously be compared, after statistical adjustment). If one city provided financial help to caregivers but many other cities did not, then an analogous RPD might be conducted with inner-city teachers). Finally, you note that multiple mental health indicators were compared for a large set of caregivers just prior to and subsequent to initiation of care (and consider an analogous CC design implemented using quality-of-life indicators with inner-city teachers). My argument: thinking in templates gives you a huge advantage over scholars who look for design precedents only within their own discipline.[3]

Design choice is constrained by access to data; consider university settings as a microcosm

Too simply, graduate school dissertations are either (1): prospective, laboratory-based RCTs (e.g., psychology, communication) using undergraduates who receive extra credit for participation; or (2) retrospective studies conducted from often large, archival datasets (e.g., Medicare, Early Childhood Longitudinal Study-Birth cohort) that typically make group contrasts (NECG, CITS) and rely on sophisticated statistical analyses like propensity score analysis. I propose an alternative strategy. Consider the university as an expanded laboratory, one that provides a microcosm for problems facing U.S. society. I claim that the very problems confronting the country writ large are mirrored within university settings. The humongous advantage: university-based data are routinely collected and available, potentially for free. The rub: students must obtain permission from university administration and reformat data for analysis. Still better, a wide range of design alternatives exists to confront problems that universities face. To whet readers' appetite for possibilities, I briefly describe five substantive areas and relevant research questions along with possible design options. (Only space limitations restrict applying multiple designs to each research question.)

A local student in the Department of Information Technology (Kang, 2014) proposed an RPD study to evaluate an alternative for teaching first semester STEM students' use of library resources. One randomly selected group of students (determined by the time period in which they had signed up) received an augmented reality, iPad version of the same tour given in the actual library; control groups received the usual walking tours. Pretest and post-test knowledge of library resources would be obtained in one intervention group and multiple control groups.

Registration for university classes is almost universally conducted by computer. When students reach a set number of completed credit hours (cut-point), the university may alter website content to address issues faced by both lower- and upper-level students. The success of such alterations (e.g., rate of subsequent drop-and-add requests and average, total number of credit hours maintained) can be evaluated using RD. The University of Michigan (Callewaert & Marans, 2017) provides an ideal environment to empirically evaluate efforts to reduce energy consumption. Since monthly energy use was reported for individual buildings, it is possible to use the CITS design. Different interventions (e.g., stickers near light switches prompted the last person leaving a classroom to turn off lights) can be introduced at staggered times across buildings. Energy use would potentially decrease soon after interventions were established in treatment but not in control buildings (until the intervention was instated in controls).

Campus movie theatres exist at most U.S. universities. With the advent of hand-held, digital devices used to assess voting preferences at exit polls, one could assess pre- and post-attitudes towards a particular movie, in a single, random-time sample of students who arrive in a particular five-minute period and receive a movie review, compared to attitudes in controls who arrive in other periods but receive no review (CC design). University development departments are in the business of encouraging alumni to provide financial support. The success of different, randomly allocated versions of web pleas (RCTs) for donations could be easily evaluated, as records of donations are routinely tallied and compiled. For more than a decade (e.g., Ayres & Nalebuff, 2007), businesses have utilized experimentally determined web displays to consumers to maximize spending (e.g., purchase airline tickets).

Common research problems and ways design-related methods can ameliorate them

Design choice does not always take the form of explicit ways to allocate participants to groups. Design-based methods have considerable potential to ameliorate common research problems. Here, I note particularly thorny problems (in italics) likely faced by researchers. For each problem, I discuss one or two partial "remedies" from the following list: (1) include multiple designs; (2) use the non-equivalent dependent variable (NEDV) design (use control variables instead of a control group; e.g., Herman & Walsh, 2011); (3) use multiple dependent variables (different kinds of outcomes or different operationalization of outcomes; e.g., Webb, Campbell, Schwartz, & Sechrest, 1966); (4) work to establish high quality covariates.

In the face of *small sample size*, combine multiple designs and provide multiple outcome measures. The primary aim is often to produce results "in the same direction" that are not statistically significantly different for each design and measure (Steiner & Wong, 2016). When *a control group is not practical*, establish control variables: conceptually similar outcome variables expected to not change after the intervention. McSweeny (1978) showed that a surcharge for local directory assistance reduced those call rates but did not reduce rates for long distance calling. When *a control group is feasible but its quality is likely to be low*, expend extra efforts to establish good covariates.[4] Shadish et al. (2008) provide an exemplary instance in which they piloted 156 questionnaire items from five theoretically based construct domains. Alone and in combination, some covariates reduced bias in the NECG design to near zero.

When *differential attrition* looms likely, the embedded design approach is especially warranted if attrition is expected to be minimal in at least one design. Based on pilot studies or studies in the existing literature, if one anticipates *a small effect size* for the primary outcome, a decision to include multiple outcomes or operationalizations (designated before data collection!) is an especially promising tactic, as some outcomes may produce statistically significant effect sizes.

The finishing touch

The palette of the design artist is enormous. In this landscape, the intellectual task of "argument-by-design" begs a cogent metaphor. I first considered the idea of "preponderance of evidence" but then remembered a wonderful example by Paul Rosenbaum (2015) that masterfully applied the idea of a crossword puzzle to illustrate how disparate but interconnected pieces of evidence can be interwoven to corroborate the potentially causal relationship between smoking and lung cancer. This metaphor is not a perfect fit; in Rosenbaum's probe of casual inference, the crossword analogy aptly included multiple designs but in different publications. Also, the different designs did not always refer to precisely the same research question.

A substantially shortened version follows. Design designations are italicized or inserted by this author. Rosenbaum's description of casual mechanism, central to his argument for causal inference, was also included.

> A controlled *randomized experiment* shows that deliberate exposure to the toxin causes this same cancer in laboratory animals.
>
> A pathology study finds these DNA-adducts in tumors of the particular cancer under study, but not in most tumors from other types of cancer.
> *(NECG)*
>
> A *case-control* study finds cases of this cancer have high levels of these DNA-adducts, whereas non-cases (so-called "controls") have low levels.

Exposure to the toxin is observed to be associated with DNA-adducts in lymphocytes in humans.

(SCD)

The crossword puzzle metaphor interweaves design logic in a rich tapestry to establish cause.

Notes

1 This title of a music album by Harry Chapin roughly translates as "truth and nonsense".
2 Full disclosure . . . I have published articles using all designs in this chapter except for SMART. Fortuitously, I learned a good deal about SMART from Daniel Almirall, a colleague of Susan Murphy, and Nick Seewald during a class I taught in the Summer Institute at the University of Michigan.
3 Template mirroring can also work "in reverse". I recently introduced a colleague to the idea of applying group, two-stage randomization to sampling design. Reasoning by analogy, consider RCTs to be like random samples and imagine quasi-experiments as non-random samples. Then compare estimates in random samples with estimates in non-random samples.
4 With retrospective data, when it is not possible to obtain pretests of dependent variables for NECG, I recently recommended covariate identification ideas germane to exploratory and confirmatory factor analysis (e.g., Gelman & Loken, 2014). Exploratory: use the research literature to identify important covariates in a random sample of existing data. Test correlations between covariates and: (1) dependent variables and (2) participant entry into intervention and control groups. Confirmatory: use covariates found to be significantly correlated with condition entry or outcome.

References

(Note: some citations may appear in the annotated bibliography.)

Ayres, I., & Nalebuff, B. (2007). Experiment. *Forbes, 180*(4), 130.
Bailey, J. S., & Burch, M. R. (2002). *Research methods in applied behavior analysis.* Thousand Oaks, CA: Sage.
Boruch, R. F. (1975). Coupling randomized experiments and approximations to experiments in social program evaluation. *Sociological Methods and Research, 4,* 31–53.
Callewaert, J., & Marans, R. W. (2017). Measuring progress over time: The sustainability cultural indicators program at the University of Michigan. In W. Leal Filho (Ed.), *Handbook of theory and practice of sustainable development in higher education* (Vol. 2., pp. 173–187). Berlin, Germany: Springer.
Campbell, D. T. (1969). Ethnocentrism of disciplines and the fish-scale model of omniscience. In M. Sherif & C. W. Sherif (Eds.), *Interdisciplinary relationships in the social sciences* (pp. 328–348). Chicago, IL: Aldine.
Cook, T. D., Shadish, W. J., & Wong, V. C. (2008). Three conditions under which observational studies produce the same results as experiments. *Journal of Policy Analysis and Management, 27,* 724–750.
Fisher, R. A. (1935). *The design of experiments.* Edinburgh, UK: Oliver & Boyd.
Frieden, T. R. (2017). Evidence for health decision making – beyond randomized, controlled trials. *New England Journal of Medicine, 377,* 465–474.

Gelman, A., & Loken, E. (2014). Data-dependent analysis – a "garden of forking paths" – explains why many statistically significant comparisons don't hold up. *American Scientist, 102*, 460–465.

Herman, P. M., & Walsh, M. E. (2011). Hospital admissions for acute myocardial infarction, angina, stroke, and asthma after implementation of Arizona's comprehensive statewide ban. *American Journal of Public Health, 101*, 491–496.

Ioannides, J. P. A., Haidich, A. B., Pappa, M., Pantazis, N., Kokori, S. I., Tektonidou, M. G., . . . Lau, J. (2001). Comparison of evidence of treatment effects in randomized and nonrandomized studies. *Journal of the American Medical Association, 286*, 821–830.

Kang, J. H. (2014). Designing studies to evaluate an orientation program using mobile augmented reality for net generation students (pp. 901–904). In *iConference 2014 Proceedings*.

Kazdin, A. E. (2011). *Single-case research designs: Methods for clinical and applied settings*. Oxford: Oxford University Press.

Kratochwill, T. R., Hitchcock, J., Horner, R. H., Levin, J. R., Odom, S. L., Rindskopf, D. M., & Shadish, W. R. (2010). *Single-case designs technical documentation*. Princeton, NJ. What Works Clearinghouse.

McSweeny, A. J. (1978). The effects of response cost on the behavior of a million persons: Charging for directory assistance in Cincinnati. *Journal of Applied Behavior Analysis, 11*, 47–51.

Morgan, S. L., & Winship, C. (2008.) *Counterfactuals and causal inference: Methods and principles for social research*. New York, NY: Cambridge University Press.

Moss, B. G., Yeaton, W. H., & Lloyd, J. E. (2014). Evaluating the effectiveness of developmental mathematics by embedding a randomized experiment within a regression discontinuity design. *Educational Evaluation and Policy Analysis, 36*, 170–185.

Open Science Collaboration. (2015). Estimating the reproducibility of psychological science. *Science, 349*(6251), aac4716–1-aac4716–8.

Rosenbaum, P. R. (2015). Cochran's causal crossword. *Observational Studies, 1*, 205–211.

Rubin, D. B. (2008). For objective causal inference, design trumps analysis. *The Annals of Applied Statistics, 2*, 808–840.

Schulz, R., Mendelsohn, A. B., Haley, W. E., Mahoney, D., Allen, R. S., Zhang, S., . . . Resources for Enhancing Alzheimer's Caregiver Health Investigators. (2003). End-of-life care and the effects of bereavement on family caregivers of persons with dementia. *New England Journal of Medicine, 349*, 1936–1942.

Shadish, W. R. (1993). Critical multiplism: A research strategy and its attendant tactics. In L. Sechrest (Ed.), *New directions for program evaluation* (Vol. 60, pp. 13–57). San Francisco, CA: Jossey-Bass.

Shadish, W. R. (2013). Propensity score analysis: Promise, reality, and irrational exuberance. *Journal of Experimental Criminology, 9*, 129–144.

Shadish, W. R. (2014). Analysis and meta-analysis of single-case designs: An introduction. *Journal of School Psychology, 52*, 109–122.

Shadish, W. R., Clark, M. H., & Steiner, P. M. (2008). Can nonrandomized experiments yield accurate answers? A randomized experiment comparing random to nonrandom assignment. *Journal of the American Statistical Association, 103*, 1334–1343.

Shadish, W. R., & Cook, T. D. (2009). The renaissance of field experimentation in evaluating interventions. *Annual Review of Psychology, 60*, 607–629.

Shadish, W. R., Cook, T. D., & Campbell, T. D. (2002). *Experimental and quasi-experimental design for generalized causal inference*. Boston, MA: Houghton Mifflin.

Shadish, W. R., Galindo, R., Wong, V. C., Steiner, P. M., & Cook, T. D. (2011). A randomized experiment comparing random to cutoff-based assignment. *Psychological Methods*, *16*, 179–191.

St. Clair, T., Cook, T. D., & Hallberg, K. (2014). Examining the internal validity and statistical precision of the comparative interrupted time series design by comparison with a randomized experiment. *American Journal of Evaluation*, *35*, 311–327.

Steiner, P. M., & Wong, V. C. (2016). *Assessing correspondence between experimental and nonexperimental results in within-study-comparisons*. Unpublished manuscript. University of Virginia, Virginia.

Trochim, W. M., Donnelley, J. P., & Arora, K. (2016). *Research methods: The essential knowledge base* (2nd ed.). Boston, MA: Cengage.

Webb, E. J., Campbell, D. T., Schwartz, R. R., & Sechrest, L. (1966). *Unobtrusive measures: Nonreactive research in the social sciences*. Chicago, IL: Rand McNally.

Wing, C., & Cook, T. D. (2013). Strengthening the regression discontinuity design using additional design elements: A within-study comparison. *Journal of Policy Analysis and Management*, *32*, 853–877.

Yeaton, W. H. (unpublished). *Redesigning designs: The emergence, evolution, and promise of embedded research designs*. Tallahassee, FL: Florida State University.

Yeaton, W. H., & Moss, B. G. (2018). A multiple design, experimental strategy: Academic probation warning letter's impact on student achievement. *The Journal of Experimental Education*, doi: 10.1080/00220973.2018.1469110

Annotated bibliography of research designs

Randomized Controlled Trial (RCT)

Friedman, L. M., Furberg, C. D., & DeMets, D. L. (1998). *Fundamentals of clinical trials* (3rd ed.). New York, NY: Springer.
Aimed for health and medical audiences but carefully outlines and describes important steps and critical issues for designing, analyzing, and interpreting experimental results. Health and medical sources often provide useful "how-to" guides for social scientists.

Berkowitz, T., Schaeffer, M. W., Maloney, E. A., Peterson, L., Gregor, C., Levine, S. C., & Beilock, S. L. (2015). Math at home adds up to achievement at school. *Science*, *350*, 196–198.
Using an iPad app, when parents of first-graders read math stories in the home, math achievement increased compared to scores in a reading control group (field experiment).

SMART (Sequential Multiple Allocation Randomized Trials)

Chakraborty, B., & Murphy, S. A. (2014). Dynamic treatment regimes. *Annual Review of Statistics and Its Applications*, *1*, 447–464.
Discusses range of possible applications of SMART designs that evaluate best follow-up practices after initially successful or unsuccessful results. Current applications are limited in the social sciences and have largely been conducted in health and medicine.

Regression Discontinuity (RD)

What works clearinghouse: Preview of regression discontinuity design standards. (2015)
   Presents conditions under which RD procedures meet WWC standards with and without
   reservations (or not at all).

Tang, Y., Cook, T. D., Kisbu-Sakarya, Y., Hock, H., & Chiang, H. (2017). The comparative
   regression discontinuity (CRD) design: An overview and demonstration of its performance relative to basic RD and the randomized experiment. *Advances in Economics, 38,*
   237–279.
   Embellishment of RD design enhances causal inference by adding pretest or control group.

Non-Equivalent Control Group (NECG)

Shadish, W. R., Clark, M. H., & Steiner, P. M. (2008). Can nonrandomized experiments yield
   accurate answers? A randomized experiment comparing random to nonrandom assignment. *Journal of the American Statistical Association, 103,* 1334–1343.
   Exemplary use of theory and pilot work to develop an extensive set of strong covariates.
   The two-stage randomization approach led to many important within-study comparison
   studies that empirically estimated selection bias.

Steiner, P. M., Cook, T. D., Shadish, W. R., & Clark, M. H. (2010). The importance of covariate selection in controlling for selection bias in observational studies. *Psychological Methods,*
   15, 250–267.
   Outlines a strategy of covariate selection to minimize selection bias. Compares design and
   statistical approaches to reduce bias.

Controlled Interrupted Time Series (CITS)

Jena, A. B., Mann, N. C., Wedlund, L. N., & Olenski, A. (2017). Delays in emergency
   care and mortality during major marathons. *New England Journal of Medicine, 376,*
   1441–1450.
   Creative use of design features buttresses conclusion that marathons increase subsequent
   hospitalization delay and mortality for acute MI infarction or cardiac arrest patients.

St. Clair, T., Hallberg, K., & Cook, T. D. (2016). The validity and precision of the comparative
   interrupted time series design: Three within-study comparisons. *Journal of Educational and
   Behavioral Statistics, 41,* 269–299.
   Discusses quality of causal inference for CITS when there is a between-groups difference
   in pretest trends (with or without correct modelling) or the numbers of pretests varies.

Interrupted Time Series (ITS):

Wong, M., Cook, T. D., & Steiner, P. M. (2015). Adding design elements to improve time
   series designs: No child left behind as an example of causal pattern-matching. *Journal of
   Research on Educational Effectiveness, 8,* 245–279.
   In the context of short ITSs, the authors examine how adding design features (e.g., control
   group, measurement features such as adding pretests or removing and reintroducing the
   intervention) can enhance causal inference.

Table 10.1 Descriptions of experimental and quasi-experimental designs

---

Randomized (RCT): O X O

(One version)   O   O

   Typically, individual participants are randomly allocated to study conditions by researchers. However, persons presenting in different time periods or intact groups may be randomly assigned. Sometimes, a governmental organization will randomly allocate (e.g., by lottery). Numerous Internet sites exist that automatize randomization (caution: allocation quality varies).

***SMART (Sequential Multiple Allocation Randomized Trials):
RCT1→RCT2, same persons***

In the first stage, random allocation occurs. Participants in intervention and control conditions who demonstrate successful and unsuccessful results are subsequently randomized (four groups).

Regression Discontinuity (RD): O_A C X O_2

   (**C** = cut-score, O_2 = post-test, O_A C O_2
   O_A = assignment variable)

Participants are assigned to intervention or control (by their actions or by a decision of staff) based on the cut-point for some continuous (usually) measure. For example, all participants at or above the cut-point receive the intervention while those below do not.

Non-Equivalent Control Group (NECG): NR O X O

   (**NR** = non-random allocation)   **NR O   O**

Participants choose a study condition based on their preference or on staff decision.

Controlled Interrupted Time Series (CITS): OOOOXOOOO

                                   OOOO OOOO (may introduce and
stagger X)

Assignment to (or withdrawal from) some intervention is based on a time point cut-off. For example, intervention participants receive intervention at a specified time while controls do not receive intervention at this same time (the intervention may be staggered such that control participants receive the intervention at a later time).

(Continued)

Table 10.1 (Continued)

Interrupted Time Series (ITS): OOOOXOOOO

Multiple pretests and posttests are measured (on the same variable) before and after implementation of an ongoing or one-time intervention.

Regression Point Displacement (RPD): OXO (*n* = 1)

$$O \quad O \ (n > 1)$$

From many treatment units (typically, groups), one (usually) unit receives intervention (ideally by random selection), while control units (*n* > 1) do not receive intervention. Pretests and posttest measures are gathered for both kinds of units. The counterfactual is a regression line.

Common Cause (CC): OXO (unit 1) . . .

OXO (unit *n*)

Multiple pretest and posttest values (prior to and subsequent to an intervention) are gathered and analyzed. There is no control group. Pretest-to-post-test, seek stable rival explanations.

Fretheim, A., Soumerai, S. B., Zhang, F., Oxman, A. D., & Ross-Degnan, D. (2013). Interrupted times-series analysis yielded an effect estimate concordant with the cluster-randomized controlled trial results. *Journal of Clinical Epidemiology, 66*, 83–87.
Compares results from two designs. An ITS is embedded within a cluster-randomized clinical trial to evaluate prescriptions for diuretics in Norwegian clinical practice.

Regression Point Displacement (RPD):

Trochim, W. M. K., & Campbell, D. T. (2013). *The regression point displacement design for evaluating community-based pilot programs and demonstration projects*. Retrieved April, 22, 2013, from www.socialresearchmethods.net/research/RPD.RPD.pdf
Definitive, never published article introduces RPD design, develops ANCOVA-based analytic procedures and illustrates range of applicability.

Kowalski, C., Yeaton, W. H., Kuhr, K., & Pfaff, H. (2016). Helping hospitals improve patient centeredness: Assessing the impact of feedback following a best practices workshop. *Evaluation & the Health Professions, 40*, 180–202.
Used RPD (embedded in a CITS design) to evaluate a performance feedback intervention given to staff in German breast cancer care hospitals.

Common Cause (CC):

Yeaton, W. H., & Thompson, C. G. (2016). Transforming the canons of John Stuart Mill from philosophy to replicative, empirical research: The common cause research design. *Journal of Methods and Measurement in the Social Sciences*, 7, 122–143.
Introduces the new CC design, suggests analytic strategies, and presents circumstances of its potential applicability.

11 Surveys and web research

Danielle R. Wald, Bradley E. Gray,
and Erin M. Eatough

Introduction

Over the last several decades, survey research methods have moved from face-to-face interviewing and pencil-and-paper surveys to email and web-based surveys. Modern researchers must continually keep informed of available tools and methods to best execute their research. Toward this end, this chapter focuses on research methods for one of the most current and popular approaches to survey research: web surveys.

Web surveys have proliferated alongside the exponential growth of Internet availability, with an estimated 85% of the United States adult population now connected to the Internet, for example (Perrin & Duggan, 2015). Web surveys are becoming one of the most preferred survey methods among psychologists today, with one study reporting that 94% of human subjects research board members in the U.S. endorse web surveys as the most commonly reviewed protocol (Buchanan & Hvizdak, 2009). Advantages of web surveys include the ability to obtain large sample sizes of data relatively inexpensively and the dynamic and interactive features that cannot be achieved via other methods. Though prolific, web surveys are complex to design and execute for a variety of reasons, including sampling, non-response, question and response formatting, and survey platform issues. In this chapter we will discuss methodological issues specific to web surveys, including a discussion of the advantages, challenges and special issues with web surveys, such as survey construction and platform selection.

Advantages of web-based surveys

There are a variety of reasons why web surveys can be of enormous benefit for collecting survey data. First, compared to other survey methods, web surveys are time and cost effective, requiring up to only a quarter of the cost of traditional methods (Heiervang & Goodman, 2011). Manual labour is reduced with web surveys because participants enter their responses directly into the web survey platform, and this data can then be automatically stored and easily exported to statistical software packages. Automatic storage reduces time demands and human error, and data can be analyzed quickly at any time in the data collection process. Survey software systems also have the capability to monitor data collection and provide feedback to the participant along the way without the need of the researcher present. For example, software systems can check whether respondents have skipped an item and then require an appropriate field entry (e.g., a numerical answer) and can also prompt participants to correct invalid responses before proceeding to the next item. These features are particularly attractive because they can reduce printing, postage and labour expenses, as well as data errors and researcher bias. Indeed, some recent evidence suggests that data collected via the web has improved reliability over face-to-face surveying (Liu & Wang, 2015).

Second, web surveys are preferred by many participants due to their ease, anonymity and convenience. In fact, participants are more comfortable disclosing personal information via web surveys due to their anonymity, allowing for greater honesty and authenticity (Naus, Philipp, & Samsi, 2009). Furthermore, the ease with which web surveys can be completed is beneficial for participants. With the assistance of survey software systems (e.g., Qualtrics, SurveyMonkey), surveys can be administered using many types of devices (e.g., computers, tablets, smartphones) allowing participants to access surveys when they desire, where they desire (e.g., home versus work), as well as the ability to pause surveys and continue with them later. In addition, web survey software systems often contain design and content features that can enhance participant experience, including the ability to incorporate rich visual content (e.g., still images, diagrams, video clips), the flexibility to customize items and their design (e.g., drop-down menus), and the personalization of each survey based on participants' previous answers (e.g., skip logic, which creates a custom path for participants based on previous responses). These capabilities are likely beneficial for both participants and researchers because they make the survey experience more enjoyable, engaging and motivating, thereby strengthening the quality of the data provided.

Finally, web surveys are particularly useful for obtaining large samples of demographically and culturally diverse participants. Because the Internet removes geographical and physical barriers, web surveys offer the capability to simultaneously collect data from numerous participants based in multiple geographic locations in the world at any hour of the day.

There are two primary routes a researcher may take to obtain their sample for a web survey: self-recruiting or the utilization of sampling services. Self-recruiting requires the researcher to recruit participants through independent means such as convenience sampling or snowball sampling methods. One advantage of self-recruiting is that it can allow for greater direct control over the resulting sample. Unique samples may be obtained through self-recruiting by using various online communities (e.g., listservs, forums, newsgroups) to recruit participants who share similar characteristics or interests. Furthermore, with the influx of individuals using social media, it is possible for researchers to easily target populations using public information, including demographic characteristics (e.g., location, education, age) and interests (e.g., "likes" and "tags"; see Kraut et al., 2004; Reips, 2002).

Alternatively, sampling services allow researchers to purchase access to panels or groups of pre-screened individuals who have consented to participate in surveys, usually for small compensation, even further reducing the time demands of executing a web survey. Different services offer different panel options and filtering features (e.g., access to specific types of populations or ability to filter by certain criteria, ability to execute different designs such as repeated measures, etc.). However, researchers are cautioned that the use of such services raises concerns surrounding data quality. Although not discussed in depth here, there has been much debate on the use of such services in the social and behavioural sciences, and we recommend researchers consult this literature when making sampling strategy decisions (see Weinberg, Freese, & MCelhattan, 2014; Crump, McDonnell, & Gurecki, 2013; Buhrmester, Kwang, & Gosling, 2011).

Challenges of web surveys

As mentioned, there are a number of methodological issues associated with surveying participants via the web, including sampling under-coverage, multiple submissions, non-serious or inattentive responding, and non-response in web surveys.

Coverage and sampling frame

Coverage error and sampling error may be particularly threatening when using web surveys to make inferences about a population (Couper, Traugott, & Lamias, 2001). Coverage error results when the sample is not representative of the frame population (the population from which the sample is drawn). While Internet access in most developed countries has rapidly increased within the past decade and the coverage error problem has reduced considerably, the "digital divide" continues to be a compelling issue, as various demographic and socioeconomic groups continue to have differential access to the Internet (Perrin & Duggan, 2015). Specifically, those who have lower levels of education or lower household income, live in rural areas, and/or are older have more limited Internet access (Perrin & Duggan, 2015). Since a small portion of individuals from these populations are unable to respond to Internet surveys, web samples used to make inferences about the frame population suffer from significant coverage error because they underrepresent these groups. Importantly, with regards to web surveys, having Internet access is not the only prerequisite for survey completion. Participants must have the necessary tools and skills needed to respond to the survey, such as having the required software (e.g., web browsers, plug-ins) and technological skills. Such potential biases in web survey sampling can impact the validity and generalizability of the data.

Possibly of greater concern is difficulty with establishing a sampling frame where all members of the frame population are measured (Couper et al., 2001).

For the large, general populations, there is no way for researchers to confidently detect the necessary size for a sampling frame. For example, with a web survey it is nearly impossible to generate a sampling frame for the general population because there is no national list of email addresses. Unlike telephone methods, which have access to random-digit dialling, there is also no standard convention that allows email addresses to be randomly sampled. However, when targeting unique populations, it may be possible to establish a sampling frame. Some online communities and organizations provide membership email lists that include a verified email address for each member (e.g., listservs). For example, collecting a representative sample of data from an organization may be feasible if all employees are required to have an accessible email address.

Even if a sampling frame can be identified, there are some important complications with web surveys versus traditional methods to consider. Whether using self-recruiting or a sampling service, it is possible that email addresses are invalid, leaving the researcher to assume the person has been contacted when in fact this is not the case. Additionally, multiple email addresses may be listed for the same person. Further, contact information may be missing, as individuals in groups, organizations or listservs may request that their email addresses not be listed or disclosed to researchers. Other complications include whitelisting requirements, firewall issues and possible overloading of intranets with large email "mailouts". Organizations frequently have inbox quotas, with emails not being received due to full inboxes.

An additional factor contributing to sampling error that is prominent in web surveys results from self-selection bias (Couper et al., 2001). Self-selection is a non-probability sampling technique where individuals select themselves for a survey, leaving the researcher with no control over the sampling selection process. Researchers commonly use self-selection to recruit participants because of difficulty obtaining participants who qualify for inclusion, are interested in the research topic and are motivated to respond to a survey. Self-selection methods, such as posting survey URLs to social media sites, can allow researchers to obtain their sample in a short amount of time with low cost. However, the sample will often inaccurately represent the frame population because not all individuals are equally able to participate. As such, it is advised that those using self-selection techniques or any other type of non-probability sampling proceed with this caveat in mind, considering the representativeness of the sample and the validity of the estimated parameters. As a recommendation, sampling methods and all sample characteristics should be reported, allowing readers to develop their own claims regarding the generalizability of the data.

Multiple submissions and non-serious responding

As mentioned, completion of web surveys is often convenient and easy. Yet this very advantage, coupled with the researcher's lack of control over respondents, may result in data errors from multiple responses from the same individual and non-serious responding. Participants may complete a survey more than once due to curiosity, boredom, intent to receive additional compensation or malicious attempts to skew the survey data by over-representing responses. Furthermore, the anonymity provided can boost honesty but also reduce participant attentiveness (Gosling & Mason, 2015), leading to false or incomprehensible responses. To combat such issues, it is advisable to create a form of identity in the survey process by requiring participants to provide a unique identifier code at the start of the survey, to include personal questions with definitive answers (e.g., birth date, birth place), and to incorporate instructional manipulation checks that detect those who are inattentive or not following instructions (Nosek, Banaji, & Greenwald, 2002). Instructions warning of punitive consequences may also be effective (Ward & Pond, 2015). Additional recommendations include filtering out duplicate responses, close examination of each submission's time to completion, searching for strings of identical responses and examining the internal consistency of responses in the data cleaning process (Gosling, Vazire, Srivastava, & John, 2004).

Non-response

Meta analyses confirm that web surveys have lower response rates than other methods (Manfreda, Berzelak, Vehovar, Bosnjak, & Haas, 2008; Shih & Fan, 2008) and that even follow-up reminders are less effective for web surveys than mail surveys (Shih & Fan, 2008). Non-response is a problematic issue in web surveys because the people who don't respond are usually different in some meaningful way from those who do. For example, college students appear to be more responsive to web surveys than other groups (Shih & Fan, 2008).

Non-response includes refusing participation altogether, early survey termination and incomplete responses (Couper et al., 2001). For example, participants may refuse to respond to a web survey because of time restraints or privacy issues or due to frustration associated with being contacted too often. They may also choose to terminate the survey because of length, ambiguous questions or sensitive questions. Accidental non-response to portions of surveys may also occur. Researchers may choose to resolve such issues by using forced-response requirements, but this may result in higher levels of attrition because participants may perceive higher demand. Alternatively, many survey software platforms allow for response-contingent pop-up messages to bring an omission to the participant's attention.

Furthermore, methods of contacting participants can have varying impact on non-response rates. For example, sending participants an automated username and password instead of making them create their own as well as ensuring there are no ambiguous characters in passwords (e.g., is O the number zero or the letter O?) can increase response rates (Crawford, Couper, & Lamias, 2001). Furthermore, frequent reminders may be effective, but there could be a tipping point where too many reminders lead participants to ignore or block the reminders. Interestingly, web survey completion rates are higher when participants respond on a computer versus a smartphone (Lambert & Miller, 2015), but text invitation vs. email invitation appear to have equivalent response rates (De Bruijne & Wijnant, 2014). Providing participants with a financial incentive (e.g., lottery, gift card) may also increase response rates, with pre-paid cash incentives sometimes counteracting non-response even better than sweepstakes entries (LaRos, & Tsai, 2014). However, this method may increase the rate of multiple responses to increase participants' chances of winning a lottery (Konstan et al., 2005). It is advised that researchers using financial incentives implement procedures that prevent participants from engaging in such behaviour (i.e., ID tracking, IP address limits or monitoring). Additional suggestions to counteract non-response through question design are offered later.

Tips for constructing an effective web survey

Despite the many advantages, not all web surveys are created equally. The construction and design of web surveys can be of utmost importance for a successful data collection effort. Here we discuss the most important concerns for web survey design specifically, although some points apply to other survey methods as well. Although outside the scope here, issues of ethics specific to web surveys (e.g., informed consent, data storage) should also be given careful consideration before a survey administration (for additional reading, see Buchanan & Hvizdak, 2009).

Content and wording

To create a successful survey, it is essential to first define the overall purpose and scope of the research project. Specifically, it is advised that one narrow down the research questions and objectives in order to decide which variables are of interest (Rosenthal & Rosnow, 2007), how they will be measured and what population should be targeted. It is important to carefully consider if a web survey (versus a telephone survey, mail survey, etc.) is the most effective way to measure the variables at hand, considering the population being targeted and potential generalizability issues that may result. For example, if studying a geriatric population, is a web survey going to be effective? If asking about highly sensitive topics, would validity be improved through in-person interviews?

If a web survey is deemed appropriate, then the details of the question content and wording should be carefully considered. This is especially significant for web surveys because they are almost always completed without the presence of the researcher (e.g., while at home or work), and there is no one available to whom they can ask questions or seek clarity. Thus, clearness of language is fundamental for the success of a web survey.

It is essential to be direct, use simple language and make directions clear to avoid confusion or improper responses. For example, we recommend avoiding double-barreled questions and biased or loaded questions, which may influence the respondent's interpretation of the question (Shadish, Cook, & Campbell, 2002). We also suggest that one clearly indicate contexts and/or specific time frames in instructions when appropriate. Because the researcher will not be available for clarification, these content issues are of even greater importance for web surveys.

Formatting

Web surveys provide researchers with a plethora of tools allowing for unparalleled creativity. Features such as the ability to combine text with imagery or videos; the wide variety of question and response formats like multiple choice, matrix tables, rank order with drag-and-drop options and sliders; the option for built-in skip logic; item randomization to reduce bias resulting from item order; and many others help counteract participant non-response and fatigue (Yun & Trumbo, 2000). However, we caution that these features should only be used to add clarity or ease of use for respondents because unfamiliar formatting can confuse, distract or bias respondents, subsequently affecting reliability. For example, slider scales have been shown to reduce response rates and increase response time, perhaps due to added cognitive demand over radio button multiple choice (Funke, 2016).

A common decision is whether to use a closed-ended or open-ended question. Closed-ended questions provide clear-cut response options and are typically ideal for between-person comparison. Open-ended questions lead to deeper, more personalized responses (Rosenthal & Rosnow, 2007), particularly in the case of web surveys (Coderre, Mathieu, & St-Laurent, 2004). The goals of the research should ultimately drive this choice.

Open-ended questions with larger answer boxes are more likely to promote longer comments (Maloshonok & Terentev, 2016). When using closed-ended items, the number of response option scale points and the labelling of those points will influence response rates, range of responses, reliability and validity. To significantly increase reliability and validity, Krosnick (1999) recommends the following: to recreate the scale exactly as it was used by previous research, if available; to divide the scale continuum evenly between response options to avoid bias or unwanted neutral answers; and to label each point on the scale with words to remove subjectivity. It may also be prudent to include a response option reflecting "not applicable" to reduce non-response to items. Research on response formatting for web surveys has suggested that the use of a radio button format (compared to slider or text entry formats) allows a reduction in the percentage of respondents who choose the "Don't know" option, but vertical or horizontal orientation of the questions' options makes no significant difference (Maloshonok & Terentev, 2016). However, participants may be more likely to choose the earliest-presented response choices due to satisficing or the primacy effect (Krosnick, 1999).

Sequencing

In addition, thoughtful ordering of the questions in a survey can reduce cognitive demand and improve reliability and validity. First, we suggest that the opening questions of the survey should be simple and unobtrusive as a way for the participant to "warm up" to the experience. Researchers will often use demographic questions for this purpose. Second, it is recommended to put the most essential and cognitively demanding questions early in the survey when participants are most engaged. Third, grouping similar questions together can reduce cognitive load. Fourth, asking of highly sensitive questions later in a survey can make the respondent more comfortable (Krosnick & Presser, 2010). Fifth, questions should be ordered such that previous questions are not influencing answers to later questions. Sixth, if it is expected that most participants will respond via smartphone, using a scrolling (one long page) versus paging (flipping page to page) design could improve response rates through a reduced response time (De Bruijne & Wijnant, 2014).

Piloting

There is debate as to whether a measure can be seamlessly transferred from one survey mode to another (e.g., paper and pencil to web survey). Some studies have concluded that the results of a given survey completed in-person, through the mail and through the Internet are generally equivalent to one another (Gosling et al., 2004). However, others have found conflicting results when testing a questionnaire across modes, including disparities in item factor loadings, scale score responses, response rates and reliability (Buchanan, 2002; Carini, Hayek, Kuh, Kennedy, & Ouimet, 2003; Cronk & West, 2002; McDonald & Adam, 2003; Naus et al., 2009). Whether these conflicting results between survey modes are due to methodological issues within these studies themselves or due to differences in how participants respond to a question while in the presence of others versus while in the comfort of their own environment (e.g., due to having more time to think about their answers; experiencing less social desirability bias and more anonymity; Kreuter, Presser, & Tourangeau, 2008) is unclear.

   To combat this, web survey items both borrowed from other survey modes or newly created should first be piloted. Piloting helps remedy potential concerns with accuracy, generalizability and other common web survey concerns, like participants losing interest, satisficing or acquiescing (Krosnick, 1999). Piloting can also help identify researcher bias unwittingly introduced through improper design of response alternatives and question context (Krosnick, 1999). Even issues like including too much scientific jargon, not providing clear instructions, or providing inaccurate information (e.g., a malfunctioning progress bar) can lead to higher non-response or inaccuracy rates in web surveys (Crawford et al., 2001) and can be remedied by careful piloting. Survey length and time to completion is also important to estimate through piloting so as to give accurate information in recruitment calls and to provide appropriate participant incentives. Dillman (2000) suggests a multi-stage survey pilot process including surveying subject experts, conducting pilot studies and retrospective interviews, and using non-researcher examinations of questions in order to help identify and address these survey concerns before data collection begins. Piloting will also allow the researcher to verify that the web survey displays properly when accessed by different web browsers or smartphones.

Survey platforms

There are more than 40 popular (and likely hundreds of other less popular) web survey software services available to help researchers create their own web surveys. To summarize each platform is beyond the scope here, and it is not our intention to direct readers to a particular platform. Instead, we suggest some topics to consider when determining which platform to use. Consider the look and feel of the survey. Many survey platforms provide templates to help researchers get started, each providing a different degree of customization beyond their provided templates. Also, consider the features needed to best execute the survey. Different platforms provide special features like skip logic, randomization, website integration, integrated data analysis, the ability to share with collaborators and saving/archiving of surveys, among others. Researchers should consider the pricing of the platform and make note of extra fees necessary for added features. They should also know whether server space to store data online is necessary or if data will be stored locally. Each platform is unique, and we recommend investing some time in selecting a platform up front in order to best match researcher needs to the platform.

Conclusion

With an exponential rise in Internet usage, the web survey has become an extremely popular data collection method among researchers. This chapter provided a broad review of the advantages and potential challenges associated with web surveys and provided tips and best practices for survey construction and execution.

References

Buchanan, T. (2002). Online assessment: Desirable or dangerous? *Professional Psychology: Research and Practice, 33*(2), 148.

Buchanan, E. A., & Hvizdak, E. E. (2009). Online survey tools: Ethical and methodological concerns of human research ethics committees. *Journal Of Empirical Research On Human Research Ethics, 4*(2), 37–48.

Buhrmester, M., Kwang, T., & Gosling, S. D. (2011). Amazon's Mechanical Turk a new source of inexpensive, yet high-quality, data?. *Perspectives on Psychological Science, 6*(1), 3–5.

Carini, R. M., Hayek, J. C., Kuh, G. D., Kennedy, J. M., & Ouimet, J. A. (2003). College student responses to web and paper surveys: Does mode matter?. *Research in Higher Education, 44*(1), 1–19.

Coderre, F., Mathieu, A., & St-Laurent, N. (2004). Comparison of the quality of qualitative data obtained through telephone, postal and email surveys. *International Journal of Market Research, 46*, 347–358.

Couper, M. P., Traugott, M. W., & Lamias, M. J. (2001). Web survey design and administration. *Public Opinion Quarterly, 65*(2), 230–253.

Crawford, S. D., Couper, M. P., & Lamias, M. J. (2001). Web surveys perceptions of burden. *Social Science Computer Review, 19*(2), 146–162.

Cronk, B. C., & West, J. L. (2002). Personality research on the Internet: A comparison of Web-based and traditional instruments in take-home and in-class settings. *Behavior Research Methods, Instruments, & Computers, 34*(2), 177–180.

Crump, M. J., McDonnell, J. V., & Gureckis, T. M. (2013). Evaluating Amazon's Mechanical Turk as a tool for experimental behavioral research. *PloS one, 8*(3), e57410.

De Bruijne, M., & Wijnant, A. (2014). Improving response rates and questionnaire design for mobile web surveys. *Public Opinion Quarterly, 78*(4), 951–962.

Dillman, D. A. (2000). *Mail and internet surveys: The tailored design method* (Vol. 2). New York, NY: John Wiley & Sons.

Funke, F. (2016). A web experiment showing negative effects of slider scales compared to visual analogue scales and radio button scales. *Social Science Computer Review, 34*(2), 244–254.

Gosling, S. D., Vazire, S., Srivastava, S., & John, O. P. (2004). Should we trust web-based studies? A comparative analysis of six preconceptions about internet questionnaires. *American Psychologist, 59*(2), 93.

Gosling, S. D., & Mason, W. (2015). Internet research in psychology. *Annual Review of Psychology, 66*(1), 877–902.

Heiervang, E., & Goodman, R. (2011). Advantages and limitations of web-based surveys: Evidence from a child mental health survey. *Social Psychiatry and Psychiatric Epidemiology, 46*(1), 69–76.

Konstan, J. A., Simon Rosser, B. R., Ross, M. W., Stanton, J., & Edwards, W. M. (2005). The story of subject naught: A cautionary but optimistic tale of Internet survey research. *Journal of Computer-Mediated Communication, 10*(2).

Kraut, R., Olson, J., Banaji, M., Bruckman, A., Cohen, J., & Couper, M. (2004). Psychological research online: Report of board of scientific affairs' advisory group on the conduct of research on the internet. *American Psychologist, 59*, 105–117.

Kreuter, F., Presser, S., & Tourangeau, R. (2008). Social desirability bias in CATI, IVR, and Web surveys the effects of mode and question sensitivity. *Public Opinion Quarterly, 72*(5), 847–865.

Krosnick, J. A. (1999). Survey research. *Annual Review of Psychology, 50*(1), 537–567.

Krosnick, J. A., & Presser, S. (2010). Question and questionnaire design. *Handbook of Survey Research, 2*, 263–314.

Lambert, A. D., & Miller, A. L. (2015). Living with smartphones: Does completion device affect survey responses?. *Research In Higher Education, 56*(2), 166–177.

LaRose, R., & Tsai, H. S. (2014). Completion rates and non-response error in online surveys: Comparing sweepstakes and pre-paid cash incentives in studies of online behavior. *Computers In Human Behavior, 34*, 110–119.

Liu, M., & Wang, Y. (2015). Data collection mode effect on feeling thermometer questions: A comparison of face-to-face and Web surveys. *Computers in Human Behavior, 48*, 212–218.

Maloshonok, N., & Terentev, E. (2016). The impact of visual design and response formats on data quality in a web survey of MOOC students. *Computers in Human Behavior, 62*, 506–515.

Manfreda, K. L., Berzelak, J., Vehovar, V., Bosnjak, M., & Haas, I. (2008). Web surveys versus other survey modes: A meta-analysis comparing response rates. *International Journal of Market Research, 50*(1), 79.

McDonald, H., & Adam, S. (2003). A comparison of online and postal data collection methods in marketing research. *Marketing Intelligence & Planning, 21*(2), 85–95.

Naus, M. J., Philipp, L. M., & Samsi, M. (2009). From paper to pixels: A comparison of paper and computer formats in psychological assessment. *Computers in Human Behavior, 25*(1), 1–7.

Nosek, B. A., Banaji, M. R., & Greenwald, A. G. (2002). E-Research: Ethics, Security, Design, and Control in Psychological Research on the Internet. *Journal of Social Issues, 58*(1), 161–176.

Perrin, A., & Duggan, M. (2015). Americans' Internet access: 2000–2015. *Pew Research Center: Internet. Science & Tech.* Retrieved from www.pewinternet. org/2015/06/26/americans-internet-access-2000–2015

Reips, U. D. (2002). Standards for Internet-based experimenting. *Experimental Psychology, 49*, 243–256.

Rosenthal, R., & Rosnow, R. L. (2007). *Essentials of behavioral research: Method and data analysis* (3rd ed.). Boston, MA: McGraw-Hill.

Shadish, W. R., Cook, T. D., & Campbell, D. T. (2002). *Experimental and quasi-experimental designs for generalized causal inference.* Boston, MA: Houghton, Mifflin, and Company.

Shih, T., & Fan, X. (2008). Comparing response rates from Web and mail surveys: A meta-analysis. *Field Methods, 20*(3), 249–271.

Ward, M. K., & Pond, S. I. (2015). Using virtual presence and survey instructions to minimize careless responding on internet-based surveys. *Computers in Human Behavior, 48*, 554–568.

Weinberg, J. D., Freese, J., & McElhattan, D. (2014). Comparing data characteristics and results of an online factorial survey between a population-based and a crowdsource-recruited sample. *Sociological Science, 1*, 292–310.

Yun, G. W., & Trumbo, C. W. (2000). Comparative response to a survey executed by post, email, & web form. *Journal of Computer-Mediated Communication, 6*(1).

12 Assessing cognitive processes

John O'Gorman, David Shum, and Candice Bowman

Introduction

Cognitive processes consist of perception, attention, memory, imagery, language, problem solving, reasoning, and decision making (Matlin, 2005). Traditionally, cognitive processes were considered distinct from emotional and motivational processes (e.g., Zajonc, 1980, 1984). More recent research, however, suggests this sharp demarcation is not feasible and 'hot cognitions' (i.e., "cognitions coloured by feeling"; Brand, 1985, p. 5) need to be recognised (see Pessoa, 2008). The study of cognitive processes has widespread significance in a number of areas of psychology, including clinical psychology (e.g., cognition and depression; Roiser & Sahakian, 2013), social psychology (e.g., persuasion; Petty & Briñol, 2008), and developmental psychology (e.g., facial expression recognition in infants; Ichikawa & Yamaguchi, 2014), and in other disciplines outside psychology, including politics (e.g., public opinion formation; Leeper & Slothuus, 2014), law (e.g., eyewitness testimony; Loftus & Palmer, 1996), and business (e.g., cognitive mechanisms in entrepreneurship; Baron, 1998).

The aim of this chapter is to provide a review of the key ways in which cognitive processes are generally assessed in psychology. Cognitive processes are assessed via different approaches to provide a complete picture of each cognitive function and to help establish corroborative evidence across different methodologies (Smith & Kosslyn, 2007). In the following sections we provide an overview of the more salient approaches to cognitive assessment (viz., psychometric, experimental, neuropsychological, and psychophysiological approach) that have been adopted by behavioural scientists and their implications for applied psychologists.

Review

Psychometric

One of the oldest approaches to the assessment of cognitive processes is the psychometric approach, which broadly is the science of psychological measurement (Jones & Thissen, 2006). Statistical techniques have been used by researchers to evaluate different theories of mental abilities (e.g., human intelligence), and this has led to extensive research and the basis for measuring cognitive processes using multi-itemed pencil-and-paper psychometric tests. In fact, the study of intelligence has been considered to be the father of psychometrics (Cattell, 1987).

In summarising almost 100 years of research pioneered by Charles Spearman and his supporters and critics, Carroll (1993) factor analysed some 460 datasets that included a wide range of psychometric tests. He concluded that Spearman was correct in proposing a general mental ability (g) factor at the highest level of abstraction, but that there are at least two further levels (or strata, as he termed them) that require consideration. Specifically, he described intelligence as a three-stratum, hierarchical model, with Stratum I (lowest level) describing narrow abilities (e.g., reading ability, spelling ability), Stratum II (middle level) describing broad abilities (viz., those proposed by Cattell, Horn, and Thurstone, including crystallised intelligence, fluid intelligence, visualisation ability), and Stratum III (highest level) describing general mental ability (viz., Spearman's g; Carroll, 1993). According to this three-stratum model, termed the Cattell-Horn-Carroll (CHC) model (Alfonso, Flanagan, & Radwan, 2005) because of the similarities between Carroll's findings and the earlier theorising of Cattell (1987) and Horn (1985), cognition involves a number of specific skills (e.g., visual memory, spatial scanning, imagery) and broader domains of functioning (e.g., visual processing).

The CHC is impressive in terms of its evidence base and the high degree of consensus among researchers in the field. Support is not unanimous, however, with some arguing a level above the second stratum but before the third should be considered (see e.g., Deary, 2012; Johnson & Bouchard, 2005; Vernon, 1965). As with all statements in science, the CHC theory has to be considered provisional, holding only so long as contrary evidence of sufficient weight is not forthcoming.

Assessment of the CHC factors can be conducted individually using face-to-face testing or with groups. The Wechsler intelligence tests for adults (Wechsler, 2008), children (Wechsler, 2003), and preschoolers (Wechsler, 2012) provide individual assessments at the third stratum in terms of a global measure of g and at the second stratum in terms of measures of crystallised knowledge (verbal comprehension), fluid intelligence, and visual processing, as well as scores for a number of individual tests at the first stratum (Benson, Hulac, & Kranzler, 2010). Group tests, such as vocabulary (e.g., ACER higher tests; Australian Council for Education Research, 1982) and the Ravens Progressive Matrices (see Carpenter, Just, & Shell, 1990) provide proxies for the crystallised and fluid ability, respectively, as well as second stratum factors (e.g., the Differential Abilities Scales [Second Edition]; see Shum, O'Gorman, Myors, & Creed, 2013).

CHC theory, as with all accounts of cognition emanating from the study of human variation, is concerned about mental abilities, and, one might argue, these are not strictly mental processes. Process implies change or movement towards an outcome of some sort. For example, encoding information can be considered a different memory process to storing information and, in turn, a different memory process to retrieving information (Matlin, 2005). Each of these processes are part of memory ability but are discrete. Controlled experimental procedures can help disentangle the discrete processes associated with a specific cognitive function, as we next describe.

Experimental approaches

Although there are no general assessment methods for experimental approaches to the assessment of cognitive processes, it is usually the case that the assessment is designed to examine a particular hypothesis, and stimulus parameters are accordingly specified by the nature of the hypothesis. Presentation of stimuli and timing of events is by computer, with special purpose software to ensure a high degree of precision.

Taking the broad ability of analogical reasoning (e.g., Red is to Stop as Green is to '?'), Sternberg (1977) argued that it can be decomposed into several mental processes. First, the terms of the analogy need to be encoded (e.g., Red is a colour, Stop is a verb); next the relation between the first pair of terms needs to be inferred (e.g., Red = Stop signal); this relation then needs to be applied or mapped onto the second pair of terms (e.g., Red and Green are colours); and finally a response must be produced (e.g., Green = Go signal). Sternberg sought to test how these processes might be involved in solving analogies by manipulating them experimentally and measuring the time taken for problem solution. For example, he presented analogies in two parts: the first part contained either no terms, two terms, or three terms; the second part contained the full analogy (Sternberg, 1982). Sternberg found that latencies increased for the first part and solutions decreased for the second part with more items. Furthermore, he found that more time was spent on encoding than on the other attribute-comparison components (i.e., inference, mapping, and application). He concluded that a greater amount of time spent on encoding may have helped improve the efficiency of the other attribute-comparison components, thus resulting in a quicker response to the problems.

Likewise, Baddeley and Hitch (1974) used an information-processing approach (i.e., the approach that likens human cognitive processes to that of computer processes) but focused on structures that might be involved in working memory. They argued that there were at least three, and later (e.g., Baddeley, 2001) four, structures that needed to be considered: *phonological loop* (the temporary storage of sounds), *visuospatial sketchpad* (the temporary storage of visual and spatial information), *central executive* (integrates information from all structures and suppresses irrelevant information), and *episodic buffer* (temporary storage of information from all structures). Again, experimental procedures were used to manipulate variables that were thought to independently influence these processes. For example, serial recall of items that are similar or different in sound might be expected to affect the auditory rehearsal of information and thus show something of the way the phonological loop operated (e.g.,

Gathercole & Baddeley, 1993). The overall functioning of these processes is thought to be reflected in working memory span, such as recalling a series of digits in the reverse order to that in which they were presented.

Digits Span Backward, a subtest of the Wechsler Adult Intelligence Scale (WAIS; Wechsler, 2008), has been used since at least the first version of the Wechsler tests to assess memory processes (see Flanagan & Harrison, 2005 for a review). Currently, *n*-back tasks are used for this purpose when precise assessment is required (see Jaeggi, Buschkuehl, Perrig, & Meier, 2010). In the *n*-back task, a series of stimuli (words, numbers, or pictures) are presented, and the participant is asked to recall or identify the item that was presented immediately prior (1-back) or the one prior to the immediately prior (2-back) and so on. Accuracy and speed of recall are both used for assessment (Jaeggi et al., 2010).

Analogies and recall are relatively complex cognitive tasks. Simpler tasks are also used, although early in the study of cognitive processes simple tasks, such reaction time (RT) and sensory discrimination, were found not to be appropriate (see e.g., Wissler, 1901). Arthur Jensen's work with discriminative RT helped resurrect these simple measures (Jensen & Munro, 1979). On this task, the participant has to respond (as quickly as possible) to one of four different coloured lights mounted on a console. Discriminative RT measures both RT and movement time (i.e., the interval between releasing the home button and pressing the stimulus button). Jensen and Munro (1979) showed that discriminative RT correlated to the order of .4 with measures of general mental ability. Hunt and Pellegrino (1985) noted that while the importance of this demonstration should not be minimised and discriminative RT should continue to be used to examine cognitive processes, its reliability as a measure is lower than is needed in a practical measure of cognition. The same might also be said of the *n*-back task (see Jaeggi et al., 2010).

A simple measure of sensory judgement that has been used with some success in studying cognition is inspection time (e.g., Kranzler & Jensen, 1989). The participant is asked to judge which of two lines is longer when the lines appear side by side but at millisecond exposure duration (e.g., 6 ms, 31 ms, or 150 ms exposure). Correct detection is defined as identifying the longer line at least 80% of the time. The exposure duration required for correct detection is used as the measure (Nettelbeck & Lally, 1976). Inspection time has been found to correlate with success in ordinary day living activities in older adults, with faster times being associated with better everyday performance (Gregory, Callaghan, Nettelbeck, & Wilson, 2009). Although the measure is apparently simple, there are reasons to expect a number of cognitive processes to be involved, which may of course be the reason for its association with practical aspects of living.

The use of working memory and RT as an index of cognitive processing brings into sharp relief neuropsychological methods of assessment, which will be discussed shortly. As noted earlier, the Digit Span Backward subtest has been part of the Wechsler tests for many years and has seen service in neuropsychological evaluations, where general mental ability may not be impaired but where discrete and specific impairments in cognitive functioning exist.

Neuropsychological approach

Experimental and psychometric methods have been combined to help eluci-
date the nature of impaired functioning as a result of developmental disorder,
brain lesion, or trauma. Much of the early work in this field adopted a clinical
approach that relied on careful observation of the individual case (e.g., Luria,
1973), and this continues to be a key feature of the professional neuropsy-
chologist's approach. Tasks that challenge a particular ability or skill are used to
determine what the person can and cannot do, and inferences are drawn about
the site of the problem, given what is known about the person's condition from
invasive and noninvasive neurological testing.

An important concept in neuropsychological assessment is executive function (EF). This concept bears more than a passing resemblance to the central
executive discussed in relation to the Baddeley and Hitch model of working
memory. EF was defined by Lezak, Howieson, Bigler, and Tranel (2012) as
"those capacities that enable a person to engage successfully in independent,
purposive, self-directed, and self-serving behavior" (p. 37). EF is underpinned
by prefrontal lobe functions (Stuss & Levine, 2002) and is central to the person's
adaptation to the physical and social environment in meaningful ways (Lezak
et al., 2012).

A number of EFs and their specific assessments have been proposed, but
a consensus has yet to be reached on defining the major EFs and the extent
they are interrelated. For instance, there is some evidence suggesting the unitary nature of EF, which can characterise the nature of frontal-lobe deficits in
patients with brain injuries (see e.g., Duncan, Johnson, Swales, & Freer, 1997).
In contrast, other evidence suggests that EF is not a unitary construct but
instead consists of multiple distinct components (e.g., Huizinga, Dolan, & Van
der Molen, 2006; Miyake et al., 2000). Miyake et al. (2000) sought to classify
methods empirically by using factor analysis of scores on a number of EF tests.
They proposed three key EFs: shifting, updating, and inhibition. They found
moderate levels of correlation among markers of these EFs but at the same time
reasonable separation and argued for a 'unity in diversity' approach. That is, EF
is not one thing but many, and each has sufficient family resemblance to make
the use of a general term such as EF meaningful.

Neuropsychological tests of specific functions have been developed over
a number of years (Chan, Shum, Toulopoulou, & Chen, 2008). Some of the
most commonly used tests include the Trail Making Test (TMT) Form B, Verbal
Fluency Test (VFT) – F, A, and S, VFT Animals category, Clock Drawing Test,
Digits Forward and Backward subtests (WAIS-IV), Stroop Test, and Wisconsin
Card Sorting Test (WCST; for a review see Chan et al., 2008). Comprehensive
batteries have also been developed over the years to test a number of functions
in the one assessment session. The Halsted-Reitan (see Allen, 2011) was one
of the earliest of these batteries. Nowadays, most such testing is computer-
based; for example, the Cambridge Neuropsychological Test Automated Battery (CANTAB) provides for the assessment of memory, executive function,

and attention, among others, using computer-based software (Fray, Robbins, & Sahakian, 1996).

Although the neuropsychological approach can help establish causal connections between cognitive deficits and specific parts of the brain, the use of neuroimaging techniques demonstrates that certain brain areas are active during performance. Moreover, neuroimaging can assist in identifying the neural mechanisms that underlie a specific cognitive function (Smith & Kosslyn, 2007).

Psychophysiological approach

Approaches to assessing cognitive processes, which have some affinities to the neuropsychological approach, are those based in electroencephalography (EEG) recording and brain imaging (e.g., functional magnetic resonance imaging [fMRI]). As with the neuropsychological approach, in the psychophysiological approach, neural functioning is thought to be central to understanding of cognition. The EEG is the older of the two, with Hans Berger providing the first EEG recording using his son as the participant in 1929. The principle employed was that the electrical activity engendered by neural functioning can be recorded from electrodes placed on the surface of the scalp if it is amplified sufficiently and displayed as voltage oscillations. This 'spontaneous' activity was subsequently shown to include discrete electrical events time-locked to stimuli in the participant's environment. For instance, a period may be defined as 100 ms before the onset of a stimulus and 1,000 ms after the onset of a stimulus (Coles & Rugg, 1996). Within this period there may be small electrical changes in neural activity reflecting the brain's response to a particular stimulus. It is these electrical changes in the brain over time that constitutes the event-related potentials (ERPs; Coles & Rugg, 1996).

After averaging the time-locked ERPs, the focus is then on identifying peaks and troughs in the resulting waveform, known as ERP components (Luck, 2005). A commonly used approach to quantify these ERP components is to determine the latency (ms) and amplitude (μV) of the peak. For example, a peak that is 300 ms post-stimulus and a positive deflection is called the P3 or P300 (Coles & Rugg, 1996). In the oddball task, for example, the participant is required to respond to infrequent targets. The P300 has been found to be sensitive to infrequent (low probability) targets, and interestingly, it is the subjective (and not the objective) probability that controls the P300 amplitude, indicating the sensitivity of the electrophysiological response to cognitive processes.

ERPs have the property of high temporal resolution (to the nearest millisecond), but their source in the brain cannot be determined with the same degree of certainty, as they result from firing in aggregations of neurons at a distance from the scalp surface where they are recorded (Luck, 2005). Brain imaging techniques (e.g., fMRI) by contrast provide very good spatial resolution (to the nearest millimetre) but poorer differentiation of events in terms of their timing (Luck, 2005; Otten & Rugg, 2005). Brain imaging in the case of fMRI relies on the facts that (a) oxygen-rich blood reacts differently from oxygen-poor blood to the pull of a magnetic field and (b) active areas of the brain receive more oxygen-rich blood. Cognitive processing that engenders neuronal activity can thus be traced to particular brain areas from the blood-oxygen-level-dependent (BOLD) signals they produce (Luck, 2005). Results are displayed as coloured maps of the brain, with areas highlighted that are relatively more and relatively less active as a result of the participant responding to experimental instructions. fMRI is safe because there is no radiation involved, and it provides excellent resolution of where activity is occurring in the brain.

Advances in measurement precision, in terms of temporal and spatial resolution and the ease of data collection, makes these neuroimaging techniques particularly suitable for examining the discrete brain areas associated with a cognitive function. More importantly, it is these innovative techniques that are likely to play an increasingly large role in future cognitive research.

Conclusion

Although a number of approaches to assessing cognitive processes have been considered, it is important to realise that the coverage is not exhaustive and that other approaches are possible. For example, behaviour genetics is being used to study cognitive functions (e.g., genes involved in prospective and retrospective memory traits; Dongés et al., 2012), and there is a tradition in developmental psychology of using tasks devised by Piaget to study the growth of cognitive capacity in children (Gottfried & Brody, 1975). If attention is confined just to the approaches that have been reviewed here, an obvious question is: What, if any, is the overlap among what appear to be different methods? For example, the CHC model of abilities identifies a number of individual difference variables in the area of cognitive functioning, and the literature on EF identifies a number of processes; but to what extent do these approaches overlap? A definite answer to this question is not yet possible. Clearly, if general mental ability has to do with the effectiveness of adapting to the environment, as Wechsler (1955) maintained, then measures of it should correlate with EF measures of planning and decision making. Findings have been mixed and, when positive, indicate that only a modest amount of the variance (e.g., 12%) in EFs is accounted for by general mental ability (see e.g., Arffa, 2007). Further work examining tests at the first and second stratum of the CHC model and collections of marker tests of EFs in which reliabilities of the various tests are accounted for are needed to answer the question with more precision.

For other approaches, substantial but not overly strong correlations have been reported. For example, discriminative RT and general mental ability correlate about .4 (Jensen & Munro, 1979). The correlation between general mental ability and inspection time is higher (Grudnik & Kranzler, 2001). Van Ravenzwaaij, Brown, and Wagenmakers (2011) argued that these findings could be incorporated into a model of information processing that postulated that the speed at which information accumulated (a parameter termed drift rate) in reaching a decision was related to general mental ability. As well as accounting for a number of existing findings, the model makes some novel predictions and provides for an extension of the research into areas in which neuroscience approaches are being used, such as ERPs.

Bringing together research in experimental cognitive psychology and neuroscience is an important goal, although the techniques currently used require a level of expertise and expense that limits research of this kind to a few laboratories. The joint use of fMRI and ERPs is an exciting new frontier of research in this regard made possible by finding technical solutions to EEG recording inside a magnetic resonance scanner (e.g., Kruggel, Wiggins, Herrmann, & von Cramon, 2000). This allows the benefits of good temporal (ERP) and good spatial resolution (fMRI) to be brought to bear in studying brain function with paradigms from the experimental cognitive approach.

The use of these various approaches in applied settings such as selection or diagnosis is largely limited to the individual difference and the neuropsychological approaches. The speed of change in technology over recent years has been such, however, that those approaches that are currently impractical, such as those based in neuroscience, should not be pushed too far out of sight.

References

Alfonso, V. C., Flanagan, D. P., & Radwan, S. (2005). The impact of Cattell-Horn-Carroll theory on test development and the interpretation of cognitive abilities. In D. P. Flanagan & P. L. Harrison (Eds.), *Contemporary intellectual assessment: Theories, tests and issues* (2nd ed., pp. 185–202). New York, NY: Guilford Press.

Allen, D. N. (2011). Halstead – Reitan neuropsychological test battery. In J. S. Kreutzer, J. DeLuca, & B. Caplan (Eds.), *Encyclopedia of clinical neuropsychology* (pp. 1201–1205). New York, NY: Springer.

Arffa, S. (2007). The relationship of intelligence to executive function and non-executive function measures in a sample of average, above average, and gifted youth. *Archives of Clinical Neuropsychology, 22*(8), 969–978. doi:10.1016/j.acn.2007.08.001

Australian Council for Education Research. (1982). *ACER Advanced Tests AL-AQ (2nd Edition) and BL-BQ*. Melbourne, Australia: Author.

Baddeley, A. D. (2001). Is working memory still working? *American Psychologist, 56*(11), 851–864.

Baddeley, A. D., & Hitch, G. (1974). Working memory. In G. Bower (Ed.), *The psychology of learning and motivation* (Vol. 8, pp. 47–89). New York, NY: Academic Press.

Baron, R. A. (1998). Cognitive mechanisms in entrepreneurship: Why and when enterpreneurs think differently than other people. *Journal of Business Venturing, 13*(4), 275–294. doi:http://dx.doi.org/10.1016/S0883-9026(97)00031-1

Benson, N., Hulac, D. M., & Kranzler, J. H. (2010). Independent examination of the Wechsler Adult Intelligence Scale—Fourth Edition (WAIS-IV): What does the WAIS-IV measure? *Psychological Assessment, 22*(1), 121–130.

Brand, A. G. (1985). Hot cognition: Emotions and writing behavior. *Journal of Advanced Composition, 6*, 5–15.

Carpenter, P. A., Just, M. A., & Shell, P. (1990). What one intelligence test measures: A theoretical account of the processing in the Raven Progressive Matrices Test. *Psychological Review, 97*(3), 404–431. doi:10.1037/0033–295X.97.3.404

Carroll, J. B. (1993). *Human cognitive abilities: A survey of factor-analytic studies*. Cambridge; New York, NY: Cambridge University Press.

Cattell, R. B. (1987). *Intelligence: Its structure, growth, and action* (Vol. 35). Amsterdam, The Netherlands; New York, NY: North-Holland.

Chan, R. C. K., Shum, D., Toulopoulou, T., & Chen, E. Y. H. (2008). Assessment of executive functions: Review of instruments and identification of critical issues. *Archives of Clinical Neuropsychology, 23*(2), 201–216. doi:10.1016/j.acn.2007.08.010

Coles, M. G., & Rugg, M. D. (1996). Event-related brain potentials: An introduction. *Electrophysiology of Mind*. Retrieved from http://l3d.cs.colorado.edu/~ctg/classes/lib/cogsci/Rugg-ColesChp1.pdf

Dongés, B., Haupt, L. M., Lea, R. A., Chan, R. C. K., Shum, D. H. K., & Griffiths, L. R. (2012). Role of the apolipoprotein E and catechol-O-methyltransferase genes in prospective and retrospective memory traits. *Gene, 506*(1), 135–140. doi:10.1016/j.gene.2012.06.067

Deary, I. J. (2012). Intelligence. *Annual Review of Psychology, 63*, 453–482.

Duncan, J., Johnson, R., Swales, M., & Freer, C. (1997). Frontal lobe deficits after head injury: Unity and diversity of function. *Cognitive Neuropsychology, 14*(5), 713–741. doi:10.1080/026432997381420

Flanagan, D. P., & Harrison, P. L. (2005). *Contemporary intellectual assessment: Theories, tests, and issues* (Vol. 2nd). New York, NY: Guilford Press.

Fray, P. J., Robbins, T. W., & Sahakian, B. J. (1996). Neuorpsychiatyric applications of CANTAB. *International Journal of Geriatric Psychiatry, 11*(4), 329–336. doi:10.1002/(SICI)1099–1166(199604)11:4<329::AID-GPS453>3.3.CO;2-Y

Gathercole, S. E., & Baddeley, A. D. (1993). *Working memory and language*. Hove, UK: Lawrence Erlbaum.

Gottfried, A. W., & Brody, N. (1975). Interrelationships between and correlates of psychometric and Piagetian scales of sensorimotor intelligence. *Developmental Psychology, 11*(3), 379.

Gregory, T., Callaghan, A., Nettelbeck, T., & Wilson, C. (2009). Inspection time predicts individual differences in everyday functioning among elderly adults: Testing discriminant validity. *Australasian Journal on Ageing, 28*(2), 87–92. doi:10.1111/j.1741–6612.2009.00366.x

Grudnik, J. L., & Kranzler, J. H. (2001). Meta-analysis of the relationship between intelligence and inspection time. *Intelligence, 29*(6), 523–535. doi:10.1016/S0160–2896(01)00078–2

Horn, G. (1985). *Memory, imprinting, and the brain: An inquiry into mechanisms*. Oxford: Oxford University Press.

Huizinga, M., Dolan, C. V., & Van der Molen, M. W. (2006). Age-related change in executive function: Developmental trends and a latent variable analysis. *Neuropsychologia, 44*(11), 2017–2036. doi:10.1016/j.neuropsychologia.2006.01.010

Hunt, E., & Pellegrino, J. (1985). Using interactive computing to expand intelligence testing: A critique and prospectus. *Intelligence, 9*(3), 207–236. doi:10.1016/0160–2896(85)90025-X

Ichikawa, H., & Yamaguchi, M. K. (2014). Infants' recognition of subtle anger facial expression: Infants' recognition of subtle facial expression. *Japanese Psychological Research, 56*(1), 15–23. doi:10.1111/jpr.12025

Jaeggi, S. M., Buschkuehl, M., Perrig, W. J., & Meier, B. (2010). The concurrent validity of the N-back task as a working memory measure. *Memory, 18*(4), 394–412. doi:10.1080/09658211003702171

Jensen, A. R., & Munro, E. (1979). Reaction time, movement time, and intelligence. *Intelligence, 3*(2), 121–126. doi:10.1016/0160–2896(79)90010–2

Johnson, W., & Bouchard, T. J. (2005). The structure of human intelligence: It is verbal, perceptual, and image rotation (VPR), not fluid and crystallized. *Intelligence, 33*(4), 393–416. doi:10.1016/j.intell.2004.12.002

Jones, L.V., & Thissen, D. (2006). A history and overview of psychometrics. In C. R. Rao & S. Sinharay (Eds.), *Handbook of statistics* (Vol. 26, pp. 1–28). Amsterdam, The Netherlands: Elsevier.

Kranzler, J. H., & Jensen, A. R. (1989). Inspection time and intelligence: A meta-analysis. *Intelligence, 13*(4), 329–347. doi:10.1016/S0160–2896(89)80006–6

Kruggel, F., Wiggins, C. J., Herrmann, C. S., & von Cramon, D.Y. (2000). Recording of the event-related potentials during functional MRI at 3.0 Tesla field strength. *Magnetic Resonance in Medicine, 44*(2), 277–282. doi:10.1002/1522–2594(200008)44:2<277::AID-MRM15>3.0.CO;2-X

Leeper, T. J., & Slothuus, R. (2014). Political parties, motivated reasoning, and public opinion formation: Parties and motivated reasoning. *Political Psychology, 35*, 129–156. doi:10.1111/pops.12164

Lezak, M. D., Howieson, D. B., Bigler, E. D., & Tranel, D. (2012). *Neuropsychological assessment* (5th ed.). New York, NY: Oxford University Press.

Loftus, E. F., & Palmer, J. (1996). *Eyewitness testimony*. Cambridge, MA; London, UK: Havard University Press.

Luck, S., J. (2005). *An introduction to the event-related potential technique*. Cambridge, MA: MIT Press

Luria, A. R. (1973). *The working brain: An introduction to neuropsychology* (2nd ed.). London, UK: Penguin.

Matlin, M.W. (2005). *Cognition* (Vol. 6). Hoboken, NJ John Wiley & Sons.

Miyake, A., Friedman, N. P., Emerson, M. J., Witzki, A. H., Howerter, A., & Wager, T. D. (2000). The unity and diversity of executive functions and their contributions to complex "frontal lobe" tasks: A Latent Variable Analysis. *Cognitive Psychology, 41*(1), 49–100. doi:doi.org/10.1006/cogp.1999.0734

Nettelbeck, T., & Lally, M. (1976). Inspection time and measured intelligence. *The British Journal of Psychology, 67*(1), 17–22. doi:10.1111/j.2044–8295.1976.tb01493.x

Otten, L. J., & Rugg, M. D. (2005). Interpreting event-related brain potentials. In T. C. Handy (Ed.), *Event-related potentials: A methods handbook* (pp. 3–16). Cambridge, MA: MIT Press.

Pessoa, L. (2008). On the relationship between emotion and cognition. *Nature Reviews Neuroscience, 9*(2), 148–158. doi:10.1038/nrn2317

Petty, R. E., & Briñol, P. (2008). Persuasion: From single to multiple to metacognitive processes. *Perspectives on Psychological Science, 3*(2), 137–147. doi:10.1111/j.1745–6916.2008.00071.x

Roiser, J. P., & Sahakian, B. J. (2013). Hot and cold cognition in depression. *CNS Spectrums, 18*(3), 139–149. doi:10.1017/s1092852913000072

Shum, D., O'Gorman, J., Myors, B., & Creed, P. (2013). *Psychological testing and assessment* (Vol. 2nd). South Melbourne, VIC: Oxford University Press.

Smith, E. E., & Kosslyn, S. M. (2007). *Cognitive psychology: Mind and brain*. Upper Saddle River, NJ: Pearson/Prentice Hall.

Sternberg, R. J. (1977). Component processes in analogical reasoning. *Psychological Review, 84*(4), 353–378. doi:10.1037/0033–295X.84.4.353

Sternberg, R. J. (1982). *Handbook of human intelligence*. Cambridge: Cambridge University Press.

Stuss, D. T., & Levine, B. (2002). Adult clinical neuropsychology: Lessons from studies of the frontal lobes. *Annual Review of Psychology, 53*, 401–433. doi:10.1146/annurev.psych.53.100901.135220

van Ravenzwaaij, D., Brown, S., & Wagenmakers, E.-J. (2011). An integrated perspective on the relation between response speed and intelligence. *Cognition, 119*(3), 381–393. doi:10.1016/j.cognition.2011.02.002

Vernon, P. E. (1965). Ability factors and environmental influences. *American Psychologist*, *20*(9), 723–733. doi:10.1037/h0021472

Wechsler, D. (1955). *Wechsler adult intelligence scale: Manual*. New York, NY: Psychological Corporation.

Wechsler, D. (2003). *Wechsler Intelligence Scale for Children-Fourth Edition (WISC-IV): Administration and scoring manual*. San Antonio, TX: Psychological Corporation.

Wechsler, D. (2008). *Wechsler Adult Intelligence Scale: Technical and interpretative manual-Fourth Edition (WAIC-IV): Administration and scoring manual*. San Antonio, TX: Pearson.

Wechsler, D. (2012). *Wechsler Preschool and Primary Scale of Intelligence-Fourth Edition*. San Antonio, TX: Psychological Corporation.

Wissler, C. (1901). The correlation of mental and physical tests. *Psychological Review*, *3*(Monograph Suppl. 16). doi:10.1037/h0092995

Zajonc, R. B. (1980). Feeling and thinking: Preferences need no inferences. *American Psychologist*, *35*(2), 151–175. doi:10.1037/0003–066X.35.2.151

Zajonc, R. B. (1984). On the primacy of affect. *American Psychologist*, *39*(2), 117–123. doi:10.1037/0003–066X.39.2.117

13 Longitudinal data collection

Christian Dormann and Christina Guthier

Introduction

Many open questions in applied psychology can be validly answered using longitudinal data. Consider the relation between job demands and burnout, which were strongly correlated in previous studies and meta-analyses (e.g., Alarcon, 2011; Nahrgang, Morgeson, & Hofmann, 2011). Most previous studies used cross-sectional analyses and regressed burnout on job demands, and a significant regression coefficient was also observed if authors controlled for age and sex, for example (e.g., White, Aalsma, Holloway, Adams, & Salyers, 2015). However, there are several related questions that cannot be answered with cross-sectional studies. For example:

1   Are there fluctuations in the strength of the demand-burnout relation over time? Does an increase in job demands directly increase burnout, or is there some kind of latency period (e.g., one month without any vacation) for job demands to affect burnout?
2   Do some employees show a trend of increasing burnout, whereas others show a constant decline over time? Is a change in burnout levels related to the initial levels of job demands and burnout?
3   Does burnout increase job demands, or do job demands cause burnout? May there even be reciprocal relations?

To answer those questions, longitudinal data are required. Longitudinal data are defined as repeated measures (at least twice) of the same variables (e.g., job demands and burnout) gathered from the same study participants (e.g., employees) over time (e.g., Zapf, Dormann, & Frese, 1996). Depending on the specific study design, longitudinal data enable (1) to identify developmental stages in the relationship between independent and dependent variables, (2) to investigate growth processes and their causes and consequences or (3) to identify possible causal relations between variables. Contrary to cross-sectional research, longitudinal designs require decisions – based on theoretical and statistical considerations – about *when* and *how frequently* to measure the variables (Mitchell & James, 2001). These decisions determine the validity of all conclusions that can be derived.

Our main purpose of this chapter is to give theoretical, methodological and analytical advice for making decisions about how to collect longitudinal data. This chapter will be divided into three sections. First, we provide a general overview of several popular longitudinal research designs in applied psychology (experimental studies, diary studies and panel studies). Second, we introduce some guidelines for longitudinal data collection, including theoretical, methodological and analytical aspects. Third, we summarize the essential considerations one should take into account before collecting longitudinal data.

Longitudinal research designs in applied psychology

Longitudinal research has recently substantially increased in the applied psychology area. Searching the PsycINFO Database for journals with "Applied & Psychology" in the title for studies using "repeated measures" or "longitudinal" or "diary" yielded 202 studies from 2001–2005, 246 studies from 2006–2010, and 331 studies from 2011–2015. Experimental and quasi-experimental research designs using repeated measures, so-called diary studies and panel studies have been particularly popular in applied psychology research. In the following three subsections we will shortly introduce the basic characteristics of experimental intervention studies, diary studies and panel studies and take a closer look at the merits and limitations of the different longitudinal study designs.

Experimental and quasi-experimental intervention studies

Experimental and quasi-experimental studies are used to assess the effect of interventions (e.g., introducing or changing job demands) on the outcome variables of interest (e.g., burnout). Such studies aim at establishing a *causal* link between an independent and dependent variable. True experiments, also known as randomized controlled trials (Thiese, 2014), are characterized by assigning each participant of the study sample *randomly* into one out of two or more separate groups (e.g., Hahn, Binnewies, Sonnentag, & Mojza, 2011; Müller, Heiden, Herbig, Poppe, & Angerer, 2016). Random assignment of individual participants is frequently impossible because, for example, interventions are performed on preexisting groups such as organizations or teams (e.g., Holman & Axtell, 2016), and this is called quasi-experimentation. In experiments and quasi-experiments, different interventions are performed on different *experimental groups* except one, which is usually referred to as the *control group*. Afterwards, possible differences in the dependent variables between the experimental and control groups are statistically compared.

Applied psychology experiments frequently involve more than a single measurement. In several studies, a pre-post design is realized in which the dependent variable is measured before and after the intervention (e.g., Holman & Axtell, 2016). Pre-post designs have several advantages including that they increase statistical power and the internal validity of quasi-experiments because they can use preexisting differences between participants as explanatory variables.

In other studies, the dependent variable is measured two or more times after the intervention (e.g., Le Blanc et al., 2007), which is usually done in order to investigate for how long the experimentally induced changes sustain.

The repeated measurement of variables is also governed by the setting in which (quasi) experiments take place. In laboratory experiments, participants may only be available shortly before and after the experiments. This is typically not the case in field experiments, which take place in naturalistic environments. Whereas student populations are frequently used in laboratory experiments, field experiments are typically conducted among the real target population of applied psychology research – for example, employees in companies. Thus, although the internal validity of laboratory experiments is highest, this is corroborated by threats to their *external validity*, which could render causal conclusions of quasi-experiments in the field more valid than true experiments in the laboratory.

There is another threat to the validity of experiments, in particular when they are conducted in a laboratory setting. Especially, the "ideal" conditions realized in laboratory experiments are usually difficult to realize in organizations and among real employees. The result is that effect sizes found in experiments are misleading regarding the degree of efficiency that could be expected for intervention studies. As Dwyer (1983, p. 327) pointed out, experiments have the capacity "to demonstrate that an effect *can* occur, whereas passive designs are more likely to capture causal relations that *are* occurring". Passive designs, in which no experimental or interventional manipulations take place, are reviewed next.

Diary studies

A diary study is a method to collect data at the daily level or even several times a day, usually over several days or even weeks, from the same study participants (Ohly, Sonnentag, Niessen, & Zapf, 2010). Diary studies are particularly suitable for measuring within-person processes or if they are aimed at ruling out person-related differences as confounders.

Whenever experimental designs cannot be realized and possible long-term effects are not of much importance, diary studies can be considered. However, almost all previous diary studies suffered from ambiguous conclusions regarding the direction of possible causal effects among focal variables because the time ordering of variables was not explicitly considered. To put it differently, although data are collected repeatedly from the same participants in diary *designs*, the *analyses* are mostly performed cross-sectionally. Hence, like in all cross-sectional analyses, occasion factors, that is, confounding variables that impact on the independent and dependent variables at the measurement occasion (e.g., current mood), are the Achilles heel of diary designs (cf. Dwyer, 1983). These occasion factors imply correlations among the variables that cannot be causally interpreted. However, the particular strength of diary studies is to reject stable variables as potential confounders by means of centering (i.e., transforming participants' variables by taking their deviation from each participant's mean value in the respective variable over time), which could make causal conclusions based on diary designs much more valid compared to more simple, cross-sectional designs.

Panel studies

Panel studies are a method to collect data repeatedly from the same individuals over a longer period of time, with measurement intervals usually varying between months or years. Panel data facilitate describing and understanding growth and developmental processes as well as causal relationships between focal variables over a longer period of time (Blossfeld, Schneider, & Doll, 2009).

Whenever experimental designs cannot be realized and causal interpretations are intended, panel designs can be considered. Recall, however, that diary designs and panel designs are conceptually similar; the differences (larger sample sizes in panel studies, more measurement occasions in diary studies) are either superficial or grounded in the statistical methods used to analyze the data. In panel studies, centering is usually not done. Therefore, stable variables which are potential confounders cannot be fully excluded. However, the particular strengths of panel designs are their inherent possibility to analyze the direction of causal effects, the possibility to model unmeasured occasion factors as possible confounding variables and the explicit consideration of time by means of autoregressive and cross-lagged effects (e.g., Dormann, 2001).

Although there are commonalities among experimental, diary and panel designs, the reasons for choosing a particular design and the intended statistical analyses could have a significant impact on the data collection. In the following section we introduce some guidelines.

Guidelines for longitudinal data collection

We adapted and expanded the guidelines for developing and evaluating longitudinal research by Polyhart and Vandenberg (2010) to address the most important aspects for longitudinal data collection in applied psychology. We divided this chapter into three sections including theoretical aspects, methodological aspects and analytical aspects.

Theoretical aspects

When designing a longitudinal study, it is very important to think about the expected change processes in advance. Researchers should be able to explain *when* and *why* causal effects are expected. For instance, one could propose that communication technology with enriched audio and video feedback helps virtual teams to effectively manage conflict at early team developmental stages, whereas at later stages rich feedback hampers efficiency (Maruping & Agarwal, 2004). Obviously, proposing such developmental stages in the relation between independent (e.g., enriched feedback) and dependent variables (e.g., efficiency) should determine the required number of measurements; in the present example at least three measurements are required because two different processes are proposed. When it is further assumed that newly composed teams change more rapidly than teams that existed for a long time, the spacing between measurement occasions should also be planned accordingly; in the present example, shorter lags between the first two occasions and longer lags between the second two occasions would be appropriate.

Furthermore, the *direction* and *rate* of change in variables could also be important. When the *direction* of change is of interest, at least three waves of data collection are required. With three or more waves, it becomes possible to identify possible trends – for example, steadily growing or declining, or curvilinear growth curves (e.g., Wu & Griffin, 2012). In addition to identifying growth processes of focal variables, growth processes can also be related to each other. For example, do people who show a linear decline in job demands also show a linear increase in well-being? This could be helpful to identify the predictors and outcomes of growth. When variables are expected to change at a high rate, the use of shorter time lags between measurement occasions is justified compared to times when variables remain relatively stable (low change rate).

The change rate or stability of variables is also affected by the way they are *conceptualized* and *measured*. Whenever researchers are interested in *actual* cognitions, emotions or behaviours, the focal variables should be conceptualized in a state-like manner and could be measured by (self-)observations of participants' momentary thoughts, feelings or activities (cf. Ohly et al., 2010). Trait-like assessments are useful when researchers want to know how people think, feel and behave *in general*, that is, across situations and time. Thus, for example, whereas a state-like measure captures what an individual actually feels (e.g., "*Right now*, I feel calm"), a trait-like measure reflects what an individual believes he or she has felt in the past (e.g., "*In general*, I feel calm"). State assessments are frequently used in diary designs, whereas trait assessments are frequently used in panel studies and interventional/experimental studies.

To summarize, substantive reasons should primarily determine how (state vs. trait), how frequent (two vs. three or more), and at what rate (separated by minutes vs. years) focal variables should be measured. This should be augmented by methodological considerations, which are discussed next.

Methodological aspects

Statistically speaking, in many instances the goal of researchers is to collect repeatedly measured data so that the *causal* effect of a previously measured independent variable on a subsequently measured dependent variable is as *strong and significant* as possible. The central methodological questions for designing a longitudinal study is *when* and *how frequently* to measure in order to achieve this goal. Ideally, researchers have sound theoretical expectations regarding the optimal timing and frequency of measurements; however, methodological considerations could add to them. Such methodological considerations could help identify stronger effects that are less likely to be confounded so that causal interpretations become more valid. Hence, designing the number of measurement occasions and time lag between them should be based on methodological considerations, too, which could increase statistical power and internal validity.

Time lags could be short or long, but there has been little agreement in the literature what a short vs. a long time lag is. Dormann and Van de Ven (2014) provided a taxonomy of time lags for stress-reactions that gives a helpful orientation for choosing the length of time lags when examining other reaction patterns in applied psychology as well. They differentiated between six time frames. The first one is called *immediate* and refers to time lags of seconds up to minutes, the second is *short-term* (hours up to one day), the third is *mid-term* (one day up to one month), the fourth is *meso-term* (one month up to one year), the fifth is *long-term* (one year up to 10 years), and the sixth is *grand-term* (more than a decade).

A typical problem with short time lags in non-experimental research is that confounding variables that impact on both independent and dependent variables may not have changed between measurement occasions. Thus, researchers should suspect that any relation between the focal variables cannot be causally interpreted. However, as we discuss in the next subsection, this problem can be at least partly solved by proper data analysis (i.e. autoregressive effects or ANCOVA).

A typical problem associated with longer time lags is sample attrition. Sample attrition reduces statistical power and may threaten internal and external validity. Problems with sample attrition are more obvious in intervention studies and panel studies compared to diary studies; intervention and panel studies typically fully exclude participants with partly missing data from analysis, whereas diary studies use all available data. Still, power remains reduced and validity is threatened through sample attrition. Both issues are rarely discussed in published studies in the applied psychology literature. These problems could be (partly) compensated post hoc by using multiple data augmentation methods (e.g., Schafer & Graham, 2002), although this is still rarely found in published studies in applied psychology (e.g., Dudenhöffer & Dormann, 2015). Since power is dramatically reduced in panel studies with long time lags, we recommend shorter time lags than those typically found in the literature (Dormann & Griffin, 2015).

For intervention studies there is no simple answer to the question of when to measure before and after the intervention. In general, statistical power is higher for shorter time lags because the observed test-retest correlation of the focal variable is higher. So even small effects become significant. However, a disadvantage of measuring the dependent variable before the intervention is that participants could become suspicious about the study aims. Measuring the focal variable shortly after the intervention might yield large effects; however, what researchers frequently would like to know is if effects sustain, and thus, they opt for longer time intervals.

Analytical aspects

After longitudinal data are collected, researchers have to decide how to statistically analyze them. Hierarchical linear modelling (HLM), cross-lagged panel analysis (CLP), and growth curve modelling (GCM) are popular current approaches in applied psychology. As long as longitudinal data across at least three measurement occasions are available, each of the three approaches is possible (HLM and CLP can also be used with two measurement occasions only). In this section, we elaborate on the possible impact of the desired analytical method on longitudinal data collection.

As just noted, three waves of data collection allow for either statistical method, but there are more or less implicit standards. Such standards rarely represent statistical or mathematical requirements, but researchers have to comply with some rules in order to have their research findings published. We subsequently discuss the use of trait vs. state measures, the number of measurements, the spacing and sample size.

Trait vs. state measures

For example, GCM is most commonly based on trait-like measures (for an exception see Hülsheger, 2016). By contrast, HLM of diary data is most commonly based on state-like measures, but many diary studies use a kind of baseline questionnaire where personality traits and trait-like counterparts of the later applied state-like measures are gathered, too. For instance, the baseline questionnaire may include a measure of trait affect (e.g., positive and negative affectivity schedule, PANAS, Watson, Clark, and Tellegen, 1988), and subsequent diary questionnaires may include the same items but with reference to the current moment or the last few hours. Like GCM, CLP analysis has for a long time almost exclusively relied on trait-like measures. More recently, some studies used short time lags between measurement occasions (e.g., two weeks, Dudenhöffer & Dormann, 2013). In such studies, time overlap would have occurred if trait-like measures were used. For instance, if participants were asked how they felt the last year, and they were asked the same question two weeks later, the two measures "overlap" by 50 out of 52 weeks. Hence, for CLP analysis, researchers tend to adjust the trait-like measures to the time lag used in order to avoid time overlap.

Number of measurements

For GCM, the number of measurement occasions determines the kind of trends that could be analyzed. With three waves of data available, only linear trends (polynomial of degree 1) could be identified, and with each additional wave polynomial trends with one additional degree could be identified.

Even if researchers aim at investigating *linear* GCM only, the number and spacing of measurement occasions is important because it is known to influence statistical power. In particular, when the overall study duration is no longer than five years (which, in fact, is the case for the early phases of *all* longitudinal studies), increasing measurement occasions substantially increases power (Rast & Hofer, 2014). Conversely, when researchers aim at GCM using state-like measures, plenty of measurement occasions separated by short time lags could be required (e.g., Hülsheger, 2016).

Most CLP analysis rests on data collected at two waves only. This is sufficient to identify possible reciprocal causal relations among variables. However, when researchers aim at identifying changes of causal patterns over time, three or more waves are required. The same applies if researchers propose more complex causal mechanisms above and beyond simple linear effects. For example, Frese and Zapf (1988) described a sleeper effect that occurs not directly after the change of the independent variable but with some delay. In order to identify such an effect, a researcher would need a three-wave model where there would be no cross-lagged effect of the independent variable expected between Wave 1 and Wave 2 but an effect between Wave 1 and Wave 3.

Whereas studies that use CLP analysis usually have few waves and many participants, studies that analyze diary data with HLM typically have more waves and fewer participants. One of the reasons is that HLM analysis could identify the effects of an independent variable on a dependent variable *for each participant individually*. For example, the strength of the effect (e.g., a regression coefficient) of job demands on burnout could vary among participants; for some, job demands do not matter much or even prevent burnout, whereas for others the effect of demands is positive and strong. Conceptually, HLM analysis involves separate regressions for every individual. When the aim is to include two predictors for one dependent variable in HLM analysis, one thus should plan to have three waves of data collection per participant. However, in general, studies using less than five occasions have become rare in recent years.

Spacing of measurements

Since most GCM relied on trait-like measures, it is not too surprising that they also relied on data with a long-term spacing involving time lags of one or even more years (e.g., Wu & Griffin, 2012). Although shorter time lags are possible, too, they could be problematic. Either the trends are very weak across a range of waves separated by short time lags (e.g., a decline in health by .001 on a 7-point scale across a day), which then would require large sample sizes to become significant, or there are strong trends (e.g., a decline in health by .1 on a 7-point scale across a day), which then impose the question of what would happen to those participants, for example, after three months (i.e., the scale would be insufficient). Of course, if there is sound theoretical reason, short spacing could and should be done (e.g., Hülsheger, 2016). For instance, it seems to be reasonable to assume that fatigue increases for most employees during the workweek and then declines during the weekend.

For most studies that apply HLM analysis to repeatedly measured data, the spacing of measurement is unimportant. The reason is that most HLM analyses do not make use of any time-related information; in fact, the waves of data collection could be shuffled without affecting the results. This is because HLM analysis treats each participant as a "sample" and the participants' measurement occasions as "cases" (i.e., a row of data in a spreadsheet). Only a few studies have used HLM analysis and considered time. For example, Dudenhöffer and Dormann (2013) used morning affect as a predictor of evening affect to analyze whether job demands as a further predictor led to a change in affect across the day. Obviously, spacing is important in such instances and has to be guided by theoretical reasons.

Although using so-called lagged variables or autoregressive effects in HLM analysis like in the study by Dudenhöffer and Dormann (2013) is rarely conducted, this is common in CLP analyses. Dormann and Griffin (2015) showed that the sizes of the autoregressive effects have a sustained impact on the size of the causal effects (cross-lagged effects). Since the size of an autoregressive effect depends on the spacing between measurement occasions, the spacing thus impacts on the causal effects, too. Hence, when researchers aim at demonstrating strong causal effects using CLP analysis, spacing of measurement occasions is highly relevant. Dormann and Griffin (2015) suggested that time lags of several months or years, which are frequently used, could be much too long. They also recommended conducting "shortitudinal" pilot studies and performing an initial CLP analysis. The results could be readily published if the hypothesized effects are significant; if they are not, the results nevertheless could be used to calculate an *optimal time lag* at which a third wave of data collection could be carried out (for details see Dormann & Griffin, 2015).

Sample size

When collecting longitudinal data, in addition to the number and spacing of measurement, sample size is also important as it determines statistical power. This is crucial because the increased validity of a longitudinal study is accompanied by shrinking effect sizes; cross-lagged effects in longitudinal studies are frequently much smaller than in effects found in cross-sectional studies. In particular, panel studies rarely yield cross-lagged effects exceeding .20. Therefore, power analysis should be carried out, and we recommend to refer to extant meta-analyses for expected effects sizes. In the absence of meta-analyses, we recommend to assume (standardized) regression coefficients not to be larger than .20 in diary designs and not to be larger than .12 in panel designs, which was the average effect in the review by Zapf et al. (1996; cf. Maxwell, Kelley, & Rausch, 2008, for power analysis of targeted regression coefficients). For an intervention study, we recommend to assume standardized mean differences between experimental groups (i.e., d) not to exceed .30.

Most well-done diary studies aim at having a sample size of $N = 100$ (and five measurement occasions; cf. Ohly et al., 2010), which is probably more driven by the Gestalt law of "a nice number" rather than power calculations. Scherbaum and Ferreter (2009) recommended not to have fewer the $N = 30$

participants because of risk of biased results. In terms of power, the results presented by these authors also suggest that increasing the sample size increases power more than increasing measurement occasions.

Conclusion

There is no simple answer to the question how to optimally collect longitudinal data. As we discussed, the answer depends on the design of the study, theoretical considerations including the size and rate of change, methodological considerations, and the statistical analysis employed. Furthermore, there are "political" factors, too, as it is usually easier to redo what others have already published successfully than to be unconventional. For instance, reviewers would probably challenge a diary design in which four randomly selected days across one year would be used to collect state-like measures among 45 participants, although there might be little reason not doing so. Rather, the data collection of most diary studies does not spread across more than four weeks, most diary studies have at least five measurement occasions these days, and sample size is close to or even above 100. Growth curve and panel studies tend to have even larger samples, the former with at least three waves and the latter with at least two waves. Sample sizes vary considerably in these studies, and we highly recommend performing a power analysis of the targeted effects. The spacing of measurements in most growth curve and panel studies tends to be larger than six months, albeit much shorter lags such as two weeks are becoming more frequent, too. We strongly believe this is a good development, as it allows for much quicker results that are nevertheless highly valid.

References

Alarcon, G. M. (2011). A meta-analysis of burnout with job demands, resources, and attitudes. *Journal of Vocational Behavior, 79*, 549–562. doi:10.1016/j.jvb.2011.03.007

Blossfeld, H. P., Schneider, T., & Doll, J. (2009). Methodological advantages of panel studies: Designing the new National Educational Panel Study (NEPS) in Germany. *Journal for Educational Research Online, 1*, 10–32.

Dormann, C. (2001). Modeling unmeasured third variables in longitudinal studies. *Structural Equation Modeling, 8*, 575–598. doi:10.1207/S15328007SEM0804_04

Dormann, C., & Griffin, M. A. (2015). Optimal time lags in panel studies. *Psychological Methods, 20*, 489–505. doi:10.1037/met0000041

Dormann, C., & Van de Ven, B. (2014). Timing in methods for studying psychosocial factors at work. In: Dollard, M., Shimazu, A., Bin Nordin, R., Brough, P., & Tuckey, M. (Eds.). *Psychosocial factors at work in the Asia Pacific* (pp. 89–116). London, UK: Springer.

Dudenhöffer, S., & Dormann, C. (2015). Customer-related social stressors: Meaning and consequences across service jobs. *Journal of Personnel Psychology, 14*, 165–181. doi:10.1027/1866–5888/a000132

Dudenhöffer, S., & Dormann, C. (2013). Customer-related social stressors and service providers' affective reactions. *Journal of Organizational Behavior, 34*, 520–539. doi:10.1002/job.1826

Dwyer, J. H. (1983). *Statistical models for the social and behavioral sciences*. Oxford: Oxford University Press.

Frese, M., & Zapf, D. (1988). Causes, coping and consequences of stress at work. In *Methodological issues in the study of work stress: Objective vs. subjective measurement of work stress and the question of longitudinal studies* (pp. 375–412). London, UK: John Wiley & Sons.

Hahn, V. C., Binnewies, C., Sonnentag, S., & Mojza, E. J. (2011). Learning how to recover from job stress: Effects of a recovery training program on recovery, recovery-related self-efficacy, and well-being. *Journal of Occupational Health Psychology, 16*, 202. doi:10.1037/a0022169

Holman, D., & Axtell, C. (2016). Can job redesign interventions influence a broad range of employee outcomes by changing multiple job characteristics? A quasi-experimental study. *Journal of Occupational Health Psychology, 21*, 284–295. doi:10.1037/a0039962

Hülsheger, U. R. (2016). From dawn till dusk: Shedding light on the recovery process by investigating daily change patterns in fatigue. *Journal of Applied Psychology, 101*, 905–914. doi:10.1037/apl0000104

Le Blanc, P. M., Hox, J. J., Schaufeli, W. B., Taris, T. W., & Peeters, M. C. (2007). Take care! The evaluation of a team-based burnout intervention program for oncology care providers. *Journal of Applied Psychology, 92*, 213–227. doi:10.1037/0021–9010.92.1.213

Maxwell, S. E., Kelley, K., & Rausch, J. R. (2008). Sample size planning for statistical power and accuracy in parameter estimation. *Annual Review of Psychology, 59*, 537–563. doi:10.1146/annurev.psych.59.103006.093735

Maruping, L. M., & Agarwal, R. (2004). Managing team interpersonal processes through technology: A task-technology fit perspective. *Journal of Applied Psychology, 89*, 975–990. doi:10.1037/0021–9010.89.6.975

Mitchell, T. E., & James, L. R. (2001). Building better theory: Time and the specification of when things happen. *Academy of Management Review, 26*, 530–547. doi:10.5465/AMR.2001.5393889

Müller, A., Heiden, B., Herbig, B., Poppe, F., & Angerer, P. (2016). Improving well-being at work: A randomized controlled intervention based on selection, optimization, and compensation. *Journal of Occupational Health Psychology, 21*, 169–181. doi:10.1037/a0039676

Nahrgang, J. D., Morgeson, F. P., & Hofmann, D. A. (2011). Safety at work: A meta-analytic investigation of the link between job demands, job resources, burnout, engagement, and safety outcomes. *Journal of Applied Psychology, 96*, 71. doi:10.1037/a0021484

Ohly, S., Sonnentag, S., Niessen, C., & Zapf, D. (2010). Diary studies in organizational research. *Journal of Personnel Psychology, 2*, 79–93. doi:10.1027/1866–5888/a000009

Ployhart, R. E., & Vandenberg, R. J. (2010). Longitudinal research: The theory, design, and analysis of change. *Journal of Management, 36*(1), 94–120. doi: 10.1177/0149206309352110

Rast, P., & Hofer, S. M. (2014). Longitudinal design considerations to optimize power to detect variances and covariances among rates of change: Simulation results based on actual longitudinal studies. *Psychological Methods, 19*, 133–154. doi:10.1037/a0034524

Schafer, J. L., & Graham, J. W. (2002). Missing data: Our view of the state of the art. *Psychological Methods, 7*, 147–177. doi:10.1037/1082–989X.7.2.147

Scherbaum, C. A., & Ferreter, J. M. (2009). Estimating statistical power and required sample sizes for organizational research using multilevel modeling. *Organizational Research Methods, 12*, 347–367. doi:10.1177/1094428107308906

Thiese, M. S. (2014). Observational and interventional study design types: An overview. *Biochemia Medica, 24*, 199–210. doi:10.11613/BM.2014.022

Watson, D., Clark, L. A., & Tellegen, A. (1988). Development and validation of brief measures of positive and negative affect: The PANAS scales. *Journal of Personality and Social Psychology, 54*, 1063–1070. doi:10.1037/0022–3514.54.6.1063

White, L. M., Aalsma, M. C., Holloway, E. D., Adams, E. L., & Salyers, M. P. (2015). Job-related burnout among juvenile probation officers: Implications for mental health stigma and competency. *Psychological Services, 12,* 291–302. doi:10.1037/ser0000031

Wu, C. H., & Griffin, M. A. (2012). Longitudinal relationships between core self-evaluations and job satisfaction. *Journal of Applied Psychology, 97,* 331–342. doi:10.1037/a0025673

Zapf, D., Dormann, C., & Frese, M. (1996). Longitudinal studies in organizational stress research: A review of the literature with reference to methodological issues. *Journal of Occupational Health Psychology, 1,* 145–169. doi:10.1037/1076–8998.1.2.145

14 Diary studies, event sampling, and smartphone apps

Joel M. Hektner

Introduction

To understand people – how they act, think, and feel, and how that is related to context – questionnaires and lab experiments are not sufficient. Psychologists also need to use methods that capture the full range of individuals' experiences in the real world. Intensive longitudinal methods (ILM), which include experience sampling, event sampling, daily diaries, ecological momentary assessment, and ambulatory monitoring, are among the most important tools at researchers' disposal for gaining understanding of people in their natural contexts. The fact that there is now a *Handbook of Research Methods for Studying Daily Life* (Mehl & Conner, 2012) indicates the tremendous growth both in the use of these methods and in varieties of methods and their purposes. What these methods have in common is their focus on people as they go about daily life in the real world, their collection of data as experience happens in as close to real time as possible, and their ability to reveal variability within the person, not just between people (Mehl & Conner, 2012).

As is the case with any method, the most important consideration in the selection of a particular type of intensive longitudinal method is whether and how it addresses the research questions. To draft good questions, researchers need to keep in mind that within-person variability may not coincide with – and may even run counter to – between-person variability (Hamaker, 2012), and so questions need to be precise enough to recognize this distinction. In any case, the types of questions most ideally suited for intensive longitudinal methods are those that concern processes and experiences that vary over a short time span, from hours to days (Conner & Lehman, 2012). Because these methods are employed in the natural environment of daily life, the rigid control and random assignment required by the experimental method are not possible, and thus descriptive and correlational questions, rather than causal questions, will need to be the focus of ILM. Bamberger (2016) gives examples of research questions well-suited to ILM, paired with appropriate sampling protocols for applied family research.

Types of intensive longitudinal methods

The various types of intensive longitudinal methods can be categorized on the basis of their location along several dimensions, as shown in Table 14.1, which is an expansion of a taxonomy started by Conner and Lehman (2012). It must be noted, however, that there are no hard and fast rules regarding the naming of particular methods, and many studies combine aspects from several prototypical methods. The most fundamental dimension is *what* the focus of the study is; what aspects of life do the constructs or variables measure? Most of these methods measure individuals' behavior (what they are actually doing or saying in the moment) as well as their inner experiences, which include their cognitions and emotions. Many also measure the context, such as the date, day of week, time of day, physical location, and presence of others. A fourth possibility along this dimension is physiological measurements, such as heart rate, blood pressure, physical activity level, or neuroendocrine levels.

Another dimension to consider is *whose perspective* is taken in collecting the data: the self or a third-person observer? Classic experience sampling method (ESM) is rooted in understanding the phenomenology of everyday life and thus takes the person's self-reported behavior, experience, and context as the most important object of study. Even if an objective observer might record different data about the person in the same moment, it is the person's own perceptions and experiences that matter for an ESM researcher. However, for other purposes, an objective perspective may be more valuable. Note that this perspective does not require the actual presence of an observer following research participants as they go about daily life. The observational perspective is achieved through instrumentation, such as audio, video, or photo recording; location (GPS) monitoring; or physiological recording.

Data from either perspective could be fundamentally quantitative (e.g., a response on a rating scale or a heart rate) or qualitative (e.g., a photo or a description of current thoughts). Thus, a third dimension to consider is that of the *form of the data*. Most qualitative data can be coded and reduced to produce numbers or categories that can be analyzed statistically, but it is still useful to maintain the distinction between a data collection process that elicits numeric data and one in which numeric data must be derived by the researcher.

The most widely recognized dimension along which intensive longitudinal methods vary is *when or at which times* data are collected. When self-reported data are collected on a variable (often random) time schedule, responses are said to be made on signal-contingent basis, because participants must be signaled by a device to complete a self-report. Observational or physiological data may be collected on a variable basis without signaling the participant. Another option is for data to be collected in fixed intervals (such as once daily in diary studies). Some instruments provide a third option, which is for continuous recording of data, such as heart activity or skin conductance. Finally, in event sampling, data are collected only when a particular event occurs. The occurrence of the event could be discerned by the participant or detected automatically by instruments the participant is asked to carry or wear.

It should be clear by now that there are two answers to the question of what the *role of the participant* is in collecting and reporting the data. Participants can take an active role, self-reporting their experiences, contexts, and behaviors and collecting their own physiological data (such as swabbing a cheek for a salivary cortisol measure). Or participants can take a passive role, doing nothing much more than wearing or carrying devices that automatically collect data without prompting or intervention from the participants.

Description and logistics of experience sampling method

Although the logistics of carrying out an ILM study will vary depending on the type of study, many aspects of implementation are similar across types. In the sections that follow, the steps necessary to implement an ESM study are described, but many of them are easily adapted for other types of studies. Aspects of implementation specific to other types of ILM will be described in subsequent sections.

Sampling time frame and signals per day

As noted in Table 14.1 and in the *Experience Sampling Method* book (Hektner, Schmidt, & Csikszentmihalyi, 2007), ESM (or ecological momentary

Table 14.1 Location of prototypical intensive longitudinal methods along several dimensions

Prototypical method	What is focus	Whose perspective	Form of data	When recorded	Role of participant
ESM	Experience Context Behavior	Self	Quantitative Qualitative	Variable	Active
DES	Experience	Self	Qualitative	Variable	Active
Diary	Experience Context Behavior	Self	Quantitative Qualitative	Fixed	Active
DRM	Experience Context Behavior	Self	Quantitative Qualitative	Fixed	Active
ECR	Experience Context Behavior	Self	Quantitative Qualitative	Event	Active
Photovoice	Experience Context	Self Observer	Qualitative	Event	Active
Activity monitoring	Behavior	Observer	Quantitative	Continuous	Passive
Ambulatory assessment	Physiological	Observer	Quantitative	Fixed Continuous	Passive Active
EMA	Experience Context Behavior Physiological	Self Observer	Quantitative	Variable	Active Passive
Acoustic sampling	Context Behavior	Observer	Qualitative	Fixed Event	Passive

assessment, EMA) is used to collect self-reported data on the participants' experiences, context, and behavior. Participants in ESM studies are typically signaled over a span of three days to three weeks, with a week being the most common (Hektner et al., 2007). Longer periods have been used when the number of signals per day is lower, and particularly in daily diary studies when there is only one self-report per day. Researchers typically signal participants from four to 10 times each day, the most common being six to eight. This leads to participants being signaled roughly once every two hours, on average, if there are assumed to be 16 waking hours. To obtain a representative sample of moments from the population of moments in daily life, a stratified random schedule is created, with the waking hours of the day divided into a number of equal-length intervals that is equal to the number of signals per day. Then a random time is chosen within each interval, with the chosen time varying each day. In order to prevent participants from being bothered by signals happening in close succession, a stipulation can be added that no two signals will be less than 30 minutes apart. The hours during which signals will occur can be the same for all members of the sample or they can be individually tailored to each person's anticipated waking hours.

Technology options

Researchers have a wide range of both hardware and software options that vary in functionality and cost. Before the advent of palmtop computers or personal digital assistants (PDAs, the forerunner to the smartphone), it was common for ESM studies to use a device to deliver signals, such as a pager or programmable wristwatch, and pen and paper for participants to read and respond to questions. Of course, these options are still available today and may be preferable in some contexts or with certain special populations. PDAs provided the advantage of combining the functions of signaling, presenting questions, and recording answers in a single device. However, these devices are now obsolete, and labs will not be able to find replacements for devices that break down. Clearly, today the smartphone is becoming the technology of choice for ESM studies. One question that researchers must resolve is whether they should acquire a fleet of phones that are then provided to participants to carry for the duration of the study or rely on participants' own smartphones. The latter choice may bias the sample by eliminating people who don't own smartphones, and it may pose challenges in finding software that will work on all different hardware platforms that people own. However, these issues are rapidly diminishing as smartphone ownership becomes normative and apps are continually being developed. Other hardware platforms are well suited for particular functions, such as the person's own computer/laptop/tablet for reporting daily diaries or other specialized devices for monitoring physical activity or physiological parameters.

There is a plethora of software options for conducting an ESM study. Conner (2015) provides a comprehensive list of these options, along with brief descriptions, pricing information, and web links for further information and ordering. Much of the information in this paragraph comes from Conner's list. One basic software option comes from web survey services, such as Qualtrics and Survey Monkey, which allow researchers to create online surveys with many different question formats. At each signal, the participant is sent a link to the survey via text messaging. Programs such as Survey Signal or Diario help researchers manage the sending of texts to multiple participants. More commonly, researchers use a dedicated app that is downloaded onto the phone. One newer app, Sensus, is free and is available for both iOS and Android operating systems. It can deliver scheduled prompts to participants as well as prompts that are triggered by an event that is detected by the phone or by an external wearable device. An app with similar functionality is mEMA (mobile EMA); it is available at three levels of pricing depending on the level of features needed. The most basic level includes some features the company claims are not available anywhere else, such as a "compliance dashboard" and the use of languages other than English. For traditional ESM studies with no passive data collection, the app called PACO (Personal Analytics Companion) has been available for a longer time and thus has been widely used. It is easy to use and free, although as with any free software, tech support may be limited.

Measurement

To determine the actual questions that will be asked of participants, researchers must once again carefully consider their research questions. Participants in ESM studies typically respond to prompts that get at behavior (e.g., "What are you doing?"), context (e.g., "Who are you with?"), and inner experience (e.g. "Rate how happy you are") at the moment of the signal (Hektner, et al, 2007). These questions can be written in a way to elicit qualitative or quantitative responses, but there are tradeoffs associated with either option. Open-ended responses will likely need to be coded by trained research assistants, requiring time and money. Providing participants with a closed-ended list of response options may be more efficient, but it requires careful consideration of which options to include and misses a lot of detail and variation.

For quantitative measurement of psychological constructs, researchers may want to find a longer questionnaire scale that was developed to measure a construct of interest and then adapt it to fit the momentary context of an ESM study. This adaptation would likely include reducing the number of questions and revising the wording to focus on the moment just prior to the signal. To insure participants do not become overburdened and then stop responding, the total number of questions should not exceed what can be answered in about two minutes. In a review of several studies, Hektner et al. (2007) found that a typical-length ESM self-report included the standard context and behavior questions, plus about 35 additional quantitative inner experience questions.

In the variation of ESM called *descriptive experience sampling* (DES), there really are no questions other than a general instruction for participants to take notes on their inner experience in response to each signal (Hurlburt, 2011). In this completely qualitative approach, no coding is conducted. Instead, researchers interview participants about their noted experiences on that same day or the immediately following day. The goal is to capture "pristine inner experience" (Hurlburt & Heavey, 2015), which does not include the cognitive processes of attention, memory, judgment, or comprehension. Thus, the interviews are used both to clarify data and also to train participants on how to apprehend and describe inner experience without these cognitive filters.

Orientation, signaling, and wrap-up

In order to fully understand the demands they are asking participants to meet, researchers should first complete the study protocol themselves, including wearing or carrying any devices and responding to all signals. The pilot test will also help researchers determine how long each self-report will take to complete. To begin the full study, researchers typically meet with participants either individually or in groups to orient them to the study procedures and provide any equipment and/or set up any necessary software. Participants should be encouraged to think about times during which it will be difficult for them to carry the device or complete a response (such as when driving or swimming), and researchers should discuss appropriate ways to handle these situations. In our studies, we tell participants to respond as soon after the signal as they can, but not to respond if 15 minutes or more have passed since the signal. If participants will be in school or at work during signaling, it may be helpful for the researcher to provide them with a letter documenting the study that they can show to an employer or teacher. Because of the burden and intrusion of participating in an ESM study, participants will need to have a higher level of motivation and commitment than they would in a standard questionnaire or lab study. Researchers will want to consider whether and how they can enhance motivation through several different avenues, such as offering compensation, emphasizing the personal insight one can gain from participation, and promoting a research alliance in which the participant partners with the researcher to further scientific understanding (Hektner et al., 2007).

At the end of the signaling period, participants will need to be debriefed. Any devices that are the property of the lab are returned. Participants may be asked to complete a brief questionnaire asking them whether their experiences during the signaling period were typical or how they were not typical. As a check on reactivity, they may also be asked if participation in the study caused their experiences to be different in any way. Some studies have also complemented the ESM data collection with interviews of participants that ask them to elaborate on specific moments of interest (e.g. Csikszentmihalyi & Schneider, 2000).

Advantages and disadvantages

Certainly, ESM and related methods are not appropriate for every research question. But for questions about relations among behavior, inner experience, and context in the moments of daily life, ESM is the method of choice. Unlike most lab or questionnaire studies, ESM research has a high degree of ecological validity due to its ability to capture information about moments in the real world in close to real time (Hektner et al., 2007; Reis, 2012). Some have noted that ESM measures of some inner experiences do not correlate very highly with corresponding questionnaire measures. For example, on questionnaires, parents tend to say they enjoy spending time with their children, whereas diary data show more negative experiences (Schwarz, 2012). Rather than anointing one method as "valid" and the other as flawed, researchers can accept both findings at face value by recognizing that they are measures of different things. One-time self-reports are filtered through lenses of reflection, beliefs, memory, and social desirability, each of which is minimized in ESM data collection. Some vital research questions would be better answered through the former and some through the latter.

One of the disadvantages of ESM is the burden it places on participants and the intrusion it brings into their daily lives. As a result, some individuals may refuse to participate at the outset, and others may begin but then reduce or stop their compliance before study completion. When this happens, it is a threat to the external validity of the study (Hektner et al., 2007). Both the human sample and the sample of moments of time may be less representative of their respective populations than we would wish them to be.

Daily diaries

Daily diaries address this problem by reducing the burden. Participants are sampled on an interval-contingent basis, and the interval is one day. Data collection can occur over a period of days to months, with two weeks being the most frequent (Gunthert & Wenze, 2012). Besides being more tolerable and less expensive, once-daily reporting is better suited than ESM to some constructs. Gunthert and Wenze (2012) suggest that behaviors and situations that occur with moderate frequency are well-suited for diary studies, such as interpersonal conflict, sexual behavior, alcohol use, and physical symptoms. Because participants are bothered only once daily, they can be asked to spend a longer time completing the report, which can contain more questions than in an ESM study. There have also been measurement tools specifically created for diary studies (e.g. Courvoisier, Eid, Lischetzke, & Schreiber, 2010; Moskowitz, 1994; Wilhelm & Schoebi, 2007). Compliance may be enhanced if participants are reminded to complete their self-reports; a daily email or text could include a web link to the survey.

Besides the self-selection bias that is also a potential problem in recruiting samples of people for ESM studies, diary studies also have a couple of unique disadvantages. One is that within–day fluctuation is lost. If participants are asked about the moods they had, they will tend to recall the more intense moods more readily than the perhaps longer lasting or more frequent periods of neutral moods (Gunthert & Wenze, 2012). The context immediately surrounding the response in a diary study is also likely to be much more homogenous than the full range of daily life contexts reported in an ESM study. Participants will likely report at the same time of day and in the same place (e.g., home, office) every day. Keeping these considerations in mind, the diary method is a valuable tool that has been used in a large body of good research, and researchers will continue to find it useful for particular purposes.

Day reconstruction method

One specific form of daily diary attempts to capture within-day fluctuation by having participants do a sort of retrospective ESM. In the day reconstruction method (DRM; Kahneman, Krueger, Schkade, Schwarz, & Stone, 2004), participants reflect on the previous day as a series of scenes or episodes. An episode is a defined activity, such as a work meeting, lunch, or watching TV, that could last from 15 minutes to two hours; the average reported episode was about one hour. Then, participants are asked a series of ESM-type questions about each episode, including context (where, who with, time of day), behavior, and inner experience (e.g. emotion ratings). In this way, the DRM assesses contiguous episodes over a full day rather than sampling discrete moments as in the ESM (Kahneman et al., 2004). Thus, it may be more accurate in providing time budget information. It also does not interrupt participants' lives and is less expensive. However, Csikszentmihalyi (2007) found some of the results of a DRM study to be questionable. Participants in the DRM study, who were studied only on work days, rated TV watching (retrospectively) as a relatively positive experience, contradicting in-the-moment evidence from many ESM studies that it is actually not. The differing results point again to the notion that retrospective reports do not measure the same thing as ESM self-reports completed in the moment and thus should not be taken as a substitute.

Event contingent recording

Research questions that are more narrowly focused on a particular behavior or experience rather than on daily life in general may be well-suited for event-contingent recording (ECR; Moskowitz & Sadikaj, 2012). In ECR, instead of completing a report in response to a signal, participants are trained to recognize when the event of interest occurs and to complete a report immediately following the event. Social interactions and health-related behaviors and experiences, such as taking a drink of alcohol, smoking a cigarette, or experiencing acute pain, have been the most common events studied with ECR. For studying social interaction, the Rochester Interaction Record (Wheeler & Nezlek, 1977) and the Social Behavior Inventory (Moskowitz, 1994) are published ECR protocols. Because participants are not waiting until the end of the day to recall events, as in the diary method, ECR may capture a more valid picture of their immediate experience. It also has the advantage of capturing every relevant event; in random signal-contingent ESM, many events of study would be missed. The key to a successful ECR study is to focus on well-defined, discrete events that occur with moderate frequency and can easily be recognized by participants. One concern is that there may be greater reactivity with respect to the event in question than there would be with standard ESM. Participants may alter both the frequency and the experiential qualities of the event when they know that every event needs to be recorded.

ECR has traditionally relied on an active participant to recognize the occurrence of the event and record information about it. However, electronic devices now make possible the passive detection of certain body movements, physiological states, or social interactions, followed by passive recording of aspects of the individual or environment. Some of these options will be described further later.

Photovoice

In one recent variation of ECR, participants are given more latitude in discerning whether a given moment constitutes a relevant event or not, and their primary means of reporting on the event is to take a photo. First described and named by Wang and Burris (1997), photovoice is a method in which participants are provided with cameras or are asked to use their own smartphone cameras for a period of time. They are asked to take photos of events or things that are relevant to a particular topic. For example, Adams and colleagues (2012) used photovoice with Australian Aboriginal people to understand meanings of food and food insecurity. In another study, African immigrant youth and elderly in the U.S. took photos that illustrated health resources and barriers to health and well-being (Adekeye, Kimbrough, Obafemi, & Strack, 2014). Participants were also provided with memo pads for their notes on each photo. During a focus group meeting, photos were projected on a screen and discussed. This process is what Wang and Burris called "voicing our individual and collective experience" (VOICE). Clearly, photovoice is not just a method of data collection but also a tool for community based participatory research (CBPR). Strack, Lovelace, Jordan, and Holmes (2010) provide a social-ecological logic model for using photovoice that includes activities and outcomes related to individual, organizational, and community levels.

Activity monitoring, ambulatory assessment, and ecological momentary assessment

Researchers can ask participants to wear or carry devices to measure a wide range of contextual, behavioral, and physiological parameters as they go about their daily lives. For example, the *Electronically Activated Recorder* (EAR; Mehl & Robbins, 2012) records ambient sounds at random times throughout the day, including the participants' own voices and those of others with whom participants interact. Similarly, a "baby cam," a video camera embedded in a headband worn by an infant, records snippets of video from the infant's natural environments (Smith, Yu, Yoshida, & Fausey, 2015). To record physical behavior, accelerometers continuously measure body movement, and data from over 27,000 children aged 3 to 18 in the International Children's Accelerometry Database show that children get less active with age (Cooper et al., 2015). Ambulatory assessment of physiological functioning can occur continuously or on a fixed interval schedule and can include recordings of heart rate, blood pressure, salivary cortisol, or skin conductance. Wilhelm, Grossman, and Müller (2012, pp. 221–222) provide a list of devices and the parameters they measure. When such measures are coupled with self-reports of experience recorded at the same time, the method is called ecological momentary assessment (EMA; Stone & Shiffman, 1994), but some researchers also use "EMA" to refer to traditional experience sampling alone. Combining and integrating capabilities across multiple devices allows for context-sensitive EMA, in which changes in location, weather, physical activity, or proximity to other people are possible triggers of further data collection (Intille, 2012).

Conclusion

Since their beginnings several decades ago, intensive longitudinal methods have contributed richly to a wide range of fields in the human sciences. This chapter provides only a glimpse of the many different types of these methods. Researchers wanting to implement one of these methods in a study will need to consult other sources for more detailed information. Beyond raising awareness of these methods, this chapter may also inspire researchers to consider new research questions associated with their topic that better capture the complexity within and across people as they live life in the real world in real time.

References

Adams, K., Burns, C., Liebzeit, A., Ryschka, J., Thorpe, S., & Browne, J. (2012). Use of participatory research and photo-voice to support urban Aboriginal healthy eating. *Health and Social Care in the Community, 20*, 497–505. doi:10.1111/j.1365–2524.2011.01056.x

Adekeye, O., Kimbrough, J., Obafemi, B., & Strack, R. W. (2014). Health literacy from the perspective of African immigrant youth and elderly: A photovoice project. *Journal of Health Care for the Poor and Underserved, 25*, 1730–1747. doi:10.1353/hpu.2014.0183

Bamberger, K. T. (2016). The application of intensive longitudinal methods to investigate change: Stimulating the field of applied family research. *Clinical Child and Family Psychology Review, 19*, 21–38. doi:10.1007/s10567-015-0194-6

Conner, T. S. (2015, May). *Experience sampling and ecological momentary assessment with mobile phones.* Retrieved from www.otago.ac.nz/psychology/otago047475.pdf

Conner, T. S., & Lehman, B. J. (2012). Getting started: Launching a study in daily life. In M. R. Mehl & T. S. Conner (Eds.), *Handbook of research methods for studying daily life* (pp. 89–107). New York, NY: Guilford Press.

Cooper, A. R., Goodman, A., Page, A. S., Sherar, L. B., Esliger, D. W., van Sluijs, E. M. F., . . . Ekelund, U. (2015). Objectively measured physical activity and sedentary time in youth: The International Children's Accelerometry Database (ICAD). *International Journal of Behavioral Nutrition and Physical Activity, 12*(113). doi:10.1186/s12966-015-0274-5

Courvoisier, D., Eid, M., Lischetzke, T., & Schreiber, W. (2010). Psychometric properties of a computerized mobile phone method for assessing daily life. *Emotion, 10*, 115–124.

Csikszentmihalyi, M. (2007). Concluding thoughts. In J. M. Hektner, J. A. Schmidt, & M. Csikszentmihalyi (Eds.), *Experience sampling method: Measuring the quality of everyday life* (pp. 277–292). Thousand Oaks, CA: Sage.

Csikszentmihalyi, M., & Schneider, B. (2000). *Becoming adult: How teenagers prepare for the world of work*. New York, NY: Basic Books.

Gunthert, K. C., & Wenze, S. J. (2012). Daily diary methods. In M. R. Mehl & T. S. Conner (Eds.), *Handbook of research methods for studying daily life* (pp. 144–159). New York, NY: Guilford Press.

Hamaker, E. L. (2012). Why researchers should think "within-person": A paradigmatic rationale. In M. R. Mehl & T. S. Conner (Eds.), *Handbook of research methods for studying daily life* (pp. 43–61). New York, NY: Guilford Press.

Hektner, J. M., Schmidt, J. A., & Csikszentmihalyi, M. (2007). *Experience sampling method: Measuring the quality of everyday life*. Thousand Oaks, CA: Sage.

Hurlburt, R. T. (2011). *Investigating pristine inner experience: Moments of truth*. Cambridge: Cambridge University Press.

Hurlburt, R. T., & Heavey, C. L. (2015). Investigating pristine inner experience: Implications for experience sampling and questionnaires. *Consciousness and Cognition, 31*, 148–159. doi:10.1016/j.concog.2014.11.002

Intille, S. S. (2012). Emerging technology for studying daily life. In M. R. Mehl & T. S. Conner (Eds.), *Handbook of research methods for studying daily life* (pp. 267–282). New York, NY: Guilford Press.

Kahneman, D., Krueger, A. B., Schkade, D. A., Schwarz, N., & Stone, A. A. (2004). A survey method for characterizing daily life experience: The Day Reconstruction Method. *Science, 306*, 1776–1780. doi:10.1126/science.1103572

Mehl, M. R., & Conner, T. S. (Eds.). (2012). *Handbook of research methods for studying daily life*. New York, NY: Guilford Press.

Mehl, M. R., & Robbins, M. L. (2012). Naturalistic observation sampling: The Electronically Activated Recorder (EAR). In M. R. Mehl & T. S. Conner (Eds.), *Handbook of research methods for studying daily life* (pp. 176–192). New York, NY: Guilford Press.

Moskowitz, D. S. (1994). Cross-situational generality and the interpersonal circumplex. *Journal of Personality and Social Psychology, 66*, 921–933.

Moskowitz, D. S., & Sadikaj, G. (2012). Event-contingent recording. In M. R. Mehl & T. S. Conner (Eds.), *Handbook of research methods for studying daily life* (pp. 160–175). New York, NY: Guilford Press.

Reis, H. T. (2012). Why researchers should think "real world": A conceptual rationale. In M. R. Mehl & T. S. Conner (Eds.), *Handbook of research methods for studying daily life* (pp. 3–21). New York, NY: Guilford Press.

Schwarz, N. (2012). Why researchers should think "real-time": A cognitive rationale. In M. R. Mehl & T. S. Conner (Eds.), *Handbook of research methods for studying daily life* (pp. 22–42). New York, NY: Guilford Press.

Smith, L. B., Yu, C., Yoshida, H., & Fausey, C. M. (2015). Contributions of head-mounted cameras to studying the visual environments of infants and young children. *Journal of Cognition and Development, 16*, 407–419. doi:10.1080/15248372.2014.933430

Stone, A. A., & Shiffman, S. (1994). Ecological Momentary Assessment (EMA) in behavioral medicine. *Annals of Behavioral Medicine, 16*, 199–202.

Strack, R. W., Lovelace, K. A., Jordan, T. D., & Holmes, A. P. (2010). Framing photovoice using a social-ecological logic model as a guide. *Health Promotion Practice, 11*, 629–636. doi:10.1177/1524839909355519

Wang, C., & Burris, M. A. (1997). Photovoice: Concept, methodology, and use for participatory needs assessment. *Health Education & Behavior, 24*, 369–387.

Wheeler, L., & Nezlek, J. (1977). Sex differences in social participation. *Journal of Personality and Social Psychology, 35*, 742–754.

Wilhelm, F. H., Grossman, P., & Müller, M. I. (2012). Bridging the gap between the laboratory and the real world: Integrative ambulatory psychophysiology. In M. R. Mehl & T. S. Conner (Eds.), *Handbook of research methods for studying daily life* (pp. 210–234). New York, NY: Guilford Press.

Wilhelm, P., & Schoebi, D. (2007). Assessing mood in daily life – structural validity, sensitivity to change, and reliability of a short-scale to measure three basic dimensions of mood. *European Journal of Psychological Assessment, 23*, 258–267.

15 Organisational interventions

Amanda Biggs

Organisational interventions explained

Organisational interventions are policies, programmes, or activities intentionally enacted by organisations to initiate some form of organisational change; for instance, to improve employee health and well-being or organisational efficiency. Specific examples of published organisational intervention evaluations include:

- supervisor training and self-monitoring intervention implemented to improve supervisors' use of family-supportive behaviours (Hammer, Kossek, Anger, Bodner, & Zimmerman, 2011);
- training programme to equip employees to manage their career progression and development, evaluated in relation to its effects on career management preparedness; depressive symptoms, exhaustion, and early retirement intentions; and work engagement and mental resources (Vuori, Toppinen-Tanner, & Mutanen, 2012);
- a suite of organisational-level changes to reduce occupation stress and turnover experienced by nurses, including the development and implementation of a nursing workload tool to assess workloads; roster audits; increased staff numbers; and increased access to staff development, clinical supervision, and support (Rickard et al., 2012);
- leadership development training to enhance upstream organisational resources, such as work culture support and strategic alignment, and improve employee well-being outcomes (Biggs, Brough, & Barbour, 2014);
- workplace health promotion interventions to improve physical activity in the workplace (Malik, Blake, & Suggs, 2014); and
- implementation of a stress risk-assessment tool to be utilised by managers to prevent organisational stress (Biron, Gatrell, & Cooper, 2010).

As organisational interventions comprise a diverse range of initiatives, researchers often use classification systems to synthesise them into meaningful categories (Biggs, Noblet, & Allisey, 2014). The most widely cited organisational intervention classification system is Murphy's (1988) tripartite framework that distinguishes between primary, secondary, and tertiary interventions. Primary strategies, such as job redesign and flexible work practices, are preventative, as they target the source of the problem, minimising its severity or removing the problem entirely. Secondary interventions, such as work skills training and stress management, aim to build an individual's skills, resources, and capacity to cope with problems, interrupting the causal chain between exposure to the problem and adverse consequences (Cooper & Cartwright, 1997). Finally, tertiary interventions, such as employee assistance programmes, are reactive and focus on dealing with the problem after it has occurred or dealing with the negative consequences of the problem (Cooper & Cartwright, 1997; Murphy, 1988).

Interventions are also distinguished based on the organisational level targeted by the strategy. Individual interventions target individual employees, aiming to modify their behaviour, resources, resilience, and responses. In contrast, organisational interventions aim to modify problematic aspects of the broader organisational environment (Bowling, Beehr, & Grebner, 2012; Giga, Noblet, Faragher, & Cooper, 2003). Expanding on this dichotomy, Nielsen and Abildgaard (2013) distinguished between interventions targeting individuals, groups, leaders, and organisational procedures/structures.

Calls for more stringent evaluations of the theoretical mechanisms underlying organisational interventions have also prompted the development of theoretically based categorisations. Burgess, Brough, Biggs, and Hawkes (under review) recently developed a theoretically derived classification of occupational health interventions based on three underlying psychosocial mechanisms proposed to affect the occupational health process: demands, resources, and recovery.

There are a multitude of techniques to choose from and numerous complex issues to consider when designing, implementing, and evaluating organisational interventions. Ideally, the process should be guided by sound theoretical principles and scientific knowledge of the targeted phenomenon and relevant methodology, whilst also being relevant to the needs of the organisational environment in which the intervention is being implemented. Unfortunately, while there is considerable knowledge of the antecedent processes of phenomena targeted by organisational interventions (e.g., stress, work engagement, turnover intentions, and productivity), there is limited or inconsistent evidence supporting the effectiveness of organisational interventions (Nielsen, Taris, & Cox, 2010). In response to this issue, Nielsen, Taris et al. (2010, p. 220) argued "one vitally important issue in intervention research is how the effectiveness of interventions can be improved".

A renewed emphasis on organisational intervention research has emerged in recent years in response to these calls to more rigorously examine factors that contribute to intervention effectiveness. This includes improved research methodology to measure the impact of interventions on targeted outcomes; the application of multi- or mixed-methods approaches to assess the impact of context and process factors that attenuate or augment an intervention's effectiveness; and an increased recognition of the value of closely examining derailed interventions, which, despite their lack of success, can provide important information about how to develop effective organisational interventions. Drawing on recent research and frameworks, this chapter will discuss the topic of designing, implementing, and evaluating organisational interventions.

Frameworks for intervention design, implementation, and evaluation

Several frameworks have been devised to assist researchers and practitioners to conduct effective organisational interventions (e.g., Biggs & Brough, 2015b; Biron & Karanika-Murray, 2014; Goldenhar, LaMontagne, Katz, Heaney, & Landsbergis, 2001; Nielsen & Abildgaard, 2013; Noblet & Lamontagne, 2009). Biggs and Brough (2015b) proposed a framework that emphasises relevant tasks, process factors, and context factors to consider across three primary intervention stages: (a) development, (b) implementation, and (c) evaluation (see also Goldenhar et al., 2001). The framework is illustrated in Figure 15.1, and the tasks within each intervention stage are discussed here in more detail.

The *development stage* provides an important foundation for the intervention and includes several activities:

1   Establish relationships with stakeholders at all levels within and external to the organisation, including senior and middle managers, employees, and union representatives. Identifying local champions who are supportive of the intervention is especially important in large, multi-faceted organisations (Biggs & Brough, 2015a).
2   Establish clear communication structures amongst key stakeholders and set guidelines for feedback about the intervention's progress.
3   Conduct a theoretically driven, contextually appropriate needs analysis, identifying risks, strengths, and vulnerable groups. Combining multiple methods of data collection can assist in obtaining an appropriate depth and breadth of information (e.g., consider using both qualitative and quantitative methods; see Brough, Brown, & Biggs, 2016). Data collected at this stage also provides a baseline assessment of outcomes that may be utilised for future pre- and post-intervention comparative purposes.
4   Develop the intervention action plan:

    a   Formulate the intervention's objectives, drawing on the issue that initially alerted the organisation to the need for an intervention, the comprehensive needs analysis, the broader strategic priorities of the organisation, and the availability of resources to support the intervention.
    b   Design specific intervention techniques and activities, according to the intervention's objectives, as well as relevant theory, research, and evidence-based practice. It is recommended that both individual- and organisational-based strategies be considered within comprehensive intervention programmes (Biggs, Noblet et al., 2014).

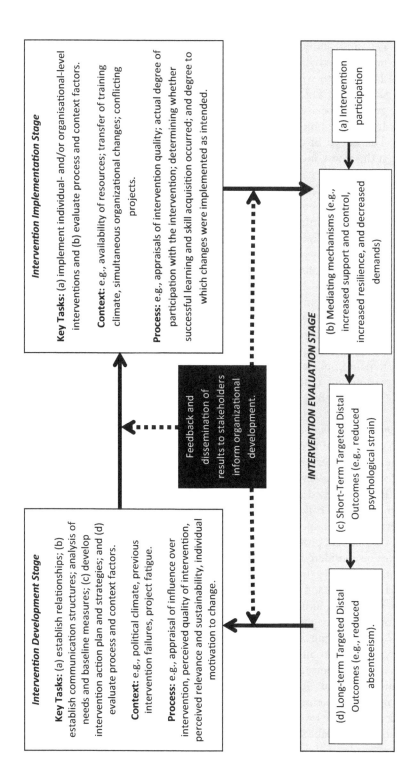

Figure 15.1 Intervention development framework adapted from Biggs and Brough (2015a)

c   Decisions about the intervention's process need to be made, including how the activities will be implemented (e.g., location, frequency, and duration); to whom they will be implemented; the roles and responsibilities of stakeholders in the intervention process; and how progress will be assessed to ensure the intervention remains on track and achieves its objectives.

d   The design of the intervention evaluation should also be considered at this point, including the time frame and method for data collection, processes for handling and analysing data, identifying evaluation participants (e.g., control versus intervention group), and operationalising the constructs to be measured.

e   Finally, the intervention (or programme) theory should be clearly articulated. The intervention theory provides a cohesive rationale for combining the objectives, activities, and methods utilised and a logical conceptualisation for how the intervention is presumed to effect change in the targeted outcomes (Adkins, Kelley, Bickman, & Weiss, 2010). A recent review of occupational health psychology interventions (Burgess et al., under review) indicated 29% of studies made no reference to the intervention's theory, supporting an earlier argument that the assumptions underlying organisational interventions "often remain implicit and unspecified, providing little in the way of explanation and rendering data amassed less meaningful" (Adkins et al., 2010, p. 399).

The *intervention implementation* stage involves implementing the intervention activities and collecting data assessing process and context factors that augment or attenuate the intervention's effectiveness. Controlling for process and context factors within intervention evaluations is increasingly being recommended, a point that is discussed in further detail later.

The intervention *evaluation* stage involves analysing data to evaluate whether the intervention produced anticipated changes, with consideration given to relevant context and process factors. It is important to note the evaluation stage should not be considered as an endpoint; rather, knowledge gained from specific intervention activities (both of the effect of the intervention on outcomes and the effect of process and context factors at each intervention stage) is intended to guide and inform future intervention activities (Cooper & Cartwright, 1997; Giga, Cooper, & Faragher, 2003; Nielsen, Randall, Holten, & González, 2010; Noblet & Lamontagne, 2009).

Finally, the model also recommends employee involvement be integrated within each intervention phase, including direct participation, representation, endorsement, and/or feedback. Executive and middle-level manager endorsement is necessary to ensure the intervention is appropriately resourced and has credibility. Employee involvement facilitates the acceptance and relevance of the intervention and enables the contribution of context-specific expertise; when integrated with the researchers' content expertise, a more thorough under-standing of relevant issues and meaningful change can be achieved (Dollard, Le Blanc, & Cotton, 2008; LaMontagne, Keegel, Louie, Ostry, & Landsbergis, 2007). However, it is important to consider whether employees are appropri-ately skilled to contribute to different intervention-related activities and ensure their involvement does not compromise the scientific rigour of the process (Brough et al., 2016).

A closer look at intervention evaluations

Intervention evaluations "involve the use of scientific methods to collect and analyse information" about an intervention "with the intent of coming to a determination about its relevance, progress, efficiency, effectiveness, and out-comes or impact" (Adkins et al., 2010, p. 396). As identified earlier in this chap-ter, evaluation planning should ideally be conducted alongside the development and implementation phases of the intervention and aligned with the interven-tion theory, objectives, and activities. Intervention evaluations provide valu-able data about whether the intervention's objectives were achieved, why and how certain outcomes occurred, whether outcomes were consistent for differ-ent subgroups, areas for programme improvement, and if an acceptable return on the investment of time and resources was achieved (Adkins et al., 2010). Continual evaluation is recommended, as a previously effective intervention may produce null or even deleterious effects in subsequent iterations of the programme. Finally, an important and often overlooked benefit of conduct-ing intervention evaluations is that they enable theoretical models to be tested (Cox & Griffiths, 2010).

Organisational evaluations take on many forms, depending on theoretical concerns, such as the focus of the intervention and its underlying theory, and pragmatic factors, such as the interests of key stakeholders, the intervention's process, and the context in which the evaluation occurs (Adkins et al., 2010). Although there is no one-size-fits-all approach to intervention evaluation, it is worth considering a comprehensive approach that assesses four intervention mechanisms: (a) targeted intervention outcomes; (b) mediating mechanisms; (c) intervention context; and (d) intervention process (Biggs & Brough, 2015b).

Evaluating intervention outcomes

The *intervention outcomes* are the individual and/or organisational conditions expected to change as a consequence of exposure to or involvement in an intervention. For example, stress management intervention outcomes might include a significant reduction in self-reported stress by employees and a reduction of stress compensation claims within the organisation. Selecting appropriate outcome measures is not always straightforward: one of the great-est challenges in intervention research is to translate intervention aims into measurable outcomes (Lipsey & Cordray, 2000). Some guidelines for selecting appropriate outcomes include:

- Select outcomes based on their alignment with the intervention's objectives, underlying theory, and activities (Adkins & Weiss, 2003; Lipsey & Cordray, 2000).
- Choose psychometrically robust outcome measures to ensure conclusions made about the intervention's effects are valid and reliable (Adkins & Weiss, 2003; Lipsey & Cordray, 2000).
- Consider the appropriate time lag between intervention exposure and measurement of outcomes: the time between measurement points should reflect the actual time lag expected for the intervention to produce change in targeted outcomes (Brough et al., 2016).
- Single-source and single-method approaches to measurement have been criticised (Eatough & Spector, 2013). Consider the possibility of measuring outcomes using more than one source/method (e.g., combining self-reported and physiological assessments of stress; Brough et al., 2016).
- Follow-up assessments of intervention effectiveness are seldom conducted but provide valuable insight into the sustainability and cost-effectiveness of the intervention and should be considered if possible (Caulfield, Chang, Dollard, & Elshaug, 2004; Murphy, 1996).

Intervention evaluations typically seek to measure change in targeted outcomes, most commonly via true- or quasi-experimental research designs (Biggs & Brough, 2015b). True experiments assess change between pre- and post-intervention measures for recipients of the intervention compared to a control group, with participants being randomly allocated to conditions (Adkins et al., 2010; Cook & Campbell, 1979). This design theoretically enables greater control over extraneous factors, such as preexisting differences between groups, allowing for a more robust determination of cause and effect attributable to the intervention (Adkins & Weiss, 2003; Griffiths, 1999). Such stringent experimental conditions are difficult to apply within an organisational context, however, as it is not always practical or ethical to randomly allocate participants to conditions (Adkins & Weiss, 2003). As a result, quasi-experimental designs, comprising non-random allocation to intervention conditions, are more commonly applied to evaluate organisational interventions (Lipsey & Cordray, 2000). Their use is justifiable given (a) their results tend to approximate the results of true experiments when appropriate statistical controls are employed to constrain pre-intervention differences; (b) even true experiments do not guarantee equivalent pre-intervention groups; and (c) neither true nor quasi-experimental designs can completely control for the influence of extraneous non-intervention factors that may influence results in complex organisational systems (Lipsey & Cordray, 2000; Salmela-aro, Näätänen, & Nurmi, 2004).

Both true- and quasi-experimental designs are utilised to assess the effectiveness of an intervention by determining whether statistically significant change occurred over time for the intervention participants compared to a control condition (i.e., null hypothesis significance testing; Burgess et al., under review). The accuracy of this decision is dependent on the validity and reliability of the research methods and measures used, valid operationalisation of constructs, correspondence between the measured time-lag and actual time lag, appropriate selection of participants and sample size, achieving sufficient power to reject the null hypothesis, and the ability to control for confounding factors (Adkins & Weiss, 2003; Burgess et al., under review). Although controlling for confounding variables reduces their influence, the success of the control is dependent on whether confounding factors are expected, identifiable, and measurable; unfortunately, this is unrealistic in organisational intervention research (Lipsey & Cordray, 2000).

The adoption of more rigorous experimental designs is a welcome response to long-standing criticisms that intervention research has lacked scientific rigour. However, determining the effectiveness of an intervention *solely* based on a dichotomous decision of significance versus non-significance, no matter how scientifically robust, has been criticised in recent years, as it provides limited information about the intervention's cost-effectiveness, the magnitude of an effect, or whether meaningful change occurred (Adkins et al., 2010; Burgess et al., under review). In a recent review of occupational health psychology interventions (Burgess et al., under review), all of the reviewed interventions were assessed via null hypothesis significance testing ($n = 59$); just over half of these evaluations reported the effect sizes ($n = 33$), and only 21 interpreted the size of the effect. Possible additions to null hypothesis significance testing include reporting and interpreting effect sizes, cost-benefits analysis, and the attainment of post-intervention outcome scores that are similar to those expected within a functional population (Adkins & Weiss, 2003; Lipsey & Cordray, 2000). For instance, studies using the General Health Questionnaire often assess the proportion of participants who were no longer "cases" after an intervention (e.g., Biggs, 2011; Gardner, Rose, Mason, Tyler, & Cushway, 2005).

Furthermore, evaluating interventions solely using null hypothesis significance testing provides little information about why the intervention succeeded or failed, the specific components that were effective, and for whom the intervention worked (or did not work). This has led to researchers advocating for more comprehensive evaluation frameworks that take into account the complexity and dynamic nature of the social environments the interventions are embedded in (e.g., Biron & Karanika-Murray, 2014; Griffiths, 1999; Nielsen & Abildgaard, 2013). Biggs and Brough (2015b) recently suggested that as well as measuring the effect of an intervention on targeted distal outcomes, researchers should consider evaluating:

1 mediating mechanisms that theoretically explain why an intervention is expected to produce change in targeted outcomes;
2 intervention context, taking into account the social system in which the intervention is embedded and its subsequent influence on intervention effects; and
3 intervention process, examining factors relating to how the intervention is conducted and the intervention's recipients.

Evaluating mediating mechanisms

Organisational interventions should be guided by sound theory; that is, a clear rationale explaining how the intervention produces change in an outcome should be articulated, and objectives, activities, and methods should be aligned with the theory (Adkins et al., 2010). Drawing on the jobs demands–resources model, for example, Biggs, Brough et al. (2014) proposed that participation in a leadership development programme would improve perceptions of leadership and work culture support (mediating mechanism), which would in turn enhance engagement and reduce strain (targeted outcome). This implies a mediated process, in which the intervention is expected to result in actual or perceived changes to outcomes (e.g., strain and engagement), via actual or perceived changes to psychosocial work characteristics (e.g., supportive leadership and work culture). These theoretical mechanisms explaining the intervention's effect on outcomes have been referred to as *micro processes, theoretical mediating mechanisms, chains of causal effect*, and *mediating proximal effects* (Biggs & Brough, 2015b; Griffiths, 1999; Nielsen & Abildgaard, 2013). Formally testing these indirect effects in an evaluation is recommended, as it contributes to knowledge of the mechanisms of change associated with targeted outcomes; these mechanisms are generalizable to other situations and enable the development of more targeted and effective future interventions (Biggs & Brough, 2015b). More broadly, it also provides an opportunity to evaluate not only the intervention itself but the underlying theory (Cox & Griffiths, 2010). Yet despite theoretical and practical justification for doing so, these underlying processes are seldom evaluated (Biggs, Brough et al., 2014; Bond & Bunce, 2001; Bunce, 1997; Griffiths, 1999; Randall & Nielsen, 2010). Some recent examples testing mediating processes include the aforementioned study by Biggs, Brough et al. (2014) and the study investigating supervisors' use of family-supportive behaviours conducted by Hammer et al. (2011).

Evaluating process and context

Recent evidence suggests the effectiveness of organisational interventions is influenced by the intervention's context and process, and it is recommended these factors be considered during each intervention phase (Biggs & Brough, 2015b; Biron & Karanika-Murray, 2014; Griffiths, 1999; Nielsen & Abildgaard, 2013). Context factors are aspects of the psychosocial environment in which interventions are conducted, while process factors are characteristics of the intervention itself or the intervention's recipients that influence the success of an intervention (Biron & Karanika-Murray, 2014). Example process and context factors are depicted in Figure 15.1.

Considering context and process factors during the design and implementation phases can provide valuable information for appropriately tailoring the intervention, enhancing the likelihood that meaningful change will occur (Biron et al., 2010; Nytro, Saksvik, Mikkelsen, Bohle, & Quinlan, 2000). Measuring and assessing these factors is also particularly important for the intervention evaluation phase, as it can explain why an intervention resulted in a particular outcome, identify which components worked, and demonstrate whether the intervention was more or less effective for different subgroups. Studies that have evaluated process and context factors, in addition to outcomes, have demonstrated that non-significant, unexpected, and inconsistent findings can be partially explained by planning and implementation issues rather than intervention failure (Biggs, Noblet et al., 2014).

Both qualitative and quantitative methods have been employed to evaluate intervention process and context. Using a quasi-experimental design and quantitative self-report measures, Hammer et al. (2011) examined whether the effect of a work-family intervention on family-supportive supervisory behaviours was greater for employees who had higher levels of work-family conflict. Nielsen, Randall, and Albertsen (2007) conducted a quantitative study showing that participants were more likely to positively appraise and engage in an intervention when they perceived they would be able to influence its process. Participants' positive appraisals of the quality and longevity of the intervention also explained the relationship between intervention participation and outcomes. Randall, Nielsen, and Tvedt (2009) developed a self-report survey to quantitatively assess five intervention process factors (e.g., line manager attitudes and actions) that correlated significantly with intervention outcomes. Finally, Biron et al. (2010) employed a qualitative study, using field notes and interviews, to evaluate an organisational intervention involving the implementation of a stress risk-assessment tool. Their study demonstrated the intervention's unexpected negative effects and low uptake of the tool was associated with flaws in the intervention's design, an unstable organisational context, and lack of ownership by stakeholders. These studies demonstrate the considerable insight to be gained by evaluating context and process factors. In particular, although experimental designs adopting null hypothesis significance testing still play an important role in determining intervention effectiveness, adopting alternate approaches (e.g., mixed-method approaches) may provide more comprehensive information about intervention outcomes, process, and context (Nielsen & Abildgaard, 2013).

Conclusion

The number of published high-quality intervention evaluations is increasing, although there is still an imbalance in favour of individual-level interventions and a lack of evidence demonstrating that organisational interventions consistently and effectively improve targeted outcomes (Biggs, Noblet et al., 2014; Nielsen, Taris et al., 2010). This is largely a result of organisational interventions being (a) hard to implement and evaluate, (b) strongly influenced by context and process factors, and (c) difficult to publish, as evaluations do not always meet acceptable levels of scientific rigour required by journals (Biggs, Noblet et al., 2014; Brough & Biggs, 2015). Growing recognition of these issues and of the value of examining derailed interventions and evaluating process and context, represents a promising avenue for future research.

Challenges conducting comprehensive interventions are notable and include, for example, the requirement to invest substantial time and resources, employee and organisational resistance to change, and sabotage from stakeholders due to intergroup conflict (Biggs & Brough, 2015a; Brough & Biggs, 2015). There are now good resources available providing information about dealing with some of these issues, and it is recommended pertinent issues be taken into account during each intervention phase (e.g., Karanika-Murray & Biron, 2015). These challenges may seem insurmountable, deterring practitioners and researchers from undertaking organisational interventions; however, overcoming the obstacles enables researchers to contribute to science via theoretical refinement and contribute to practice by developing evidence-based strategies to improve working conditions (Adkins et al., 2010, p. 395).

This chapter discussed frameworks and tips for intervention design, implementation, and evaluation, to ensure intervention strategies are theoretically sound, contextually appropriate, and evidence-based. It also advocated for the use of scientifically rigorous evaluations of outcome effects but argued the sole reliance of null hypothesis significance testing to evaluate intervention effectiveness misses an opportunity to explain why, how, and for whom an intervention works.

References

Adkins, J. A., Kelley, S. D., Bickman, L., & Weiss, H. M. (2010). Program evaluation: The bottom line in organizational health. In J. C. Quick & L. E. Tetrick (Eds.), *Handbook of occupational health psychology* (2nd ed., pp. 395–415). Washington, D.C.: American Psychological Association.

Adkins, J. A., & Weiss, H. M. (2003). Program evaluation: The bottom line in organizational health. In J. C. Quick & L. E. Tetrick (Eds.), *Handbook of occupational health psychology* (pp. 399–416). Washington, DC: American Psychological Association.

Biggs, A. (2011). *A longitudinal evaluation of strain, work engagement, and intervention strategies to address the health of high-risk employees.* Doctoral Thesis, Griffith University, Brisbane, Australia.

Biggs, A., & Brough, P. (2015a). Challenges of intervention acceptance in complex, multi-faceted organizations: The importance of local champions. In M. Karanika-Murray & C. Biron (Eds.), *Derailed organizational stress and well-being interventions: Confessions of failure and solutions for success.* (pp. 151–158). London, UK: Springer.

Biggs, A., & Brough, P. (2015b). Explaining intervention success and failure: What works, when, and why? In M. Karanika-Murray & C. Biron (Eds.), *Derailed organizational stress and well-being interventions: Confessions of failure and solutions for success.* (pp. 237–244). London, UK: Springer.

Biggs, A., Brough, P., & Barbour, J. P. (2014). Enhancing work-related attitudes and work engagement: A quasi-experimental study of the impact of a leadership development intervention. *International Journal of Stress Management, 21*(1), 43–68. doi:10.1037/a0034508

Biggs, A., Noblet, A., & Allisey, A. (2014). Organisational interventions. In M. F. Dollard, A. Shimazu, R. Bin Nordin, P. Brough, & M. R. Tuckey (Eds.), *Psychosocial factors at work in the Asia Pacific* (pp. 355–376). New York, NY: Springer.

Biron, C., Gatrell, C., & Cooper, C. L. (2010). Autopsy of a failure: Evaluating process and contextual issues in an organizational-level work stress intervention. *International Journal of Stress Management, 17*(2), 135–158. doi:10.1037/a0018772

Biron, C., & Karanika-Murray, M. (2014). Process evaluation for organizational stress and well-being interventions: Implications for Theory, Method, and Practice. *International Journal of Stress Management, 21*(1), 85–111.

Bond, F. W., & Bunce, D. (2001). Job control mediates change in work-reorganization intervention for stress reduction. *Journal of Occupational Health Psychology, 6*(4), 290–302. doi:10.1037//1076–8998.6.4.290

Bowling, N. A., Beehr, T. A., & Grebner, S. (2012). Combating stress in organizations. In G. P. Hodgkinson & J. K. Ford (Eds.), *International review of industrial and organizational psychology* (Vol. 27, pp. 65–88). Chichester, West Sussex, UK: John Wiley & Sons. doi:10.1002/9781118311141

Brough, P., & Biggs, A. (2015). The highs and lows of occupational stress intervention research: Lessons learnt from collaborations with high-risk industries. In M. Karanika-Murray & C. Biron (Eds.), *Derailed organizational stress and well-being interventions: Confessions of failure and solutions for success* (pp. 263–270). London, UK: Springer.

Brough, P., Brown, J., & Biggs, A. (2016). *Improving criminal justice workplaces: Translating theory and research into evidence-based practice.* Oxon, UK: Routledge.

Bunce, D. (1997). What factors are associated with the outcome of individual-focused work-site stress management interventions? *Journal of Occupational and Organizational Psychology, 70,* 1–17.

Burgess, M. G., Brough, P., Biggs, A., & Hawkes, A. J. (under review). A systematic review of health psychology interventions.

Caulfield, N., Chang, D., Dollard, M. F., & Elshaug, C. (2004). A review of occupational stress interventions in Australia. *International Journal of Stress Management, 11*(2), 149–166. doi:10.1037/1072–5245.11.2.149

Cook, T. D., & Campbell, D. T. (1979). *Quasi-experimentation: Design and analysis for field settings.* Boston, MA: Houghton-Mifflin.

Cooper, C. L., & Cartwright, S. (1997). An intervention strategy for workplace stress. *Journal of Psychosomatic Research, 43*(1), 7–16. doi:http://dx.doi.org/10.1016/S0022-3999(96)00392-3

Cox, T., & Griffiths, A. (2010). Work-related stress: A theoretical perspective. In S. Leka & J. Houdmont (Eds.), *Occupational health psychology* (pp. 31–56). Hoboken, NJ: Wiley-Blackwell.

Dollard, M. F., Le Blanc, P. M., & Cotton, S. J. (2008). Participatory action research as work stress intervention. In K. Näswall, J. Hellgren, & M. Sverke (Eds.), *The individual in the changing working life* (pp. 353–379). Cambridge, UK: Cambridge University Press.

Eatough, E. M., & Spector, P. E. (2013). Quantitative self-report methods in occupational health psychology research. In R. R. Sinclair, M. Wang, & L. E. Tetrick (Eds.), *Research methods in occupational health psychology: Measurement, design, and analysis* (pp. 248–267). New York, NY: Routledge.

Gardner, B., Rose, J., Mason, O., Tyler, P., & Cushway, D. (2005). Cognitive therapy and behavioural coping in the management of work-related stress: An intervention study. *Work & Stress, 19*(2), 137–152. doi:10.1080/02678370500157346

Giga, S. I., Cooper, C. L., & Faragher, B. (2003). The development of a framework for a comprehensive approach to stress management interventions at work. *International Journal of Stress Management, 10*(4), 280–296. doi:10.1037/1072–5245.10.4.280

Giga, S. I., Noblet, A. J., Faragher, B., & Cooper, C. L. (2003). The UK perspective: A review of research on organisational stress management interventions. *Australian Psychologist, 38*(2), 158–164. doi:10.1080/00050060310001707167

Goldenhar, L. M., LaMontagne, A. D., Katz, T., Heaney, C., & Landsbergis, P. (2001). The intervention research process in occupational safety and health: An overview from the national occupational research agenda intervention effectiveness research team. *Journal of Occupational and Environmental Medicine, 43*, 616–622.

Griffiths, A. (1999). Organizational interventions: Facing the limits of the natural science paradigm. *Scandinavian Journal of Work, Environment, and Health, 25*(6), 589–596. doi:10.5271/sjweh.485

Hammer, L. B., Kossek, E. E., Anger, W. K., Bodner, T., & Zimmerman, K. L. (2011). Clarifying work-family intervention processes: The roles of work-family conflict and family-supportive supervisor behaviors. *Journal of Applied Psychology, 96*(1), 134–150. doi:10.1037/a0020927

Karanika-Murray, M., & Biron, C. (2015). *Derailed organizational stress and well-being interventions: Confessions of failure and solutions for success*. London, UK: Springer.

LaMontagne, A. D., Keegel, T., Louie, A. M., Ostry, A., & Landsbergis, P. (2007). A systematic review of the job-stress intervention evaluation literature, 1990–2005. *International Journal of Occupational and Environmental Health, 13*, 268–280.

Lipsey, M. W., & Cordray, D. S. (2000). Evaluation methods for social intervention. *Annual Review of Psychology, 51*, 345–375. doi:10.1146/annurev.psych.51.1.345

Malik, S. H., Blake, H., & Suggs, L. S. (2014). A systematic review of workplace health promotion interventions for increasing physical activity. *British Journal of Health Psychology, 19*, 149–180. doi:10.1111/bjhp.12052

Murphy, L. R. (1988). Workplace interventions for stress reduction and prevention. In C. L. Cooper & R. Payne (Eds.), *Causes, coping, and consequences of stress at work* (pp. 301–399). New York, NY: Wiley.

Murphy, L. R. (1996). Stress management in work settings: A critical review of the health effects. *American Journal of Health Promotion, 11*(2), 112–135.

Nielsen, K., & Abildgaard, J. S. (2013). Organizational interventions: A research-based framework for the evaluation of both process and effects. *Work & Stress*. doi:10.1080/02678373.2013.812358

Nielsen, K., Randall, R., & Albertsen, K. (2007). Participants' appraisals of process issues and the effects of stress management interventions. *Journal of Organizational Behavior, 28*, 793–810. doi:10.1002/job.450

Nielsen, K., Randall, R., Holten, A., & González, E. R. (2010). Conducting organizational-level occupational health interventions: What works? *Work & Stress, 24*(3), 234–259. doi:10.1080/02678373.2010.515393

Nielsen, K., Taris, T. W., & Cox, T. (2010). The future of organizational interventions: Addressing the challenges of today's organizations. *Work & Stress, 24*(3), 219–233. doi:10.1080/02678373.2010.519176

Noblet, A. J., & Lamontagne, A. D. (2009). The challenges of developing, implementing, and evaluating interventions. In S. Cartwright & C. L. Cooper (Eds.), *The Oxford handbook of organizational well being* (pp. 467–496). Oxford: Oxford University Press. doi:10.1093/oxfordhb/9780199211913.003.0019

Nytro, K., Saksvik, P. O., Mikkelsen, A., Bohle, P., & Quinlan, M. (2000). An appraisal of key factors in the implementation of occupational stress interventions. *Work & Stress, 14*(3), 213–225. doi:10.1080/02678370010024749

Randall, R., & Nielsen, K. (2010). Interventions to promote well-being at work. In S. Leka & J. Houdmont (Eds.), *Occupational health psychology* (pp. 88–123). Hoboken, NJ: Wiley-Blackwell.

Randall, R., Nielsen, K., & Tvedt, S. D. (2009). The development of five scales to measure employees' appraisal of organizational-level stress management interventions. *Work & Stress, 23*(1), 1–23. doi:10.1080/02678370902815277

Rickard, G., Lenthall, S., Dollard, M. F., Opie, T., Knight, S., Dunn, S., . . . Brewster-Webb, D. (2012). Organisational intervention to reduce occupational stress and turnover in hospital nurses in the Northern Territory, Australia. *Collegian, 19*(4), 211–221.

Salmela-aro, K., Näätänen, P., & Nurmi, J. (2004). The role of work-related personal projects during two burnout interventions: A longitudinal study. *Work & Stress, 18*(3), 208–230. doi: 10.1080/02678370412331317480

Vuori, J., Toppinen-Tanner, S., & Mutanen, P. (2012). Effects of resource-building group intervention on career management and mental health in work organizations: Randomized controlled field trial. *Journal of Applied Psychology, 97*(2), 273–286. doi:10.1037/a0025584

Section 3

The nitty gritty

Data analysis

This third section of the book contains eight chapters discussing the most common data analysis methods employed by applied psychology researchers and those in related fields. Again, these chapters are not written as specific 'how to do' guides (but provide further reading to assist you to sources such guides). Instead, each chapter discusses the key issues, relevant arguments, and main literature justifying each data analysis technique. This section aims to install an understanding of *why* you could employ a specific method of data analysis, before you advance to the 'how to do' guides. Chapter 16 provides an essential discussion of the most common methods to manage missing data, and Chapter 17 describes the key stages in data preparation before the fun of actual data analysis begins. Chapter 18 focuses on two common qualitative data analysis methods: *content analysis and thematic analysis* and Chapter 19 describes the key point to consider when conducting 'real' data analysis. Chapters 20 to 23 discuss advanced quantitative data analysis methods: *mediation analysis and conditional process models* (Chapter 20) *structural equation modelling* (Chapter 21) *multilevel analyses* (Chapter 22) and *social network analysis* (Chapter 23).

16 Managing missing data

Concepts, theories, and methods

Rachel Davis, Stefano Occhipinti, and Liz Jones

Introduction

Missing data are a common occurrence in research, and although researchers would prefer a complete dataset, the realistic chances of this occurring are almost nil. Sometimes participants may refuse to answer particular survey questions; others times, questions may have been overlooked. Alternatively, a participant may not know how to respond to a question, or a question may not be applicable to their situation. Missing data pose problems because most standard data analytic techniques require a complete dataset (Chen & Åstebro, 2003); thus, a variety of methods for handling missing data have been developed. However, missing data dealt with incorrectly can do more harm than good, producing answers that are unreliable, inefficient and biased (Schafer & Graham, 2002). The following chapter will introduce the core concepts for understanding missing data in applied research, describe the traditional methods still currently utilised by the discipline and introduce modern methods to effectively manage missing data. Finally, this chapter will also provide a brief introduction to how such modern methods of handling missing data are being applied to create new types of efficiency designs called *planned missing data designs*.

Missing data can occur at several different levels of a study (Newman, 2014). On the one hand, *unit missingness* refers to when a research unit[1] does not provide any information and the entire measurement is missing. Examples include when a participant refuses to participate, does not meet inclusion criteria or is not available at the time of data collection (Schafer & Graham, 2002). Unit missingness is often interpreted as a study's response rate. *Construct missingness*, on the other hand, is when partial data are available, but one or more instruments (e.g., a test) in the measurement are missing (Newman, 2014). Some examples include refusing to answer questions about a specific construct or stopping a measurement midway through. In applied psychology where multi-item instruments are common, *item missingness* may also occur, which is when some items relating to a construct are completed and other items are missing (Newman, 2014). Finally, specific to longitudinal designs, research can also have *wave missingness*, which is when participants do not complete all wave measurements (Graham, Cumsille, & Shevock, 2012). A special case of *wave missingness*

Table 16.1 Example dataset with single-item covariate, a multi-item predictor, and single-item criterion

ID	Wave 1					Wave 2				Wave 3			
	COV	$X.1_1$	$X.2_1$	$X.3_1$	Y_1	$X.1_2$	$X.2_2$	$X.3_2$	Y_2	$X.1_3$	$X.2_3$	$X.3_3$	Y_3
1	NA	3	4	2	5	5	6	4	4	4	5	7	5
2	19	NA	NA	NA	3	4	5	6	4	6	7	5	4
3	56	3	5	4	4	3	2	5	5	4	3	5	3
4	35	4	5	4	5	6	7	5	5	6	6	5	4
5	NA	NA	NA	NA	NA	NA	NA	NA	NA	NA	NA	NA	NA
6	26	3	3	1	2	2	2	3	1	3	4	4	5
7	25	4	5	3	2	3	4	5	3	5	4	4	4
8	18	NA	3	1	4	4	4	5	4	4	5	6	5
9	22	1	4	1	1	NA	NA	NA	NA	2	1	3	1
10	23	2	3	4	2	NA	NA	NA	NA	NA	NA	NA	NA

Note. Participants 1 and 2 are examples of construct missingness, participant 5 shows unit missingness, participant 8 shows item missingness, and participants 9 and 10 are examples of wave missingness, with 10 being an example of attrition.

is when a participant leaves a study and does not complete the subsequent data collection waves; this is often referred to as *attrition* or *dropout*. For example, attrition can occur when participants who are recontacted refuse to remain in the particular study or are unable to be contacted again due to changes in residency, emigration or death. Attrition can also occur due to sampling procedures where only participants who completed the previous wave are invited to participate in the subsequent wave. Therefore, in longitudinal research, missing data can occur for a single item on a multiple-item scale; an entire instrument, either as a single item variable or a whole scale; for a particular wave of measurement; or for all measurements. Table 16.1 presents an example on how these forms of missingness translate into a hypothetical dataset.

Hypothetical study

To illustrate more abstract concepts, a hypothetical study is presented here. Imagine that a researcher seeks to understand what influences people's engagement in the workplace – specifically, how supervisory coaching and the availability of professional development opportunities can influence an employee's level of work engagement. Work engagement can be measured using the Utrecht Work Engagement Scale (UWES; Schaufeli, Bakker, & Salanova, 2006), which consists of 17 items, among them *I get carried away when I am working*, with participants responding according to a six-point scale, ranging from 0 (*never*) to 6 (*always*). Supervisory coaching can be measured using a scale developed by Graen and Uhl-Bien (1991), which consists of five items, among them *My supervisor uses his/her influence to help me solve my problems at work*, with participants responding according to a five-point scale, ranging from 1 (*never*)

to 5 (*always*). To examine the impact of professional development opportunities, the researcher may collect data from two types of organisations: those that
provide developmental opportunities to their employees and those that do not.
When collecting the data, the researcher finds that information on supervisory
coaching is completed, but information on employees' work engagement is
sometimes missing.

Theory of missing data: moving from *what* is missing to *why* it is missing

To be able to choose an appropriate method for handling missing data, one must
first understand the theory behind it. Most datasets are, or can be, arranged in a
matrix form, where rows correspond to participants and columns represent scale
items or research variables (Schafer & Graham, 2002). Statistically, missing data can
be defined as an incomplete data matrix that occurs when one or more participants in a sample do not respond to all items (Newman, 2014). For any dataset, a
series of vectors R can be created to identify what is known and what is unknown.
That is, each element R_{ij} in the data-matrix R would take the value of 1 if a variable has data and 0 if it is missing (Graham, 2009). R then can be treated as having
a probability distribution that can describe the rates and patterns of missing values.
These patterns of missing data capture the relationships between missingness and
the values of the missing items themselves (Schafer & Graham, 2002).

Examining the patterns of missing data, Rubin (1976) proposed three *missingness mechanisms*, or probabilistic explanations, for why data are missing. When
the probability of missingness is dependent on observed data but not unobserved data, the missing data are considered to be *missing at random* (MAR). That
is, missing values on a particular variable X can be related to other measured
variables but not to the underlying values of X. Using the hypothetical study,
an example of data missing under MAR would be if respondents who scored
low on the supervisory coaching scale were more likely to have missing data on
the work engagement scale. It is important to note here that the word *random*
in MAR conveys a different meaning to what most psychologists understand
about the word (Graham, 2009). In psychology, *random* is often associated with
the idea of *randomness* or the lack of any pattern or predictability. The mechanism MAR suggests that once the effect of observed variables has been controlled for, the remaining patterns of missingness are completely random (that
is, they do not depend on another unobserved variable). Returning to the
hypothetical example, once the effects of other measured variables – in this case,
supervisory coaching – are controlled for, the probability of data being missing
becomes completely random.

A special case of MAR is what is known as *missing completely at random*
(MCAR), which is when the probability of missingness is not dependent on
either observed or unobserved data. That is, the missing values on variable X
are unrelated to the underlying values of X as well as other measured variables
and thus can be seen as a random sample of all values. Using the hypothetical

study, data can be considered MCAR if participants accidently missed a page of questions on a survey or were absent the day of data collection. It is important to also note that the missingness in MCAR may still be related to unmeasured variables, just not measured ones. Both MCAR and MAR are what Rubin (1976) described as *ignorable mechanisms*, in the sense that unbiased parameter estimates are able to be obtained using an appropriate statistical model.

By contrast, the final pattern of missingness is known as *missing not at random* (MNAR) and is when the probability of missingness depends upon unobserved data and is considered to be non-ignorable. That is, missing data on a particular variable, X, is related to the underlying values of that variable. In the hypothetical example, data would be considered MNAR if the missing data in the work engagement scale were primarily from employees who are not very engaged at work. Similarly, if employees who had quite high work engagement appeared to have high attrition rates, this too is an example of MNAR, as the cause of missingness is due to the variable itself.

Rubin's (1976) framework for describing missing data has become the foundation of missingness theory, and the implications of the missingness mechanisms become apparent when examining the performance of different missing data methods. As with most statistical procedures, meeting certain analytic assumptions will determine the quality of the inferences one can make (Peugh & Enders, 2004). Similarly, different missing data methods require certain missingness mechanisms to produce unbiased and efficient parameter estimates. Therefore, at a practical level, Rubin's (1976) mechanisms can be viewed as assumptions that can dictate the conditions in which a missing data method will provide optimal performance (Peugh & Enders, 2004).

Traditional methods for managing missing data

Researchers employ a variety of methods to manage missing data in their research. Before the advent of modern procedures, most researchers relied on ad hoc methods that involved editing the dataset to give an appearance of completeness, so that they could continue with their analysis (Schafer & Graham, 2002). Commonly used methods to manage missing data included deletion (removal of participants with missing data) and single imputation (imputing values for missing items). However, these methods were not grounded in theory and have been widely criticised (e.g. Wilkinson & Task Force on Statistical Inference, 1999). Despite more appropriate methods now being available, many substantive researchers still routinely employ these older methods (Baraldi & Enders, 2010). The following section provides a quick overview of some of the most common traditional missing data methods that are widely used and describes the circumstances in which they provide effective results.

Case deletion

One of the most common methods for handling missing data is to discard participants that have incomplete data. *Listwise deletion*, also known as *complete case analysis*, removes any case with missing data and conducts the analysis only on units that have complete data for all the variables under consideration (Graham, 2009). Most standard statistical software programs use this method as the default if missing data are left untreated. Listwise deletion is a simple method to understand and perform; however, the reduction in sample size also results in a reduction in statistical power and can become nontrivial when large amounts of data are missing. Additionally, by only including units with complete data in the analysis, the sample may no longer represent an accurate selection of the population, which can influence estimation. Therefore, if the data is not MCAR, listwise deletion can produce biased parameter estimates.

A similar approach called *pairwise deletion*, or available case analysis, aims to partially reduce the amount of power lost in listwise deletion by discarding participants on an analysis-by-analysis basis. This results in a different set of participants being used to calculate different parameters (Peugh & Enders, 2004). Pairwise deletion is often described in relation to a covariance matrix, which is when each parameter is calculated using all participants having data on two variables. The limitation to pairwise deletion is that comparing analyses within a study can become problematic, as a different subset of participants are being used for each analysis. Additionally, a covariance matrix produced using pairwise deletion may not be positive definite, which can become problematic in multivariate analyses that rely on a covariance matrix (such as structural equation modelling). For the same reasons as listwise deletion, pairwise deletion also produces biased estimates when the missing data are not MCAR.

Averaging available items

Often in applied research, the variables of interest cannot be reliably measured by a single item; thus, multi-item scales are used. Multiple items can be averaged out to create a more reliable measure of the construct based on the assumption that items are "equally reliable measures of a unidimensional trait" (p. 157; Schafer & Graham, 2002). If data are missing at the item level, calculating an average of the remaining items is often preferred as opposed to reporting the entire scale as missing (McDonald, Thurston, & Nelson, 2000). Standard statistical software programs also use this method as the default when computing averages with missing values from several items. This method, although widespread, has little empirical research available on its effectiveness. Theoretically, however, averaging available items creates a mixture of averages based upon different numbers of items (n's), which can lead to an increase in the scale's variance and thus a decrease in the scale's reliability. Moreover, this can increase bias in parameter estimates, and a decrease in statistical power, even when the data is MCAR. That is, averaging available items can produce biased estimates, regardless of the missing data mechanism.

Single imputation

To avoid the reduction in statistical power that case deletion incurs, single imputation methods aim to retain units by replacing the missing values with an approximate value. Single imputation produces what appears to be a complete dataset that is available to be analysed by standard statistical software. Additionally, imputing once at the beginning ensures that all analyses are examining the same sample. Imputation can also make use of the information in the observed data to help predict more accurate imputed values, which can help increase precision. There are a variety of single imputation methods, with the common methods being: *unconditional mean imputation, regression imputation* and *stochastic regression imputation.*

Mean imputation

Unconditional mean imputation is where the missing values are replaced with the arithmetic mean for that variable (Roth, Switzer, & Switzer, 1999). Although at face value the mean seems a logical choice, imputing a constant number for all missing values in a variable decreases the variability of that variable. Additionally, since only the variable in question is used to help predict values, the imputed scores have no relationship with other variables, thus also decreasing the variable's covariance with other variables. Therefore, using mean imputation will produce biased estimates for any parameter, except for the mean, regardless of the missingness mechanism.

Regression imputation

Regression imputation, also known as *conditional mean imputation*, replaces a missing value with a predicted score calculated from a linear regression equation using other variables as predictors (McDonald et al., 2000). At its simplest, a bivariate regression can be performed using complete cases, where the variable with missing data is the criterion and the complete variable the predictor. The resulting regression equation can then generate predicted scores for the participants with missing data on the criterion. This method can be seen as an improvement over unconditional mean imputation, as information from other variables is being used to predict cases. However, regression imputation creates a dataset where imputed values always lie right on the regression line, whereas actual data almost always deviate by some amount (the residual component). Therefore, similar to unconditional mean imputation, this method produces biased parameter estimates despite the missingness mechanism, as the imputed scores will have a reduced variability and an overestimated correlation. Additionally, imputed scores will truncate the overall residual score, which will result in an underestimated standard error.

Stochastic regression imputation

Stochastic regression imputation attempts to restore the error variance lost using regression imputation. This is completed by adding a random residual score to each predicted value within a regression model. Adding in an error component allows unbiased parameter estimates under both MCAR and MAR assumptions. While this method can provide unbiased parameter estimates under non-MNAR conditions, there is, however, no adjustment in measuring the degree of uncertainty due to the missing values, which can result in standard errors being understated. Because stochastic regression imputation uses observed information to predict values, as well as including an error component, this method is sometimes described as the historical precursor to modern methods of managing missing data (Little & Rubin, 2002; Peugh & Enders, 2004).

Modern methods for managing missing data

Researchers have developed several modern methods to manage missing data that are based on a sound statistical framework (Collins, Schafer, & Kam, 2001). These methods produce efficient parameter estimates and accurate measures of statistical uncertainty under non-MNAR conditions (Peugh & Enders, 2004). Empirical support for these methods continues to grow, as does the availability of these procedures, through a variety of software packages. When the assumptions underlying these procedures are met, they are able to restore much of the statistical power and eliminate bias. Even when the assumptions are not met, modern methods produce improved estimates and standard errors over the older, ad hoc methods (Little & Rubin, 2002).

Expectation maximisation (EM) algorithm

To more easily understand the mechanisms behind how *multiple imputation* (MI) and *maximum likelihood* (ML) handle missing data, it is first best to understand what is meant by an EM algorithm, which produces maximum likelihood estimates, and how algorithms can be used in treating missing data (Graham, 2009). A plethora of different EM algorithms are available for different purposes; however, they can all be described as iterative procedures that repeat between two stages – reading in raw data and producing a different product. For handling missing data, this becomes reading in the raw data with missing values and producing a maximum likelihood variance-covariance matrix and vector of means. Specifically, the procedure first assigns estimates of missing values based on the values of other variables; that is, it imputes values using regression imputation as described previously. Parameter estimates (variance, covariance and means) are then calculated based on the current values (the E step). Using this new covariance matrix, new regression equations are calculated that are used to update the missing values for the E step of the next iteration (the M step). This two-stage process (estimating and updating equations) continues until the elements in the covariance matrix stop changing. That is, the changes between iterations become trivial. In this sense, EM algorithms are a type of Markov chain where information in a particular stage is dependent upon the previous one.

Logically then, using the converged data from the covariance matrix, EM algorithms can be used to impute missing data. EM algorithms do provide unbiased parameter estimates under non–MNAR conditions; however, the technique does not include a method of adjusting the standard error as part of its procedure, and thus error terms become largely underestimated. So, although this approach alone is more sophisticated than previous imputation methods, the issue of increased type II error, as found in stochastic regression imputation, still exists.

Multiple imputation (MI)

MI can be seen as the logical extension of single imputation, especially that of stochastic regression imputation, where each missing value is replaced by a set of appropriate values ($m > 1$), creating m complete datasets, which can then all be analysed by standard statistical software (Schafer & Graham, 2002). By analysing each dataset separately, multiple sets of parameter estimates and standard errors are produced. By combining the results from these datasets, unbiased parameter estimates and adjusted uncertainty measures are obtained under non–MNAR conditions. The MI method consists of three steps: an imputation phase, an analysis phase and a pooling phase.

In the imputation phase a specified number of datasets are created by generating several different estimates for the missing values. Many algorithms can be used to accomplish this; however, for normally distributed data, a data-augmentation (DA) procedure is widely used (Baraldi & Enders, 2010). Similar to an EM algorithm, DA uses a two-step iterative process to impute and create the multiple datasets. In the imputation step, DA simulates the missing data based on current parameter estimates; and in the posterior step, parameters are calculated given the current imputed data. However, rather than simply running the iterative procedure until the estimates have converged (such as in EM algorithms), MI uses different copies of the dataset that the process produces in each iteration, each of which contain unique estimates of the missing values. The fact that the imputed values differ across datasets is what sets MI apart from single imputation methods such as stochastic regression imputation. This is because the multiple datasets allow more accurate standard errors to be calculated. As DA is part of the Markov chain Monte Carlo family of algorithms, where information from one step is based on the previous step, two adjacent steps are more similar to each other than two random draws from a population would be. Therefore, to ensure that the datasets are independent from others, a large number of iterations lapse before a dataset is saved. This ensures that each dataset is akin to being a random sample from the population (Graham, 2009).

After the imputation phase, the analysis phase performs the appropriate statistical analysis on each dataset using the same techniques as if there were no missing data. This phase will yield several estimates of each parameter as well as several estimates of the standard error. Finally, in the pooling phase, the estimates are combined into a single set of values, which can be reported. To accurately combine the results collected in the analysis phase, Rubin (1987) described a procedure that ensures unbiased parameter estimates and adjusted standard errors. Parameter estimates are pooled by calculating the arithmetic mean of the estimates from each dataset. However, as seen in Equation 16.1, calculating the pooled standard error involves a combination of the standard errors collected from the imputed datasets (within-imputation variance) as well as a component that measures the variance across datasets (between-imputation variance).

$$SE = \sqrt{W + B + \frac{B}{m}} \qquad (16.1)$$

Equation 16.2 presents how the within-variance standard error is calculated, where t denotes the particular dataset and m the total number of datasets. Equation 16.3 presents the calculation of between variance standard error, where O is the parameter estimate for dataset t and $\overline{\theta}$ is the average parameter estimate across datasets.

$$W = \frac{\sum SE_t^2}{m} \qquad (16.2)$$

$$B = \frac{\sum (\widehat{\theta}_t - \overline{\theta})^2}{m - 1} \qquad (16.3)$$

As with stochastic regression imputation, the aim of MI is to restore the error variance that is lost from regression imputation, as imputed values always lie exactly along the regression line. MI retains the attractiveness of single imputation but solves the issue of understating uncertainty. Similar to single imputation, MI allows researchers to proceed with familiar analyses and software that require complete data. Although the analysis and pooling procedures appear tedious, most software packages that run MI tend to automate these steps so that, similar to other analytical procedures, calculating them by hand is rarely required.

Maximum likelihood (ML)

Unlike other methods that aim to either discard cases or fill in the missing values prior to the analysis, ML estimation simultaneously deals with missing data and estimates parameters and standard errors (Graham, 2009). ML estimation is a procedure that uses all available data to identify the parameters and standard errors that have the highest, or *maximum*, probability of producing the sample data (Collins et al., 2001). ML estimation is often described as *full-information maximum likelihood* (FIML) because it uses all observed information to produce results with the highest probability. ML estimation can produce unbiased parameter estimates as well as adjusted standard errors under non-MNAR conditions. The process aims to minimise the standardised distance between the parameter of interest, such as a mean, and the observed data points, using a log likelihood function. In this way, it is conceptually similar to ordinary least squares estimation, where the aim is to identify regression coefficients that minimise the distance between the collective actual and predicted scores. Whereas other methods for handling missing data have the aim of obtaining a complete dataset so that they can proceed with the analysis, ML estimation does not require a full dataset. Rather, it can estimate parameters without discarding information and without imputing information.

Conceptually, ML estimation borrows information from complete variables to identify the most likely values of the population parameters. Using the hypothetical example, suppose that supervisory coaching and work engagement are positively correlated. This relationship would suggest that the presence of a low score on supervisory coaching would indicate that a missing value on work engagement would also be low, had it been observed. This leads to ML estimation making a downward adjustment to the course grade mean, compared to a method such as listwise deletion, which would produce an estimate that is too high as it ignored the cases with missing values. Like MI, most software packages that implement ML tend to be automated and sometimes set as the default way of handling missing data in certain analyses (such as some multi-level modelling (MLM) programs; see Chapter 22, this volume).

Evaluations of the missing data methods

Missing data can be handled in multiple ways, and certain factors such as the type and amount of missing data will determine which method will provide the researcher with acceptable results. Graham (2009) provided three basic criteria for evaluating different methods for handling missing data. First, the method should produce unbiased parameter estimates. Second, there should be an appropriate method of measuring uncertainty around the parameter estimates. Finally, the method should have good statistical power. Table 16.2 presents a

Table 16.2 Evaluation of missing data methods

Missing data method	Evaluation methods		
	Unbiased parameter estimates	*Measuring uncertainty*	*Good statistical power*
Deletion methods			
Listwise deletion	Only under MCAR	No	No
Pairwise deletion	Only under MCAR	No	No
Single imputation methods			
Mean imputation	No	No	Yes
Regression imputation	No	No	Yes
Stochastic regression imputation	Under MCAR and MAR	No	Yes
Modern methods			
EM algorithm	Under MCAR and MAR	Yes	No
Multiple imputation	Under MCAR and MAR	Yes	Yes
Maximum likelihood estimation	Under MCAR and MAR	Yes	Yes

summary comparing each of the discussed methods using these three criteria. What can be surmised from this table is that both MI and ML perform better under Graham's (2009) criteria for evaluating missing data methods as compared to traditional methods. However, it is also important to note that these modern methods are not a panacea for handling missing data. They still rely on missing data assumptions, and can be sensitive to deviations from the assumed model (Schafer & Graham, 2002).

Planned missing data designs

Unplanned missing data refers to when there is data loss that is not part of the research design and is outside the researcher's control (Collins, 2006). The methods described in the previous section all aim to counteract the unplanned missingness to allow researchers to continue to analyse their data without bias. Planned missing data, on the other hand, refers to when data loss becomes part of the research design. There are many costs associated with conducting research, most especially for longitudinal studies (Lewis-Beck, Bryman, & Liao, 2003; see also Chapter 13, this volume, for a specific discussion). Methodologists have attempted to maximise efficiency by creating research designs that are cost effective and efficient without placing undue limits on what is actually studied. These research designs fall under the term *efficiency designs* (Graham, Taylor, Olchowski, & Cumsille, 2006). Some efficiency designs target a study's sampling method, with some well-known designs including random sampling, Latin square design, and cohort sequential design (Graham, Taylor, & Cumsille, 2001; Graham et al., 2006). Other research designs focus on measurement, such as matrix sampling (Shoemaker, 1971). With the developments in missing data methods, research designs which at one point would not have seemed feasible are now quite practical. These designs combine well-known ideas regarding sampling and measurement, with theories of missing data mechanisms and effective ways that new analyses can handle it. These designs fall under the term *planned missing data designs*. Incorporating a planned missing data design allows researchers to reduce the testing burden placed on its participants (Rhemtulla, Jia, Wu, & Little, 2014). Additionally, this leads to higher quality data with truncated practice and fatigue effects and reduced unplanned missing data (Harel, Stratton, & Aseltine, 2011).

The basic concept behind planned missing data designs is that participants are not asked every single question or at all possible measurement waves; and this is evidenced in the generic three-form design originally developed for cross-sectional studies (Graham et al., 2006). The three-form design can reduce the workload of research participants primarily via allowing researchers to collect information on more items without changing the number of questions asked of each respondent (Graham, 2009). The idea behind the three -form design is that each participant is asked a manageable number of questions, but the questions given to each participant vary. This allows data to be collected on a large number of items all of which are then available for the analysis. With this design, items are divided into four sections: X, A, B and C. Sections are then

Table 16.3 Three-form design for planned missing data

	Item set received by respondents			
	X	A	B	C
Form 1	1	1	1	0
Form 2	1	1	0	1
Form 3	1	0	1	1

Note. 1 = data present, 0 = data missing.

either given or not given to participants as illustrated in Table 16.3. Considering the availability of the missing data methods described earlier, the data produced by this design can be easily analysed, as the missingness is known to be missing MCAR (Graham et al., 2001). Similar designs to the three -form design include the split questionnaire survey design, which involves 11 different forms and six item sets (as opposed to three forms and four item sets in the three-form design). Adapted for longitudinal research, the three-wave design can either reduce the number of items in each wave (Rhemtulla et al., 2014) or reduce the number of waves (Graham et al., 2001).

The primary aim of the three form design is to be able to collect more information from participants without reducing the quality of the information. Alternatively, another planned missing data design, called the two-method design, aims to increase a study's validity (Garnier-Villarreal, Rhemtulla, & Little, 2014). As the name suggests, the two-method design utilises two different forms of measurement for the key variable of interest: a highly valid yet expensive measurement and a second inexpensive (but less valid) measure. All participants are measured on the inexpensive measure and only a small sample are administered the expensive measure. The result, as depicted in Table 16.4, is a large sample of participants who have "missing data" on the expensive measure. This design allows researchers to increase the validity of large-scale research by including a gold-standard reference group. Used alternatively, the design can bring expensive small-sample research into the domain of affordable large-sample research. By using planned missingness it allows to balance cost, efficiency and validity of measurement.

Conclusion

Missing data is an issue that all applied researchers must manage and having a good understanding about how to effectively analyse incomplete data is paramount. A plethora of methods for coping with missing information in a dataset has become available; however, the effectiveness of each method can vary drastically depending upon the circumstances. Suitable methods for handling missing data include MI and ML, both of which are becoming increasingly available in statistical software packages including SPSS, SAS, M*plus* and R. Although not a panacea for handling missing data, as they still rely on various assumptions,

Table 16.4 Two-method design for planned missing data

	Measurement type	
	Less expensive, less valid measure	*Highly expensive, more valid measure*
Participant 1	1	1
Participant 2	1	0
Participant 3	1	0
Participant 4	1	0
Participant 5	1	1
Participant 6	1	0
Participant 7	1	1
Participant 8	1	0
Participant 9	1	0
Participant 10	1	0

Note. 1 = data present, 0 = data absent

these modern methods continue to outperform the more traditional methods under differing conditions. Furthermore, core concepts and modern missing data methods are now being considered in the design stages of a study with planned missing data designs.

Note

1 Although the term *research unit* can range from organisations and schools to individual people, most often in applied psychology the research unit is an individual person and thus will be referred to as such henceforth.

References

Baraldi, A. N., & Enders, C. K. (2010). An introduction to modern missing data analyses. *Journal of School Psychology, 48*(1), 5–37. doi:10.1016/j.jsp.2009.10.001

Chen, G., & Åstebro, T. (2003). How to deal with missing categorical data: Test of a simple Bayesian method. *Organizational Research Methods, 6*(3), 309–327. doi:10.1177/1094428103254672

Collins, L. M. (2006). Analysis of longitudinal data: The integration of theoretical model, temporal design, and statistical model. *Annual Review of Psychology, 57*(1), 505–528. doi:10.1146/annurev.psych.57.102904.190146

Collins, L. M., Schafer, J. L., & Kam, C. M. (2001). A comparison of inclusive and restrictive strategies in modern missing data procedures. *Psychological Methods, 6*(4), 330–351. doi:10.1037/1082–989X.6.4.330

Garnier-Villarreal, M., Rhemtulla, M-J., & Little, T. D. (2014). Two-method planned missing designs for longitudinal research. *International Journal of Behavioral Development, 38*(5), 411–422. doi:10.1177/0165025414542711

Graen, G. B., & Uhl-Bien, M. (1991). The transformation of professionals into self-managing and partially self-designing contributors: Toward a theory of leadership-making. *Journal of Management Systems, 3*(3), 25–39. Retrieved from http://digitalcommons.unl.edu/managementfacpub/16

Graham, J. W. (2009). Missing data analysis: Making it work in the real world. *Annual Review of Psychology, 60*(1), 549–576. doi:10.1146/annurev.psych.58.110405.085530

Graham, J. W., Cumsille, P. E., & Shevock, A. E. (2012). Methods for handling missing data. In I. B. Weiner, J. A. Schinka, & W. F. Velicer (Eds.), *Handbook of psychology: Research methods in psychology* (pp. 109–141). Hoboken, NJ: Wiley.

Graham, J. W., Taylor, B. J., & Cumsille, P. E. (2001). Planned missing-data designs in analysis of change. In L. M. Collins (Ed.), *New methods for the analysis of change* (pp. 335–353). Washington, DC: American Psychological Association.

Graham, J. W., Taylor, B. J., Olchowski, A. E., & Cumsille, P. E. (2006). Planned missing data designs in psychological research. *Psychological Methods, 11*(4), 323–343. doi:10.1037/1082–989X.11.4.323

Harel, O., Stratton, J., & Aseltine, R. (2011). *Designed missingness to better estimate efficacy of behavioral studies.* Paper presented at the National Center for Health Statistics, Tenth Conference on Health Survey Research Methods, Hyattsville, MD.

Lewis-Beck, M. S., Bryman, A., & Liao, T. F. (2003). *The SAGE encyclopedia of social science research methods* (Vol. 2). London, UK: Sage.

Little, R. J. A., & Rubin, D. B. (2002). *Statistical analysis with missing data.* New York, NY: John Wiley & Sons.

McDonald, R. A., Thurston, P. W., & Nelson, M. R. (2000). A Monte Carlo study of missing item methods. *Organizational Research Methods, 3*(1), 71–92. doi:10.1177/109442810031003

Newman, D. A. (2014). Missing data: Five practical guidelines. *Organizational Research Methods, 17*(4), 372–411. doi:10.1177/1094428114548590

Peugh, J. L., & Enders, C. K. (2004). Missing data in educational research: A review of reporting practices and suggestions for improvement. *Review of Educational Research, 74*(4), 525–556. doi:10.3102/00346543074004525

Rhemtulla, M-J., Jia, F., Wu, W., & Little, T. D. (2014). Planned missing designs to optimize the efficiency of latent growth parameter estimates. *International Journal of Behavioral Development, 38*(5), 423–434. doi:10.1177/0165025413514324

Roth, P. L., Switzer, F. S., & Switzer, D. M. (1999). Missing data in multiple item scales: A Monte Carlo analysis of missing data techniques. *Organizational Research Methods, 2*(3), 211–232. doi:10.1177/109442819923001

Rubin, D. B. (1976). Inference and missing data. *Biometrika, 63*(3), 581–592. doi:10.1093/biomet/63.3.581

Rubin, D. B. (1987). *Multiple imputation for nonresponse in surveys.* New York, NY: John Wiley & Sons.

Schafer, J. L., & Graham, J. W. (2002). Missing data: Our view of the state of the art. *Psychological Methods, 7*(2), 147–177. doi:10.1037/1082–989X.7.2.147

Schaufeli, W. B., Bakker, A. B., & Salanova, M. (2006). The measurement of work engagement with a short questionnaire: A cross-national study. *Educational and Psychological Measurement, 66*(4), 701–716. doi:10.1177/0013164405282471

Shoemaker, D. M. (1971). *Principles and procedures of multiple matrix sampling* (Technical Report 34). Inglewood, CA: Southwest Regional Laboratory. Retrieved from http://eric.ed.gov/?id=ED057100

Wilkinson, L., & Task Force on Statistical Inference. (1999). Statistical methods in psychology journals: Guidelines and explanations. *American Psychologist, 54*(8), 594. doi:10.1037/0003–066X.54.8.594

17 Data preparation

Stefano Occhipinti and Caley Tapp

Introduction

Researchers are rarely presented with data in a form ready to submit to statistical procedures. Some processing will almost certainly be required before analysis, and the analyst is well advised to keep a close eye on matters, as many of the decisions are far from routine. The process is a broad one and is appropriately called *data preparation*. In this chapter, readers will find an outline of what encompasses data preparation and a set of guidelines as to how to proceed optimally. Just as one size never fits all, one approach to data preparation will never meet all needs.

In our experience of consultation, many assume erroneously that data preparation is merely *data cleaning*, in which the procedures such as log transformations, usually gleaned from an early chapter of a statistics text, are applied robotically to misbehaving data. Rather, the process begins much earlier and can be said to cover many of the procedures from when the responses are recorded to when the data is analysed. For example, some of the most important evidence for the appropriateness of a linear regression model will come from inspection of the residuals that are only obtained once the analysis has been run.

Many of the analyses conducted by applied psychology researchers, such as ordinary least squares (OLS) regression and ANOVA, derive from the general linear model (GLM; Scheffé, 1959; Searle, 1971). The underlying statistical assumptions, although only a part of the data preparation process, have many commonalities. Accordingly, the guide that follows is biased to some extent towards these types of analyses. However, it will be seen that much of the material is applicable to any form of statistical modelling.

Goals of data preparation

Data preparation can seem like a confusing and arbitrary set of procedures intended to change oddly shaped curves into pleasing and symmetrical ones. However, it should be a time for considering whether the data are in the best form to provide evidence to assess the research questions. Data preparation is not a single, standalone module that occurs prior to analysis and *irrespective of the type of* analysis; rather it must be integrated both with the research questions and the analyses chosen to address them. The two related components of this process are to check, first, whether data are in a condition to be submitted to the statistical model at all, and second, whether the model is the best or most appropriate one. Although these two components are roughly ordered, the analyst must undoubtedly iterate and oscillate between them. A dataset that contains many errors or gaps in responses or variables distributed haphazardly cannot provide the basis for defensible results. However, the observable aspects of the distribution of variables or residuals, such as skewness, clusters of outliers or evident nonlinearity, may not be blemishes in the data to be rectified if possible, but instead vital evidence as to the nature of the sample or population. This is true whether the analyses are *t*-tests or growth curves. It follows that data preparation is not a procedure to remove all the perceived imperfections of a dataset, leaving idealised, perfect variables. Nor should it be assumed that clever application of procedures like transformations will license the analyst to ignore the appropriate analytic model for the data. In these cases, the best outcome of properly conducted data preparation is to point out the reasons why the initial analytic plans may no longer be appropriate.

Phases in data preparation

In performing data preparation we strongly advise avoiding the point and click menus of the chosen statistical software. Almost all commonly used software has a command language (*syntax*) that allows statistical procedures to be specified like computer programs. Although it may be tempting to use the menus, in data preparation a clear audit trail is essential (e.g., to be able to go back and note who was dropped and why). Careful, well annotated use of the command language of the software will allow us always to take the original, untouched dataset and run the exact set of procedures taken to come up with the final results. This will be very important later in checking and perhaps justifying results and conclusions to critics. As well, the command language is likely to allow a considerably more efficient workflow in that repetitive tasks can be specified very simply and errors that arise can be identified and fixed more easily at the source. If consultation is required, beware the consultant who does not or cannot write out the syntax for their procedures.

Examining data before running any analysis

Prior to fitting a model, the sample data must be examined fairly closely. Contrary to popular belief, this is not to assess whether the data *are normal or not* or whether *there are outliers or not*. Instead, the first task is to seek to answer the following questions by examining the outcome variable and the predictors in turn.

1   *Does the sample approximate what is known about the population from which it has been drawn?* There is a trick hiding in this question. What the average researcher may consider to be a population is different to what a

statistician may think. Statistical populations are sets of scores and not of the respondents who gave those scores. Bearing this in mind, one could expect the underlying population parameters to be normal if the variable is a measure of a physical trait such as height or a cognitive one such as maths ability. Also, many noncontroversial attitude items may be distributed normally in the population. The sample scores derived on these variables ought to appear normally distributed. If so, rejoice and move on. If not, the reasons *why* not are important. Perhaps the sampling frame has resulted in an uncommonly extreme group of respondents. No satisfactory solution can be applied statistically in these cases. By contrast, some items, for perfectly good reasons, may not elicit normally distributed responses in a sample. Very common examples are variables measuring socially undesirable quantities, such as overt prejudice (e.g., containing items such as *I just don't like members of Group X*) or traditional sexism. In many cases, these tend to show a slight to moderate skew in the direction away from the socially desirable end. This is because many participants may respond in a way that minimises the socially undesirable response, resulting in a concentration of scores at that end of the scale. If this turns out to be the case, the best approach is to make a note to check the variable when performing later diagnostics. There is a very good chance that the robustness of GLM procedures will have alleviated problems. If distributional issues are extreme or unexpected, then a more extreme solution, such as creating one or more dummy variables (see later) may be attempted.

2　**Do the variables follow a clearly non-normal but otherwise systematic distribution?** Some items in a questionnaire will not ever elicit a normal distribution. After a steady diet of normal, theory-based OLS analyses in statistics courses, this can be a shock! For example, frequency-of-use data is known for not being normal. We shouldn't expect it to be so. It often follows a *Poisson* distribution. If a respondent is asked, *How many times did you do X in the last week?* and *X* is not an extremely common behaviour, the odds will be that most people haven't done it at all or only did it a small number of times, and relatively few did *X* many times. For example, how frequently do you go to the doctor? Once a year? Twice a year? Once a month? What if you have a chronic illness or care for someone who does? Imagine the pattern: over a period of six months, most people would hardly go to the doctor, while a very few would go frequently. In these cases, researchers may either need to transform the variable into a series of meaningful categories or dummies or to adopt a statistical model (e.g., ordinal regression family) that actually fits the data (if more information on this approach is required, texts such as that by Agresti, 2013 will be of use). This choice will be affected by the role and importance of the variable in the analysis plan and the budget (in both time and money). Is there money for a consultant? Is this type of variable going to figure prominently in this or future projects? These and other questions will help to clarify the likely path. In this case, transformations are of dubious value and likely to add interpretational difficulties to distributional ones.

3   *Are there groups of scores in your data that do not seem to belong with the others (i.e., does your sample potentially represent more than one underlying population)?* This is a different question than *Are there outliers?* It cannot be answered by looking at one variable and wondering which scores are ±3.29 standard deviations from the mean. A case must be considered in the context of their complete response pattern, especially on key demographic and other informative variables. For example, is there a subgroup of participants who are particularly high in education attainment but low in income? Do most of the women in the sample share a narrow range of values on some characteristic that is much more varied in the men? These and other questions may be harder to find initially and may come up later when more targeted analyses such as moderation are attempted. However, at this early stage, it is worth examining more carefully the distributions and cross-tabulations (or scatterplots) of the important variables. For example, if a focal variable is gender, be sure also to examine any known correlates of gender in the dataset, such as income or perhaps education. If a complex sample structure is uncovered, this may flag the need for expert consultation or at least a re-evaluation of the analytic plan to incorporate grouping.

Practical pre-analysis checklist

Having considered and examined the data as appropriate in search of answers to the broad questions listed earlier, the next step is to address the practicalities of the analyses. In real data analysis (see Chapter 19 in this volume), the analyst will not find that a smooth delineation exists between strictly statistical and methodological or practical issues. The next list reflects this. Instead of a neat linear progression, it is best considered as a somewhat iterative, hesitant process. This process encompasses two broad steps: (a) does the dataset contain anything that is more or less an error – a typo, a mistake in scale calculations? and (b) are there already issues like floor or ceiling effects that will likely be reflected as more substantial problems later in terms of skew or perhaps influential data?

1   Before examining the data, the researcher should be sure that there is an ID variable in the data that is a unique numerical value for each separate case. If so, it will always be possible to sort and re-sort the data or to merge new variables or cases and so forth. An ID variable will also greatly facilitate record-keeping during the whole of data preparation. It is important to keep note of any problematic participants, as there will be a need to identify those who appear to be problematic across several variables in the dataset. The whole dataset provides context for the individual variables, so keeping notes will allow easy identification of consistently problematic participants.

2   If data has been transcribed from hard copy participant protocols (i.e., survey booklets or similar), select a random subset and check that the protocol

is accurately reflected in the dataset. For example, when entering psychological rating scale data from a hard copy, did the transcriber accidentally punch keys in the wrong row of the numeric keypad? If more errors arise than expected, then it is prudent to conduct more substantial checks.

3   Request histograms for continuous variables and bar charts for discrete and/or nominal variables, as appropriate. Request means, standard deviations (SDs), minimum, maximum and number of observations for each variable. This step may reflect a more detailed version of any examinations already conducted to answer the questions in the previous section. This will provide early warning for the potential data problems listed in Table 17.1.

4   At this point, attempt to deal with the identified issues. The remedies may be as simple as correcting coding errors or recoding some variables into meaningful dummy variables (see later).

5   Run bivariate scatterplots of some key variables, both focal variables for the analyses and demographic variables like age that could be expected to have stable, known relationships with other constructs (e.g., income). If the data is composed of many scales, scale scores may not yet have been computed, and it is acceptable to focus on simple measured variables that are already in the dataset. This approach provides clues that there are odd or unexplained patterns in the data. Does a scale contain notorious items that tend to elicit

Table 17.1 Common data problems and ways to detect them

Data problem	Comments
Floor effects	• Mean very low and close to the lower end of the scale.
	• Using a clinical scale with nonclinical participants can cause this.
Ceiling effects	• Mean very high and close to the top of the scale.
	• Classically, this is evidence of a too easy task.
Non-normality	• Mean less than the *SD* is a classic positive skew pattern with data bunched at the bottom.
	• If *SD* is greater than the difference between mean and maximum score on scale, then there is negative skew.
	• As a rough guide, twice the *SD* should be the distance between each of minimum and maximum and the mean, respectively, for a normal distribution.
	• Beware! Bimodality in the data will not be picked up by just looking at the numbers, hence examine distributions
Bimodality	• Histogram will show two (or more) peaks of frequency. This is usually a sign that there are two or more subgroups in the data. Were data gathered in two distinct ways or from different sampling frames? Is there reason to suspect there should actually be two underlying populations?
Data entry errors	• Out-of-range values (e.g., 8 on a 1–5 scale) for minimum or maximum.
	• Implausible values on open scales (e.g., 99 drinks per week). These require some knowledge of the underlying construct to interpret.
	• Impossible values on an open-ended scale (e.g., negative values for number of times a behaviour was performed).

a particular response pattern? Are there reverse coded items? How do these appear when plotted against more straightforward items? Is there evidence of extreme responses that may be related to bad faith responding? For example, the authors once found in a dataset a respondent claiming to be a 14-year-old male who consumed 110 standard drinks a week and was of a religion of very low representation in the population. Close inspection of the protocol revealed evidence of response sets and patterned responding (e.g., using opposite scale extremes on alternate items irrespective of the item wording). The appropriate action was to delete this respondent from the data. Deleting participants in this way should be noted in any report on the analyses. If there are more than a proportional handful of deleted respondents, this may be evidence of systematic problems with the project and should be examined further. It is worth taking some time to move systematically through the dataset at this step, before full analyses are begun. Any extreme cases or other anomalies found now will almost certainly show up later in diagnostic checks. By removing them now, the chance is lessened of such anomalous respondents obscuring any real issues and patterns in the data.

6   Now is the time to methodically reverse code items, as required. Using a systematic naming convention, such as *r_oldvarname*, create new variables.

7   Obtain alpha coefficients, if required, now, while the raw items are available. Address any issues that alpha analyses have thrown up – some poorly behaved items may need to be dropped if possible.

8   Compute scale scores. Save a reduced version of the dataset containing only (a) the variables that to be used in the analyses and (b) the participants who have been retained. Data hygiene is important, but allow for later potential changes in emphasis. It will be evident at this point that the more carefully planned the analyses aligning closely with the research questions, the clearer the path forward is.

Diagnostics: assessing the outcome after running a regression

Data preparation does not end when the analyses proper begin; the boundary between preparation and analysis is indistinct. The early stages of analysis, after a model has been fitted, provide residuals, the analysis of which is the core of diagnostics (e.g., Bollen & Jackman, 1985; Stevens, 1984). To reiterate, here we make the assumption that the applied psychology researcher is primarily using GLM statistics, such as regression and ANOVA. There is a wide variety of plots and scores available in this part of the analysis, and we discuss the key scores following recommendations of Stevens (1984) in psychology and Bollen and Jackman (1985) in sociology. Most textbook chapters on regression diagnostics owe their content to these works. Next is a summary and guide to the most commonly used quantities. Importantly, the following does not address the issue of significance tests for diagnostics. With the applied researcher in mind, the emphasis is firmly upon the types of graphical plots and patterns of scores across cases that may signal problems ahead. The topic of regression diagnostics is a vast one (e.g., the classic book length treatment is by Cook and Weisberg, 1982), but many procedures may be overkill in typical, relatively small *N* applied studies. The goal is to search for *recurring patterns*, indicating problematic cases or variables.

It is important to remember that diagnostic evaluation of the residuals precedes simple transformations of any and all predictors on the basis of potential skewness or other similar reasons. First, if the aforementioned stages of data preparation have been conducted carefully, many issues will already have been identified. Second, the presence of mild to moderate skew may simply not cause any serious problems. Given the robustness of GLM analysis to such issues and provided no further influential data points are discovered, the analysis may often proceed as is. When analysing the residuals, we pay particular attention to a series of quantities that signal the presence of cases (i.e., sets of individual participant scores) that may be exerting undue influence on the parameters of the model (i.e., in a regression, particularly the *b*-weights). The diagnostics listed alert us to the presence of such cases. As well, inspection of various plots may alert the researcher to violations of other assumptions.

Studentised residuals

Residuals are the part of each person's score that is not accounted for by the regression. A case's residual is positive if regression underestimated the actual score and negative if there was an overestimate. Residuals account for the uncertainty of prediction, and they should be centred around zero and normally distributed. Studentised residuals have been standardised with the estimated standard error of the residuals. The upshot is that cases with a studentised residual greater in absolute value than approximately 3.3 are less likely to occur than one in a thousand times (i.e., corresponding to an alpha level of .001) and are considered outliers. Residuals greater than this absolute value should be noted but should *not* be automatically deleted. Most software will print out extreme residual scores and will provide a histogram of the residuals to illustrate the shape of the distribution.

Mahalanobis distance (D)

Cases may also represent outliers in terms of the all the predictors at once, and these are called multivariate outliers. To gauge the occurrence of such cases, Mahalanobis *D*, a generalisation of the concept of *Z* scores, is used. It is a standardised and weighted measure of the distance of any point from the joint mean of all the component variables (i.e., predictors in a regression model). In regression, Mahalanobis *D* provides a sense of how different a given case is in comparison to the rest of the sample, from the perspective of all the predictors at once (i.e., not from the perspective of the outcome variable), and most software will print out the most extreme values.

Leverage

The raw components of leverage are known as the h values and come from the hat matrix (Bollen & Jackman, 1985). As well as actual listed values of leverage (in the form of Mahalanobis distance; see previous section), it is useful to inspect a histogram of h values, as this can illustrate cases that are far away from predictor means. The values of h are all positive, unlike residuals, and the lower bound is zero. This gives a naturally skewed histogram of leverage values that ought to show that most cases are bunched at the low or zero end of the scale. A few may well occur in extreme areas towards the right of the plot. In a more complex dataset with many predictors, it may not be possible to identify individual cases with potentially problematic levels of leverage without making use of this plot. Cases with high leverage should be noted.

Cook's distance (D)

According to Stevens (1984), Cook's D

> is a measure of the change in the regression coefficients that would occur if this case was omitted, thus revealing which cases are most influential in affecting the regression equation. It is affected by both the case being an outlier on y and on the set of the predictors.
>
> (p. 341)

Influence is a function of both distance and leverage. Having *solely* a very high distance (i.e., extreme residual, indicating the case is very poorly explained by the regression equation) or a very high leverage (i.e., high Mahalanobis D or h value, indicating that the case lies far from the others in the sample from the perspective of the predictors) does not necessarily mean that the case will affect the regression coefficients by changing what they would otherwise have been. By contrast, having high values on both measures at once suggests that the case is influential. Cook's D is sensitive to this interplay – it is a weighted product of studentised residuals and Mahalanobis D. Cases with high values of Cook's D should be noted.

Partial regression plots

These are scatterplots that look like ordinary bivariate scatterplots but are a form of residual plot. On an intuitive basis, partial plots show the regression between each predictor (X_k) and the criterion (Y), in turn, where both Y and the particular X_k have been adjusted for the effects of the remaining predictors. This is another useful way to find any cases that may pose problems of influence in the context of one of more predictors, as they will stand apart from the main scatter. Partial plots can help to isolate influence issues that may arise from perhaps one or two predictors.

Scatterplot of standardised residuals (Y-axis) and predicted scores (X-axis)

A great deal of information is available from these plots. For the heterogeneity assumption, the residuals should be constant across predicted values. Practically, the shape of this plot should be rectangular and not fan shaped (or any other irregular shape). For the linearity assumption, they should not show a pronounced curvature across predicted values. If nonlinearity is found unexpectedly, inspection of the scatterplots of each individual predictor and the outcome is warranted to locate the source.

Creating dummy variables

Dummy coded variables are an extremely useful data preparation tool, and the researcher is advised to be familiar with them (for a more detailed discussion of dummy variables in regression, the reader is directed to a graduate-level regression text such as Cohen, Cohen, West, and Aiken, 2003, or Pedhazur, 1997). They represent a binary attribute and are coded either 0 or 1. Formally, dummy variables have a type of *binomial distribution*, which is beyond the scope of this chapter (for further information, see, for example, Agresti, 2013). Practically, dummy variables can be included as predictors in any regression (e.g., linear, logistic, ordinal) or similar procedure without modification. Some of the useful properties of dummy variables are: (a) mutually exclusive and exhaustive categories; (b) a meaningful zero point (i.e., if 1 = psychologist is member of clinical college, then 0 is the set of psychologists who definitely do not share that property); and (c) equal interval. Dummy variables are any preexisting binary variable that has been coded in the dataset as 0 and 1 (i.e., not 1 and 2 or anything else), such as public vs. private schooling, female vs. male sex. However, dummies may also be created by recoding a more complex variable. This may be required because a variable is best split into two categories because of distributional concerns or analytic preferences. For example, of all the types of educational level reported in a sample, the researcher may decide that the only meaningful comparison is between those who have and have not completed high school. As well, where there are ordinal or nominal categorical variables that have been collected or created later when inspecting the data, dummies can be used to render variables amenable to analysis. For example, an income variable may be very messily distributed with multiple modes. The researcher may decide to create a series of ordinal categories instead. In turn, the categories can be recoded into a set of dummies (see next) and incorporated into regression analysis as predictors.

Categorical variables can also be recoded into a *set* of dummy variables representing all the logical information in the original categorical variable. This is true of both ordinal (e.g., educational levels) and nominal (e.g., marital status) variables. It is immaterial whether the categories were naturally occurring in the data or if they were created by the researcher. To create sets of dummy variables, the rule applied is, *if there are c categories in a categorical variable, c − 1 dummies are needed to completely represent the grouping information.* For example, a researcher has collected marital status with 3 levels, where 1 = married in a registered marriage; 2 = cohabiting, and 3 = not married. Two dummies are needed, as there are three categories. A dummy representing the people in a registered marriage is created by recoding the marital status variable into a new variable where 1 = respondent was married in a registered marriage (i.e., 1 on the original variable) and 0 = everyone else. A second dummy, representing those in a co-habiting relationship is created by recoding the same marital status variable into another new variable where 1 = respondent is cohabiting (i.e., 2 on the original variable) and 0 = everyone else. A moment's reflection will show that those who responded 3 on the original variable, the *not marrieds*, will be the only group to score zero simultaneously on both of the new dummies. This logical property of dummy variables is used extensively in statistical analyses where dummies represent categorical information in models that would otherwise require continuous predictors only. It does not matter statistically which category is left out in dummy creation. Practically, researchers usually leave out the category representing the reference group against whom they wish to compare the responses of the other groups. Dummy variables are useful to prevent the waste of data that would otherwise not be able to be used in statistical analyses.

Conclusion

The data preparation stage offers a chance to examine and, if necessary, to remediate the obtained data before analysis. The logic of the stage involves seeking to isolate the individual (or sets of) cases that may cause the statistical analyses to be invalid and then to assess whether more serious violations of assumptions remain. Together, the procedures discussed here will enable the researcher to understand their data better and to avoid proceeding with costly and critical analyses while data errors remain.

References

Agresti, A. (2013). *Categorical data analysis* (3rd ed.). Hoboken, NJ: John Wiley & Sons.

Bollen, K. A., & Jackman, R. (1985). Regression diagnostics: An expository treatment of outliers and influential cases. *Sociological Methods and Research, 13,* 510–42. doi:10.1177/0049124185013004004

Cohen, J., Cohen, P., West, S. G., & Aiken, L. S. (2003). *Applied multiple regression/correlation analysis for the behavioral science.* New York, NY: Routledge.

Cook, R. D., & Weisberg, S. (1982). *Residuals and influence in regression.* New York, NY: Chapman and Hall.

Pedhazur, E. J. (1997). *Multiple regression in behavioral research: Explanation and prediction.* Fort Worth: Harcourt Brace College Publishers.

Scheffé, H. (1959). *The analysis of variance.* New York, NY: John Wiley & Sons.

Searle, S. R. (1971). *Linear models.* New York, NY: John Wiley & Sons.

Stevens, J. P. (1984). Outliers and influential data points in regression analysis. *Psychological Bulletin, 95,* 334–344. doi:10.1037/0033–2909.95.2.334

18 Content analysis and thematic analysis

Kimberly A. Neuendorf

Introducing content analysis and thematic analysis

Message analyses

Content analysis and thematic analysis are two prominent methods used for the analysis of message content. Both have been defined in various ways and have been applied to a wide range of phenomena. This chapter will focus on key definitions and applications useful for those involved in applied psychology research.

The two methods have similarities – both involve codes and coding (Ahuvia, 2001), that is, a process of representing message content with abbreviated, convenient symbols. These codes may be applied to messages by human investigators (coders) or, in the case of some content analyses, by computer programs that use predefined search algorithms. The messages to be coded may be (a) an already-existing set of messages, such as postings to the "Men's Room" bulletin board of an online fertility support group (Malik & Coulson, 2008), "fitspiration" images posted on Instagram (Tiggemann & Zaccardo, 2016), or popular pornographic videos (coded for aggressive and sexual behaviors; Bridges et al., 2010); or they may be (b) messages newly created by research participants, such as open-ended questionnaire responses in surveys and experiments, interview responses, dream analysis reports, focus group transcripts, transcripts of customer service interactions, or responses within such personality assessment strategies as Rorschach testing and thematic apperception tests (TAT) (Weiner & Greene, 2017). Clearly, for the latter class of messages (b), there will be important considerations that precede the application of content analysis or thematic analysis – i.e., the research design and protocol including the questions participants are asked or procedures executed on them and an appropriate plan for the selection of participants.

Both methods may also attempt to tap both manifest (i.e., directly observable variables) and latent (i.e., unobservable constructs) content (Joffe & Yardley, 2004). Both methods should be applied only after research questions or hypotheses have been forwarded, in order to appropriately guide the analysis. And, as Joffe and Yardley (2004) note, both methods are taxing and time consuming.

There are no shortcuts to a properly conducted, painstaking investigation of messages using either thematic analysis or content analysis.

But the two methods also have important differences. Historically, content analysis has followed a paradigm of positivism, with chiefly quantitative techniques used, dating to the early twentieth century (Berelson, 1952; Neuendorf, 2002; Smith, 2000). More recent variations have introduced "qualitative content analysis" (Altheide & Schneider, 2013; Mayring, 2014; Schreier, 2012; Vaismoradi, Turunen, & Bondas, 2013), which actually has many characteristics in common with other qualitative analyses of messages, including thematic analysis. Thematic analysis, an addition to the options for message analysis in psychology in the 1970s, developed from within a more constructivist paradigm (although some argue that it is positivist in its requirement that assertions ought to be supported with evidence) and an emphasis on an interpretive approach to largely qualitative techniques[1] (Guest, MacQueen, & Namey, 2012; Merton, 1975).

Thematic analysis assumes that the recorded messages themselves (i.e., the texts) are the data, and codes are developed by the investigator during close examination of the texts as salient themes emerge inductively from the texts. These codes most often consist of words or short phrases that symbolically assign an "essence-capturing, and/or evocative attribute" (Saldaña, 2016, p. 4) and are viewed interactively, to be modified throughout the coding process by the investigator. While the investigator may begin the thematic analysis process with "templates" (a set of *a priori* codes), the epistemological roots of the technique dictate that these codes need to be flexible, able to be modified as the analysis progresses (King, 2004). The conclusion of the thematic analysis is the identification of a (hopefully) saturated set of themes (i.e., no additional themes are found from additional data; Ando, Cousins, & Young, 2014) and a meaningful "codebook" or other compilation of findings that documents the structure of codes and themes, with the validity of the findings paramount. The frequency of occurrence of specific codes or themes is usually not a main goal of the analysis.

Content analysis (in its most common, quantitative form) assumes that the messages (texts) are the phenomena to be examined and provide the units of data collection – the data are the recorded occurrences of specified codes as applied to these units. Codes are developed *a priori* in a primarily deductive process and then applied in relatively objective fashion by trained coders whose intercoder reliability is viewed as critical, or via an automated computer-assisted coding process. The codes are most often numeric, usually representing categories of a nominal variable, but may alternatively represent levels of a metric variable. The conclusion of the typical content analysis is the statistical summarization and analysis of the coded variables across many units of analysis.

It should be noted that the *a priori* coding scheme of a content analysis has often been developed at least in part through a process very much like thematic analysis – an inductive step of deriving salient variables and their codes from the pool of message content to be studied. This is particularly true of investigations in which scant existing theory or past research guides the content analyst in the development of a coding scheme. In all instances, investigator "immersion" in the message content being studied is recommended as a first step for both thematic analysis and content analysis (Clarke & Braun, 2014; Neuendorf, 2017).

Thematic analysis

Defining thematic analysis

Thematic analysis has been defined broadly as "a way of seeing" and "making sense out of seemingly unrelated material" (Boyatzis, 1998, p. 4). Braun and Clarke (2006) identify it as a method for identifying and analyzing patterns of meaning in a dataset (i.e., texts).[2] The process is seen as organic and reflexive, requiring an "engaged, intuitive" investigator who considers "the ways in which they are *part* of the analysis. . . [making] TA a personal, and sometimes even emotional, experience" (Braun, Clarke, & Terry, 2015, p. 107). The goal is to develop a *story* from the texts of interest. The investigator notes patterns and themes from the coded texts and from this may construct a codebook, a structured compendium of codes that includes a description of how codes interrelate (Guest et al., 2012, p. 50). Coding categories often form a hierarchy of categories (Joffe & Yardley, 2004). The end result of a thematic analysis will highlight the most salient "constellations" of meanings present in the texts (Joffe, 2012). Themes may be presented in a map, indicating processes or hierarchy among the themes (Braun, Clarke, & Terry, 2015).

The typical process of thematic analysis

Clarke and Braun (2014; see also Braun & Clarke, 2006, and Braun, Clarke, & Rance, 2015, pp. 188–189) present a recursive six-phase process for thematic analysis:

1 Familiarising oneself with the data (text; may be transcriptions) and identifying items of potential interest
2 Generating initial codes that identify important features of the data relevant to answering the research question(s); applying codes to the dataset (segmenting and "tagging") consistently; collating codes across segments of the dataset
3 Searching for themes; examining the codes and collated data to identify broader patterns of meaning
4 Reviewing themes; applying the potential themes to the dataset to determine if they tell a convincing story that answers the research question(s); themes may be refined, split, combined, or discarded
5 Defining and naming themes; developing a detailed analysis of each theme
6 Producing a report; weaving together the analytic narrative and data segments, relating the analysis to extant literature

Boyatzis' widely cited volume (1998) provides a comprehensive treatment of the process of developing codes and the full process of thematic analysis. Altheide and Schneider (2013) outline the process of developing themes and frames for the analysis of media content. And Saldaña (2016) provides a detailed guide of the "how to" of coding for qualitative analysis.

In addition to the development of codes and the identification of themes, other analytic techniques may assist in constructing the story of the data (Guest et al., 2012), such as word searches and key-word-in-context (KWIC) output. For this, computer adjuncts are employed, called QDAS (qualitative data analysis software) or CAQDAS (computer-assisted qualitative data analysis). Programs such as NVivo 11, Atlas.ti, and QDA Miner provide organizing power and give basic quantitative summaries as well (see Joffe & Yardley, 2004). The typical QDAS functions include the facilitation of the creation of a codebook with definitions and examples, the application by the investigator of codes, comments, and memos to text ("text" may also include images and multimedia content), the retrieval of content segments that have been coded, and visual representations of co-occurrence relationships among codes (e.g., via network concept mapping, dendrograms, or cluster analysis).

While interrater/intercoder reliability is not routinely assessed in thematic analyses, some scholars argue that this ought to be part of the process (Boyatzis, 1998; Joffe & Yardley, 2004). Some investigators have indeed included a consideration of reliability by employing additional analysts for comparative purposes (e.g., Chambers et al., 2013).

Examples of thematic analysis

Examples of thematic analyses show the range of message content that may be examined and the types of findings that are typical. In all cases, themes are an outcome, and these themes may be further subdivided or combined in a hierarchical or process-based model.

Tierney and Fox (2010) sought to discover the perspective of individuals who have lived with an "anorexic voice." Twenty-two participants from three UK self-help organizations participated, providing accounts in the form of poems, letters, and reflections/descriptive narratives. Initial analyses produced 135 codes, which were grouped into 10 categories, such as "attacking sense of self," "demanding and harsh task master," and "breaking free." Further, three stages of the "voice" were identified in a model of change from positive to negative: "being drawn into the relationship"; "ensnared in the relationship"; and "life without the relationship."

In a study of online support groups of individuals with Parkinson's disease, Attard and Coulson (2012) studied a random sample of postings in four discussion forums over the years 2003–2010. The 1,013 messages in the sample revealed six major themes and 16 subthemes. For example, the theme "Welcome to the land of the Parky people" included the subthemes of "comfort in numbers," "empathy and understanding," and "friendship formation"; the theme "It's like a graveyard at the moment," included the subthemes of "lack of replies," "symptom restrictions," and "a lack of personal information."

Open-ended written responses to the query "How would you define sexual satisfaction?" were the focus of a thematic analysis by Pascoal, Narciso, and Pereira (2014). They developed a three-level hierarchical thematic map from codes derived from responses generated by 760 heterosexual participants. Their main themes (at the highest, or third, level) were "personal sexual well-being" and "dyadic processes," with the latter divided into three subthemes (at the second level) and five codes (at the first level).

Content analysis

Defining content analysis

A brief definition of content analysis has been proposed by this author: "The systematic, objective, quantitative analysis of message characteristics" (Neuendorf, 2017, p. 1).[3] Content analysis may be applied to *any* message content. Analyses may be as complex as for any other quantitative study, including predictive regression analyses and structural equation models (e.g., Neuendorf et al., 2010; Sultan & Wong, 2011)

Human-coded content analysis vs. CATA

Content analysis may be executed by human coding according to a predefined coding scheme or by computer program using a predefined set of search dictionaries and algorithms (often termed computer-aided text analysis, or CATA). For all types of quantitative content analysis, the construction of an *a priori* coding scheme is important. Examples of coding schemes may be found at the Content Analysis Guidebook Online (http://academic.csuohio.edu/neuendorf_ka/content/; Neuendorf, 2017).

The typical process of content analysis

As delineated in Neuendorf (2017), the typical steps in the execution of a content analysis are:

1   Theory and rationale
2   Conceptualizations – identification of variables to be included in the study and conceptual definitions of them derived from theory, past research, and possible emergent variables from an inductive examination of the message content
3   Operationalizations (measures) – should match the variables' conceptualizations
4   Establishment of coding scheme – either a codebook and coding form (for human coding) or a set of original or predefined dictionaries (for CATA)
5   Sampling – deciding on the population of messages to be studied and sampling an (optimally) representative subset of messages for the study

6   Coder training and pilot intercoder reliability assessment
7   Coding
8   Final intercoder reliability assessment
9   Tabulation and reporting

Psychometric content analysis

Of particular interest to psychologists has been the application of content analysis to psychometrics, the quantitative measurement of psychological characteristics. While self-report inventories are perhaps the most common method of psychometric assessment, a second main way is via performance-based measures (Weiner & Greene, 2017). The latter includes assessment via Rorschach testing, thematic apperception tests (TAT), figure-drawing methods, and sentence completion methods. The scoring of the output of these techniques matches the process of quantitative content analysis – i.e., raters/coders are trained on a coding scheme, and their interrater reliability is assessed (Jenkins, 2017; Weiner & Greene, 2017).

Smith et al. (1992; see also Smith, 2000) presents a large volume of predefined coding schemes for the nonclinical measurement of psychological characteristics called thematic content analysis. The volume began with a focus on the needs of scholars coding TAT outcomes but was expanded to include coding open-ended survey responses, archival historical documents, and everyday verbal materials such as conversations, reports of dreams, and transcripts of TV programs. Coding schemes include power motivation, intimacy motive, and psychological stances toward the environment, among many others. Content analysis has also been used to assess psychometrics for clinical purposes, as with the coding scheme developed by Gottschalk and colleagues. The CATA form of this scheme, PCAD, is described in the next section.

CATA options

There are dozens of available computer-aided text analysis (CATA) programs (see Neuendorf, 2017, for a fuller list and comparison chart). Some of the more useful CATA programs that show the range of options are:

PCAD (Psychiatric Content Analysis and Diagnosis)

The application of content analysis to an individual's naturally occurring communication (e.g., speech or writing) in order to assess mental states, emotions, and neuropsychiatric indicators to provide preliminary diagnostics for psychiatric purposes was the life's work of Louis Gottschalk. With his team, he first developed an elaborate human-coded scheme, with a computer-driven system (PCAD) the eventual outcome (Gottschalk, 1995; Gottschalk & Bechtel, 2007; 2008). The 40 PCAD measures include 14 subscales for depression, cognitive impairment, and six anxiety subscales. Unlike most other content analyses (and thematic analyses), PCAD is designed for idiographic purposes.[4] That is, the 40 measures are applied to an individual in order to produce "candidate diagnoses for consideration" for that individual. For example, President Ronald Reagan was found to exhibit a "significant increase" in cognitive impairment between the 1980 and 1984 presidential debates (although Gottschalk held the release of the findings until 1987; Romney, 1997).

LIWC2015 (Linguistic Inquiry and Word Count)

Devised as an automated method to detect important differences among essays by individuals who had undergone traumatic experiences, LIWC has since been used in a wide array of other applications (Pennebaker, 2011; Pennebaker et al., 2015). LIWC uses dozens of dictionaries to measure linguistic and paralinguistic dimensions, relativity dimensions, psychological constructs (e.g., affective processes, such as anger; cognitive processes, such as inhibition), and other constructs. Pennebaker and Chung (2009) applied LIWC to texts authored by al-Qaeda leaders Osama bin Laden and Ayman al-Zawahiri, comparing their speech with that of other extremist groups, concluding that bin Laden increased his cognitive complexity and emotionality after 9/11 and that post-2003 the use of anger and hostility words by both al-Qaeda leaders was much higher than that for other extremist groups.

Profiler Plus

Profiler Plus is a "general purpose text analytics (natural language processing) system" that allows for multi-pass, rule-based analyses of text, relying on substantial researcher input and specification rather than machine learning (socialscience.net/tech/profilerplus.aspx). The platform offers a number of coding schemes that have already been created for applied projects, such as Leadership Trait Analysis and conceptual/integrative complexity. A number of Profiler Plus coding schemes are computerized adaptations of psychometric measures presented in the Smith et al. (1992) volume, including need for achievement, need for affiliation, and need for power. User-created, custom coding schemes may also be devised.

Yoshikoder

The freeware Yoshikoder is particularly useful for analysts who are constructing their own CATA dictionaries. Yoshikoder performs basic functions, such as word counts, dictionary term counts/data, KWIC, and concordances, making it a good vehicle via which to learn the typical process and principal functions of CATA. The program provides options for the use of both predefined dictionaries and custom dictionaries (http://yoshikoder.sourceforge.net/).

Additional examples of content analyses

Additional examples of content analyses show the range of message content that may be examined and the types of findings that are typical. Both human-coded and CATA examples show how predefined coding schemes and CATA dictionaries are employed to produce quantitative data for analysis.

Tiggemann and Zaccardo (2016) conducted a human-coded content analysis of 600 images on Instagram marked with the "fitspiration" hashtag. Their *a priori* coding scheme included measures of body type, activity, objectification, and inspirational and dysfunctional quotes. Intercoder reliability was acceptable for each of the 11 measured variables. Results included the finding that most images of women represented only one body type – thin (75.2%) and visibly toned (56.2%). Further, a majority of images were found to include objectifying elements (56%).

Responses to semi-structured interviews were the content analyzed in Stahl and Caligiuri's (2005) study of coping strategies employed by expatriate managers while on international assignment. Interviews were conducted with 116 German managers in Japan or the U.S. A coding scheme comprised of 30 different variables (i.e., types of coping strategies) was developed via a combination of inspection of past literature and emergent codes from an examination of the interview transcripts. All variables in the coding scheme were found to have acceptable intercoder reliability. The most frequently reported coping strategies were "emphasizes the positive in a difficult situation," "tries to control the situation by taking initiative," and "intentionally violates cultural norms." The 30 strategies were further divided into two types: problem-focused ($k = 14$) and emotion-focused ($k = 16$). Combining these data with additional self-report survey data from the 166 managers, the investigators found that the prediction of cross-cultural adjustment from the use of problem-focused coping strategies was moderated by cultural distance and position level.

Bligh, Kohles, and Meindl (2004) examined how elements of the speeches of President George W. Bush changed in response to the post-9/11 environment. The CATA program DICTION (www.dictionsoftware.com/; Hart, 2014), which was designed to examine the linguistic characteristics of political speech, was applied to 74 speeches collected from the official White House website ($n = 39$ pre-9/11 and $n = 35$ post-9/11). Six of the 31 predefined dictionary-based measures in DICTION were the focus. In ANCOVA statistical analyses, it was found that the post 9/11 speeches were significantly more likely to incorporate references to collectives, faith, patriotism, and aggression and less likely to reference ambivalence (after controlling for speech length and word variety). There was no pre/post difference found for the measure of optimism.

Blended approaches

Thematic analysis and content analysis each has its own set of characteristics that might be viewed as advantages, and each has limitations (see Braun & Clarke,

2013). Thematic analysis produces a depth of understanding of the meaning of a set of texts. The investigator is the instrument, and reliability among investigators is not typically assessed.[5] For content analysis, a main assumption is that a coding scheme is independent of the individual perspective of an investigator. The instrument is not the investigator but rather the coding scheme, which is not adaptable during the final coding process. Reliability between coders is paramount.

Increasingly, scholars have called for mixed-methods research, integrating qualitative and quantitative approaches in a single study (Guest et al., 2012), as well as the triangulation of methods across studies. A purposeful pairing of qualitative and quantitative analyses has obvious advantages, given the complementary goals of each (Gray & Densten, 1998; Hardy, Harley, & Phillips, 2004).

Some scholars have recognized this complementarity. Fereday and Muir-Cochrane (2006) called for a hybrid approach to thematic analysis, including both deductive and inductive coding. Walker, van Jaarsveld, and Skarlicki (2017) utilized a mixed-method approach to analyzing customer service employee incivility toward customers. Brough, O'Driscoll, and Biggs (2009) provide an example of a hybrid approach to content analysis and thematic analysis in which an initial, *a priori* content analysis coding scheme based on theoretic and practical considerations was supplemented by additional codes derived in an iterative, emergent process of thematic analysis. The analysis examined responses to semi-structured interviews with parents who had returned to work within a year of the birth of a child. The resulting scheme was assessed for reliability by the inclusion of an additional coder. The study exemplified the viability of a blended approach to message analysis.

Conclusion

The utility of message analysis techniques, including the oft-used content analysis and thematic analysis, has been demonstrated in hundreds of studies across disciplines, including applied psychology. These two sets of methods produce different types of conclusions, with content analysis providing quantitative, objective, reliable measures about messages and thematic analysis most typically resulting in qualitative, inductive, conclusions about themes in message content. The two types may be seen as complementary, each providing a different perspective on a set of messages. As the volume of recorded messages continues to grow, notably online, applications of these two message analysis techniques will become increasingly important.

Notes

1   The distinction between quantitative and qualitative might be viewed as "a rather thin and discreet line. . . [as] most qualitative studies do contain some kind of quantitative information (numbers)" (Schedler & Mudde, 2010, pp. 418–419). Elsewhere, I recommend applying the labels of quantitative and qualitative separately to the phenomenon

under investigation and to the analytical strategies used to describe or summarize the phenomenon. For example, the typical task of *quantitative* measurement is to assign numerical values to *qualities* of a phenomenon (Neuendorf, 2017).

2   Beyond thematic analysis, other examples of wholly qualitative methods include phenomenological analysis, grounded theory, hermeneutic analysis, narrative analysis, discourse analysis, and conversation analysis (see Alhojailan, 2012; Harper & Thompson, 2012; Rohleder & Lyons, 2015; Smith, J. A., 2008). Thematic analysis is reported to be compatible with the overarching methodologies of various qualitative research approaches (e.g., phenomenology).

3   The more detailed definition given in my textbook on content analysis follows:

> Content analysis is a summarizing, quantitative analysis of messages that follows the standards of the scientific method (including attention to objectivity – intersubjectivity, *a priori* design, reliability, validity, generalizability, replicability, and hypothesis testing based on theory) and is not limited as to the types of variables that may be measured or the context in which the messages are created or presented.
>
> (Neuendorf, 2017, p. 17)

4   However, some investigators have used the PCAD measures on multiple cases for nomothetic purposes (for the distinction between idiographic and nomothetic approaches, see Te'eni, 1998, and Weiner & Greene, 2017). For example, Smith (Smith, S. S., 2008) applied measures from PCAD, as well as from Profiler Plus, to 96 instances of threatening communication from FBI case files. Among other findings, she reported that threateners exhibiting less ambivalent hostility (from PCAD) and higher conceptual complexity (from Profiler Plus) were more likely to act on their threat.

5   Some scholars have proposed processes of reliability and validity assessment in thematic analysis by the inclusion of additional, independent reviewers to validate themes and to indicate level of reliability of feedback across reviewers (Alhojailan, 2012). However, these techniques, more closely aligned with positivist perspectives, are not routinely part of thematic analysis.

References

Ahuvia, A. (2001). Traditional, interpretive, and reception based content analyses: Improving the ability of content analysis to address issues of pragmatic and theoretical concern. *Social Indicators Research, 54*, 139–172.

Alhojailan, M. I. (2012). Thematic analysis: A critical review of its process and evaluation. *West East Journal of Social Sciences, 1*(1), 39–47.

Altheide, D. L., & Schneider, C. J. (2013). *Qualitative media analysis* (2nd ed.). Thousand Oaks, CA: Sage.

Ando, H., Cousins, R., & Young, C. (2014). Achieving saturation in thematic analysis: Development and refinement of a codebook. *Comprehensive Psychology, 3*, Article 4.

Attard, A., & Coulson, N. S. (2012). A thematic analysis of patient communication in Parkinson's disease online support group discussion forums. *Computers in Human Behavior, 28*, 500–506.

Berelson, B. (1952). *Content analysis in communication research*. New York, NY: Hafner.

Bligh, M. C., Kohles, J. C., & Meindl, J. R. (2004). Charting the language of leadership: A methodological investigation of President Bush and the crisis of 9/11. *Journal of Applied Psychology, 89*, 562–574.

Boyatzis, R. E. (1998). *Transforming qualitative information: Thematic analysis and code development*. Thousand Oaks, CA: Sage.

Braun, V., & Clarke, V. (2006). Using thematic analysis in psychology. *Qualitative Research in Psychology, 3*, 77–101.

Braun, V., & Clarke, V. (2013). *Successful qualitative research: A practical guide for beginners*. London, UK: Sage.

Braun, V., Clarke, V., & Rance, N. (2015). How to use thematic analysis with interview data. In A. Vossler & N. Moller (Eds.), *The counselling and psychotherapy research book* (pp. 183–197). London, UK: Sage.

Braun, V., Clarke, V., & Terry, G. (2015). Thematic analysis. In P. Rohleder & A. C. Lyons (Eds.), *Qualitative research in clinical and health psychology* (pp. 95–113). Houndmills, Basingstoke, Hampshire, UK: Palgrave Macmillan.

Bridges, A. J., Wosnitzer, R., Scharrer, E., Sun, C., & Liberman, R. (2010). Aggression and sexual behavior in best-selling pornography videos: A content analysis update. *Violence Against Women, 16*, 1065–1085.

Brough, P., O'Driscoll, M. P., & Biggs, A. (2009). Parental leave and work-family balance among employed parents following childbirth: An exploratory investigation in Australia and New Zealand. *Kōtuitui: New Zealand Journal of Social Sciences Online, 4*(1), 71–87. doi: 10.1080/1177083X.2009.9522445

Chambers, S. K., Schover, L., Halford, K., Ferguson, M., Gardiner, R. A., Occhipinti, S., & Dunn, J. (2013). ProsCan for couples: A feasibility study for evaluating peer support within a controlled research design. *Psycho-Oncology, 22*, 475–479. doi:10.1002/pon.2110

Clarke, V., & Braun, V. (2014). Thematic analysis. In A. C. Michalos (Ed.), *Encyclopaedia of quality of life and well-being research* (pp. 6626–6628). Dordrecht, The Netherlands: Springer.

Fereday, J., & Muir-Cochrane, E. (2006). Demonstrating rigor using thematic analysis: A hybrid approach of inductive and deductive coding and theme development. *International Journal of Qualitative Methods, 5*(1), 80–92.

Gottschalk, L. A. (1995). *Content analysis of verbal behavior: New findings and clinical applications*. Hillsdale, NJ: Lawrence Erlbaum.

Gottschalk, L., & Bechtel, R. (2007). *Psychiatric content and diagnosis: The PCAD 3*. Brighton, MI: GB Software.

Gottschalk, L. A., & Bechtel, R. J. (Eds.). (2008). *Computerized content analysis of speech and verbal texts and its many applications*. New York, NY: Nova Science.

Gray, J. H., & Densten, I. L. (1998). Integrating quantitative and qualitative analysis using latent and manifest variables. *Quality & Quantity, 32*, 419–431.

Guest, G., MacQueen, K. M., & Namey, E. E. (2012). *Applied thematic analysis*. Thousand Oaks, CA: Sage.

Hardy, C., Harley, B., & Phillips, N. (2004). Discourse analysis and content analysis: Two solitudes? *Qualitative Methods: Newsletter of the American Political Science Association Organized Section on Qualitative Methods, 2*(1), 19–22.

Harper, D., & Thompson, A. R. (Eds.). (2012). *Qualitative research methods in mental health and psychotherapy*. Malden, MA: John Wiley & Sons.

Hart, R. P. (Ed.). (2014). *Communication and language analysis in the corporate world*. Hershey, PA: IGI Global.

Jenkins, S. R. (2017). Not your same old story: New rules for Thematic Apperceptive Techniques (TATs). *Journal of Personality Assessment, 99*, 238–253. doi:10.1080/00223891.2016.1248972

Joffe, H. (2012). Thematic analysis. In D. Harper & A. R. Thompson (Eds.), *Qualitative research methods in mental health and psychotherapy* (pp. 209–223). Chichester, West Sussex, UK: Wiley-Blackwell.

Joffe, H., & Yardley, L. (2004). Content and thematic analysis. In D. F. Marks & L. Yardley (Eds.), *Research methods for clinical and health psychology* (pp. 56–68). London, UK: Sage.

King, N. (2004). Using templates in the thematic analysis of text. In C. Cassell & G. Symon (Eds.), *Essential guide to qualitative methods in organizational research* (pp. 256–270). London, UK: Sage.

Malik, S. H., & Coulson, N. (2008). The male experience of infertility: A thematic analysis of an online infertility support group bulletin board. *Journal of Reproductive and Infant Psychology, 26*, 18–30.

Mayring, P. (2014). *Qualitative content analysis: Theoretical foundations, basic procedures and software solutions.* Klagenfurt, Austria. Retrieved from www.ssoar.info/ssoar/handle/document/39517

Merton, R. K. (1975). Thematic analysis in science: Notes on Holton's concept. *Science, 188*, 335–338.

Neuendorf, K. A. (2002). *The content analysis guidebook.* Thousand Oaks, CA: Sage.

Neuendorf, K. A. (2017). *The content analysis guidebook* (2nd ed.). Thousand Oaks, CA: Sage.

Neuendorf, K. A., Gore, T. D., Dalessandro, A., Janstova, P., & Snyder-Suhy, S. (2010). Shaken and stirred: A content analysis of women's portrayals in *James Bond* films. *Sex Roles, 62*, 747–761.

Pascoal, P. M., Narciso, I. S. B., & Pereira, N. M. (2014). What is sexual satisfaction? Thematic analysis of lay people's definitions. *Journal of Sex Research, 51*(1), 22–30.

Pennebaker, J. W. (2011). *The secret life of pronouns: What our words say about us.* New York, NY: Bloomsbury Press.

Pennebaker, J. W., Boyd, R. L., Jordan, K., & Blackburn, K. (2015). *The development and psychometric properties of LIWC2015.* Austin, TX: University of Texas at Austin. doi:10.15781/T29G6Z

Pennebaker, J. W., & Chung, C. K. (2009). Computerized text analysis of Al-Qaeda transcripts. In K. Krippendorff & M. A. Bock (Eds.), *The content analysis reader* (pp. 453–465). Thousand Oaks, CA: Sage.

Rohleder, P., & Lyons, A. C. (Eds.). (2015). *Qualitative research in clinical and health psychology.* Houndmills, Basingstoke, Hampshire, UK: Palgrave Macmillan.

Romney, L. (1997, January 8). UCI given $1.5 million by Psychiatry Dept. founder. *Los Angeles Times.* Retrieved from http://articles.latimes.com/1997-01-08/local/me-16606_1_university-officials

Saldaña, J. (2016). *The coding manual for qualitative researchers* (3rd ed.). London, UK: Sage Publications Ltd.

Schedler, A., & Mudde, C. (2010). Data usage in quantitative comparative politics. *Political Research Quarterly, 63*, 417–433.

Schreier, M. (2012). *Qualitative content analysis in practice.* Thousand Oaks, CA: Sage.

Smith, C. P. (2000). Content analysis and narrative analysis. In H. T. Reis & C. M. Judd (Eds.), *Handbook of research methods in social and personality psychology* (pp. 313–335). Cambridge, UK: Cambridge University Press.

Smith, C. P. (Ed.), in association with Atkinson, J. W., McClelland, D. C., & Veroff, J. (1992). *Motivation and personality: Handbook of thematic content analysis.* Cambridge, UK: Cambridge University Press.

Smith, J. A. (Ed.). (2008). *Qualitative psychology: A practical guide to research methods.* London, UK: Sage.

Smith, S. S. (2008). Risk assessment of threatening communications from FBI case files using Gottschalk-Gleser content analysis scales. In L. A. Gottschalk & R. J. Bechtel (Eds.), *Computerized content analysis of speech and verbal texts and its many applications* (pp. 111–121). New York, NY: Nova Science Publishers, Inc.

Stahl, G. K., & Caligiuri, P. (2005). The effectiveness of expatriate coping strategies: The moderating role of cultural distance, position level, and time on the international assignment. *Journal of Applied Psychology, 90*, 603–615.

Sultan, P., & Wong, H. Y. (2011). Service quality in a higher education context: Antecedents and dimensions. *International Review of Business Research Papers, 7*(2), 11–20.

Te'eni, D. R. (1998). Nomothetics and idiographics as antonyms: Two mutually exclusive purposes for using the Rorschach. *Journal of Personality Assessment, 70,* 232–247.

Tierney, S., & Fox, J. R. E. (2010). Living with the "anorexic voice": A thematic analysis. *Psychology and Psychotherapy: Theory, Research and Practice, 83,* 243–254.

Tiggemann, M., & Zaccardo, M. (2016). "Strong is the new skinny": A content analysis of #fitspiration images on Instagram. *Journal of Health Psychology,* 1–9. doi:10.1177/135910531 663943

Vaismoradi, M., Turunen, H., & Bondas, T. (2013). Content analysis and thematic analysis: Implications for conducting a qualitative descriptive study. *Nursing and Health Sciences, 15,* 398–405.

Walker, D. D., van Jaarsveld, D. D., & Skarlicki, D. P. (2017). Sticks and stones can break my bones but words can also hurt me: The relationship between customer verbal aggression and employee incivility. *Journal of Applied Psychology, 102,* 163–179.

Weiner, I. B., & Greene, R. L. (2017). *Handbook of personality assessment* (2nd ed.). Hoboken, NJ: John Wiley & Sons.

19 'Real' analyses

Carlo Tramontano and Roberta Fida

Introduction

The aim of this chapter is to provide a description of the most common analytical approaches used in quantitative research. In order to provide the reader with examples of research 'in practice', throughout the chapter we will take the perspective of a researcher, Mary, and we will describe the analytical processes she may use to address the different research questions and to test the corresponding hypotheses. More specifically, Mary is interested in ethics in higher education and is assessing these four research questions: *What are the frequencies of the different types of cheating behaviours? Is cheating behaviour more frequent among females or males? Is cheating behaviour more common in some specific faculties? What are the factors that hinder or foster the engagement in cheating behaviour?*

As we will describe in the following sections, each of these questions leads to a specific analytical approach: describing a phenomenon (e.g., frequencies of different forms of cheating behaviour), testing for group differences (e.g., gender and faculties differences), investigating relationship (e.g., association of cheating behaviour with other variables) and predicting outcomes (e.g., cheating behaviour as an outcome of other variables).

Describing a phenomenon

Based on the literature review Mary has undertaken before designing the research, she prepared an online questionnaire comprising the following sections:

- Information sheet and consent form;
- demographic information: gender, age, ethnicity, parents' educational level;
- background information: faculty, current academic year;
- cheating behaviour: four items asking the students to rate how frequently they engaged respectively in plagiarism, use of crib notes, seeking hints and unauthorised collaborations on a scale from 1, corresponding to 'never', to 5, corresponding to 'always';
- academic self-efficacy: five items asking students to rate how confident they perceived themselves in each of the statements using a five-point Likert

scale from 1, corresponding to 'not confident at all', to 5, corresponding to 'completely confident';

- moral disengagement: five items asking the students to rate their level of agreement with each of the items, using a five-point Likert scale from 1, corresponding to 'agree not at all', to 5, corresponding to 'totally agree'.

After obtaining the ethical approval from the ethics board of her university, Mary forwarded a link to all students enrolled in her university ($N = 15,000$). Overall, 10,000 students answered the questionnaire. As a preliminary step Mary describes the sample.[1] Specifically, as initial information she computes the response rate that is the proportion of students who actually completed the questionnaire, given the total number of students initially contacted. Based on the results of the research, Mary has a response rate of:

$$\frac{10,000 \ (\textit{number of students who filled in the questionnaire})}{15,000 \ (\textit{number of students who were initially contacted})} \times 100 = 67\%$$

She then describes the respondent sample characteristics. These variables are not equivalent in terms of measurement levels (i.e., nominal, ordinal, interval and ratio); hence, different types of indices are computed. Specifically, gender, ethnic group and faculty are discrete *nominal* variables, including a range of categories that are mainly qualitative in nature and cannot be sorted in any specific order. For these variables, Mary reports the frequency, the corresponding percentage of each category, and the *mode* that is the most frequent categories for each variable.

Other variables in the questionnaire are assessed at a higher level of measurement. For example, the parents' level of education is a discrete *ordinate* variable, meaning that the corresponding numerical values can be sorted. For this type of variable, Mary, along with frequency, percentage of each category and the mode, reports also the *median*. This index of central tendency denotes the category that splits the variable distribution in half. In contrast, age is a continuous quantitative variable measured at *ratio* level, and accordingly Mary reports the *range* (i.e., the lowest and the highest values within the sample under study), the *mean* (i.e., the average score) and the *standard deviation* (or the *variance*) that is a measure of the variability around the mean within the sample. Overall, the sample descriptive statistics are reported in a specific paragraph of the research summary (or scientific paper/dissertation) and could also be included in a table. For example, Mary writes:

Overall, 10,000 students (53.5% female) participated in the research (response rate: 67%). They ranged in age between 17 and 42 years old, with a mean age of 19 (SD = 4.23). The majority of students are enrolled in social sciences (38.9%), while 28.3% are in health sciences, 17.2% in science, and 15.6% arts and humanities. Furthermore, the majority of the sample comprises first-year undergraduate students (36.1%), while the remainder are second-year undergraduate students (28.2%), third-year undergraduate students (19.6%) and postgraduate (16.1%).

Table 19.1 Sample descriptive statistics

		f (%)	Range (Min-Max)	M (SD)
Gender	Male	4,650 (46.5)		
	Female	5,350 (53.5)		
Age			17–42	19 (4.23)
Faculty	Social sciences	3,890 (38.9)		
	Health sciences	2,830 (28.3)		
	Science	1,720 (17.2)		
	Arts and humanities	1,560 (15.6)		
Year of course	1 UG	3,610 (36.1)		
	2 UG	2,820 (28.2)		
	3 UG	1,960 (19.6)		
	PG	1,610 (16.1)		

Note. f = frequency; Min-Max = minimum and maximum; M = mean; SD = standard deviation; 1 UG = first-year undergraduate; 2 UG = second-year undergraduate; 3 uG = third-year undergraduate; PG = postgraduate

Describing cheating behaviour

Cheating behaviour was measured, as previously mentioned, on a scale from 1 to 5. This type of scale is usually referred to as *Likert scale* and is often used in survey-based research to ask participants to rate, for example, their frequency, agreement, or liking with each scale item. Formally, this type of variable is a discrete *ordinal* variable; however, under certain assumptions, it is possible to treat this type of variable 'as if' it was continuously measured at *interval level*. This is possible when the number of categories is large enough (at least five), the variable is normally distributed (see Table 19.1), and the sample size is adequate (e.g., Babakus, Ferguson, & Jöreskog, 1987; Bollen & Barb, 1981; Breckler, 1990; Maurer & Pierce, 1998; Tabachnick & Fidell, 2014). Accordingly, Mary describes cheating behaviours by analysing frequency and percentage of each form of misconduct, along with the mode, median and mean, with the corresponding standard deviation. In addition, Mary also reports the mean and standard deviation of the overall cheating behaviour score.

Referring to this table Mary writes:

> *Between 50 and 60% of the students reported to have engaged sometimes in some forms of cheating behaviour; between 15 and 24% on a few occasions; between 14 and 23% quite a bit; between 2 and 5% never; and only between 1 and 4% often. Overall, in the sample under study, the cheating behaviour average score is about 3 (SD 1.3).*

Testing for group differences

Mary now wants to explore whether there are gender differences in cheating behaviour. To this end she runs a *t*-test for independent samples. Specifically, the statistical hypotheses she is testing are:

h_0(**null hypothesis**): $\mu_{male} = \mu_{female}$ – that is, males and females in the population have the same mean in cheating behaviour;

h_1(**alternative hypothesis**): $\mu_{male} \neq \mu_{female}$ – that is, males and females in the
population differ in cheating behaviour.

As shown in the alternative hypothesis, Mary is not positing any specific
differences between males and females, hence in this case we refer to h_1 as a
bidirectional hypothesis. If she would have had a specific idea about the direction
of the differences, she could have posited a *unidirectional hypothesis*. For example,
Mary could have hypothesised $\mu_{male} > \mu_{female}$ if she expects males to engage more
frequently in cheating or, alternatively, $\mu_{female} > \mu_{male}$ if she expects females to
engage more frequently in cheating.

As shown in Table 19.3, Mary reports the means of cheating behaviour separately for the two groups (i.e., females and males), the value for *t* and the associated level of significance. Setting the significance level at $\alpha = .05$ (*two-tails*),
Mary can reject the null hypothesis and conclude that males engage significantly more frequently in cheating behaviour than females (because the mean
score for males is *significantly* higher than the mean scores for females). Along
with this information Mary could also include the *effect size* that is a measure
of the strength of the difference, as expressed by the Cohen's *d* index (typically
used when groups have similar sample size and standard deviations). Generally,
values of Cohen's *d* are considered small when $< .20$, medium when between
.20 and .50, or large when $> .50$ (Cohen, 1988).

Table 19.2 Cheating behaviour descriptive statistics

	(1)	(2)	(3)	(4)	(5)	Mo	Me	M(SD)
Plagiarism	500	2400	5000	2000	100	(3)	(3)	2.88 (1.3)
	(5%)	(24%)	(50%)	(20%)	(1%)			
Use of crib notes during test	400	2000	6000	1400	200	(3)	(3)	2.90 (1.3)
	(4%)	(20%)	(60%)	(14%)	(2%)			
Seeking hint during a test	200	1500	6000	1900	400	(3)	(3)	3.08 (1.4)
	(1%)	(15%)	(60%)	(19%)	(4%)			
Unauthorised collaborations on an	200	1800	5500	2300	200	(3)	(3)	3.05 (1.3)
assignment	(2%)	(18%)	(55%)	(23%)	(2%)			
Overall cheating behaviour								2.98 (1.3)

Note. (1) = Never; (2) = On a few occasion; (3) = Sometimes; (4) = Quite a bit; (5) = Often; Mo = mode;
Me = median; M = mean; SD = standard deviation

Table 19.3 Results of *t*-test for independent samples

	Females – M (SD)	Males – M (SD)	t	p
Cheating behaviour	2.7 (1.3)	3.2 (1.7)	16.33	.001

Note. M = mean; SD = standard deviation.

To test for gender differences, instead of the *t*-test, Mary could have conducted a one-way ANOVA analysing the Fisher's *F* and the associated level of significance. In this case she reports the *F* value, the degrees of freedom, the level of significance and the effect size, as expressed by the η^2, summarising the percentage of variance for the dependent variable explained. When comparing two groups on one variable, $t = \sqrt{F}$, *t*-test or the one-way ANOVA are equivalent.

Mary now wants to compare student's cheating behaviour across faculties (i.e., social science, health science, science and arts and humanities). Since there are more than two groups, Mary wisely opts to use the one-way ANOVA, providing a simultaneous comparison between the four groups (for a more detailed explanation, see Fields, 2009). Specifically, the statistical hypotheses associated with Fisher's *F* are:

h$_0$ (null hypothesis): $\mu_{ss} = \mu_{hs} = \mu_s = \mu_{ah}$ – that is, students from different faculties have the same mean in cheating behaviour;

h$_1$ (alternative hypothesis h1): $\mu_{ss} \neq \mu_{hs}$ or $\mu_{ss} \neq \mu_s$ or $\mu_{ss} \neq \mu_{ah}$ or μ_{hs} $\mu_{ss} \neq \mu_{hs}$ or $\mu_{ss} \neq \mu_s$ or $\mu_{ss} \neq \mu_{ah}$ or $\mu_{hs} \neq \mu_s$ or $\mu_{hs} \neq \mu_{ah}$ $\mu_s \neq \mu_{ah}$ – that is, students from at least two faculties have different means in cheating behaviour.

As shown, with the ANOVA, if we rejected the null hypothesis we cannot identify in which faculty cheating behaviour is significantly more frequent than others, so we would need to explore *post hoc* tests. This will allow the researcher to run *pairwise comparisons* to specifically test all the possible combinations of groups. Post hoc tests in this example are basically a procedure to run pairwise *t*-tests to determine which groups are equal and which are significantly different from each other. Since on the same dataset Mary will compare six pairs, she needs to adjust the level of significance by using Bonferroni's correction. Hence, she sets the significance level at $\alpha = .008$ (.05/6).

An important note of caution for Mary when testing these group differences is that one of the assumption for both *t*-test and ANOVA is the normality of the dependent variable. *What does this mean?* This means that the frequency distribution for engagement in plagiarism in her sample should be approximable to the normal (or Gaussian) distribution, also known as the 'bell curve' due to its shape. *How can Mary verify this?* A first indication can derive from the graphical representation (i.e., histogram) of the frequency distribution for engagement in plagiarism. In addition, it is possible to analyse the skewness and the kurtosis of the distribution. Skewness refers to the symmetry of the frequency distribution, with distribution considered *positively skewed* when lower categories have greater frequencies versus *negatively skewed* when higher categories have greater frequencies. Kurtosis refers to the shape of the peak of the distribution. Distributions are defined as *leptokurtic* when the data are highly concentrated around the mean, resulting in a sharp peak of the curve (i.e., data tend to be mainly concentrated in a limited range of values, with options around the tail(s) particularly underrepresented). In contrast, distributions are defined as *platykur-tic* when the data are spread across the range of variable categories resulting in a relatively flat peak of the curve (i.e., data tend to be spread across the possible values, with options around the tails particularly overrepresented).

When analysing descriptive statistics for the specific frequency distribution, almost any statistical package allows the researcher to have indices for skewness and kurtosis along with mean and standard deviation. As a rule of thumb, values for both indices that are lower than one in absolute value ($< |1|$, meaning values ranging between -1 and $+1$) are considered adequate to assume that there is a normal distribution, although in some cases a cut-off value of $|1.5|$ also has been suggested.

What happen if this assumption is not verified? Do not panic! There are some transformations that can be applied to the data in order to improve the normality of the distribution. For example, in case of a positively skewed distribution, in which lower categories have greater frequencies, the scores x on the variable can be transformed in their reciprocal $\dfrac{1}{x}$ (in case of strong skewness) or by using the logarithmic function $\log x$ or the root square $\sqrt{x}$ (in case of moderate skewness). In case of a negatively skewed distribution, in which higher categories have greater frequencies, the scores x on the variable can be similarly transformed $1/k - x$; $\mathrm{Log}(k - x)$; $\mathrm{root}(k -- x)$, where k is equal to $1 +$ the highest value in the distribution. Furthermore, ANOVA analysis is considered robust for violations of normality; that is, even if the dependent variable is not perfectly normally distributed, results tend to be quite reliable, but it is good practice to interpret the findings with some caution. Notwithstanding this, when the violation of normality is particularly evident and is not negligible, an alternative analytical strategy should be pursued (e.g., non-parametric analysis).

Investigating relationships between the variables

Progressing in her investigation, Mary also wants to explore the association between cheating behaviour and academic self-efficacy (i.e., students' beliefs about their ability to manage their academic activities) and academic moral disengagement (i.e., cognitive mechanisms students may use to temporarily silence their moral control and engage in deviant conduct). A measure of association provides information about whether and how two measures co-vary, that means whether the increase in one measure corresponds with an increase (positive correlation) or a decrease (negative correlation) in the other. Hence, there is not a hypothesis of causation (i.e., A *causes* B) but just of co-variation (i.e., A and B 'move' together). Accordingly, the hypotheses Mary is testing are:

h_0 **(null hypothesis):** there is no association between the variables (correlation coefficient $= 0$);

h_1 **(alternative hypothesis h1):** there is a significant association between the variables (correlation coefficient $\neq 0$).

Since the variables under study are measured at interval level (five-point Likert scales), Mary analyses the *Pearson's r* that is the correlation index used for variables assessed on interval or ratio scale. Mary's results produce the following associations, summarised in Table 19.4:

Table 19.4 Correlations among the study variables

	(1)	(2)	(3)
Academic self-efficacy (1)	1	−0.31	−0.35
Moral disengagement (2)	−0.31★★	1	.40
Cheating behaviour (3)	−0.35★★	.40★★	1

Note. ★*p* <. 05; ★★ *p* < .01

The correlation matrix is a square matrix with as many rows (an equal number of columns) as the number of variables under study (in this case 3 × 3). It is also a symmetric matrix with respect to the main diagonal. Since the correlation coefficients are a measure of co-variation and the correlation between A and B is the same as the one between B and A ($r_{AB} = r_{BA}$), when presenting the correlation matrix, only the values below or above the principal diagonal are reported. In addition, the correlation between one variable and itself is obviously perfect ($r_{AA} = 1$); this information in the principal diagonal is usually omitted in the table, since it is tautological and irrelevant. In reference to this correlation table Mary reports:

> *Academic self-efficacy, moral disengagement and cheating behaviour are significantly associated to each other. In particular cheating behaviour negatively correlates with academic self-efficacy (r = −.31) and positively correlates with moral disengagement (r = .40). Hence, the more students engage in cheating behaviour, the less they perceived themselves as able to manage their academic activities (and vice versa) and the more they are prone to silence their moral control to engage in deviant conduct, and vice-versa. Furthermore, academic self-efficacy and moral disengagement shows a significant negative association (r = −.31), meaning that the more students perceived themselves as able to manage their academic activities the less they are prone to silence their moral control, and vice-versa.*

Please note that should Mary be interested in exploring the associations between variables that are assessed at a different measurement level, she should refer to alternative indices, depending on the specific type of variables under study. Specifically:

- *Spearman's rho*: for correlations between two ordinal variables;
- *Kendal's tau*: like rho, it is used for two ordinal variables;
- *point-biserial coefficient*: when one of the two variables is dichotomous and the other is continuous; and
- *tetrachoric coefficient phi*: when both variables are dichotomous.

However, all these indices, independently from their specific formulas and procedures for calculation, vary between -1 (i.e., perfect negative correlation) and $+1$ (i.e., perfect positive correlation), with 0 indicating the absence of association (i.e., A and B 'move' independently from each other). In sum, the sign of the correlation index provides information about the direction of the relationship (positive vs. negative), while the absolute value of it provides information about the strength of the relationship. According to the guidelines available in the literature, the association is considered weak for values below .10, moderate for values between .10 and .30, medium for values between .30 and .50, and strong for values greater than .50 (Cohen, 1988).

Predicting outcomes

So far, Mary has established a co-variation between academic self-efficacy, moral disengagement and cheating behaviour. However, relying on social cognitive theory, she has a more specific hypothesis testing whether academic self-efficacy and moral disengagement are two significant antecedents of cheating behaviour. To test this hypothesis, after exploring the correlation among these three variables, Mary runs a multiple regression analysis that examines the linear relationship between the two independent variables (quantitative or dichotomous) and her dependent variable (at least on an interval scale, although alternative approaches do exist that could be implemented with dichotomous or ordinal variables). A regression analysis provides Mary with regression coefficients (β_i), expressing the relationship between the dependent and each independent variable, after controlling for the others. These coefficients, differently from correlation coefficients, express a non-symmetrical and unidirectional relationship, in which it is hypothesised that values in the dependent variable are influenced by values in the independent variable and not vice-versa. In relation to her study, Mary posits this set of hypotheses:

$h_{0 \text{ self-efficacy}}$ **(null hypothesis)**: $\beta_{\text{self-efficacy}} = 0$; self-efficacy does not significantly affect cheating behaviour;

$h_{1 \text{ self-efficacy}}$ **(alternative hypothesis h1)**: $\beta_{\text{self efficacy}} \neq 0$; self-efficacy does significantly affect cheating behaviour.

$h_{0 \text{ moral disengagement}}$ **(null hypothesis)**: $\beta_{\text{moral disengagement}} = 0$; moral disengagement does not significantly affect cheating behaviour;

$h_{1 \text{ moral disengagement}}$ **(alternative hypothesis h1)**: $\beta_{\text{moral disengagement}} \neq 0$; moral disengagement does significantly affect cheating behaviour.

Mary produces the following results in Table 19.5:

Table 19.5 Summary of the results from multiple regression analysis

	b	β	p
Academic self-efficacy	$-.27$	$-.25$	.001
Moral disengagement	.34	.31	.001

The unstandardised regression coefficient (b) is expressed in the same measurement units as the variables and can then be difficult to interpret. For this reason, what is generally reported is the *standardised regression coefficient* (β), which represents the expected change in the standardised dependent variable for a change of one standard deviation in the independent variable. Similar to correlation coefficients, these regression coefficients can vary from −1 (perfect negative association) and +1 (perfect positive association), with 0 indicating the absence of relationship (i.e., self-efficacy and cheating behaviour 'move' independently from each other). The sign of the regression coefficients provides information about the direction of the relationship (positive vs. negative), while the absolute value of it provides information about the strength of the relationship. Based on the results, Mary writes:

> *Results of the multiple regression attested that both academic self-efficacy and moral disengagement significantly affect cheating behaviour. In particular, the former hinders it (−.25) and the latter fosters it (.31).*

In addition to this Mary, is also reporting the R^2 (varying between 0 and 1) expressing the proportion of variability of the dependent variable that is explained overall by the independent variables. Accordingly, assuming R^2 is equal to .17 in her analysis, she writes:

> *Overall, both self-efficacy and moral disengagement explained 17% of the variance of cheating behaviour.*

Conclusion

This chapter provided a brief overview of a process of data analysis 'in practice'. We did not discuss the preliminary steps prior to data analyses which Mary would follow. In particular, missing value analysis and data preparation are essential actions to undertake and are discussed in detail in Chapters 16 and 17 of this volume. This chapter emphasises the need for researchers to have a clear idea of what they want to investigate, since their hypotheses and the research design will direct the specific analytical approach to be used, working under the assumption that statistical analysis should be always considered not as an end in itself but as a means to address research problems.

Note

1 Please note that all the data presented in this chapter are completely fictitious. Tables and statistics are reported exclusively as examples and do not reflect actual findings.

References

Babakus, E., Ferguson, C. E., & Jöreskog, K. G. (1987). The sensitivity of confirmatory maximum likelihood factor analysis to violations of measurement scale and distributional assumptions. *Journal of Marketing Research, 24*, 222–228.

Bollen, K. A., & Barb, K. H. (1981). Pearsons' R and coarsely categorised measures. *American Sociological Review, 46*, 232–239.

Breckler, S. J. (1990). Application of covariance structure modelling in psychology: Cause of concern. *Psychological Bulletin, 107*, 260–273.

Cohen, J. (1988). *Statistical power analysis for the behavioral sciences*. Hillsdale, NJ: Lawrence Erlbaum.

Field, A. (2009). *Discovering statistics using IBM SPSS statistics* (4th ed.). London, UK: Sage.

Maurer, J., & Pierce, H. R. (1998). A comparison of Likert scale and traditional measures of self-efficacy. *Journal of Applied Psychology, 83*, 324–329.

Tabachnick, B. G., & Fidell, L. S. (2014). *Using multivariate statistics* (6th ed.). Essex, UK: Pearson Education Limited.

20 Mediation analysis and conditional process models

*Joshua L. Howard, Patrick D. Dunlop,
and Michael J. Zyphur*

Introduction

One fundamental goal of the social and applied sciences is to improve our understanding of how an independent variable or predictor (X) relates to a dependent variable or outcome of interest (Y). As a simple example, industrial and organizational psychologists have long taken an interest in investigating the relations of individual differences such as personality traits and cognitive ability with organizationally relevant outcomes such as job performance (Schmidt & Hunter, 1998), resulting in practical advice for personnel selection. However, scientific enquiry has evolved from simply investigating the presence, absence, or strength of relations between two variables to understanding the *processes* that tie variables together; that is, understanding why, how, or through what mechanisms X affects Y, such as through a mediating variable (M), such that X affects Y indirectly via M (Judd & Kenny, 1981).

For this purpose, the influential article by Baron and Kenny (1986) popularized the term "mediation" within the applied sciences, triggering a boom in the investigation of process models – here, we use the term "process model" synonymously with "mediation model," "mediation analysis," or "indirect effects model." Indeed, Rucker, Preacher, Tormala, and Petty (2011) reported that 59% of articles published in the *Journal of Personality and Social Psychology*, and 65% of articles in the *Personality and Social Psychology Bulletin* between 2005 and 2009 included at least one mediation analysis. Nonetheless, as Hayes (2009) noted, there is evidence of substantial misunderstanding with regard to the appropriateness of the different approaches researchers can employ to evaluate process models (see also Hayes & Scharkow, 2013).

This chapter familiarizes the reader with the principles of process models and currently recommended steps for testing mediation hypotheses contained therein. In doing so, we first commence with an overview of the basic principles of process models and then provide a review of common methods to test indirect effects in process models, along with recommendations for researchers. We then provide an account of the ways in which basic process models can be extended to test more complex processes, including conditional process models. We conclude with a brief discussion of several critical conceptual and methodological issues that should be considered when working with process models.

The basic process model

Process models concern mediation hypotheses and are used to answers questions concerning *how* or *why* X affects Y. For this, relevant terms include "mechanisms," "causal chains," "processes," "mediators," or "indirect effects." Implicit in each of these terms is the notion that X is *causing* Y through the mechanisms, causal chains, processes, mediators, or in the form of indirect effects that are operationalized in a model. To illustrate, Figure 20.1 depicts three causal models. Figure 20.1A represents a simple hypothesis that X *directly* causes Y (i.e., X has a *direct effect* on Y), with c representing the magnitude of this causal relation. Without any additional paths for Y to affect X, c is also the *total effect* of X on Y. On the other hand, the two models depicted in Figures 20.1B and 20.1C are process models.

In its most basic form, a process model involves a single mediating variable M that transmits the effect of the independent variable (X) on the outcome (Y). In specifying such a model, the researcher proposes that X has an *indirect effect* on Y *through the mediator* M. Figure 20.1B shows an indirect effect model wherein X only affects Y through M; that is, the indirect effect is the *only* process that ties X to Y, so that the *total effect* of X on Y is comprised of an indirect effect only (with no direct effect of X on Y). The magnitude of the indirect effect is equal to the product of the two paths constituting the $X \rightarrow M \rightarrow Y$ relationship, namely $a \times b$. When an indirect effect equals a total effect, the relationship is sometimes referred to as "full" or "complete" mediation, since M is hypothesized to completely account for (i.e., fully or completely mediate) the effect of X on Y. To describe why a mediated or indirect effect is operationalized as the product of paths such as $a \times b$, consider equations for Y and M that omits intercepts and residuals but roughly correspond to Figure 20.1B as follows:

$$M = a \times X$$
$$Y = b \times M$$

so that with substitution the indirect effect of X on Y can be shown as follows:

$$Y = b \times (a \times X) = a \times bX$$

This result can also be described substantively. Consider a case where a human resources practice such as a high performance reward system is put in place (X), which in turn affects employee motivation (M) with an effect $a = .5$. This

Figure 20.1A Direct effect

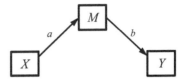

Figure 20.1B Indirect effect

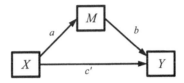

Figure 20.1C Direct and indirect effects

Note. A direct effect model (1A) and two simple process models incorporating an indirect effect only (1B) and a direct and indirect effect (1C)

increase of .5 for employee motivation then increases job performance (*Y*), with an effect b = .5. In the end, the total increase in job performance *Y* due to the high performance reward system *X* is only .25 because the initial increase of .5 in motivation *M* is multiplied by .5 when transmitted to *Y*. The crucial idea is that increasing *X* changes *M* by some amount a (e.g., .5), and this change is then weighted by the amount of change that *M* causes in *Y* b (i.e., .5), resulting in the indirect effect $a \times b$.

Figure 20.1C shows a direct and indirect effect model, incorporating a *direct* path from *X* to *Y*, denoted as c' and an *indirect* path through *M* $a \times b$. In models like this, *M* does not completely explain why or how *X* causes *Y*. Instead, *X* still remains a direct cause of *Y* after accounting for the mediator *M* (or at least other possible mediators that would account for this direct effect are unmeasured). This kind of model is sometimes called "partial mediation" because the total effect includes a direct and indirect effect (i.e., after accounting for *M*, an effect of *X* on *Y* remains).

Common approaches to testing indirect effects in process models

When using data to test process models, researchers estimate the indirect effects that represent the process by which *X* affects *Y*. As described earlier in the simple process models, this indirect effect is the product of the parameters a and b in Figures 20.1B and 20.1C. Therefore, the null hypothesis in process models is that the indirect effect of *X* on *Y* through *M* is zero, or $a \times b = 0$. Testing this hypothesis has generated substantial debate. Historically, the three most common approaches to this test are the *causal steps* approach (Baron & Kenny, 1986;

Judd & Kenny, 1981), the *Sobel* test (Sobel, 1982), and resampling techniques known as *bootstrapping* (Bollen & Stine, 1990; Lockwood & MacKinnon, 1998) although Bayes, Monte Carlo, and partial posterior *p*-value approaches are also possible but are far less common (see Biesanz, Falk, & Savalei, 2010; Preacher & Selig, 2012).

The causal steps method marked the beginning of widespread tests for mediation (owing to Baron & Kenny, 1986; Judd & Kenny, 1981). However, we do not cover this approach due to space constraints and because this approach suffers from multiple problems that more recent approaches overcome (see Fritz, Cox, & MacKinnon, 2015; MacKinnon, Lockwood, Hoffman, West, & Sheets, 2002). The same is true of the Sobel test, which various authors have recommended avoiding because of its poor performance (see Hayes, 2009; Hayes & Scharkow, 2013).

Instead of these approaches, a better performing and today the most common approach to testing indirect effects in process models relies on a resampling method known as the bootstrap. Bootstrapping works by treating an observed sample of N units as if it were a population, sampling with replacement N units to estimate an indirect effect. Then, this process is typically repeated 10,000 times to estimate the sampling distribution of the product $a \times b$ (Hayes, 2009, recommends at least 5,000). This method is useful because it is non-parametric, which is to say it does not make *a priori* assumptions about the distribution of $a \times b$. The result is an accurate sampling distribution and a statistically powerful method for detecting indirect effects. Furthermore, the greater power of the bootstrap increases as sample sizes decrease (Mallinckrodt, Abraham, Wei, & Russell, 2006).

Using the bootstrapped sampling distribution of the product $a \times b$, tests of mediation or indirect effects are typically conducted by constructing a confidence interval (CI) and rejecting the null hypothesis $a \times b = 0$ when the CI does not contain zero. The estimation of such CIs can rely on two competing approaches – the percentile-based bootstrap CI and the bias-corrected bootstrap CI. The percentile bootstrap arranges all estimates of the indirect effect $a \times b$ from the bootstrapping procedure, arranged from smallest to largest. The CI is then constructed using the middle 95% of scores to represent the 95% CI (although CIs of any width can be estimated by retaining the desired middle percentage of $a \times b$ estimates). However, as Efron and Tibshirani cautioned (1993), the bootstrapped sampling distribution is not normally distributed, and therefore CIs estimated from this distribution will be biased, which can be corrected. The bias-corrected bootstrap CI adjusts for this non-normal distribution.

A simulation study by MacKinnon et al. (2004) compared several resampling methods, including the percentile bootstrap and bias-corrected percentile bootstrap. The bias-corrected bootstrap had the greatest statistical power to detect true effects, although it was also prone to type I errors. The CI bootstrap procedure was found to have relatively high power levels but lower Type-I error rates compared to the bias-corrected bootstrap. These results are supported by both Hayes (2013) and Zhang (2014), who found that bootstrapped CIs performed better than non-bootstrapped procedures and that the bias-corrected bootstrap is the most outright powerful test for indirect effects. However the percentile bootstrap CI represents a strong balance between statistical power and type I error; Biesanz et al. (2010) agree with using the percentile-based bootstrap over the bias-corrected bootstrap on various grounds.

In sum, the percentile bootstrap CIs and bias-corrected bootstrap CIs are the most commonly used and recommended methods for testing indirect effects (Hayes, 2009, 2013). In comparisons of their performance for testing indirect effects in process models, authors often recommend using the percentile-based bootstrap as a favorable compromise between statistical power and type I error rate. However, studies with particularly low statistical power (i.e., where sample sizes are small or effect sizes are expected to be small) may favor the use of the bias-corrected bootstrap CIs, whereas the more balanced percentile-based bootstrap is likely sufficient and desirable for more adequately powered studies. In practice, bootstrapping indirect effects is available in most contemporary statistical packages that can undertake structural equation modeling (SEM) for estimating process models, including AMOS, SAS, Stata, SPSS, LISREL, R, and M*plus*. SPSS users can also download the PROCESS package by Hayes (2013), which can analyze certain process models using the SPSS graphical user interface.

Extended process models

Both of the process models in Figures 20.1B and 20.1C incorporate only one mediating variable. Process models can be easily extended, however, to incorporate multiple mediators. Some illustrative examples of extended process models (also known as multiple mediation models) are shown in Figures 20.2A–20.2C. Figure 20.2B depicts a process model that incorporates two mediators, M_1 and M_2, which transmit in parallel the effect of X onto Y. A researcher who specifies a model like this proposes that X has an *indirect effect* on Y *through both mediators* M_1 and M_2. Thus, there are two *specific indirect effects* to estimate, namely $X \rightarrow M_1 \rightarrow Y$ (i.e., $a \times b$) and $X \rightarrow M_2 \rightarrow Y$ (i.e., $c \times d$). The bootstrapping method can be used to estimate each of these effects in order to establish CIs around the estimates (Preacher & Hayes, 2008). In specifying models like this, researchers may be interested in evaluating each indirect effect separately or jointly, either estimating two specific indirect effects (e.g., $a \times b$ and $c \times d$) or a single *total indirect effect* (e.g., $a \times b + c \times d$) to determine either the unique indirect effects or the total indirect effect of X on Y. Also, as with the simpler models in Figures 20.1B and 20.1C, parallel process models can include a direct path from X to Y based on the theorized effect of X on Y and tested using typical SEs and/or model fit indices in an SEM. This "optional" path is shown in gray in Figure 20.2A.

Figure 20.2B depicts a process model that incorporates two mediators that transmit, in sequence, the effect of X on Y. That is, in specifying this model, a researcher proposes that X affects M_1, which then in turn affects M_2, which then in turn affects Y. In other words, X ultimately affects Y through its effects

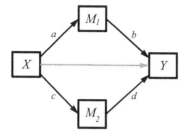

Figure 20.2A Parallel process model

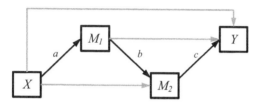

Figure 20.2B Serial process model

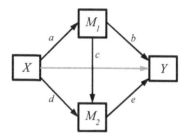

Figure 20.2C Hybrid process model

on M_1, through M_1's effect on M_2, and through M_2's effect on Y. In this model, the indirect effect of X on Y is equal to the product of the three paths, that is $a \times b \times c$, and CIs for this effect can be estimated using the bootstrapping method described earlier. Note that there are also two other indirect effects in this model that can also be estimated, namely $X{\rightarrow}M_1{\rightarrow}M_2$ (i.e., $a \times b$) and $M_1{\rightarrow}M_2{\rightarrow}Y$ ($b \times c$). Again, depending on the researcher's theoretical perspective, direct paths from X to Y, X to M_2 and M_1 to Y might also be included (these "optional" paths are shown in gray in Figure 20.2B).

Finally, Figure 20.2C depicts a model incorporating two mediators that operate in parallel and in a sequence. A researcher specifying this model proposes that X affects M_1 (i.e., the path denoted by a) and M_2 directly (path d), but also that X affects M_2 indirectly through M_1 ($a \times c$). In turn, this model operationalizes three mechanisms by which X affects Y: $X{\rightarrow}M_1{\rightarrow}Y$ ($a \times b$); $X{\rightarrow}M_2{\rightarrow}Y$ ($d \times e$);

and $X{\rightarrow}M_1{\rightarrow}M_2{\rightarrow}Y$ ($a \times c \times e$). Each of these specific indirect effects can be evaluated separately, *and* the total indirect effect can be evaluated using the bootstrap method described earlier. Again, researchers may wish to consider including a direct path from X to Y.

Note that, in principle, all of the process models mentioned can be extended indefinitely to incorporate any number of mediators that operate in parallel, in sequence, or both. Further, process models can be extended to incorporate multiple independent variables and outcomes with the principles of estimating and statistically evaluating the indirect effects remaining unchanged. However, even extended process models are not able to fully describe all possible intervening variable relationships, leading to the addition of conditional (or moderating) relationships as represented in conditional process models.

Conditional models

In addition to understanding the mechanisms that tie an independent variable X to an outcome Y, researchers are also often interested in understanding the *conditions* under which a relationship between X and Y is present vs. absent, positive vs. negative, or strong vs. weak. To this end, researchers can specify conditional (or moderation) models. Conditional models propose that the strength (and perhaps direction) of a relation between two variables depends on the state of at least one "conditional" variable or moderator W. Such models are therefore concerned with addressing questions regarding *when*, for *whom*, or *where* X causes Y.

Figure 20.3A shows a diagram of a basic conditional model whereby the relationship of X and Y is conditional on the state of a third variable, W (often called a "moderator"). The path from W ends at the path from X to Y to depict W influencing the causal effect of X on Y (i.e., *W changes the effect* of X on Y). Much has already been written about testing moderation hypotheses, and thus we refer interested readers to this work, such as Cohen, Cohen, West, and Aiken's (2003) classic text on multiple regression analysis. Here, we simply summarize procedures for testing conditional hypotheses in process models involving indirect effects.

Importantly, we note that it is not sufficient for a researcher to merely propose that W moderates the relation of X with Y; the researcher must also be clear about the nature of the conditional effect that is expected. For example, a researcher might hypothesize that when or where there are high levels of W,

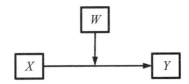

Figure 20.3A Simple conditional model

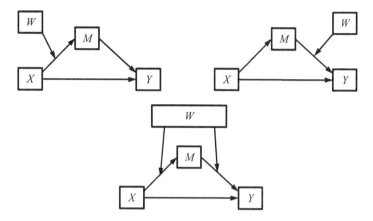

Figure 20.3B Three simple conditional process models

the effect of X on Y will be amplified. Alternatively, high or low levels of W might be hypothesized to alleviate, eliminate, or reverse an effect of X on Y (Dawson, 2014).

In order to test a conditional hypothesis, the researcher must establish two things. First, they must ascertain whether there is statistical evidence of a conditional effect (see Cohen et al., 2003). Second, if there is evidence of a conditional effect (i.e., an interaction), they must examine whether the *form* of the interaction is consistent with what was hypothesized. Again, readers are referred to Cohen et al. (2003) for advice, but the basic principle is that researchers should examine (perhaps via visual plots) the relation of X and Y after fixing the value of W to a meaningful low versus high number (researchers often choose one standard deviation below the mean for convenience, but it is preferable to select a meaningful value). This procedure is often called inspecting the "simple slopes" of X on Y at different levels of W. To generate these simple slope plots, we encourage readers to consult the useful set of downloadable Excel sheets developed by Jeremy Dawson (www.jeremydaw son.co.uk/slopes.htm).

Conditional process models

Process models and conditional models can be combined to form what are now often termed conditional process models (Hayes & Preacher, 2013) or models integrating mediation and moderation (Holland, Shore, & Cortina, 2016). In general terms, a conditional process model is one that incorporates causal mechanisms that tie an independent variable X to an outcome Y and where at least one of the mediating mechanisms involving M is conditional on the state of a moderator variable W. In other words, conditional process models propose that the presence, size, or direction of *at least one indirect effect* depends on the state of a moderator (Edwards & Lambert, 2007). Three simple examples of conditional process models are depicted in Figure 20.3B. These models all involve one mediator (M) that is hypothesized to partially explain why or how X causes Y, and each model incorporates one moderator variable W that moderates the effect of X on M, the effect of M on Y, or both effects.

Note that, though not depicted in Figure 20.3B, a researcher might hypothesize that W moderates the effect of X on Y. Thus, in the simplest case involving just four variables, X, Y, M, and W, there are six possible conditional process models that a researcher could specify. Further, like the process models described earlier, conditional process models can also be extended to incorporate additional mediators, additional moderators, additional independent variables, additional outcomes and higher order moderation effects (i.e., moderators of moderating relations). It is easy to appreciate that these models can become very complex even with relatively few variables (Hayes & Preacher, 2013).

Research into conditional process models in the organizational sciences was no doubt heavily influenced by the publication of Edwards and Lambert's (2007) review, along with their analytical recommendations. Other authors (e.g., Hayes & Preacher, 2013; Preacher, Rucker, & Hayes, 2007) have since offered supplementary advice on the analyses of conditional process models using contemporary statistical software. As space prohibits a comprehensive account of the appropriate analyses of conditional process models, we encourage researchers to refer to these useful resources. Here, we explain the general principles that govern conditional process hypothesis testing.

Appropriate conditional process hypothesis testing is essentially a hybrid of conditional hypothesis testing and process hypothesis testing. Recall that a conditional process model proposes that the size and perhaps direction of an indirect effect is contingent on the state of a moderator variable. Thus, in principle, the test of the conditional process hypothesis involves fixing the moderator to a meaningful high value and undertaking a test of the proposed indirect effect at that level, and then fixing the moderator to a meaningful low value and undertaking a test of the proposed indirect effect at that level. This procedure should be undertaken for all proposed conditional processes in the model. Researchers should report the indirect effects at both the high and low values of the moderator, along with CIs from a bootstrapping procedure (Holland et al., 2016). *Mplus* users may wish to refer to Hayes and Preacher (2013) for practical advice and example syntax.

Further methodological and analytical considerations

Researchers of any type of process models must always consider that these models, at their core, assume that the proposed relationships are causal. This may seem obvious, but it has significant implications for the planning, design, and implementation of research on causal processes. Antonakis, Bendahan, Jacquart, and Lalive (2010) explained that social and applied science literature has often failed to satisfy the assumptions that permit causal interpretations, and in doing so, yielded results that are likely to be meaningless.

In order for a *causal* relationship between X and Y to be inferred, it must satisfy the following three criteria; (a) X must precede Y temporally, (b) X must reliably correlate with Y, and (c) the relationship between X and Y must not be explained by other causes (Kenny, 1979). Statistics packages *allow* researchers to evaluate process models using data collected from cross-sectional research designs (e.g., where a sample of people completes a survey). However, cross-sectional designs must assume that condition (a) is satisfied. Longitudinal research, which can model variables over multiple time points to establish temporal order of effects, is relatively scant within the social and applied sciences. To further this point, Antonakis et al. (2010) described how the issue of reverse causality, or simultaneity, is often overlooked in social scientific research and requires more longitudinal research in order to clarify for any particular set of relationships (see also Chapter 13 in this text for a detailed discussion about longitudinal data collection; Dormann & Guthier, 2018). Authors such as MacKinnon, Fairchild, and Fritz (2007) and Preacher (2015) have addressed statistical methods for strengthening the assumption that X precedes Y in great detail. Cross-lagged data collected over three or more time points is a straightforward, although time and resource intensive, method for establishing temporal relationships. Half-longitudinal and latent longitudinal designs are also possible for data containing two time points. While clearly less desirable than true longitudinal data (i.e., with three or more observations over time) these half-longitudinal methods present stronger support for temporal ordering than standard cross-sectional research and therefore should be more widely adopted.

In relation to assumption (c), the omission of variables that are causes of *any* mediators in a process model *or* the outcome variable can also potentially bias the parameter estimates observed and hence the estimates of the indirect effect, to the point where any parameter estimate is essentially meaningless (Antonakis et al., 2010). Fiedler, Schott, and Meiser (2011) described a range of situations where this assumption is likely breached in field research, and therefore the casual assumption of mediation analysis jeopardized. As such, the role of strong and well-reasoned theorizing about included and excluded variables is emphasized. Indeed, the issue of causality can perhaps only be resolved through strong research design rather than through data analysis, as was discussed in detail in Chapter 2 in this text (Brough & Hawkes, 2018).

Conclusion

In summary, process and conditional process models are useful and widely used. Taking these approaches requires bootstrapping procedures are used regardless of whether a simple process model or a more advanced extended conditional process model is estimated. Researchers using these methods must also assure that issues of causality in these models are taken seriously by demonstrating causal relationships rather than simply assuming these exist.

References

Antonakis, J., Bendahan, S., Jacquart, P., & Lalive, R. (2010). On making causal claims: A review and recommendations. *The Leadership Quarterly, 21*, 1086–1120.

Baron, R. M., & Kenny, D. A. (1986). The moderator-mediator variable distinction in social psychological research: Conceptual, strategic, and statistical considerations. *Journal of Personality and Social Psychology, 51*, 1173–1182.

Biesanz, J. C., Falk, C. F., & Savalei, V. (2010). Assessing mediational models: Testing and interval estimation for indirect effects. *Multivariate Behavioral Research, 45*(4), 661–701.

Bollen, K. A., & Stine, R. (1990). Direct and indirect effects: Classical and bootstrap estimates of variability. *Sociological Methodology, 20*, 115–140.

Brough, P., & Hawkes, A. (2018). Designing impactful research. In P. Brough & S. Occhipinti (Eds.), *Advanced research methods for applied psychology: Design, analysis and reporting.* London, UK: Taylor & Francis.

Cohen, J., Cohen, P., West, S. G., & Aiken, L. S. (2003). *Applied multiple regression/correlation analysis for the behavioral sciences* (3rd ed.). Mahwah, NJ: Lawrence Erlbaum.

Dawson, J. F. (2014). Moderation in management research: What, why, when, and how. *Journal of Business and Psychology, 29*, 1–19. doi:10.1007/s10869-013-9308-7

Dormann, C., & Guthier, C. (2018). Longitudinal data collection. In P. Brough & S. Occhipinti (Eds.), *Advanced research methods for applied psychology: Design, analysis and reporting.* London, UK: Taylor & Francis.

Edwards, J. R., & Lambert, L. S. (2007). Methods for integrating moderation and mediation: A general analytical framework using moderated path analysis. *Psychological methods, 12*(1), 1.

Efron, B., & Tibshirani, R. J. (1993). *An introduction to the bootstrap.* New York, NY: Chapman & Hall.

Fiedler, K., Schott, M., & Meiser, T. (2011). What mediation analysis can (not) do. *Journal of Experimental Social Psychology, 47*, 1231–1236.

Fritz, M. S., Cox, M. G., & MacKinnon, D. P. (2015). Increasing statistical power in mediation models without increasing sample size. *Evaluation and the Health Professions, 38*, 343–66.

Hayes, A. F. (2009). Beyond Baron and Kenny: Statistical mediation analysis in the new millennium. *Communication Monographs, 76*, 408–420.

Hayes, A. F. (2013). *Introduction to mediation, moderation, and conditional process analysis.* New York, NY: Guildford Press.

Hayes, A. F., & Preacher, K. J. (2013). Conditional process modeling: Using structural equation modeling to examine contingent causal processes. In G. R. Hancock & R. O. Mueller (Eds.), *Structural equation modeling: A second course* (2nd ed.). Greenwich, CT: Information Age Publishing.

Hayes, A. F., & Scharkow, M. (2013). The relative trustworthiness of inferential tests of the indirect effect in statistical mediation analysis does method really matter? *Psychological Science, 24*, 1918–1927.

Holland, S. J., Shore, D. B., & Cortina, J. M. (2016). Review and recommendations for integrating mediation and moderation. *Organizational Research Methods, 20*(4), 686–720. doi:10.1177/1094428116658958

Judd, C. M., & Kenny, D. A. (1981). Process analysis estimating mediation in treatment evaluations. *Evaluation Review, 5*, 602–619.

Kenny, D. A. (1979). *Correlation and causality.* New York, NY: Wiley-Interscience.

Lockwood, C. M., & MacKinnon, D. P. (1998). Bootstrapping the standard error of the mediated effect. In *Proceedings of the Twenty-third Annual SAS Users Group International Conference* (pp. 997–1002). Cary, NC: SAS Institute.

MacKinnon, D. P., Lockwood, C. M., & Williams, J. (2004). Confidence limits for the indirect effect: Distribution of the product and resampling methods. *Multivariate Behavioral Research*, *39*, 99–128.

MacKinnon, D. P., Lockwood, C. M., Hoffman, J. M., West, S. G., & Sheets, V. (2002). A comparison of methods to test mediation and other intervening variable effects. *Psychological Methods*, *7*(1), 83.

MacKinnon, D. P., Fairchild, A. J., & Fritz, M. S. (2007). Mediation analysis. *Annual Review of Psychology*, *58*, 593.

Mallinckrodt, B., Abraham, W. T., Wei, M., & Russell, D. W. (2006). Advances in testing the statistical significance of mediation effects. *Journal of Counseling Psychology*, *53*, 372.

Preacher, K. J. (2015). Advances in mediation analysis: A survey and synthesis of new developments. *Annual Review of Psychology*, *66*, 825–852.

Preacher, K. J., & Hayes, A. F. (2008). Asymptotic and resampling strategies for assessing and comparing indirect effects in multiple mediator models. *Behavior Research Methods*, *40*, 879–891.

Preacher, K. J., Rucker, D. D., & Hayes, A. F. (2007). Addressing moderated mediation hypotheses: Theory, methods, and prescriptions. *Multivariate Behavioral Research*, *42*(1), 185–227.

Preacher, K. J., & Selig, J. P. (2012). Advantages of Monte Carlo confidence intervals for indirect effects. *Communication Methods and Measures*, *6*(2), 77–98.

Rucker, D. D., Preacher, K. J., Tormala, Z. L., & Petty, R. E. (2011). Mediation analysis in social psychology: Current practices and new recommendations. *Social and Personality Psychology Compass*, *5*, 359–371.

Schmidt, F. L., & Hunter, J. E. (1998). The validity and utility of selection methods in personnel psychology: Practical and theoretical implications of 85 years of research findings. *Psychological Bulletin*, *124*, 262–274.

Sobel, M. E. (1982). Asymptotic confidence intervals for indirect effects in structural equation models. *Sociological Methodology*, *13*, 290–312.

Zhang, Z. (2014). Monte Carlo based statistical power analysis for mediation models: Methods and software. *Behavior Research Methods*, *46*, 1184–1198.

21 Structural equation modelling

Yanyun Yang

Overview

Structural equation modelling (SEM) is a flexible statistical approach and encompasses a variety of interrelated techniques including but not limited to path analysis, confirmatory factor analysis, structural regression model, longitudinal growth curve model, multiple-sample SEM, and multilevel SEM. In conjunction with advances in computing capacity and the advent of free-access and commercial software, SEM has become increasingly popular in psychological research for testing *a priori* hypotheses among observed or latent variables. Appropriately or not, SEM may also be called covariance structure modelling, covariance structure analysis, causal modelling, or LISREL modelling. Many widely used statistical techniques such as multiple regression, ANOVA, and MANOVA can be viewed as special cases of SEM. In this chapter, I briefly introduce SEM by constructing and fitting an example model, emphasize the assumptions and basic principles of SEM, discuss some current issues in SEM, and conclude with a very brief overview of some other structural equation models that have been used in psychological research. I assume that readers are familiar with path analysis, measurement theory, factor analysis, and basic concepts and principles of SEM. Kline (2016) is an exemplary nontechnical introductory textbook for applied researchers who are new to SEM.

An introduction to SEM: an example model

A postgraduate researcher majoring in psychology is interested in investigating the relationship between the perception of stressful situations and the use of a problem-solving coping strategy among college students. The researcher hypothesizes that when individuals perceive stressful situations during their daily lives, they tend to take actions to actively cope with the stress. However, such a relationship is mediated by a stress-related personality trait: resilience. Specifically, stress would activate individuals' trait resilience, buffer the effect of stress, and promote individuals' motivation to cope (Siegel, 1999). To test this hypothesis, the researcher selects well-known scales for measuring three latent constructs: *perceived stress*, *trait resilience*, and *coping*. Each scale contains three sub-scales, and the sub-scale scores are used as measurement indicators of latent constructs. The hypothesized model of associations among these variables is visualized by a path diagram in Figure 21.1. Although not shown, the hypothesized model can also be expressed using a set of regression equations or in matrix form (cf. Bollen, 1989).

Measurement indicators are represented in rectangles; latent variables are represented in ovals. The hypothesized directional relationships among variables are indicated by single-headed arrows. The variance and covariance of variables are indicated by double-headed curves. Excluding the mean structure from the analysis, this model has 20 parameters, denoted by Greek letters: six loading parameters $(\lambda_{s2}, \ldots, \lambda_{c3})$, nine variances of measurement errors $(\psi_{s1}, \ldots, \psi_{c3})$, two path coefficients connecting latent factors (β_{rs}, β_{cr}), one variance of exogenous factor (ϕ_s), and two variances of disturbances associated with the endogenous factors (φ_r, φ_c). A model should be identified in order to be testable. In an identified model, each of the parameters (i.e., 20 in this example) has a unique solution that is a function of variance and covariance among measurement indicators. According to common heuristic rules, this model is identified: (1) all latent variables are given a scale (unit loading identification in this example); (2) the model degrees of freedom are equal to or greater than zero, that is, *df* ≥ 0; (3) three latent factors are related and each latent factor is measured by at least two indicators; and (4) the hypothesized relationships among latent factors are recursive. These rules are necessary requirements for a structural regression model to be identified. An under-identified model is not testable. *Model under-identification* may occur mathematically or empirically. A model is mathematically under-identified if *df* < 0. Empirical under-identification is typically caused by particular characteristics of the data (e.g., a nearly perfect correlation between two variables). See Green and Yang (in press) and Kenny and Milan (2012) for nontechnical discussions and illustrations of model identification issues in SEM.

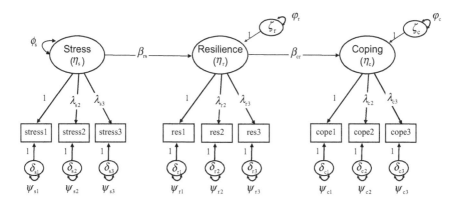

Figure 21.1 Hypothesized relationships among stress, resilience, and coping

Table 21.1 Covariance matrix for the nine measurement indicators

	stress1	stress2	stress3	res1	res2	res3	cope1	cope2	cope3
stress1	1.658								
stress2	.966	3.455							
stress3	.864	1.533	5.400						
res1	−.075	−.261	−.278	4.198					
res2	−.074	−.275	−.170	1.085	1.893				
res3	−.175	−.244	−.434	.713	.401	1.330			
cope1	.327	.175	.389	.968	.427	.0146	4.158		
cope2	−.004	−.044	−.005	.710	.352	.278	.896	1.772	
cope3	.194	−.019	−.018	.822	.287	.266	.818	.736	1.985

The researcher has collected data from 300 college students. The covariance matrix for the nine measurement indicators is shown in Table 21.1. The researcher fitted the hypothesized model to the sample data using maximum likelihood (ML) estimation method using the M*plus* 8 software (Muthén & Muthén, 1998–2017). The obtained results produced a chi-square statistic of $\chi^2 = 28.36$, $df = 25$, $p > .05$, CFI = .989, TLI = .985, RMSEA = .021, and SRMR = .045, indicating an adequate model-data fit based on the cutoff values suggested by Hu and Bentler (1999). The standardized parameter estimates are shown in Figure 21.2. The standardized path coefficients from *stress* to *resilience* and from *resilience* to *coping* were −.16 ($p < .05$) and .57 ($p < .05$), respectively. The indirect effect from *stress* to *coping* through *resilience* and its confidence intervals was approximated using biased-corrected bootstrap method with 1,000 bootstrap samples. The estimate was −.12 with 95% C.I. of [−.366, .048]. The researcher concluded that the hypothesized mediational relationship is not supported by the data.

The step procedure described here is quite typical to applied researchers: construct the model based on research hypotheses; determine that the model is identified; select good measurement instruments; collect data from either a convenience sample (more often than not) or through a simple random sampling procedure (preferred); analyze the model (often the default estimation method ML) using an available SEM software; evaluate the model-data fit; and interpret the parameter estimates if the model fits the data well; otherwise, revise the model until an adequate fit is reached (e.g., by examining the modification indices). This step procedure is well laid out in introductory SEM textbooks (e.g., Kline, 2016) and is not the focus of this chapter. Instead, I use this example model as a context to discuss three key issues in SEM. These three issues by no means exhaust all important issues in SEM, but they are the common issues which post-graduate students especially have identified as requiring clarification. I rephrase the three issues in the following three questions: Is ML appropriate for my SEM analysis? Can I still use the conventional cutoffs of CFI, TLI, RMSEA, etc. to evaluate my model if I use estimation methods other than ML? The number of individual items is large, but my sample size is not large enough

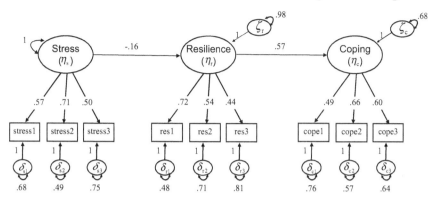

Figure 21.2 Standardized parameter estimates for the example model

to include all individual items in the analysis; may I aggregate item scores for each subscale and use the aggregated scores in the SEM analysis? Next I provide a brief summarization of current literature in these areas.

Estimation methods in SEM

Once a model is determined to be identified and sample data are collected, an estimation method should be chosen to analyze the hypothesized model. Maximum likelihood (ML) estimation method is by far the most frequently used method in SEM and is the default option in SEM software including EQS, M*plus*, AMOS, SAS Proc Calis, LISREL, and lavaan in R. ML is a *normal-theory estimator*; its statistical properties are well known and its empirical performance in SEM is well studied. ML is an iterative procedure searching for the estimates of model parameters such that the likelihood of obtaining the given data is maximized and the discrepancy between the observed covariance matrix and the model-reproduced covariance matrix is minimized (Bollen, 1989; Enders, 2010). The minimization of the discrepancy is quantified by fit function F_{ML}. For a given sample size n, $T = (n - 1) \times F_{ML}$. The T statistic is used to test $H_0 : \Sigma = \hat{\Sigma}$. Failure to reject the H_0 indicates a good model-data fit.

ML relies on distributional and structural assumptions. First, data are continuous and follow multivariate normal distribution in the population. Second, the hypothesized model is consistent with the true model in the population. When these assumptions are met, the sample T statistic follows asymptotically a central chi-square distribution: $T \sim \chi^2$ (*df*, 2*df*). SEM software prints the T statistic as a chi-square statistic. However, both of these assumptions are rarely met in reality. Data collected from psychological and achievement measures tend to demonstrate various degrees of asymmetry (Micceri, 1989). It is also not uncommon in SEM applications that ordinal variables (e.g., Likert-type scale data) are treated as continuous when the number of response categories is large (e.g., ≥ 5; cf. Finney & Distefano, 2013). In addition, the true model is unknown in reality, and the hypothesized model might be faulty. Extensive studies (e.g., Bollen, 1989; Chou, Bentler, & Satorra, 1991; Curran, West, & Finch, 1996) have shown that applying ML to multivariate non-normal data results in biased estimates of model parameters, standard errors, and model chi-square statistic. Consequently, all fit indices that are chi-square-based (e.g., CFI, TLI, RMSEA) are inaccurate. Next I provide a review of alternative estimation methods that do not require multivariate normality assumption.

Robust maximum likelihood

One alternative to ML is robust ML (Satorra & Bentler, 1994). This method yields parameter estimates that are identical to those from ML. However, the model chi-square statistic and standard errors of parameter estimates are adjusted by a scaling factor, which is a function of multivariate kurtosis and model complexity (Satorra & Bentler, 1994). Bentler (2006) suggested that multivariate kurtosis "larger than 3 provide evidence of nontrivial positive kurtosis, though modelling statistics may not be affected until values are 5, 6, or beyond" (p. 106). But robust ML may perform worse than ML when the sample size is small (Yang & Liang, 2013).

Weighted least squares

The second alternative to ML is weighted least squares (WLS), also known as asymptotically distribution free (ADF) estimator (Browne, 1984; Muthén, 1984). The WLS fit function contains a weight matrix, which is a consistent estimator of the asymptotic covariance matrix of the variance and covariance among the observed variables. WLS involves an inversion of the entire weight matrix to obtain model parameter estimates. Thus, WLS estimation is computationally demanding, the model is complex (e.g., Curran et al., 1996; Muthén & Kaplan, 1992; Olsson, Foss, Troye, & Howell, 2000). This estimation method is not recommended unless the sample size involved in the analysis is very large, even when the data are multivariate normal (e.g., Curran et al., 1996; Hu, Bentler, & Kano, 1992).

Diagonally weighted least squares and unweighted least squares

Diagonally weighted least squares (DWLS; Christoffersson, 1977; Muthén, du Toit, & Spisic, 1997) and unweighted least squares (ULS; Muthén et al., 1997) can be used for ordinal data. In psychological research based on survey or questionnaire, data collected from participants are often ordinal, so these two estimators and the accompanying issues have received much attention within the SEM literature. DWLS and ULS analyze thresholds and polychoric correlations (or tetrachoric correlations for dichotomous data). Both estimators adopt *underlying normal variable assumption* (Raykov & Marcoulides, 2015) by assuming that a continuous, normally distributed variable underlies the ordinal variable. This is a restrictive assumption; it is not testable for a single ordinal variable but may be implied through testing a higher dimensional normality such as bivariate normality (see Jöreskog, 2005; Muthén & Hofacker, 1988; Raykov & Marcoulides, 2008; Raykov & Marcoulides, 2015).

Nevertheless, two steps are taken for analyzing models with ordinal variables (e.g., Jöreskog & Sörbom, 1996; Muthén & Muthén, 1998–2017). The first step is to estimate thresholds and polychoric correlations based on the observed contingency table. The most frequently used method for estimating thresholds and polychoric correlations is ML (Olsson, 1979). This method is currently implemented in *Mplus* and lavaan and works reasonably well when the sample size is sufficiently large and the probability of obtaining any response pattern between any pair of ordinal variables is not too small (Olsson, 1979; Savalei, 2011). Some authors have recommended using Bayesian methods to estimate polychoric correlations, especially for analysis with small sample size (e.g., Choi, Kim, Chen, & Dannels, 2011), and have developed a stand-alone program for this purpose (Choi, Chen, & Kim, 2009). In the second step, the estimated thresholds and polychoric correlations are analyzed by using DWLS or ULS. Because DWLS and ULS use zeros in off-diagonal elements in the weight matrix, they are less computationally demanding. However, the resulting chi-square statistic deviates asymptotically from the target chi-square distribution. Therefore, robust corrections are needed to adjust chi-square statistic (Muthén, du Toit, & Spisic, 1997). In *Mplus* and lavaan in R, DWLS is implemented as WLSMV if both the mean and variance of the chi-square statistic is adjusted, and WLSM if only the mean of the chi-square statistic is adjusted. Similarly, the ULS estimator is implemented as ULSMV due to the robust correction on both the mean and variance of the chi-square statistic. Both estimators work reasonably well in terms of parameter estimation under the conditions that thresholds and polychoric correlations are accurately estimated.

Evaluation of model-data fit

As an essential step in SEM analysis, issues surrounding model-data fit evaluation have received much attention. Parameter estimates would not be interpreted if the model does not fit adequately to the data. In addition to the chi-square statistic, several fit indices have been proposed. Each index reflects a unique aspect of model-data misfit. No single specific index exists that works for all models (Hu & Bentler, 1999; Marsh, Hau, & Wen, 2004). However, applied researchers often determine "adequate fit" based on conventional cutoff values of fit indices and use these cutoffs universally. The most influential article regarding cutoff values of fit indices is undoubtedly Hu and Bentler (1999). The search for a "Hu and Bentler (1999)" article in the Google Scholar engine resulted in 45,000 citations in December 2017. Through a simulation study, Hu and Bentler examined type I error rates and power of various fit indices and suggested a set of cutoff values. Although the simulation study contains a large number of conditions, only continuous data with ML estimator was considered, and the only population models manipulated in the study were confirmatory factor analysis models with 15 items. Hu and Bentler (1999) warned that these suggested cutoff values may not work well under conditions other than those examined in their study. Xia (2016) and Xia and Yang (2018) showed that at the population level, DWLS, ULS, and ML do not result in the same values of RMSEA, CFI, and TLI when the same datasets are fitted to the same model. Other simulation studies (e.g., DiStefano & Morgan, 2014; Garrido, Abad, & Ponsoda, 2015; Yang & Xia, 2015; Yu, 2002) have also shown that no universal cutoff values work across all conditions for DWLS. Nevertheless, these methodological and empirical evaluation studies do not seem to discourage the use of conventional cutoff values for the fit indices. Interested readers may also want to review a special issue in 2007 in the *Journal of Personality and Individual Difference* for an interesting debate on whether fit indices should or should not be used for model-data fit evaluation.

Aside from the debate on the issue of cutoff values for fit indices, methodologists have recently revisited the population definition of chi-square-based fit indices (RMSEA, CFI, and TLI) and their sample performance when the analysis model is mis-specified and when estimators other than ML are applied. When robust ML is used for non-normally distributed continuous data, the chi-square statistic is adjusted by a scaling factor. CFI, TLI, and RMSEA are correspondingly adjusted. These rescaled fit indices are reported in the current SEM software such as M*plus* and lavaan. However, both Brosseau-Liard, Savalei, and Li (2012) and Brosseau-Liard and Savalei (2014) found that when the model is mis-specified, the rescaled fit indices converge to different population values that are a function of non-normality of the data. They proposed non-normality correction versions of these fit indices and evaluated the performance of these correction indices in simulation studies. Their results showed that the corrected version of the fit indices performed reasonably well across different sample sizes, model types, and mis-specification types. Similarly, both Xia (2016) and Xia and Yang (in press) extended this logic to DWLS with ordinal data and produced comparable conclusions: chi-square-based fit indices converge to different population values that are a function of threshold values when the model is mis-specified. More methodological and evaluation studies as well as software implementation of new development are needed.

Use of item parcelling in SEM

Readers may have noticed that in the example model, subscale scores instead of individual item scores are used as measurement indicators of latent constructs. If the researcher had used individual items, it would have resulted in a very complex model, which posits a challenge for analyzing the model with the data collected from only 300 participants. The researcher would have also questioned the appropriateness of ML given that many individual items were anchored on a limited number of response categories (e.g., < 5). Mostly for practical reasons, in many SEM applications a subset of items is aggregated (most often by summing across item scores or computing an average) into a smaller number of parcels. The parcels are then used as measurement indicators of latent factors (e.g., Bagozzi & Edwards, 1998; Kishton & Widaman, 1994). Use of parcelling has triggered some philosophical debates, which is well articulated in Little, Cunningham, and Shahar (2002):

> From a conservative philosophy of science perspective, parceling is akin to "cheating" because modeled data should be as close to the response of the individual as possible in order to avoid the potential imposition, or arbitrary manufacturing, of a false structure. . . . From liberal philosophical perspective, measurement process is defined by the researchers; therefore, the level of aggregation used to represent the measurement process is a matter of choice and justification on the part of the investigator.
>
> (pp. 152–153)

Despite these debates, parcelling techniques have been widely used in empirical SEM studies. A review conducted by Bandalos and Finney (2001) found that about 20% of the empirical SEM studies used parcelling procedures; the percentage varied across journals ranging from 9% in the *Journal of Marketing Research* to 25% in *Applied Psychological Measurement* to 60% in the *Journal of Educational Measurement*. Compared to the item-level analysis, use of parcelling in SEM is appealing for three main reasons: it reduces model complexity, requires smaller sample sizes, and obviates non-normality issues (Little et al., 2002). If a researcher opts for the liberal philosophical perspective and decides to use parcels in SEM, then the researcher should also consider an appropriate technique to create parcels. Several parcelling techniques are available: random assignment, factorial algorithm, internal consistency approach, and domain representative approach (see Little et al., 2002). The former two are for unidimensional scales and the other two are for multidimensional scales. A key concern of using parcels is: does parcelling affect model-data fit evaluation and other parameter estimates in the model (e.g., path coefficients from *stress* to *resilience* and from *resilience* to *coping*)? A handful of studies have focused on this issue, mainly on confirmatory factor analysis models or structural regression model (e.g., Bandalos, 2008; Sass & Smith, 2006; Sterba, 2011).

Extension models in SEM

The example model I provided is a conventional structural regression model and can be viewed as a combination of path analysis and confirmatory factor analysis. In the past two decades, conventional SEM has been extended to include mean structure (e.g., ANOVA, MANOVA, longitudinal SEM), integrate with Bayesian approach (Bayesian SEM), accommodate multilevel data (multilevel SEM), and handle missing data, to name a few. I conclude this chapter with a very brief overview of SEM analysis with mean structure and Bayesian SEM and provide references for readers who want to pursue other issues further. Missing data analysis and multilevel analysis are covered in Chapter 16 and Chapter 22 in this book, respectively. For specific treatment of missing data analysis and multilevel SEM, see also Enders (2010), Heck and Thomas (2015), and Stapleton (2013).

SEM analysis with mean structure

Traditional ANOVA and MANOVA can be viewed as special types of SEM analysis with both covariance/correlation and mean structures. When conducting ANOVA or MANOVA within the SEM framework, means are specified as either equal (in the constrained model) or unequal (in the unconstrained model) across groups. The tenability of equal means across groups is determined based on likelihood ratio test and Wald statistics (Green & Thompson, 2006; Hancock, 2001; Hancock, Lawrence, & Nevitt, 2000; Yuan & Bentler, 2006). In the analysis, homogeneity of error variance or equal covariance matrix across groups is not assumed; instead, they can be tested because error variances and covariances are model parameters. SEM analysis should include both covariance and mean structures when testing longitudinal growth trajectory on latent constructs that are measured repeatedly over time. Linear, quadratic, and piece-wise growth trajectories are commonly seen in psychological research. Longitudinal growth modelling can also be used in treatment/control experimental settings (e.g., Little, 2013; Muthén & Curran, 1997). SEM analysis should also include both covariance/correlation and mean structures when comparing latent factor mean(s) across multiple groups through multiple-sample factor analysis. The step procedure for conducting multiple-sample factor analysis is well discussed in Millsap (2011).

Bayesian structural equation modelling

Bayesian structural equation modelling has increased in popularity in the last two decades (e.g., Asparouhov & Muthén, 2010; Lee, 2007). Bayesian SEM is based on Bayes' theorem, which states that the posterior distribution of model parameters is proportional to the product of the prior distribution of model parameters and data likelihood. Different from frequentist estimators, a Bayesian approach assumes that each model parameter is not a constant; instead, it follows a specific type of distribution. Users select prior distribution for model parameters which can range from informative to non-informative, depending on how confident the users understand the model parameters. Commonly, *posterior distribution* of model parameters are empirically approximated using Markov chain Monte Carlo (Gilks, Richardson, & Spiegelhalter, 1996) algorithms such as a Gibbs sampler (Geman & Geman, 1984). The central tendency of the posterior distribution (e.g., mean, mode, median) is then chosen as the parameter estimate. Bayesian SEM is appealing for not only its flexibility of handling complex models but also its satisfactory performance with small samples (e.g., Asparouhov & Muthén, 2010; Lu, Chow, & Loken, 2016).

Conclusion

SEM is a very flexible statistical framework to analyze *a priori* relationships among observed/latent variables. In conjunction with the advances of computer capacity and availability of SEM software, SEM will continue enjoying its popularity in psychological research, and new issues and methods will be emerged. In the context of the running example, I provide an introduction to the basic principles of SEM analysis, discuss three current issues including estimation methods, model-data fit evaluation, and use of parcelling, and provide a very brief overview of SEM analysis with mean structure and Bayesian SEM. I by no means have discussed all issues and techniques in SEM. Readers are strongly recommended to periodically check the recent development, debates, issues, and applications in SEM in journals such as *Educational and Psychology Measurement, Multivariate Behavioral Research, Organizational Research Methods, Psychological Methods*, and *Structural Equation Modeling*, to name a few.

References

Asparouhov, T., & Muthén, B. O. (2010). *Bayesian analysis using Mplus: Technical implementation*. Retrieved from www.statmodel.com/download/Bayes3.pdf

Bandalos, D. L. (2008). Is parceling really necessary? A comparison of results from item parceling and categorical variable methodology. *Structural Equation Modeling, 15*(2), 211–240.

Bandalos, D. L., & Finney, S. J. (2001). Item parceling issues in structural equation modeling. In G. A. Marcoulides & R. E. Schumacker (Eds.), *New developments and techniques in structural equation modeling* (pp. 269–293). Mahwah, NJ: Lawrence Erlbaum.

Bagozzi, R. P., & Edwards, J. R. (1998). A general approach for representing constructs in organizational research. *Organizational Research Methods, 1*(1), 45–87.

Bentler, P. M. (2006). *EQS 6 structural equations program manual*. Encino, CA: Multivaraite Software, Inc.

Bollen, K. A. (1989). *Structural equations with latent variables*. New York, NY: John Wiley & Sons.

Brosseau-Liard, P. E., & Savalei, V. (2014). Adjusting incremental fit indexes for nonnormality. *Multivariate Behavioral Research, 49*(5), 460–470.

Brosseau-Liard, P. E., Savalei, V., & Li, L. (2012). An investigation of the sample performance of two nonnormality corrections for RMSEA. *Multivariate Behavioral Research, 47*(6), 904–930.

Browne, M. W. (1984). Asymptotic distribution free methods in the analysis of covariance structures. *British Journal of Mathematical and Statistical Psychology, 37*(1), 62–83.

Choi, J., Kim, S., Chen, J., & Dannels, S. (2011). A comparison of maximum likelihood and Bayesian estimation for polychoric correlation using Monte Carlo simulation. *Journal of Educational and Behavioral Statistics, 36*(4), 523–549.

Choi, J., Chen, J., & Kim, S. (2009). *BayesPCC (v 3.0.0): A standalone Microsoft Windows software program for estimating polychoric correlation matrices using Bayesian estimation methods* [Computer software].

Chou, C. P., Bentler, P. M., & Satorra, A. (1991). Scaled test statistics and robust standard errors for non-normal data in covariance structure analysis: A Monte Carlo study. *British Journal of Mathematical and Statistical Psychology, 44*(2), 347–357.

Christoffersson, A. (1977). Two-step weighted least squares factor analysis of dichotomized variables. *Psychometrika, 42*, 433–438.

Curran, P. J., West, S. G., & Finch, J. F. (1996). The robustness of test statistics to nonnormality and specification error in confirmatory factor analysis. *Psychological Methods, 1*(1), 16–29.

DiStefano, C., & Morgan, G. B. (2014). A comparison of diagonal weighted least squares robust estimation techniques for ordinal data. *Structural Equation Modeling, 21*(3), 425–438.

Enders, C. K. (2010). *Applied missing data analysis*. New York, NY: Guilford Press.

Finney, S. J., & DiStefano, C. (2013). Nonnormal and categorical data in structural equation modeling. In G. R. Hancock & R. O. Mueller (Eds.), *A second course in structural equation modeling* (2nd ed., pp. 439–492). Charlotte, NC: Information Age Publishing.

Garrido, L. E., Abad, F. J., & Ponsoda, V. (2015). Are fit indexes really fit to estimate the number of factors with categorical variables? Some cautionary findings via Monte Carlo simulation. *Psychological Methods, 21*(1), 93–111.

Geman, S., & Geman, D. (1984). Stochastic relaxation, Gibbs distributions, and the Bayesian restoration of images. *IEE Transactions on Pattern Analysis and Machine Intelligence, PAMI-6*(6), 721–741.

Gilks, W. R., Richardson, S., & Spiegelhalter, D. J. (Eds.). (1996). *Markov chain Monte Carlo in practice*. London, UK: Chapman & Hall.

Green, S. B., & Thompson, M. S. (2006). Structural equation modeling for conducting tests of differences in multiple means. *Journal of Psychosomatic Medicine, 68*, 706–717.

Green, S. B., & Yang, Y. (in press). Empirical underidentification with the bifactor model: A case study. *Educational and Psychological Measurement*. doi:10.1177/0013164417719947

Hancock, G. R. (2001). Effect size, power, and sample size determination for structured means modeling and MIMIC approaches to between-groups hypothesis testing of means on a single latent construct. *Psychometrika, 66*, 373–388.

Hancock, G. R., Lawrence, F. R., & Nevitt, J. (2000). Type I error and power of latent mean methods and MANOVA in factorially invariant and noninvariant latent variable systems. *Structural Equation Modeling, 7*, 534–556.

Heck, R. H., & Thomas, S. L. (2015). *An introduction to multilevel modeling techniques: MLM and SEM approaches using Mplus* (3rd ed.). New York, NY: Routledge.

Hu, L., & Bentler, P. M. (1999). Cutoff criteria for fit indexes in covariance structure analysis: Conventional criteria versus new alternatives. *Structural Equation Modeling, 6*(1), 1–55.

Hu, L., Bentler, P. M., & Kano, Y. (1992). Can test statistics in covariance structural analysis be trusted? *Psychological Bulletin, 112*(2), 351–362.

Jöreskog, K. G. (2005). *Structural equation modeling with ordinal variables using LISREL*. Lincolnwood, IL: SSS Scientific Software International, Inc.

Jöreskog, K. G., & Sörbom, D. (1996). *LISREL 8: User's reference guide*. Lincolnwood, IL: SSS Scientific Software International, Inc.

Kenny, D. A., & Milan, S. (2012). Identification: A non-technical discussion of a technical issue. In R. Hoyle (Ed.), *Handbook of structural equation modeling* (pp. 145–163). New York, NY: Guilford Press.

Kishton, J. M., & Widaman, K. F. (1994). Unidimensional versus domain representative parceling of questionnaire items: An empirical example. *Educational and Psychological Measurement, 54*(3), 757–765.

Kline, R. B. (2016). *Principles and practice of structural equation modeling* (4th ed.). New York, NY: Guilford Press.

Lee, S-Y. (2007). *Structural equation modeling: A Bayesian approach*. London, UK: John Wiley & Sons.

Little, T. D. (2013). *Longitudinal structural equation modeling*. New York, NY: Guilford Press.

Little, T. D., Cunningham, W. A., & Shahar, G. (2002). To parcel or not to parcel: Exploring the question, weighing the merits. *Structural Equation Modeling, 9*(2), 151–173.

Lu, Z. H., Chow, S. M., & Loken, E. (2016). Bayesian factor analysis as a variable-selection problem: Alternative priors and consequences. *Multivariate Behavioral Research, 51*(4), 519–539.

Marsh, H. W., Hau, K-T., & Wen, Z. (2004). In search of golden rules: Comment on hypothesis-testing approaches to setting cutoff values for fit indexes and dangers in over-generalizing Hu and Bentler's (1999) findings. *Structural Equation Modeling, 11*(3), 320–341.

Micceri, T. (1989). The unicorn, the normal curve, and other improbable creatures. *Psychological Bulletin, 105*(1), 156–166.

Millsap, R. E. (2011). *Statistical approaches to measurement invariance.* New York, NY: Routledge.

Muthén, B. O. (1984). A general structural equation model with dichotomous, ordered categorical, and continuous latent variable indicators. *Psychometrika, 49*, 115–132.

Muthén, B. O., & Curran, P. J. (1997). General longitudinal modeling of individual differences in experimental designs: A latent variable framework for analysis and power estimation. *Psychological Methods, 2*, 371–402.

Muthén, B. O., & Hofacker, C. (1988). Testing an assumptions underlying tetrachoric correlations. *Psychometrika, 53*, 563–578.

Muthén, B. O., & Kaplan, D. (1992). A comparison of some methodologies for the factor analysis of non-normal Likert variables: A note on the size of the model. *British Journal of Mathematical and Statistical Psychology, 45*(1), 19–30.

Muthén, L. K., & Muthén, B. O. (1998–2017). *Mplus user's guide* (8th ed.). Los Angeles, CA: Muthén & Muthén.

Muthén, B. O., du Toit, S., & Spisic, D. (1997). *Robust inference using weighted least squares and quadratic estimating equations in latent variable modeling with categorical and continuous outcomes.* Retrieved from www.statmodel.com/download/Article_075.pdf

Olsson, U. (1979). Maximum likelihood estimation of the polychoric correlation coefficient. *Psychometrika, 44*(4), 443–460.

Olsson, U. H., Foss, T., Troye, S. V., & Howell, R. D. (2000). The performance of ML, GLS, and WLS estimation in structural equation modeling under conditions of misspecification and nonnormality. *Structural Equation Modeling, 7*(4), 557–595.

Raykov, T., & Marcoulides, G. A. (2008). *An introduction to applied multivariate analysis.* New York, NY: Taylor & Francis.

Raykov, T., & Marcoulides, G. A. (2015). On the relationship between classical test theory and item response theory: From one to the other and back. *Educational and Psychological Measurement, 76*(2), 325–338.

Sass, D. A., & Smith, P. L. (2006). The effects of parceling unidimensional scales on structural parameter estimates in structural equation modeling. *Structural Equation Modeling, 13*(4), 566–586.

Satorra, A., & Bentler, P. (1994). Corrections to test statistics and standard errors in covariance structure analysis. In A. V. Eye & C. C. Clogg (Eds.), *Latent variables analysis: Applications for developmental research* (pp. 399–419). Thousand Oaks, CA: Sage.

Savalei, V. (2011). What to do about zero frequency cells when estimating polychoric correlations. *Structural Equation Modeling, 18*(2), 253–273.

Siegel, D. J. (1999). *The developing mind: How relationships and the brain interact to shape who we are.* New York, NY: Guilford Press.

Stapleton, L. M. (2013). Using multilevel structural equation modeling techniques with complex sample data. In G. R. Hancock & R. O. Mueller (Eds.), *Structural equation modeling: A second course* (pp. 521–561). Greenwich, CT: Information Age Publishing.

Sterba, S. K. (2011). Implications of parcel-allocation variability for comparing fit of item-solutions and parcel-solutions. *Structural Equation Modeling, 18*, 554–577.

Xia, Y. (2016). *Investigating the chi-square-based model-fit indexes for WLSMV and ULSMV estimators* (Unpublished doctoral dissertation). Florida State University, Orlando, Florida.

Xia, Y., & Yang, Y. (in press). The influence of number of categories and threshold values on fit indices in structural equation modeling with ordered categorical data. *Multivariate Behavioral Research*.

Xia, Y., & Yang, Y. (2018). RMSEA, CFI, and TLI in structural equation modeling with ordered categorical data: The story they tell depends on estimation methods. *Behavior Research Methods*. doi: 10.3758/s13428-018-1055-2

Yang, Y., & Liang, X. (2013). Confirmatory factor analysis under violations of distributional and structural assumptions. *International Journal of Quantitative Research in Education, 1*(1), 61–84.

Yang, Y., & Xia, Y. (2015). On the number of factors in exploratory factor analysis for ordered categorical data. *Behavior Research Methods, 47*(3), 756–772.

Yu, C. Y. (2002). *Evaluating cutoff criteria of model-fit indexes for latent variable models with binary and continuous outcomes* (Doctoral dissertation). University of California, Los Angeles.

Yuan, K.-H., & Bentler, P. M. (2006). Mean comparison: Manifest variable versus latent variable. *Psychometrika, 71*, 139–159.

22 Multilevel analyses

Duygu Biricik Gulseren and E. Kevin Kelloway

Introduction

Social systems are most often composed of individuals who interact with other individuals within a hierarchical or nested structure. Thus, children are nested within families, students within classrooms and employees within departments or work groups. Accordingly, although our data collection may focus on individuals, the observations will not be independent – individuals within a group may share similarities – a family environment, a workplace or a supervisor. Data analytic techniques that ignore this non-independence can lead to misleading conclusions (Austin, Goel, & van Walraven, 2001; Browne & Rasbash, 2004). For example, Kelloway (2014) presents an example of three groups with mean differences across the groups. Correlating the individual scores results in a correlation greater than .95, although the within-group correlation of the same variables is 0 in each group. In this case, the strong correlation results from group- rather than individual-level effects.

Multilevel analysis is the analytical technique that researchers use to interpret data collected from nested structures (also known as multilevel models, hierarchical linear models or mixed models). In nested structures, individuals are organized in groups or clusters, and the resulting individual observations are not independent. There is a growing trend to use multilevel analyses in both organizational behavior (Bliese & Jex, 2002; Klein, Dansereau, & Hall, 1994; Klein, Tosi, & Cannella, 1999; Kozlowski & Klein, 2000) and public health (Bliese & Jex, 2002; Diez-Roux, 1998; Greenland & Robins, 1994; Schwartz, 1994) in recognition of the nested nature of the data. Compared to linear regression models, multilevel models assume that (1) subjects are not independent, (2) subjects are hierarchically organized, and (3) subjects in the same cluster share common influences. In contrast, traditional analytical techniques such as analysis of variance or regression assume that two observations are independent. When applied to multilevel data, the violation of the assumption of independence results in an inflated rate or type 1 errors (e.g. Austin et al., 2001; Bliese & Jex, 2002; Kelloway, 2014; Peugh, 2010; Snijders & Bosker, 1999).

The objective of this chapter is to consider the implications of these observations for research. In particular, we provide an overview of multilevel models and their applications. The chapter is organized into three sections. In the first section, we provide background information about the forms of multilevel structures. In the second section, we discuss different types of multilevel models. In the last section, we introduce the statistical applications of multilevel models.

Multilevel structures

Hierarchical designs: Multilevel structures can be either hierarchical or non-hierarchical. Perhaps the simplest structure is a two-level hierarchical structure. Two-level hierarchical structures require two conditions: (1) there should only be one higher-level unit and (2) individuals in this unit should only be nested in this unit (Rashbash, 2008). Consider, for example, employees working in a bank. Although there are multiple bank branches, most employees will work in one and only one branch of the bank. In this example, the employee is the level-1 unit and the branch is the higher-level or level-2 unit.

Other types of nesting also occur. For example, one could collect data from a group of individuals over a period of time using a repeated measures design (see, for example, Wong & Kelloway, 2016). This is also a two-level hierarchical structure, but now the time of measurement is the level-1 unit and the individual is the level-2 unit.

It is easy to see that more complex hierarchical designs are possible (Browne & Rasbash, 2004). For example, one could collect data from bank employees every six months for two years. This would represent (at minimum) a three-level design in which time constitutes the first level, individuals the second level and the bank branch the third level. One could, in principle, extend the hierarchy even further (e.g., branches could be nested within region, regions with country, etc.), although, both conceptually and pragmatically, our focus is often limited to two or three levels of hierarchy.

Non-hierarchical structures: Social structures are usually more complicated than the simple hierarchical models discussed previously. Individuals may not belong to one and only one group in real life. For example, a patient can see multiple physicians for different illnesses. Employees may work on multiple units or in multiple departments. We call such structures non-hierarchical structures. Non-hierarchical structures are characterized by individuals being members of more than one higher-level unit.

In general, there are two types of non-hierarchical structures: (1) cross-classified structures or (2) multiple membership structures (Rashbash, 2008). Cross-classified structures are defined as models with crossed factors (Van den Noortgate, De Boeck, & Meulders, 2003). In other words, in cross-classified models, lower level units can be nested under multiple higher-level units, pairs or combinations of higher-level units at different levels. These models can be very complex in nature. For example, imagine a company whose branches exist in multiple cities. For this model to be three-level hierarchical, we would expect employees reporting to supervisors who work for a particular branch. However, in real life some of these employees report to supervisors who work in the corporate office, not the branch they work at. This would be an example of a cross-classification structure.

On the other hand, multiple membership refers to the models in which lower level units are nested in multiple higher-level units (Hill & Goldstein, 1998; Rasbash & Browne, 2001). For example, a branch manager of a bank can report to more than one supervisor for different tasks, such as reporting employee performance scores to the human resources director and reporting financial performance of the branch to the finance director. The frequency of the relationships between the bank manager and directors differ. He or she can give monthly reports to the finance director, whereas employee performances can be reported once a year. In multiple membership models, this difference is accounted for by using a weighting scheme (Browne, Goldstein, & Rasbash, 2001). A different weight is assigned to different memberships. In our example, this weight should be proportional to the frequency of the reporting.

Repeated measures cross-classification structures are the combination of repeated measures design and cross-classification structures. For instance, assume that employees' performance is evaluated by different parties at different times. At time 1, supervisors who work in the same department, and at time 2, human resource personnel evaluate the performance of the same employee. Even though the variable at the lowest level of the hierarchy is performance score of the employees, the mathematical model describing these relationships will be highly complex.

Multilevel models

Imagine a study in which we investigate the relationship between pay rates and motivation levels of employees. If we were to employ traditional linear regression to test this relationship, we would simply fit our data into a single line.

The mathematical representation of linear regression is:

$$Y_i = \beta_0 + \beta_1 x_i + \varepsilon_i \qquad (22.1)$$

However, if we know that employees work in groups, then it is reasonable to suspect that there might also be group differences in motivation attributable to other influences (e.g., leadership, team cohesion). The simplest way to start modeling this hierarchical structure is with a random intercept model. In **random intercept models**, we have separate regression lines for every higher-level unit (Austin et al., 2001). Each group will have its own intercept. However, the slope is constant across groups (Austin et al., 2001; De Leeuw & Meijer, 2008). Thus, a random intercept model allows for group differences in motivation but estimates a fixed effect of pay on motivation that is constant across groups.

The mathematical representation of the random intercept models is as follows:

$$Y_{ij} = \beta_{0j} + \beta_{1j} x_{ij} + \varepsilon_{ij} \quad \text{where} \quad (22.2)$$

$\beta_{0j} = \beta_0 + u_j$ and when we assume that (22.3)

$$u_{0j} \sim N\left(0, \sigma^2_{u0}\right) \text{ and } e_{0ij} \sim N\left(0, \sigma^2_{e0}\right)$$

A more complex model would allow for different intercepts and different slopes for each group, suggesting that groups differ in motivation and that the effect of pay on motivation is different for different groups. **Random slope models** allow both the intercepts and the slopes of the regression lines belonging to each same higher-level unit vary (Austin et al., 2001; De Leeuw & Meijer, 2008; Kelloway, 2014). In effect, such models estimate multiple regression lines, testing the same relationship from different populations. However, in random slopes models, we take the average regression relationship and interpret the whole dataset in relation to the average regression line (Austin et al., 2001). This means the correlation between the slope and the intercept is negative. Generally, if the intercept of a regression line is high, its slope will tend to be low and vice versa. In other words, employees with high levels of motivation at the average pay will not have a motivation boost as much as the employees with low levels of motivation at the average pay as pay rate increase. The mathematical representation of the random slopes models is:

$$Y_{ij} = \beta_{0j} + \beta_{1j}x_{ij} + \varepsilon_{ij} \qquad \text{where } 22.4$$

$$\beta_{0j} = \beta_0 + u_j \quad (5) \qquad \text{and} \qquad \beta_{1j} = \beta_1 + u_{1j} \quad (6) \text{ when we assume that}$$

$$u_{0j} \sim N\left(0, \Omega_u\right), \ u_{ij} \sim N\left(0, \Omega_u\right)$$

$$\varepsilon_{0ij} \sim N\left(0, \sigma^2_{e0}\right), \qquad \text{and} \qquad \Omega_u = (\sigma^2_{u0}, \sigma_{u01}, \sigma^2_{u1})$$

Thus far, we have assumed that our dependent and independent variables are measured at the same level of the hierarchy. That is, both motivation and pay are measured at the individual level of analysis. However, in **full multilevel models, we can incorporate higher-level effects into the regression**. In essence, we utilize two sets of separate regression equations in full multilevel models (Austin et al., 2001). In the first set of regression models, we examine the relationship between pay and motivation for employees working under each leader separately (i.e., within groups). In the second set of regression models, we use a higher-level variable (i.e., leadership) to explain the variation between groups.

In these models the focus is on the relationship between two variables at the same level (e.g., individual level, group level or organizational level). However, in **cross-level models**, we look at the relationships between variables at different levels of the hierarchy (Bliese & Jex, 2002). Since most of the cross-level models test how higher-level variables influence lower-level outcomes, Kozlowski and Klein (2000) call these models 'top-down process models'. In the literature, there are three types of cross-level models: (1) cross-level direct-effect models, (2) cross-level moderation models, and (3) frog pond models (Kozlowski & Klein, 2000).

Models in which we investigate the effect of higher-level independent variables on the lower-level dependent variable (e.g., organizational culture) are called **cross-level direct-effect models** (Bliese & Jex, 2002; Chan, 1998; James, Demaree, & Wolf, 1984; Kozlowski & Hattrup, 1992; Kozlowski & Klein, 2000; Ostroff, 1993). Regressing employees' customer service performance level on organizational culture would be an example for cross-level direct-effect models. Researchers also use other types of group variables such integral variables (i.e., group size) or contextual variables (Bliese & Jex, 2002; Susser, 1994). This means higher-level variables can sometimes be calculated by using the individual-level data (e.g., we can calculate the team's motivation by taking the mean of employees' motivation levels; Bliese & Jex, 2002).

Cross-level moderator effects occur when the relationship between two lower-level variables is influenced by a higher-level variable (Aguinis, Gottfredson, & Culpepper, 2013; Kozlowski & Klein, 2000). The question of how organizational culture affects the relationship between long work hours and employee stress can be an example for cross-level interaction effects. Kozlowski and Klein (2000) argued that it is also possible to formulate a cross-level moderator model in which a lower-level variable moderates the relationship between higher- and lower-level variables because, in each model, researchers test the direct and interactional effects of higher- and lower-level variables on the lower-level outcome. To test this model, researchers employ a two-step procedure. In the first step they estimate the variability in the predictor and outcome relationship for every single group separately to see if the variation is as big as would be expected by chance. In the second step, researchers search for a higher-level variable to explain the variation around the slope (Bliese & Jex, 2002).

Unlike cross-level moderation effects, in **frog pond models**, researchers investigate the standing of a variable (e.g., individual) in his or her higher-level unit (e.g., group; Bliese & Jex, 2002; Kozlowski & Klein, 2000). For example, work-family conflict is a subjective evaluation. Even though both of the partners in a marriage may work for eight hours a day, one of them can experience work-family conflict more than the other (this makes one of the partners the big frog in a small pond). We can investigate the relationship between work hours and work-family conflict in relation to the other partner in a marriage using a frog pond model. To test the frog pond models, researchers subtract the group mean from the individual's score (i.e., group mean centering; Bliese & Jex, 2002; Bryk & Raudenbush, 1992; Snijders & Bosker, 1999). Bliese and Jex (2002) advised that we should use frog pond models only if we have strong theoretical justifications, because in order to have meaningful results, the difference between groups must be meaningful, too (George & James, 1993). Relational constructs such as power in relationships, insecurity or perceived stress can be meaningful concepts for frog pond models. For example, Jiang, Probst, and Benson (2014) studied academic staff working at a university with severe budget cuts. Although the job satisfaction and commitment decreased and perceptions of psychological contract breach and turnover intentions increased in both groups, participants who worked in the departments less effected by the budget cuts reported higher levels of negative outcomes. They concluded that frog pond models are meaningful in work stress research (Jiang, Probst, & Benson, 2014).

Multilevel mediation and moderation models

Researchers offer different statistical methods to test the different multilevel mediation models such as multilevel modeling for 2–1–1 (e.g., Pituch & Stapleton, 2008) and 1–1–1 (e.g., MacKinnon, 2008), ordinary least squares and multilevel modeling for 2–2–1 (e.g., Raykov & Mels, 2007) and structural equation modeling for 1–2–1 (e.g., Bauer, 2003) designs. In these models the first digit refers to the independent variable, the second digit is the mediator and the third digit is the independent variable. Additionally, the values of each digit refer to the level of the variables. For example, in 1–2–1 model the predictor and the outcome are at Level 1 and the mediator is at Level 2. However, Preacher, Zyphur, and Zhang (2010) noted that multilevel structural equation modeling (ML-SEM) may be more suited to testing mediation models than traditional forms of mixed model regressions. Assume that we will test a 2–1–1 model, which is called to be a conflated model by Preacher, Zyphur, and Zhang (2011). In such a case, we start by testing the relationship between the outcome and the predictor as follows:

$$\text{Level 1,} \qquad Y_{ij} = \beta_{oj} + r_{ij} \tag{22.7}$$

$$\text{Level 2,} \qquad \beta_{oj} = \gamma_{0j} + \gamma_{01} X_j + u_{oj} \tag{22.8}$$

In the second step, we regress mediator on the predictor.

$$\text{Level 1,} \qquad M_{ij} = \beta_{oj} + r_{ij} \tag{22.9}$$

$$\text{Level 2,} \qquad \beta_{oj} = \gamma_{00} + \gamma_{01} X_j + u_{oj} \tag{22.10}$$

In the final step, we regress both mediator and the outcome on the predictor.

$$\text{Level 1,} \qquad Y_{ij} = \beta_{oj} + \beta_{1j} M_{ij} + r_{ij} \tag{22.11}$$

$$\text{Level 2,} \qquad \beta_{oj} = \gamma_{00} + \gamma_{01} X_j + u_{oj} \tag{22.12}$$

$$\beta_{1j} = \gamma_{10} \tag{22.13}$$

Traditional moderation analysis in a single-level model is as simple as follows:

$$Y = \beta_0 + \beta_1 X + \beta_2 M + \beta_3 XM \tag{22.14}$$

However, this equation is more complex in multilevel models. Most of the multilevel models test an effect of the lower-level (e.g., individual) or higher-level (e.g., group-level) variable on another lower-level variable. In multilevel moderation models, moderators can be either a lower-level or a higher-level variable. In the following sections, we will discuss multilevel moderation models using a predictor and an outcome at the lower level and the moderator at the higher level as an example.

Aguinis and his colleagues (2013) suggested that multilevel moderation analyses can be conducted in four-steps. This four-step model is an application of same-level moderation models to a multilevel model perspective. In the first step (i.e., null model), the relationship between the predictor and the outcome is established. Since both the predictor and the outcome are at Level 1, a basic equation can be written as follows:

Level 1: $\quad Y_{ij} = \beta_{0j} + r_{ij}$ (22.15)

Level 2: $\quad \beta_{0j} = \gamma_{00} + u_{oj}$ (22.16)

Level 1 and Level 2 combined: $\quad Y_{ij} = \gamma_{00} + u_{oj} + r_{ij}$ (22.17)

The second step, which is referred as random intercept and fixed slope model (Aguinis et al., 2013), involves understanding the variance across each group. Since we are interested in the within-team variance in this step, we force our slopes for each team to be a fixed value. The equations of this step are as follows:

Level 1: $\quad Y_{ij} = \beta_{0j} + \beta_{1j}(X_{ij} - \bar{X}_j) + r_{ij}$ (22.18)

Level 2: $\quad \beta_{0j} = \gamma_{00} + \gamma_{01}(W_j - \bar{W}) + u_{oj}$ (22.19)

Level 2: $\quad \beta_{1j} = \gamma_{10}$ (22.20)

Level 1 and Level 2 combined: $Y_{ij} = \gamma_{00} + \gamma_{10}(X_{ij} - \bar{X}_j)$
$$+ \gamma_{01}(W_j - \bar{W}) + u_{oj} + r_{ij}$$ (22.21)

As Aguinis and his colleagues suggested (2013), in the third step, researchers can examine the between-group variances. To do so, a random intercept and random slope model are built. The equations of this step are as follows:

Level 1: $\quad Y_{ij} = \beta_{0j} + \beta_{1j}(X_{ij} - \bar{X}_j) + r_{ij}$ (22.22)

Level 2: $\quad \beta_{0j} = \gamma_{00} + \gamma_{01}(W_j - \bar{W}) + u_{oj}$ (22.23)

Level 2: $\quad \beta_{1j} = \gamma_{10} + u_{1j}$ (22.24)

Level 1 and 2 combined: $Y_{ij} = \gamma_{00} + \gamma_{10}(X_{ij} - \bar{X}_j) + \gamma_{01}(W_j - \bar{W})$
$$+ u_{1j}(X_{ij} - \bar{X}_j) + u_{oj} + r_{ij}$$ (22.25)

In the final step, the effect of the higher-level moderator on the relationship between the predictor and the outcome is tested as follows:

Level 1: $Y_{ij} = \beta_{0j} + \beta_{1j}(X_{ij} - \bar{X}_j) + r_{ij}$ (22.26)

Level 2: $\beta_{0j} = \gamma_{00} + \gamma_{01}(W_j - \bar{W}) + u_{oj}$ (22.27)

Level 2: $\beta_{0j} = \gamma_{10} + \gamma_{11}(W_j - \bar{W}) + u_{1j}$ (22.28)

Level 1 and 2 combined: $Y_{ij} = \gamma_{00} + \gamma_{10}(X_{ij} - \bar{X}_j) + \gamma_{01}(W_j - \bar{W})$
$$+ \gamma_{11}(X_{ij} - \bar{X}_j)(W_j - \bar{W}) + u_{oj}$$
$$+ u_{1j}(X_{ij} - \bar{X}_j) + r_{ij} \qquad (22.29)$$

On the other hand Preacher, Zhang, and Zyphur (2016) argued that the steps suggested by Aguinis and his colleagues (2013) are problematic because in these steps higher- and lower-level effects are not separated from each other and handled individually. In contrast, they propose that the best way to conduct a multilevel moderation analysis is multilevel structural equation modeling. In their article, Preacher and his colleagues (2016) discussed that for the same level interaction, latent moderated structural equation models (LMS) are recommended, while for cross-level interaction, traditional random coefficient prediction (RCP) is the most effective method (for detailed explanations, please refer to Preacher et al., 2016).

Multilevel structural equation modeling

Similar to linear regression, we can use a multilevel modeling framework to test structural equation models. Combining both of the techniques, researchers can investigate the factor structure of a higher-level latent construct using individual level observations. Additionally, ML-SEM allows researchers to test a mediation model with variables at the different levels of the hierarchy (Mehta & Neale, 2005). Finally, researchers can also examine both linear and nonlinear multilevel structural equation models (Schermelleh-Engel, Kerwer, & Klein, 2014).

In contrast to multilevel models, observations are assumed to be independent in structural equation models. Researchers overcome this problem by modeling the multilevel data in accordance with its clustered nature and applying structural equation modeling techniques to these data (Goldstein & McDonald, 1988; Longford & Muthén, 1992; Muthén, 1990, 1994; Muthén & Satorra, 1995; Ryu & West, 2009). Hox (2013) suggested that researchers should inspect the between-group variance before running ML-SEM. If the variation between groups is small, then ML-SEM is redundant.

Assume that we are going to investigate the effect of branch performance on employees' motivation in a bank branch. We will also test if human resources (HR) initiatives such as bonus pay and extra vacation days provided by the organization mediate this relationship. Branch performance and HR initiatives are both at the second level in this hierarchy. However, employee performance is an individual level variable. Additionally, performance is a latent variable which we can measure using performance indicators such as goal achievement, sales numbers, number of customers added to the bank's customer database and supervisor and customer ratings. To understand a bank branch's performance, we need to measure each employee's performance. We can conduct a confirmatory factor analysis (CFA) using the performance indicators as the observed variables for each employee. Then we can conduct another CFA using employees' individual performance scores to understand the branch's performance, because CFA and multilevel modeling are equal in terms of means and covariance structures (Mehta & Neale, 2005). There is only one difference between conducting individual and branch level CFA: At the branch level, we can only use latent variables (i.e., individual performance scores) because we estimated the individual performance in the previous step. Contrary to branch performance, we can conduct a third CFA to test the model fit for HR incentives, using observed variables at the second level. We are ready to test the structural model after these steps. This method of testing ML-SEM is the traditional two-step approach (Rabe-Hesketh, Skrondal, & Zheng, 2007).

Repeated measures analysis

Traditionally, data collected by repeated measures design are analyzed either using ANOVA or MANOVA depending on the research question. As discussed in the earlier sections of this chapter, traditional approaches have some limitations such as the need to eliminate the case with missing data and the need to have equivalent time intervals between measurements or independent observations. Additionally, some researchers assume that the multilevel mediation and multilevel SEM approaches described by Preacher and his colleagues (2010) simply apply within group analyses. However, the critical point in repeated measures analysis is to incorporate time as a separate parameter.

Repeated measures designs employ growth curves that are the trajectories of change over time. In repeated measures multilevel analysis, the first step is to decide if univariate or multivariate growth processes will be employed (Heck, Thomas, & Tabata, 2013). In other words, we should decide how many growth curves we will be interested in for this analysis. In the second stage, effect of time (e.g., interval, number of time points) should be considered. This also means adding the time as a variable in the dataset. Researchers usually encapsulate the effect of time in polynomials when demonstrating growth models (Hox, Moerbeek, & van de Schoot, 2010). When the rate of change is constant, they use linear models. The rate of change may not be constant between different time intervals in real life. In such cases, higher order polynomials can be utilized (Heck et al., 2013). However, there is a trade-off here. Although higher order polynomials lead to more accurate predictions, they are difficult to interpret. To overcome this barrier, the general practice is to incorporate up to the highest polynomial that exists in the model (Heck et al., 2013). After obtaining the change trajectory by time, researchers consider the between-subject varia- bles (i.e., higher-level variables) that can influence the growth curve (Raykov & Marcoulides, 2012). Note that in repeated measures design, researchers assume that higher-level factors are stable over time, whereas level-1 factors are subject to change.

Conclusion

For many years researchers have made simplifying assumptions (i.e., the inde- pendence of observations) that allowed the use of well-known statistical tech- niques but that may have resulted in inappropriate conclusions. The growing popularity and accessibility of multilevel modeling allows researchers to more accurately reflect the complex nature of their data. Moreover, the use of such techniques allows us greater precision in identifying where (i.e., at what level) and how (i.e., the form of the relationships) the effects in which we are inter- ested occur.

References

Aguinis, H., Gottfredson, R. K., & Culpepper, S. A. (2013). Best-practice recommendations for estimating cross-level interaction effects using multilevel modeling. *Journal of Manage- ment, 20*, 1–39.

Austin, P. C., Goel, V., & van Walraven, C. (2001). An introduction to multilevel regression models. *Canadian Journal of Public Health, 92*(2), 150–154.

Bauer, D. J. (2003). Estimating multilevel linear models as structural equation models. *Journal of Educational and Behavioral Statistics, 28*(2), 135–167.

Baron, R. M., & Kenny, D. A. (1986). The moderator – mediator variable distinction in social psychological research: Conceptual, strategic, and statistical considerations. *Journal of Per- sonality and Social Psychology, 51*(6), 1173–1182.

Bliese, P. D., & Jex, S. M. (2002). Incorporating a mulitilevel perspective into occupational stress research: Theoretical, methodological, and practical implications. *Journal of Occupa- tional Health Psychology, 7*(3), 265–276.

Browne, W. J., Goldstein, H., & Rasbash, J. (2001). Multiple membership multiple classifica- tion (MMMC) models. *Statistical Modelling, 1*(2), 103–124.

Browne, W., & Rasbash, J. (2004). Multilevel Modeling. In M. A. Hardy & A. Bryman (Eds.), *Handbook of data analysis* (pp. 459–479). London, UK: Sage.

Bryk, A. S., & Raudenbush, S. W. (1992). *Hierarchical linear models.* Newbury Park, CA: Sage Publications.

Chan, D. (1998). Functional relations among constructs in the same content domain at different levels of analysis: A typology of composition models. *Journal of Applied Psychol- ogy, 83*(2), 234–246.

De Leeuw, J., & Meijer, E. (2008). Introduction to multilevel analysis. In *Handbook of multi- level analysis* (pp. 1–75). London, UK: Springer.

Diez-Roux, A. V. (1998). Bringing context back into epidemiology: Variables and fallacies in multilevel analysis. *American Journal of Public Health, 88*(2), 216–222.

George, J. M., & James, L. R. (1993). Personality, affect, and behavior in groups revisited: Comment on aggregation, levels of analysis, and a recent application of within and between analysis. *Journal of Applied Psychology, 78*, 798–804.

Goldstein, H., & McDonald, R. P. (1988). A general model for the analysis of multilevel data. *Psychometrika, 53*(4), 455–467.

Greenland, S., & Robins, J. (1994). Invited commentary: Ecologic studies – biases, misconceptions, and counterexamples. *American Journal of Epidemiology, 139*(8), 747–760.

James, L. R., Demaree, R. G., & Wolf, G. (1984). Estimating within-group interrater reliability with and without response bias. *Journal of Applied Psychology, 69*(1), 85–98.

Jiang, L., Probst, T. M., & Benson, W. L. (2014). Why me? The frog-pond effect, relative deprivation and individual outcomes in the face of budget cuts. *Work & Stress, 28*(4), 387–403.

Heck, R. H., Thomas, S. L., & Tabata, L. N. (2013). *Multilevel and longitudinal modeling with IBM SPSS*. London, UK: Routledge.

Hill, P. W., & Goldstein, H. (1998). Multilevel modeling of educational data with cross-classification and missing identification for units. *Journal of Educational and Behavioral Statistics, 23*(2), 117–128.

Hox, J. J., Moerbeek, M., & van de Schoot, R. (2010). *Multilevel analysis: Techniques and applications*. London, UK: Routledge.

Hox, J. J. (2013). Multilevel regression and multilevel structural equation modeling. In T. D. Little (Ed.), *The Oxford handbook of quantitative methods* (Vol. 2, pp. 281–294). Oxford: Oxford University Press.

Kelloway, E. K. (2014). *Using Mplus for structural equation modeling: A researcher's guide*: Thousand Oaks, CA: Sage.

Klein, K. J., Dansereau, F., & Hall, R. J. (1994). Levels issues in theory development, data collection, and analysis. *Academy of Management Review, 19*(2), 195–229.

Klein, K. J., Tosi, H., & Cannella, A. A. (1999). Multilevel theory building: Benefits, barriers, and new developments. *Academy of Management Review, 24*(2), 248–253.

Kozlowski, S., Hattrup, K., & Schmitt, N. (1992). A disagreement about within-group agreement: Disentangling issues of consistency versus consensus. *Journal of Applied Psychology, 77*(2), 161–167.

Kozlowski, S. W., & Klein, K. J. (2000). A multilevel approach to theory and research in organizations: Contextual, temporal, and emergent processes. In S. W. Kozlowski & K. Klein (Eds.), *Multilevel theory, research, and methods in organizations: Foundations, extensions, and new directions* (pp. 0–39). San Francisco, CA: John Wiley & Sons.

Longford, N. T., & Muthén, B. O. (1992). Factor analysis for clustered observations. *Psychometrika, 57*(4), 581–597.

MacKinnon, D. P. (2008). *Introduction to statistical mediation analysis*. London, UK: Routledge.

Mehta, P. D., & Neale, M. C. (2005). People are variables too: Multilevel structural equations modeling. *Psychological methods, 10*(3), 259–284.

Muthén, B. (1990). Moments of the censored and truncated bivariate normal distribution. *British Journal of Mathematical and Statistical Psychology, 43*(1), 131–143.

Muthén, B. O. (1994). Multilevel covariance structure analysis. *Sociological Methods & Research, 22*(3), 376–398.

Muthén, B. O., & Satorra, A. (1995). Complex sample data in structural equation modeling. *Sociological Methodology*, 267–316.

Ostroff, C. (1993). The effects of climate and personal influences on individual behavior and attitudes in organizations. *Organizational Behavior and Human Decision Processes, 56*(1), 56–90.

Peugh, J. L. (2010). A practical guide to multilevel modeling. *Journal of School Psychology, 48*(1), 85–112.

Pituch, K. A., & Stapleton, L. M. (2008). The performance of methods to test upper-level mediation in the presence of nonnormal data. *Multivariate Behavioral Research, 43*(2), 237–267.

Preacher, K. J., Zhang, Z., & Zyphur, M. J. (2016). Multilevel structural equation models for assessing moderation within and across levels of analysis. *Psychological Methods, 21*(2), 189–205.

Preacher, K. J., Zyphur, M. J., & Zhang, Z. (2010). A general multilevel SEM framework for assessing multilevel mediation. *Psychological Methods, 15*(3), 209–233.

Rabe-Hesketh, S., Skrondal, A., & Zheng, X. (2007). Multilevel structural equation modeling. In S-Y. Lee (Ed.), *Handbook of latent variable and related models* (pp. 209–227). Amsterdam, The Netherlands: Elsevier.

Rashbash, J. (Producer). (2008). *Multilevel structures and classifications.* Retrieved from www.cmm.bris.ac.uk/lemma

Rasbash, J., & Browne, W. J. (2001). Non-hierarchical multilevel models. In A. Leyland & H. Goldstein (Eds.), *Multilevel modelling of health statistics.* Chichester, UK: John Wiley & Sons.

Raykov, T., & Marcoulides, G. A. (2012). *A first course in structural equation modeling.* London, UK: Routledge.

Raykov, T., & Mels, G. (2007). Lower level mediation effect analysis in two-level studies: A note on a multilevel structural equation modeling approach. *Structural Equation Modeling, 14*(4), 636–648.

Ryu, E., & West, S. G. (2009). Level-specific evaluation of model fit in multilevel structural equation modeling. *Structural Equation Modeling, 16*(4), 583–601.

Schermelleh-Engel, K., Kerwer, M., & Klein, A. G. (2014). Evaluation of model fit in nonlinear multilevel structural equation modeling. *Frontiers in Psychology, 5*, 181.

Schwartz, S. (1994). The fallacy of the ecological fallacy: The potential misuse of a concept and the consequences. *American Journal of Public Health, 84*(5), 819–824.

Snijders, T., & Bosker, R. (1999). *Multilevel analysis: An introduction to basic and applied multilevel analysis.* London, UK: Sage.

Susser, M. (1994). The logic in ecological: I. The logic of analysis. *American Journal of Public Health, 84*(5), 825–829.

Van den Noortgate, W., De Boeck, P., & Meulders, M. (2003). Cross-classification multilevel logistic models in psychometrics. *Journal of Educational and Behavioral Statistics, 28*(4), 369–386.

Wong, J. H. K., & Kelloway, E. K. (in press). What happens at work stays at work? Workplace supervisory social interactions and blood pressure outcomes. *Journal of Occupational & Health Psychology.*

23 Social network analysis

Alan Sloane and Seamus O'Reilly

Introduction

Following a brief overview of the origins of social network analysis (SNA), we consider research questions that are often addressed using SNA concepts and methods. We then introduce the basic elements in an SNA research design. Next, we discuss and explain the major measures and methods used in graph theoretical and in statistical SNA methods, followed by a short discussion of the use of qualitative and mixed methods. The chapter concludes with practical advice on software packages and signposts to further reading and resources.

Origins and historical development

Although the earliest work in SNA is attributed to the classical sociologist Simmel (whose work on the dynamics of triads remains influential), the methodological origin of the field lies in the development of "sociometry" by the psychologists Jacob Moreno and Helen Jennings in the 1930s (Jennings, 1943; Moreno, 1934). Their ideas and methods were taken up and developed by a diverse group of psychologists, anthropologists, and organisational researchers including Warner, Roethlisberger, Lewin, and Bavelas, through to the 1950s. Progress, however, was constrained by technical barriers in computation and visualisation. With increasing access to computers and software from the 1970s onwards, innovation and adoption of SNA progressed rapidly. SNA today remains a field that is marked by intense methodological development and a growing diversity of application across the physical and social sciences (Borgatti, Mehra, Brass, & Labianca, 2009) and beyond (Pinter-Wollman et al., 2014).

Research questions in SNA

There are two dimensions along which the most common network research questions may be categorised: purpose and process. Purpose is the familiar distinction between descriptive ("What?" "Who?") and explanatory ("How?" "Why?") questions. Examples of descriptive network questions might be "Who in this classroom friendship network are the most sought-after as friends?" or

"In what ways does the structure of the informal advice-giving network differ from that of the formal reporting network in this organisation?" Such questions require the choice of appropriate network measures, their calculation, and the use, often, of statistical methods in further analysis. Examples of explanatory (or associational) questions might be "How does the popularity of actors differ based on their gender?" or "How well does the structure of the reporting network predict that of the advice-giving network?" Again, these require the choice of network measures and (usually) also of actor attributes. These questions, however, also require the determination of which variables are independent and which dependent, as well as the choice of suitable methods for assessing and quantifying the presence and strength of associations between the variables. Table 23.1 gives a more detailed typology of explanatory network questions.

Cell (I) contains questions that ask about interactions between pairs of actors (dyadic interactions). In cell (III) are personal (or ego) network questions, where we calculate network measures for each actor and may use multivariate statistical techniques (e.g., logistic regression) to answer the questions. Cells (II) and (IV) address what Provan et al. (2007) termed "whole network" questions. Methods that may be applied to such questions are described in a later section.

Process denotes a variety of interactional processes that have been theorised as acting at either micro- or macro-levels within groups and networks of actors. Micro-processes are those at the level of the individual (actor) or in the small neighbourhood of direct ties surrounding an actor. Macro-processes are those operating within larger groups or across the full network. At the micro-level, frequently encountered processes include those involving the individual actor (monadic), those between two actors (dyadic) and those within groups of three actors (triadic). Examples of monadic processes are those of "popularity" (also "preferential attachment", or what Merton (1968) called "the Matthew effect") and "activity". The first of these is usually operationalized by the network measure of in-degree (the sum of ties directed inwards to an actor) and the second by out-degree (the sum of ties outward from an actor to others). Dyadic processes include "reciprocity" – the tendency for directed ties to be returned – and "homophily" – the tendency for ties to form between pairs of actors who are similar in respect of some ascribed or acquired attribute, for example race, social attitudes, or cultural behaviour. Triadic processes that are commonly theorised include "transitivity" (or "closure"), where, for example, friends of

Table 23.1 Explanatory network research questions

Independent Variable (Antecedent)	Dependent variable (outcome)	
	Actor (individual)	Network (collectivity)
Actor (attributes)	(I) Dyadic interactions	(II) Whole networks
Network (metrics)	(III) Personal networks	(IV) Whole networks

Source: adapted from Provan, Fish, & Sydow (2007, p. 483)

friends are likely to become direct friends, and "brokerage", where the "middleman" in a triad keeps the other two actors disconnected from one another. At the macro-level, important processes include the tendency of networks to develop into subgroups within which the actors are strongly interconnected but across which connections are weaker. Another important macro-level process is that of "selection", in which actors prefer ties to others they perceive as being similar. Selection will, of course, over time, give rise to distinct subgroups, as in Heider's (1946) "Structural Balance" theory and its further development (Cartwright & Harary, 1956; Davis, 1967; Harary, 1953). Finally, many studies have investigated processes of "influence" (or "contagion") in which the existence of network ties gives rise to the adoption of similar attitudes or behaviours by those actors connected through chains of ties across the network.

Research design for SNA

A research design for SNA has four elements (Knoke & Yang, 2008, p. 9):

1   the choice of sampling units;
2   the form of relations;
3   the relational content; and
4   the level of data analysis.

The sampling unit refers both to the "higher-level system" that is the setting of the study and also to the "lower-level entities" that constitute the nodes or actors in the network (Knoke & Yang, 2008, p. 10). The "form of relation" is decomposed by Knoke and Yang into "relational content" and "relational form". Content is the nature of the relationship, e.g., supplier, customer, advisor; and form captures properties of the relations between pairs of actors, e.g., frequency, value, strength. The relational content that the researcher chooses to study is usually based on theoretical considerations. Each type of relational content can be viewed as determining a separate network. Alternatively, multiple types of relations may be considered at the same time (a "multiplex" or "multilayer" network). The relations in a network may be recorded as directed or undirected (symmetric). Further, the relational form may be recorded as simply the presence or absence of a tie (binary) or as a numeric representation of the tie's value (valued/weighted or signed). Finally, the "level of analysis" describes the type of network study: dyadic, egocentric, or whole (complete).

Knoke and Yang also emphasised that, for any observational network research, a crucial question is one of boundary specification: "Where does a researcher set the limits when collecting data on social relations that, in reality, may have no obvious limits?" (Knoke & Yang, 2008, p. 15). Laumann, Marsden, and Prensky (1983) distinguished between a "nominalist" specification, in which the researcher's theoretical framework determines the boundary, and a "realist" boundary specification, in which the researcher accepts the boundaries experienced by the actors in the network.

SNA has developed a range of analytic measures that represent and operationalise the concepts and processes described earlier and that measure the nature of actors' position or of patterns of relations. We place these measures into six general categories: three fundamental and three more complex. We describe each of these categories briefly and detail important measures and methods for the first three in the following section.

Network visualisation

Visualisations (or "sociograms", as they were called by Moreno and Jennings) are visual displays that give insight into the overall structure of the network and may draw attention to substructures and patterns, to "important" actors, and to outliers. Various layout algorithms may be used, but the ones that probably typify SNA are those based on "spring-embedder" algorithms (Freeman, 2005).

Position

Many of these techniques are concerned with the notion of centrality and the various measures that have been devised to represent that concept. Such techniques generally focus at the actor-level. Measures of cohesion may focus attention on individual actors or small groups of actors (reciprocity among dyads or transitivity among triads), or they may be more concerned with the overall network structure (triad census).

Subgroup

These techniques are concerned with the presence (or absence) of "meso-level" structure within the network (subgroups, components, etc.). They focus attention also both at the network level in terms of whether and how the network is composed of subgroups and at the actor level in terms of which actors are members of a particular subgroup and the subgroups of which a particular actor is a member.

Role

This is the operationalisation of the concept of "role" (Merton, 1957) defined in terms of the SNA technique of "regular equivalence classes" (White, Boorman, & Breiger, 1976). As with groups, determination of a set of roles within a network gives rise to a "partition" of the network, i.e., an assignment of the actors in the network to an enumerated set of subnetworks. Thus, it again provides a meso-level view on the network.

Block and core-periphery models

The concept of "block models" (including "core-periphery models") may be seen as a generalisation of equivalence (Doreian & Batagelj, 2005). These techniques are somewhat different in that they assess whether the network as a whole "fits" a pre-specified, theoretically driven, ideal type of network structure.

Whole network metrics

Many measures have been developed that characterise aspects of an entire network's structure, and these may be applied to support cross-network comparative analysis. Examples are density, centralization, fragmentation, and the clustering coefficient devised by Watts & Strogatz (1998) to characterise networks with the "small-worlds" property of global connectivity.

Graph theoretic methods

The mathematical concepts underlying most of the measures and methods in SNA are drawn from graph theory. A social network can be represented in two equivalent ways – as a graph of nodes and edges (or arcs, in a directed network) or as an adjacency matrix that records the ties between pairs of actors. Because a network has an algebraic representation as a matrix, techniques of linear algebra can be used to determine many measures – path lengths, node degrees, connectivity, and more. In addition, computational algorithms developed in numerical linear algebra can be applied to the calculation of SNA measures.

Visualisation (sociograms)

Figure 23.1 presents a visualisation of the network of inter-organisational ties among small businesses, laid out using the *Ucinet spring-embedder*. The visualisation gives us an impression of the overall structure of the network, suggesting, for example, the existence of a small number of central actors and of several distinct subgroups. These characteristics would be explored further and confirmed using measures such as centrality, brokerage, and cliques.

Position

Centrality

One of the main concerns of social network analysis has been with notions of "centrality" – identifying which actors are most "important" or "powerful" within the network. While there are many ways to conceptualise and to measure centrality, three measures have come to be seen as "canonical": degree, closeness, and betweenness (Freeman, 1978).

Degree-centrality is the simplest measure: the number of connections to or from that actor (node). In a directed network, we distinguish between in-degree – connections from other actors to the focal actor – and out-degree – connections from the focal actor outwards to other actors.

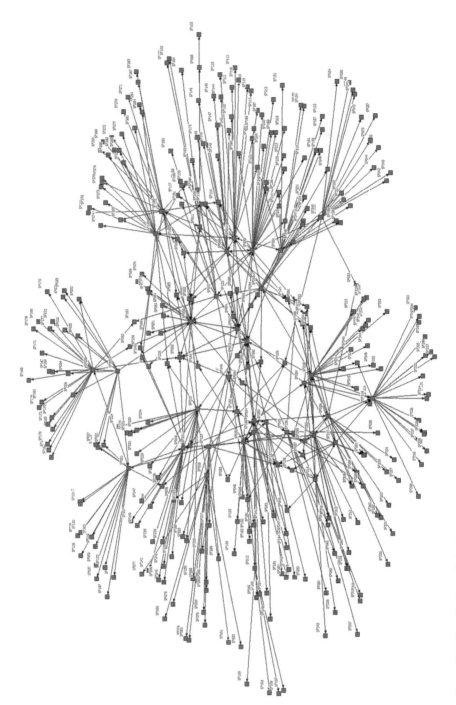

Figure 23.1 Visualisation of a business network

Betweenness-centrality is a measure of position along the most efficient (shortest) paths for information to flow. Thus, betweenness is often favoured as a centrality measure when considering the network as a medium through which information flows. An actor with high betweenness is likely to have high influence in terms of spreading information or, conversely, to exercise control over information diffusion. Figure 23.2 illustrates the use of this measure in the business network introduced in Figure 23.1. Because "betweenness" in this network measures knowledge flow, the figure highlights the influential role of the three circled actors: the first two are retailers, and the third is a peer but one who was perceived by the others as a "role model".

Closeness-centrality measures how close on average an actor is to all the other members of the network. Therefore, it again measures aspects of the flow of information within the network: "we normally think of nodes with low closeness scores as being well-positioned to obtain novel information early, when it has the most value" (Borgatti, 2005, p. 59). Many other measures of centrality have been proposed (Borgatti & Everett, 2006; Everett & Borgatti, 2010). Depending on the relational content, the research's theoretical orientation, and the specific research questions, it may be appropriate to choose one of those other measures or to explore the data using additional measures.

Brokerage

A different positional concept is that of "brokerage". The idea here is that an actor can occupy a position of importance not by being directly connected but by being the "middleman" who controls or brokers interaction between distinct parts of the network. Burt (1992) developed a set of measures (redundancy, constraint, efficiency, and effectiveness) delineating different aspects of an actor's local network neighbourhood and of what he termed "structural holes". Gould and Fernandez (1989) developed a different set of brokerage measures which they applied to the flow of information between subgroups in the network, and they labelled the resulting positions as "coordinator", "itinerant", "gatekeeper", "representative", or "liaison".

Subgroup

The identification of cohesive subgroups is typically an important focus in SNA. Frank (1995) surveyed a wide range of SNA research in sociology and social psychology and predicted that:

* actors will feel the greatest social "solidarity" with those who are also members of the same subgroup(s);
* actors will tend to act in the same ways as their co-members; and
* members of the subgroup will relate in similar ways towards the rest of the network.

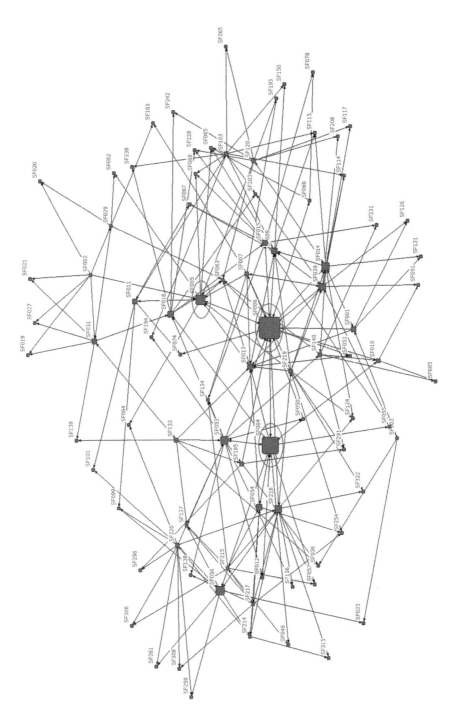

Figure 23.2 Business network – betweenness–centrality

All these ideas are related to process and norms and thus constitute three distinct consequences of subgroup membership. Similarly, because there are many different conceptions of cohesiveness, there are many ways of defining subgroups. In the following discussion, we categorise these definitions as being based on connection or on flow. Note also that, while there are measures for calculating "goodness of fit", there are no commonly applied methods of inference to determine the (external) validity of a given partition into subgroups. The analyst must exercise judgement in choosing a "good" subgrouping, guided, for example, by theory or by prior research.

Connection: cliques and related methods

Cliques are the first formal definition proposed for subgroups (Luce & Perry, 1949) and are in many ways the simplest: a clique is a maximal subgraph where every member is directly connected to every other member. In practice, analysis of the clique structure of a network is complicated, because in most social networks there are many cliques, and the cliques overlap. In terms of social structure, cliques are interpreted as representing very strong and close groupings – each member has ties to every other member of the group, and an actor's identity is bound up in the pattern of cliques of which he/she is a member. Because the criterion of complete one-to-one connection used in determining cliques is so strict, it is unlikely to be realistic in larger networks, and therefore a number of ways of relaxing it have been proposed, for example *n-cliques* (Alba, 1973), *n-clans* (Mokken, 1979), *k-plexes* (Seidman & Foster, 1978), and *k-cores* (Seidman, 1983).

Flow: Girvan–Newman "communities"

Subgroups based on flow result in a "top-down" hierarchical subdivision of the network into subgroups divided by those edges which most concentrate flow, i.e. those which form "bridges" between more internally cohesive regions. Girvan and Newman's (2002) *community detection* algorithm is a popular example of this approach. This algorithm works by iteratively subdividing the network along the edges with the highest value of edge-betweenness.[1] Consequently, it suggests that the subgroups which result are natural "communities" within which interaction is locally concentrated. Newman and Girvan (2004) later proposed a measure of goodness of fit termed *modularity*. When the method works well we should observe a clear local maximum of modularity as a function of the number of subgroups, and practice is to choose a subgrouping close to the one that maximises modularity. Figure 23.3 illustrates the result of Girvan and Newman's method applied to the small-business network of Figure 23.2.

There are many other methods of defining and calculating subgroups include factions, hierarchical clustering of geodesics, and lambda sets. In many cases the choice of method will be theoretically driven, but in others the researcher may wish to proceed in a more exploratory way or to compare results obtained using different methods.

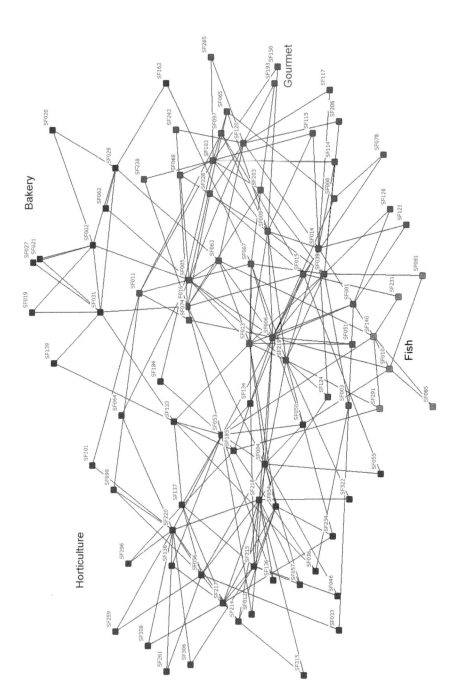

Figure 23.3 Girvan and Newman's method applied to the network of Figure 23.2

Statistical methods

The measures and methods described to this point are oriented principally towards descriptive studies, although network measures collected for whole-networks or for ego-networks may be utilised in explanatory statistical analyses. Explanatory network methods, especially those which seek to explain or predict networks as outcomes (dependent variables) – i.e., those in cells (II) and (IV) of Table 23.1 – are inherently more complex. This section outlines three such methods: *quadratic assignment procedure* (Dekker, Krackhardt, & Snijders, 2007; Krackhardt, 1987, 1988), *ERGMs* (Robins, Snijders, Wang, Handcock, & Pattison, 2007), and *stochastic actor-oriented longitudinal models* (Snijders, van de Bunt, & Steglich, 2010). All of these methods are inferential in that they allow comparison of the observed network (outcome) to a distribution of "random" networks. The first proposed model of a random network is termed the *Bernoulli or Erdős-Rényi random graph* (Erdős & Rényi, 1959). In this model, all ties are assumed equally likely to arise. This assumption is not, however, a realistic model for observed social networks, because these have much greater structure. Moreover, network statistics (for example, degree or transitivity) in observed social networks never fit a normal distribution. Neither are they independent observations, because they are subject to interaction and collinearity in ways dependent on the deep structure of network ties. All the methods described next, therefore, rely on some form of computational simulation in order to derive a representative distribution, similar to statistical jack-knife or bootstrap techniques.

The quadratic assignment procedure (or QAP) (Dekker et al., 2007; Krackhardt, 1987, 1988) generates a distribution of random but similar networks by permuting the rows and columns of the adjacency matrix. The distribution of networks will consequently have the same density and degree distributions as the observed network. This procedure is implemented in Ucinet, and it allows testing of monadic (attribute) and dyadic hypotheses – for example popularity or homophily – as well as testing comparisons between networks representing different relations among the same set of actors – for example, between the networks created by formal and informal organisational relations.

Exponential random graph models (ERGMs or p^* models; Robins et al., 2007; Snijders, 2011) allow modelling of the network based on monadic, dyadic, and also on triadic processes (such as transitivity or brokerage). They consequently support explanations of how the observed network represents the outcome of different micro-level processes. Such models are comparable to multivariate linear models in that one obtains estimates of significance, relative effect sizes, and overall goodness of fit for the model. The researcher can thus measure, for example, the significance and strength of status homophily while controlling for gender or organisational seniority.

Stochastic actor-oriented models (SAOM's) are used to develop longitudinal models of networks, in which there are multiple measurements of a network at successive points in time. These models are similar to ERGMs in the typology of Table 23.1 and also in their internal computational methods, and an analogy is often made to multivariate regression in terms of how these models are interpreted. A particularly important application of these models is in the study of network evolution, and of the co-evolution of network structure and actor attributes or behaviour. Comparison of the parameters of the fitted model can allow quantification of the relative importance of the processes of selection or influence on how the network structure has developed and the actors' attributes have changed – examples include Gremmen, Dijkstra, Steglich, and Veenstra (2017), Kalish, Luria, Toker, and Westman (2015), Mercken, Steglich, Sinclair, Holliday, and Moore (2012), Schaefer, Kornienko, and Fox (2011), and Steglich, Snijders, and West (2006).

Qualitative and mixed methods

While social network analysis has been perceived generally as a quantitative methodology, in more recent years a group of researchers have developed an explicitly qualitative approach (Hollstein, 2011; Hollstein & Straus, 2006). There is, moreover, a long-standing empirical tradition of combining both qualitative and quantitative methods in network research, for example in the work of the Manchester anthropologists of the 1950s (Barnes, 1954; Bott, 1957; Mitchell, 1969). Thus, in recent years, mixed-method approaches have been a notable methodological development in SNA (Bellotti, 2014; Domínguez & Hollstein, 2014).

Software for social network analysis

Most of the major statistical programs incorporate some functions for SNA, either through user-written extensions (Grund, 2015; Miura, 2012) or additional modules (IBM Corporation, 2012; SAS Institute Inc., 2013), and there are a large number of specialised commercial packages available. Most academic research, however, utilises either *Ucinet* (Borgatti, Everett, & Freeman, 2017), which has very inexpensive academic and student licencing, or *Pajek* (Batagelj & Mrvar, 2017), which is free. *Ucinet* (and *NetDraw*, for visualisation) provides all the most widely used SNA procedures including QAP. *Pajek* (Batagelj & Mrvar, 2017) is similar but specialises in the analysis and visualisation of large networks. The programs *Visone* (Brandes & Wagner, 2017), *Gephi* (Bastian, Heymann, & Jacomy, 2016), and *ORA* (Carley, 2017) are oriented more strongly towards visualisation. *NodeXL* (Smith et al., 2010) – an add-in to Microsoft Excel – has specialised facilities for importing and analysing data from social-media. Within the *R* programming system, the packages *network/sna* (Butts, 2015, 2016) and *igraph* (Csardy, 2015) are probably the most well-known of those used for SNA. Statistical modelling of networks with ERGMs can be done using the standalone program *pnet* (Robins, 2013; Wang, Robins, & Pattison, 2009) or in *R* with the *statnet* packages (Goodreau, Handcock, Hunter, Butts, & Morris, 2008; Handcock, Hunter, Butts, Goodreau, & Morris, 2003; Handcock, Hunter, Butts,

Goodreau, & Morris, 2008). Stochastic actor-oriented models are implemented by *RSiena* (Ripley, Snijders, Preciado, Boda, & Vörös, 2017; Snijders, 2017), which again is an *R* package.

Further reading: textbooks and websites

The primary academic society devoted to the development of SNA is the International Network for Social Network Analysis (INSNA; insna.org). The society organises or sponsors annual conferences in North America, Europe, and Asia and publishes the premier methodological journal in the field, *Social Networks*. It also runs an active mailing list, SOCNET, which supports lively and collaborative discussions and answers to questions. There are likewise active mailing lists for the Ucinet and Pajek programs. Another specialised journal in the field is *Network Science*, which has an orientation towards the work of mathematicians and physicists working in the field of social physics. Many of this group of researchers also make pre-prints and working-papers available in the physics. soc-ph category of arXiv.org (https://arxiv.org/list/physics.soc-ph/recent).

Nowadays there are many excellent SNA textbooks available at both introductory and advanced levels. Introductory texts include Knoke and Yang (2008), Prell (2011), Robins (2015), Scott (2017), and Yang, Keller, and Zheng (2016). Wasserman and Faust (1994) remain the established classic in the area of graph-theoretic methods. Carrington and Scott (2010) provide a broad overview of a range of topics from theory to methods of sampling and data-collection. There are texts that describe SNA with a focus on specific software – Ucinet (Borgatti, Everett, & Johnson, 2013), Pajek (de Nooy, Mrvar, & Batagelj, 2011), NodeXL (Hansen, Shneiderman, & Smith, 2011), pnet (Robins, Lusher, & Koskinen, 2012) and the *R* system (Kolaczyk & Csárdi, 2014). Finally, Barabási (2016), Easley and Kleinberg (2010), and Newman (2010) are well-known texts in the network science (social physics) tradition.

Note

1 Edge-betweenness is analogous to betweenness-centrality, as was defined earlier, but calculated for edges rather than for nodes.

References

Alba, R. D. (1973). A graph-theoretic definition of a sociometric clique. *Journal of Mathematical Sociology*, *3*(1), 113–126. https://doi.org/10.1080/0022250X.1973.9989826

Barabási, A.-L. (2016). *Network science*. Cambridge, UK: Cambridge University Press.

Barnes, J. A. (1954). Class and committees in a Norwegian Island parish. *Human Relations*, *7*(1), 39–58. https://doi.org/10.1177/001872675400700102

Bastian, M., Heymann, S., & Jacomy, M. (2016). *Gephi – the open graph viz platform [0.9.1]*. Paris, France: The Gephi Consortium. Retrieved from https://gephi.org/

Batagelj, V., & Mrvar, A. (2017). *Pajek: Program for large network analysis (Version 5.01)*. Retrieved from http://mrvar.fdv.uni-lj.si/pajek/

Bellotti, E. (2014). *Qualitative networks: Mixed methods in sociological research*. London, UK: Routledge.

Borgatti, S. P. (2005). Centrality and network flow. *Social Networks, 27*(1), 55–71. https://doi. org/10.1016/j.socnet.2004.11.008

Borgatti, S. P., & Everett, M. G. (2006). A graph-theoretic perspective on centrality. *Social Networks, 28*(4), 466–484. https://doi.org/10.1016/j.socnet.2005.11.005

Borgatti, S. P., Everett, M. G., & Freeman, L. C. (2017). *ucinet for Windows: Software for social network analysis (Version 6.631)*. Harvard, MA: Analytic Technologies. Retrieved from https://sites.google.com/site/ucinetsoftware/home

Borgatti, S. P., Everett, M., & Johnson, J. C. (2013). *Analyzing social networks*. London, UK: Sage.

Borgatti, S. P., Mehra, A., Brass, D. J., & Labianca, G. (2009). Network analysis in the social sciences. *Science, 323*(5916), 892–895. https://doi.org/10.1126/science.1165821

Bott, E. J. (1957). *Family and social network* (1st ed.). London, UK: Tavistock.

Brandes, U., & Wagner, D. (2017). *visone (Version 2.17)*. Konstanz, Germany: University of Konstanz. Retrieved from www.visone.info/

Burt, R. S. (1992). *Structural holes: The social structure of competition*. Cambridge, MA: Harvard University Press.

Butts, C. T. (2015). *Package "network" (Version 1.13.0)*. Irvine, CA: UC Irvine. Retrieved from https://cran.r-project.org/web/packages/network/network.pdf

Butts, C. T. (2016). *Package "sna" (Version 2.4)*. Irvine, CA: UC Irvine. Retrieved from https://cran.r-project.org/web/packages/sna/sna.pdf

Carley, K. M. (2017). *ORA (Version 3)*. Pittsburgh, PA: Center for Computational Analysis of Social and Organizational Systems (CASOS), Carnegie Mellon University. Retrieved from www.casos.cs.cmu.edu/projects/ora/

Carrington, P., & Scott, J. (Eds.). (2010). *The Sage handbook of social network analysis*. Thousand Oaks, CA: Sage.

Cartwright, D., & Harary, F. (1956). Structural balance: A generalization of Heider's theory. *Psychological Review, 63*(5), 277–293. https://doi.org/10.1037/h0046049

Csardy, G. (2015). *Package "igraph" (Version 1.0.1)*. Retrieved from http://igraph.org/r/

Davis, J. A. (1967). Clustering and structural balance in graphs. *Human Relations, 20*(2), 181–187. https://doi.org/10.1177/001872676702000206

de Nooy, W., Mrvar, A., & Batagelj, V. (2011). *Exploratory social network analysis with Pajek* (Expanded edition). Cambridge, UK: Cambridge University Press.

Dekker, D., Krackhardt, D., & Snijders, T. A. (2007). Sensitivity of MRQAP tests to collinearity and autocorrelation conditions. *Psychometrika, 72*(4), 563–581. https://doi.org/10.1007/s11336-007-9016-1

Domínguez, S., & Hollstein, B. (Eds.). (2014). *Mixed methods social networks research: Design and applications*. Cambridge, UK: Cambridge University Press.

Doreian, P., & Batagelj, V. (2005). *Generalized blockmodeling*. Cambridge, UK: Cambridge University Press.

Easley, D., & Kleinberg, J. (2010). *Networks, crowds, and markets: Reasoning about a highly connected world*. New York, NY: Cambridge University Press.

Erdős, P., & Rényi, A. (1959). On random graphs. I. *Publicationes Mathematicae Debrecen, 6*, 290–297.

Everett, M. G., & Borgatti, S. P. (2010). Induced, endogenous and exogenous centrality. *Social Networks, 32*(4), 339–344. https://doi.org/10.1016/j.socnet.2010.06.004

Frank, K. A. (1995). Identifying cohesive subgroups. *Social Networks, 17*(1), 27–56. https://doi.org/10.1016/0378-8733(94)00247-8

Freeman, L. C. (1978). Centrality in social networks conceptual clarification. *Social Networks, 1*(3), 215–239. https://doi.org/10.1016/0378-8733(78)90021-7

Freeman, L. C. (2005). Graphic techniques for exploring social network data. In P. J. Carrington, J. Scott, & S. Wasserman (Eds.), *Models and methods in social network analysis* (pp. 248–269). Cambridge, UK: Cambridge University Press.

Girvan, M., & Newman, M. E. J. (2002). Community structure in social and biological networks. *Proceedings of the National Academy of Sciences of the United States of America*, *99*(12), 7821–7826. https://doi.org/doi:10.1073/pnas.122653799

Goodreau, S. M., Handcock, M. S., Hunter, D. R., Butts, C. T., & Morris, M. (2008). A statnet tutorial. *Journal of Statistical Software*, *24*(9), 1–27. https://doi.org/10.18637/jss.v024.i09

Gould, R. V., & Fernandez, R. M. (1989). Structures of mediation: A formal approach to brokerage in transaction networks. *Sociological Methodology*, *19*, 89–126. https://doi.org/10.2307/270949

Gremmen, M. C., Dijkstra, J. K., Steglich, C. E. G., & Veenstra, R. (2017). First selection, then influence: Developmental differences in friendship dynamics regarding academic achievement. *Developmental Psychology*, *53*(7), 1356–1370. https://doi.org/10.1037/dev0000314

Grund, T. (2015). *Social network analysis using Stata* (United Kingdom Stata Users' Group Meetings 2015 No. 21). Stata Users Group. Retrieved from https://ideas.repec.org/p/boc/usug15/21.html

Handcock, M. S., Hunter, D. R., Butts, C. T., Goodreau, S. M., & Morris, M. (2003). *statnet: Software tools for the statistical modeling of network data*. Seattle, WA: Statnet Project. Retrieved from http://statnetproject.org/

Handcock, M. S., Hunter, D. R., Butts, C. T., Goodreau, S. M., & Morris, M. (2008). statnet: Software tools for the representation, visualization, analysis and simulation of network data. *Journal of Statistical Software*, *24*(1), 1548–7660. https://doi.org/10.18637/jss.v024.i01

Hansen, D. L., Shneiderman, B., & Smith, M. A. (2011). *Analyzing social media networks with Node-XL: Insights from a connected world*. Burlington, MA: Morgan Kaufmann.

Harary, F. (1953). On the notion of balance of a signed graph. *Michigan Math*, *2*(2), 143–146. https://doi.org/10.1307/mmj/1028989917

Heider, F. (1946). Attitudes and cognitive organization. *The Journal of Psychology*, *21*, 107–112. https://doi.org/10.1080/00223980.1946.9917275

Hollstein, B. (2011). Qualitative approaches. In J. Scott & P. J. Carrington (Eds.), *The SAGE handbook of social network analysis* (pp. 404–417). London, UK: Sage.

Hollstein, B., & Straus, F. (Eds.). (2006). *Qualitative netzwerkanalyse: Konzepte, methoden, anwendungen*. Wiesbaden: VS Verlag für Sozialwissenschaften.

IBM Corporation. (2012). *IBM SPSS modeler social network analysis 15 user guide*. Armonk, NY: IBM Corporation.

Jennings, H. H. (1943). *Leadership and isolation: A study of personality in interpersonal relations*. New York, NY: Longmans, Green and co.

Kalish, Y., Luria, G., Toker, S., & Westman, M. (2015). Till stress do us part: On the interplay between perceived stress and communication network dynamics. *Journal of Applied Psychology*, *100*(6), 1737–1751. https://doi.org/10.1037/apl0000023

Knoke, D., & Yang, S. (2008). *Social network analysis* (2nd ed.). Thousand Oaks, CA: Sage.

Kolaczyk, E. D., & Csárdi, G. (2014). *Statistical analysis of network data with R*. New York, NY: Springer.

Krackhardt, D. (1987). QAP Partialling as a test of spuriousness. *Social Networks*, *9*(2), 171–186. https://doi.org/10.1016/0378-8733(87)90012-8

Krackhardt, D. (1988). Predicting with networks: Nonparametric multiple regression analysis of dyadic data. *Social Networks*, *10*(4), 359–381. https://doi.org/10.1016/0378-8733(88)90004-4

Laumann, E. O., Marsden, P. V., & Prensky, D. (1983). The boundary specification problem in network analysis. In R. S. Burt & M. J. Minor (Eds.), *Applied network analysis* (pp. 18–34). Thousand Oaks, CA: Sage Publications.

Luce, R. D., & Perry, A. D. (1949). A method of matrix analysis of group structure. *Psychometrika, 14*(2), 95–116. https://doi.org/10.1007/BF02289146

Mercken, L., Steglich, C., Sinclair, P., Holliday, J., & Moore, L. (2012). A longitudinal social network analysis of peer influence, peer selection, and smoking behavior among adolescents in British schools. *Health Psychology, 31*(4), 450. https://doi.org/10.1037/a0026876

Merton, R. K. (1957). Priorities in scientific discovery: a chapter in the sociology of science. *American Sociological Review, 22*(6), 635–659.

Merton, R. K. (1968). The Matthew effect in science. *Science, 159*(3810), 56–63. https://doi.org/10.1126/science.159.3810.56

Mitchell, J. C. (1969). *Social networks in urban situations: Analyses of personal relationships in Central African towns.* Manchester: Manchester University Press.

Miura, H. (2012). Stata graph library for network analysis. *The Stata Journal, 12*(1), 94–129. Retrieved from www.stata-journal.com/sjpdf.html?articlenum=st0248

Mokken, R. (1979). Cliques, clubs and clans. *Quality & Quantity: International Journal of Methodology, 13*(2), 161–173. https://doi.org/10.1007/BF00139635

Moreno, J. L. (1934). *Who shall survive? A new approach to the problem of human interrelations* (Vol. 58). Washington, DC: National and Mental Disease Publishing Co.

Newman, M. E. J. (2010). *Networks: An introduction.* Oxford: Oxford University Press.

Newman, M. E. J., & Girvan, M. (2004). Finding and evaluating community structure in networks. *Physical Review E, 69*(2), 026113. https://doi.org/10.1103/PhysRevE.69.026113

Pinter-Wollman, N., Hobson, E. A., Smith, J. E., Edelman, A. J., Shizuka, D., de Silva, S., . . . McDonald, D. B. (2014). The dynamics of animal social networks: Analytical, conceptual, and theoretical advances. *Behavioral Ecology, 25*(2), 242–255. https://doi.org/10.1093/beheco/art047

Prell, C. (2011). *Social network analysis: History, theory and methodology*: London, UK: Sage.

Provan, K. G., Fish, A., & Sydow, J. (2007). Interorganizational networks at the network level: A review of the empirical literature on whole networks. *Journal of Management, 33*(3), 479–516. https://doi.org/10.1177/0149206307302554

Ripley, R. M., Snijders, T. A. B., Preciado, P., Boda, Z., & Vörös, A. (2017). *Manual for RSiena (Version 1.1–307).* Retrieved from www.stats.ox.ac.uk/~snijders/siena/RSiena_Manual.pdf

Robins, G. L. (2013). A tutorial on methods for the modeling and analysis of social network data. *Journal of Mathematical Psychology, 57*(6), 261–274. https://doi.org/10.1016/j.jmp.2013.02.001

Robins, G. L. (2015). *Doing social network research: Network-based research design for social scientists.* London, UK: Sage.

Robins, G. L., Lusher, D., & Koskinen, J. (Eds.). (2012). *Exponential random graph models for social networks.* Cambridge, UK: Cambridge University Press.

Robins, G. L., Snijders, T. A. B., Wang, P., Handcock, M. S., & Pattison, P. E. (2007). Recent Developments in exponential random graph (p$\star$) models for social networks. *Social Networks, 29*(2), 192–215. https://doi.org/10.1016/j.socnet.2006.08.003

SAS Institute Inc. (2013). *SAS/GRAPH® 9.4: Network visualization workshop.* Cary, NC: SAS Institute Inc.

Schaefer, D. R., Kornienko, O., & Fox, A. M. (2011). Misery does not love company network selection mechanisms and depression homophily. *American Sociological Review, 76*(5), 764–785. https://doi.org/10.1177/0003122411420813

Scott, J. (2017). *Social network analysis* (4th ed.). London, UK: Sage.

Seidman, S. B. (1983). Network structure and minimum degree. *Social Networks, 5*(3), 269–287. https://doi.org/10.1016/0378-8733(83)90028-X

Seidman, S. B., & Foster, B. L. (1978). A graph-theoretic generalization of the clique concept. *Journal of Mathematical Sociology*, *6*(1), 139–154. https://doi.org/10.1080/00222 50X.1978.9989883

Smith, M. A., Ceni, A., Milic-Frayling, N., Shneiderman, B., Mendes Rodrigues, E., Leskovec, J., & Dunne, C. (2010). *NodeXL*. Social Media Research Foundation. Retrieved from www.smrfoundation.org/nodexl/

Snijders, T. A. B. (2011). Statistical models for social networks. *Annual Review of Sociology*, *37*(1), 131–153. https://doi.org/10.1146/annurev.soc.012809.102709

Snijders, T. A. B. (2017). *RSiena* (Version 1.1–307). Retrieved from www.stats.ox.ac. uk/~snijders/siena/siena_r.htm

Snijders, T. A. B., van de Bunt, G. G., & Steglich, C. E. G. (2010). Introduction to stochastic actor-based models for network dynamics. *Social Networks*, *32*(1), 44–60. https://doi. org/10.1016/j.socnet.2009.02.004

Steglich, C., Snijders, T. A., & West, P. (2006). Applying SIENA: An illustrative analysis of the coevolution of adolescents' friendship networks, taste in music, and alcohol consumption. *Methodology: European Journal of Research Methods for the Behavioral and Social Sciences*, *2*(1), 48. https://doi.org/10.1027/1614-2241.2.1.48

Wang, P., Robins, G. L., & Pattison, P. E. (2009). *PNet: Program for the simulation and estimation of exponential random graph models*. Melbourne, Australia: Melbourne School of Psychological Sciences, the University of Melbourne. Retrieved from www.melnet.org.au/pnet/

Wasserman, S., & Faust, K. (1994). *Social network analysis: Methods and applications*. Cambridge, UK: Cambridge University Press.

Watts, D. J., & Strogatz, S. H. (1998). Collective dynamics of "small-world" networks. *Nature*, *393*(6684), 440–442. https://doi.org/10.1038/30918

White, H. C., Boorman, S. A., & Breiger, R. L. (1976). Social structure from multiple networks. I. Blockmodels of roles and positions. *American Journal of Sociology*, *81*(4), 730–780.

Yang, S., Keller, F. B., & Zheng, L. (2016). *Social network analysis: Methods and examples*. Thousand Oaks, CA: Sage.

Section 4

Research dissemination

This final section of the book contains two chapters discussing the three main ways your research results can be disseminated: via *publications* (Chapter 24) and in an *academic thesis* and an *organisational report* (Chapter 25). These two chapters discuss the key requirements and considerations for each method of research dissemination and include, for example, the relatively new concept adopted by many universities of *thesis by publication*.

24 Publishing your research

Craig McGarty and Zoe C. Walter

Introduction: why, where and how to publish?

Although we have some strong views about many of the issues we cover in this chapter, surprisingly, perhaps, we want to start with the warning that we are not suggesting you should follow *all* of our advice. Just as the work that academics publish can involve contested and conflicted positions, the same is true about publishing itself. We are not saying that there are no right or wrong answers, but we are saying that there are many cases where the same answer will be right or wrong at different times. The standards and practices that apply in sub-disciplines of applied psychology are part of the real richness of the field. Our standards come from our experiences as social psychologists who keep a keen eye on other fields, such as political psychology (both authors) and clinical psychology (Walter). We have formed our views about publication practices and standards in the fields we are interested in by observing, listening to and discussing with colleagues. Our task is not to convince you to adopt the practices we prefer but to help you to take the same steps in your own field.

As you will see, this chapter addresses three key questions: why you should publish, where to publish, and how to publish. Despite our caveat that we might not give you straight answers: what more could you want to know?

Why publish?

Our first question may surprise you: "Of course I want to publish if I don't want to perish!" Although the life-preserving functions of publications may be overstated, there are indeed powerful reasons for publishing. Publications, especially publications in applied psychology, represent new knowledge, and the stock of that knowledge is surprisingly thin even on vitally important and controversial topics. It is not uncommon to find large industrialised cities or even entire nations where there is no psychological publication record on some topics or where publications are hopelessly dated or methodologically flawed.

Despite the importance of publications for advancing human knowledge, it is not the case that any publication is better than no publication. There is no point teaching content to students or informing practice or policy, if the ideas lack scientific merit and rigour. That is why peer-reviewed publication is the gold standard for academic activity. It might seem convenient and appealing to drop your ideas on the Internet or blurt them to the media, but that can also be grossly irresponsible and contrary to the ethical and practical standards applying to psychologists (such as the Australian Code for the Responsible Conduct of Research, 2007). Peer review protects you and the public from mistakes by at least providing the guarantee that independent experts have judged the new knowledge to be of sufficient value to be shared, and without that safeguard it is generally better to remain silent (especially on topics that can have deep impact on people's lives). Balanced against that, there is no point having great ideas without telling them to other people. Turning Kurt Lewin on his head: there is nothing so impractical as an unpublished theory.

Along with the why of publishing is the when. The time to publish is now. If you are doing a PhD, then the opportunity to think deeply about a topic gives you a platform to do really good work. Your publications in the PhD and post-PhD phase may well be the most successful you ever do and can establish the rest of your career. Completing a PhD is a gruelling and long process, and so doing anything that can make that process easier should be embraced; many of the pressures of doing a PhD can be alleviated by publishing papers as you go. Publishing as you go has the benefits of making you consistently work on your writing, divides your thesis into manageable sections and allows access to expert feedback on your research and ideas for future studies (see the previous section on the peer-review process), and you come out of the PhD with a healthy track record of publications. Additionally, provided you have good supervision, this allows you to gain familiarity with the publishing procedure, such as how to write to journal editors, pitch articles and respond to reviewers, while in a supportive environment with less pressure. But get ready to deal with rejection and the extra work that comes with revise and resubmits.

You might also be limited in when you publish by who you work with. Working with industry partners can be a fruitful and practical endeavour. Industry partnerships are a growing source of funding for academic research, and if done correctly can be mutually beneficial to all parties. However, the data you collect may be the property of an industry partner who wants a report but not a journal article. This can impose restrictions on what you are able to publish. If you are planning to conduct research with an industry partner, the earlier you have these conversations, the better. Understanding what is in the contract and what you are legally allowed to publish and in what outlets is an important consideration before signing a contract with an industry partner (and it should be covered in the ethics protocol used to conduct the research). If in doubt, seek advice. Universities have liaison officers and a legal team that can assist with these matters.

Where to publish

You will have many options for publications. The main scholarly forms of publication in psychology are peer-reviewed journals, conferences and books/chapters. Peer-reviewed journals are the prestige form in psychology, and we would recommend that over a five-year period you should aim to have more papers published than you have chapters and conference presentations combined. If you find yourself veering far away from that, stop and take stock. It may be worth asking if a week-long trip for a conference is time better spent writing, or whether agreeing to write a chapter will take the time you need to commit to having your project data published. In each case, asking yourself the question should not presume the answer (if you are reading this chapter and concluding that you should spend all your time writing and never go to conferences, then you are not reading carefully enough). The decision of where to publish should be in mind before you start to write your paper. You want the message to resonate with the audience, and it is easiest to do that when you have an idea of where you want your research to be seen (for a consideration of a range of factors – in fact an actual model of how to select journals to submit to – see Knight & Steinbach, 2008).

Journals are often ranked by bibliometric indices based on citations – those same indices are often used to rank researchers and their universities. This is a controversial practice but difficult to avoid – you want your work to be cited, and on average it helps to publish where people will see your research. Citation counts come from the number of references; if your paper has a hundred references, then it needs a hundred cites to break even (and that is why you cannot compare citations rates across academic fields – if you work in pure mathematics, where people write papers with single authors and 20 references, then your work will be less highly cited). It is very common for a paper to have zero citations for a number of years, and a small number of papers receive large numbers of citation. This means that the distribution of citation rates is highly skewed, so the median is a better indicator of the expected number of citations for a paper (unfortunately, lots of people who should know better use the mean citation).

The best-known measure of citation is the *journal impact factor* (or IF) used by Web of Science (Clarivate Analytics, n.d. orig. 1994). There are alternatives to the IF such as Scopus's SNIP – source normalised impact per paper (see Beatty, 2016). This is the average number of citations for a year of papers in a journal in the last two years. McGarty (2000) suggests this statistic is inappropriate for psychology. This is partly because it takes longer than two years for a paper to have genuine impact in psychology due to the time it takes to secure funding, conduct and publish research. McGarty (2000) suggests the five-year impact factor is more appropriate (but note that most psychology academics who follow impact factors will rely on the two-year impact factor despite its limitations for the field). As a rule of thumb, aim for most of your academic stream publications to be in journals with a five-year impact greater than 2.0; that will tend to put your papers in the top half.

Another statistic that is used (questionably) to rate researchers and journal is the H-index. H (Hirschfield) numbers are counts of papers with a certain number of cites or more. A researcher with an H number of 20 has 20 papers with 20 or more cites. These numbers are intensely biased against junior researchers. It is worth being aware of them, as people may be using them to judge you (funding bodies such as the Australian National Health and Medical Research

Council do not allow their use for assessing grant applications except as part of a broad range of indicators; NHMRC, 2017). H indices can come from sources such as Web of Science and Scopus. Google Scholar has a better coverage of books and book chapters publications. Citation statistics from Google Scholar are available from Harzing's (2017) *Publish or Perish* software.

Books tend to be of lower value in psychology than peer-reviewed journals. That is not our view but an assessment of the value placed on journal articles and books by research evaluation exercises for psychology. Book and book chapters can, however, provide a space to express views in longer form. If you are going to publish in books and book chapters, make sure that you are working with outlets and people that you respect. If the publisher is one you have never heard of then that automatically suggests you need to find out more. If the editor of a book is not a respected academic on the topic of that book, then you need to ask whether your work is in the right place. Specifically, you should avoid publishers who offer to publish your thesis before anyone at the publishing house has read it. Also avoid "predatory" journals that appear to offer open access but are actually just after money.

Another key outlet to present your research is at conferences, via either an oral or poster presentation. Presenting either format at a conference provides the opportunity to disseminate your research at various stages of development, from preliminary findings to data that is being written for publication. This allows you to not only show your work but to receive instant feedback and may open up collaboration opportunities. As with publishing in journals, look at the fit of your research and where the research will get the most traction when making decisions about where to present. Additionally, know your audience and tailor your presentation to that audience. Most conferences require you to submit an abstract several months in advance, and thus require planning.

Research engagement with a broader audience outside of academia is increasingly being used as a metric for academic success. This can be seen in the Research Excellence Framework (HEFCE, 2014) in the United Kingdom, which now includes case studies for examples of research impact as part of the assessment. In this case, "impact" refers to the effect of research outside academia (so impact factors do not measure research impact in this sense). In addition to developing a portfolio of peer-reviewed publications, universities are looking for researchers who have an ability to communicate and engage within the public arena. You may also want the fantastic work you have been doing to be read more broadly than the audience that frequent the journals you are publishing in. Thus, it is important to learn skills in communicating and publishing in other outlets, such as media and social media. Commonly, this comes in the form of media statements about published research, writing an evidenced-based article on an issue close to your research (e.g., an article in The Conversation), and disseminating your publications on social media (e.g., Twitter) and career networking (e.g., LinkedIn, Research Gate) sites. This type of engagement is not just about getting more citations and views of scholarly articles (although it will hopefully help you disseminate your publications), it can enhance research collaboration and public engagement. That is, communicating your research through other outlets can help you connect with others and makes your research accessible to communities outside of academia (although one should be following the points outlined earlier, first and foremost).

Our general advice is that you should try to publish in outlets that the academics that you respect value. If you do not know what the people you respect value, then you desperately need to find out, because there is no surer sign that you are not engaged in a scholarly community. Start a conversation. Ask colleagues what they think of journals, and then evaluate those responses. If the response is "Have you seen the impact factor? It's terrible!" then your colleague may not be telling you much about a journal that they may have never read, but they may be giving you useful information as to how impact factors are regarded by that colleague. A tip on a change of editorial policy ("they are really open to qualitative research/ replication studies") may be even more valuable.

How to publish

The advice we can offer on how to publish excellent research is surprisingly straightforward. We will provide the advice generally and then drill down to some specific tips for conference presentations. Publishing excellent research involves following the standards of excellent research practice that are detailed elsewhere in this book (such as the principles outlined in Chapter 2 by Brough and Hawkes). If your research has been guided by theory, follows ethical guidelines, uses valid and reliable methods, is innovative and has practical implications, then there is every chance that you can create excellent publications. If you struggle to remember why you did the research and what you did, or if you have difficulty telling yourself what is good and new about your research, then the best writing practices in the world will avail you little. There is a one-way street from excellent research to excellent publications. It is far, far better to start the research afresh than to seek to publish deficient research – deficient publications that will sit next to your name for the rest of your career (that is also a good reason to make sure that the reference details in your publications are accurate).

If you are travelling on the "excellent research road", then the problem becomes one of communication. Here we think we can scarcely do better than to encourage you to follow Grice's (1975) maxims of effective communication: be truthful, be relevant, be as concise as possible while conveying the relevant information, and be clear. A good publication is one that meets those standards. Being truthful entails following open science practices. Say exactly what you did, why you did it, and what you found (with additional information readily available to readers in supplementary online materials). If you embrace the spirit of the previous sentence in your scientific communication, you will find you are complying with open science standards. The Open Science Framework (Nosek et al. 2017) provides the following standard advice for reviewers:

> I request that the authors add a statement to the paper confirming whether, for all experiments, they have reported all measures, conditions, data exclusions, and how they determined their sample sizes. . . .
>
> Given this clear and widely available set of expectations do not wait to be told to do this. Be proactive and supply the information before you submit.

In the case of applied psychology, "being relevant" generally also means providing guidance for practitioners on the implications of the findings for human welfare. The principle of truthfulness is paramount here. Do not overstate the relevance of your findings but remember also that if modesty is false, then there is no place for it in scientific communication. Being as concise as possible is the most difficult of the maxims to follow. It can be hard to decide what information is relevant and how much detail to provide. Other papers in the field will often provide a guide, as do bodies such as the Open Science Foundation. In general, though, it is crucial that readers should be able to access all of the information they might need (not just the information you choose to provide).

The matter of clarity of style is a personal one. Our advice again here is to follow the standard of communication in your field. Many recent graduates follow (undergraduate) writing guidelines that were outdated many years ago. Adopt the writing style used by top researchers in your field rather than that recommended by your first-year lecturer (who may be wise but might work in a completely different field to you).

For what it is worth, our preference is for communications that present a coherent narrative (without ever letting the need for the narrative to be coherent to get in the way of the truth). That story is usually of the form "We had this idea, we collected these data, we found these results, and we think this is what it means". We can call that the Story of Imrad (introduction, methods, results and discussion), but in a short conference presentation you will not have the chance to tell as much of the background as you would in a journal article. Again, you need to make sure the narrative you choose to deliver fits within the range of expectations of your audience. You might wish to tell the story of your personal voyage of discovery or of the tribulations of the research process, but you need to ask whether the audience will be interested in that. Although time will be racing by as you speak, it is unlikely that your audience is subjectively experiencing the same thing (you may have been to some brilliant talks, but how often do you find yourself thinking "I wish this speaker had a longer time slot?").

When you give an oral conference presentation, it is important to be as engaging and clear as possible. Have three to five take-away messages that you want the audience to remember and try to convey a coherent story. When preparing slides, remember less is more (a general rule of thumb is about one slide per minute of talk), and pictures or graphs are more memorable and easier to follow than a wall of text, but make sure you have that wall of text to hand so that you can provide details if requested.

When you prepare and present a conference poster, you should be wary of trying to include too much information. You want a poster that can be easily understood at a glance (the main message at least), with clear results. Be prepared to summarise the poster for anyone who stops to have a look, and have further information and a copy of your poster (e.g., a handout or a QR code) on hand for people who would like more detail. Some of the people viewing your poster will want to read the detail and then ask questions. Others will prefer a rundown from you. The audience member gets to choose.

Conclusion

In conclusion we would say your task when receiving advice is to EVALUATE the advice, not to TAKE the advice. Even though we have given you some generic standards and guides, we are not committed to all of them ourselves. We think you and everybody else will be happier if you work to the standards of applied psychologists, whom you respect and whose performances and practices you seek to emulate. If you find their advice differs from ours, then listen to them more carefully.

References

Beatty, S. (2016). *Journal Metrics in Scopus: Source Normalized Impact per Paper (SNIP)*. Retrieved November 22, 2017, from https://blog.scopus.com/posts/journal-metrics-in-scopus-source-normalized-impact-per-paper-snip

Clarivate Analytics. (n.d. orig. 1994). *The Clarivate analytics impact factor*. Retrieved November 22, 2017, from https://clarivate.com/essays/impact-factor/

Grice, H. P. (1975). Logic and conversation. In P. Cole & J. Morgan (Eds.), *Syntax and semantics. 3: Speech acts* (pp. 1–48). New York, NY: Academic Press.

Harzing, A. W. (2017). *Publish or perish*. Retrieved from www.harzing.com/pop.htm

Higher Education Funding Council for England. (2014). *REF impact*. Retrieved from November 22, 2017, from www.hefce.ac.uk/rsrch/REFimpact/

Knight, L. V., & Steinbach, T. A. (2008). Selecting an appropriate publication outlet: A comprehensive model of journal selection criteria for researchers in a broad range of academic disciplines. *International Journal of Doctoral Studies, 3*, 59–79.

McGarty, C. (2000). The citation impact factor in social psychology: A bad statistic that encourages bad science? *Current Research in Social Psychology, 5*, 1–16.

NHMRC. (2017). *Principles, obligations and conduct during peer review*. Retrieved November 1, 2017, from www.nhmrc.gov.au/book/guide-peer-review-2017/4-principles-obligations-and-conduct-during-peer-review

Nosek, B. A., Simonsohn, U., Moore, D. A., Nelson, L. D., Simmons, J. P., Sallans, A., & LeBel, E. P. (2017). Standard reviewer statement for disclosure of sample, conditions, measures, and exclusions. *Open Science Framework*. Retrieved November 30, 2017, from https://osf.io/hadz3/

25 Producing an academic thesis and an organisational report

Toni Fowlie, Maree Roche, and Michael O'Driscoll

Introduction

There is an overwhelming amount of literature available on how to write a thesis, and it is often difficult for students to decide where to begin to read and, furthermore, to decide which of this information is relevant. This chapter attempts to summarise the most relevant information and present some common problems and challenges often faced by students in the write-up phase of their thesis. It is not a 'how-to' guide; rather, it presents helpful information and advice surrounding writing a thesis. Additionally, this chapter provides advice on how to present the research as a report to organisations who have participated in the research.

Producing an academic thesis

Reading in preparation for thesis writing

While there are many 'how-to' guides available which offer advice on how to write a research thesis, it is important for students to not get carried away with trying to read everything (McBride, 2009), as this takes up valuable time that could be used for writing. There are, however, several things that should be read by the student which will make thesis writing a lot smoother. Students should read any guidelines or documents surrounding thesis writing that have been issued by their institution. Different institutions have different variations on certain aspects of the thesis process, and thus reading the protocols will give students an idea of what is expected. The institution may also be able to provide guidelines of what the examiners will be looking for when marking the thesis. Reviewing previous theses from the department in which the student is enrolled can also be informative.

Certain topics that students should be familiar with before embarking on the writing journey include the layout of a thesis, the academic writing style, grammar and formatting, and referencing. Having a sound understanding of these will enable them to concentrate on the content of their writing. For theses in psychology, it is highly recommended that students consult the Publication Manual of the American Psychological Association (American Psychological Association, 2010).

The importance of planning

Having a detailed timeline established from the very beginning of the thesis process will ensure that the writing phase of the thesis runs as smoothly as possible. Having set dates for when specific chapters are due allows supervisors to encourage students to keep on schedule. It is also useful to make a detailed plan of each chapter before commencing writing, as this will ensure that important concepts are not overlooked and will prevent random movement between ideas (Holtom & Fisher, 1999). This also provides supervisors with an idea of the direction students are intending each chapter to take.

Structuring the thesis and writing style

One of the simplest ways to structure a psychology thesis is to follow what is commonly referred to as 'the basic science structure' (Carter, Kelly, & Brailsford, 2012, p. 17). This model follows the layout of front cover, acknowledgements, abstract, table of contents, list of figures, list of tables, main body, references and appendices.

The main body of the thesis will be organised into several chapters. The number of chapters will be dependent on the student's particular research, but generally includes four major topics: introduction, method, results and discussion (Carter et al., 2012). The introduction will generally include a discussion of the theoretical model to be tested in the research, along with specific hypotheses and their underlying rationale. The method chapter focuses on the sample, measures and procedures utilised in the research. Findings from the research are presented in the results chapter, although sometimes there may be a need to have more than one results chapter, especially if the research includes both cross-sectional and longitudinal data or is a combination of quantitative and qualitative data. The discussion chapter incorporates a summary of the major findings, discussion of the potential explanations for the findings, theoretical and practical implications of the research, limitations in the research (e.g. the sample or research design), and some general conclusions regarding the contributions of the findings to the literature.

Although this structure works well for the majority of students, the nature of the particular research being undertaken should have priority over this basic model (Carter et al., 2012). Joyner, Rouse and Glatthorn (2013) believe that the thesis should be organised in a way that enables the findings to be communicated to the reader in the simplest way possible. For instance, in some theses, especially those with a more qualitative approach, the results and discussion sections may sometimes be merged.

Writing style and formatting

When it comes to beginning to write their thesis, many students often report that they would rather not begin writing until their research is underway and they feel they have something relevant to write about (Murray, 2011). However, this approach may delay writing even longer (Murray, 2011), which can mean a lot of rushed writing as the due date for the thesis submission draws nearer. Murray (2011) suggested using writing prompts to begin the writing process, such as 'My project is about. . .', rather than the more formal 'Research questions'. Writing prompts such as these can help develop ideas and build confidence (Murray, 2011). It is important for students to try to make progress with their writing as often as possible. Writing every day – even if it is only one or two paragraphs – is still progress towards the end result. Additionally, checking references and quotations on days where students feel as though they are too tired to write will enable them to continue to make progress on their thesis.

Academic writing has its own rules and conventions, which should be followed. Three major conventions are clarity, objectivity and justification of arguments (Oliver, 2014). When writing the thesis, it is important to keep in mind who the readers will be (Hartley, 1997). For example, the examiners of the thesis may not be from the same discipline as the student (Murray, 2011). This means that the writing needs to be coherent so that the reader can easily understand the research (Hartley, 1997). Students should also be concise, which means using words that have the exact meaning that the writer intends them to have, avoiding ambiguous words where possible, and writing concisely. Clarity also involves structuring the thesis in a logical and systematic order (Joyner et al., 2013).

As a general rule, academic writing is objective, meaning it must be free of personal feelings and beliefs of the researcher (Oliver, 2014), although in qualitative investigations it may be appropriate to insert personal reflections. Supervisors will advise on the appropriateness of including these types of reflection. Arguments need to be justified, whether through theoretical logic or previous findings. When citing material to support arguments, students should only cite sources that they have read, should cite primary sources rather than secondary sources where possible, and should not deliberately misinterpret the source just to support their arguments (Joyner et al., 2013).

The student should also keep in mind that even though the evidence presented may support a particular claim, it should not be presented as an absolute truth (Oliver, 2014). In psychology, it is generally difficult to know that something is true with complete certainty; thus, the general approach in academic writing is a cautious one (Oliver, 2014). For example, words such as *always, never, clearly* and *obviously* should typically be avoided, as statements which include these words can often easily be disproved. Instead, terms such as *assume, suggest, appear* and *generally* should be used, as they are more cautious and more applicable.

Often students get confused about whether they should be writing in the first or third person. Traditionally, scholarly writing is written in the third person voice, as this separates the researcher from the research and portrays the results as being more objective (Oliver, 2014). Although third person is still widely preferred, the use of first person has become acceptable in certain situations (Oliver, 2014). In theses with a more qualitative perspective, writing in the first person may be totally acceptable; supervisor(s) can advise on which approach is most appropriate. Students also should be consistent with tenses. Normally, past tense is used for the introduction/literature review chapter and the methods chapter, whereas present tense is used for the results and discussion chapters (Joyner et al., 2013). It is also important to use gender-neutral language so that assumptions are not unfairly made about one gender over another (Oliver, 2014).

Using a referencing software such as *Endnote* or *Zotero* is advantageous for several reasons. Referencing software allows students to keep a database of the sources they have read and cited. The software also allows bibliographies to be generated in any citation style and accurately cites these sources throughout the thesis, which saves considerable amounts of time. Often the software is free or available freely to students through their institution. Use of such software is often more efficient and effective than any 'manual' citation system.

Theses including publications

A thesis including publications is a relatively new mode for completing a thesis. This format is a thesis that incorporates papers authored/co-authored by students that have been submitted/accepted for publication in peer-reviewed academic journals. This type of thesis is known as a thesis-by-publication or a thesis-with-publication. Theses including publications still require the manuscript to work as an 'integrated whole' (Massey University, n.d, p. 2), and thus they must contain framing texts (Kumpulainen, 2008) to link together the separate research papers and to illustrate the overall theme. Each institution has its own guidelines surrounding how many research papers must be submitted and/or published. Some institutions require the articles to be published and some for them to be accepted, and others only require them to be submitted. Some combination of these is common. Therefore, before choosing this format of thesis, it is important that students check these requirements with their institution, as well as discussing this option with their supervisors.

There are both advantages and disadvantages with undertaking this thesis structure. Advantages include the acquisition of skills in preparing and submitting work for publication. This means that students can graduate with a degree and a publication record (Kumpulainen, 2008). Publishing research in peer-reviewed journals allows students to engage with the broader scientific community and to be mentored in the process of academic publishing. Students also learn valuable lessons, such as the ability to accept critical comment outside of the supervisor domain (The University of Sydney, 2015).

Although they are becoming more popular, theses including publications have some associated problems (Jackson, 2013). Disadvantages of this format include the difficulty of conveying coherence between the different articles and the time delay in waiting for co-authors to review and contribute and for journals to provide editorial decisions (The University of Sydney, 2015). It is also argued that it is often challenging to determine the candidate's contribution to the overall submission due to the co-authorship nature of a thesis including publications (Jackson, 2013). It is therefore important to consider several factors before choosing this type of thesis, including the requirements of the institution, the research topic, intellectual property, and co-authorship (Robins & Kanowski, 2008).

The student-supervisor relationship and other support networks

The student-supervisor relationship is extremely important, as the relationship continues from the very beginning of the thesis through to submission of the thesis, and potentially beyond this (Rountree & Laing, 1996). Therefore, the importance of establishing this relationship from the very beginning of the research is a priority. It is vital that this relationship is successful, as feelings towards the relationship can cross over to feelings about the thesis (Rountree & Laing, 1996). Because this relationship can be complex (Oliver, 2014), to ensure success it is important that the roles of students and the supervisors are well defined.

Communication is important in the student-supervisor relationship. Being clear from the beginning about what is expected from one another will help minimise misunderstandings (Holtom & Fisher, 1999). An important task for students is to reduce confusion by clarifying several things from the beginning. Student need to establish what their supervisors expect of them, and what they expect from their supervisors (White, 2011). Students are also responsible for asking for reassurance from their supervisors. An easy way to do this is to provide a list of questions when submitting drafts to the supervisor. These questions could include (Oliver, 2014, p. 70):

- Is the writing style too formal, too informal or just about right?
- Are there places where first-person singular could be used?
- Are the academic arguments sound?
- Overall, is the standard of the work at the appropriate academic level?

Within the first few weeks of thesis enrolment, three things should be established: regularity of student-supervisor meetings; time required for supervisors to read and review drafts (White, 2011); and the number of drafts the supervisor is willing to review.

Developing successful supervision

To make the supervision relationship function as smoothly as possible, White (2011) suggested that students should:

- ensure the supervisor's previous comments have been addressed before submitting the next draft;
- ensure that drafts have as few grammatical errors as possible;

- be receptive to constructive criticism;
- be prepared and prompt at meetings;
- keep supervisors informed of individual circumstances that are likely to affect the thesis process;
- remain enthusiastic and positive about the thesis; and
- approach the supervisors with any concerns they have.

Other support networks

Students cannot expect to meet with their supervisors several times a week; thus, having other support networks could benefit students. It is important, however, that students are open with their supervisors about additional support they are seeking. This ensures that supervisors do not feel that students are seeking help without their knowledge.

The use of library resources is vital for success at the postgraduate level, and therefore getting to know the way around the library is necessary for thesis completion (Rountree & Laing, 1996). Libraries usually offer tutorials on how to use the catalogue system and computer software, where to find certain collections in the library and borrowing protocols for special materials (Rountree & Laing, 1996). Identifying their subject librarian is also an excellent way for students to be able to tap into resources that they may not normally find themselves. If they make their subject librarian aware of their research, the librarian may be able to access hard-to-get resources and can keep a look out for any material new to the library (Rountree & Laing, 1996).

External mentors may be beneficial for certain aspects of the thesis such as help with reading lists. Seeking help from external mentors may also help students if their supervisors do not know much about a particular area (Kwan, 2009). However, as mentioned earlier, students need to advise their supervisors about consulting external mentors. Forming support groups with fellow students is a useful way for students to discuss challenges encountered over the course of their theses in a non-threatening environment (White, 2011). These meetings can be more facilitative and open than meetings between supervisors and students (White, 2011) and can help combat feelings of isolation (Conrad, 2006).

Students can also be involved in thesis writing groups, which can cultivate writing skills and enhance productivity (Ferguson, 2009) and could also lead to peer review systems (Aghaee & Hansson, 2013). The purpose of peer review systems is to improve the quality of thesis manuscripts by students giving feedback for improvement on the basic aspects of the manuscript (Aghaee & Hansson, 2013). This allows for the supervisors' time to be used more efficiently. Students, however, need to be wary about the accuracy of the information received from fellow students. It is wise for students to view advice given with a bit of scepticism and to double check things with their supervisor.

Common problems and challenges

This section covers some of the most common problems and challenges that thesis students often face. These can include mismanagement of time and resources, procrastination and loss of motivation. These problems and challenges are important to address, as they can often lead to students not completing their thesis on time. Some ways to obviate these difficulties are also suggested.

One of the most common problems thesis students face is not allowing enough time for particular parts of their research and thesis production. The time needed for tasks such as analyses, writing, editing and printing are often underestimated, which ultimately may create stress as the thesis submission date draws nearer. Creating a detailed timeline will ensure that these tasks progress properly.

Thesis students often have to overcome procrastination and loss of motivation at some point during their thesis. It is not unusual for them to try to avoid tasks that they find unpleasant or difficult to do. Common ways to overcome procrastination include setting specific goals and breaking up large tasks into smaller pieces to make the overall writing task more manageable. Students' desire for perfectionism can also lead to procrastination with thesis writing. Students should concentrate on getting their work and thoughts onto paper and then reworking it to make it 'perfect'.

Writing an organisational report

At the conclusion of writing a thesis, it is often necessary for students to write a feedback report for organisations who participated in the research. Students should understand that providing feedback is a 'critical part of the "psychological contract"' (Brewerton & Millward, 2001, p. 177), and if this is violated, it can mean that the student's 'future relationship with the company is severely jeopardised as are future research prospects for other students and the educational institutes of which they are part' (Brewerton & Millward, 2001, p. 177).

When writing the organisational report, there are a few things to keep in mind. Firstly, it needs to be established who will be reading the report. Identifying the key reader will ensure that the writing style and manner is appropriate. For example, different people within organisations have different levels of understanding of certain subjects and topic areas. If the reader of the report is a professional within the same field as the research, they are likely to have a good understanding of the topic. However, if the reader is not familiar with the topic area, then more background information may need to be provided.

Secondly, any complex jargon related specifically to the research needs to be omitted and replaced with everyday terms (that is, simple language). If there are certain terms that cannot be replaced (for instance, where replacing them is likely to change the meaning and interpretation), they need to be clearly explained. It may also be useful to provide a glossary of terms at the end of the report. Thirdly, it is important that no one can be identified, whether that be the organisations who took part in the research or specific research participants. It is also important to make sure there is nothing defamatory to the organisation (or specific people) in the report. It may be that the results are not what the organisation wants to hear, and thus it is essential to write these results in a sensitive way (Brewerton & Millward, 2001).

Other issues to focus on include grammar, spelling and formatting consistency throughout the report. Frequent mistakes will cause the report to look unprofessional and will undermine the importance of the research findings. The report should be presented in an attractive way that is user friendly. Lastly, students should include a cover letter which thanks the organisation for their participation and which includes their contact details, in case the organisation has any further queries. Before sending the report, students should get final approval from their supervisor.

The organisational report should include an executive summary. An executive summary's purpose is similar to that of an abstract, yet its content may be quite different. The summary should precede the report and should spell out what was done; how, when and why it was done; who was involved; what was found; what the practical implications are; and what is recommended. The executive summary may also be used to provide feedback to those who actually completed the research (i.e., participants who completed surveys or who were involved in interviews) and therefore needs to be worded in a way that the 'average worker' can understand. This may mean that students need to write two separate executive summaries: one for the organisation and one for the participants. The report for participants should also include sections on the research background, methods, results, practical implications, recommendations and conclusions.

Conclusion

To conclude, there is a lot of literature on how to write a thesis, and this chapter aimed to extract the most relevant information. It has also addressed common problems and challenges that thesis students often face and suggested some ways to overcome these difficulties. An example of how to present research to organisations was also provided. This chapter has not attempted to be a 'how to write a thesis' guide. The publications listed under 'Further Readings' provide good practical advice on how to write a thesis.

Further readings

James, E. A., & Slater, T. (2014). *Writing your doctoral dissertation or thesis faster.* Thousand Oaks, CA: Sage.

Murray, R. (2011). *How to write a thesis* (3rd ed.). London, UK: McGraw-Hill Education.

Oliver, P. (2014). *Writing your thesis* (3rd ed.). Los Angeles, CA: Sage.

White, B. (2011). *Mapping your thesis: The comprehensive manual of theory and techniques for masters and doctoral research.* Camberwell, VIC: ACER Press.

References

Aghaee, N., & Hansson, H. (2013). Peer portal: Quality enhancement in thesis writing using self-managed peer review on a mass scale. *International Review of Research in Open and Distance Learning, 14*(1), 186–203. Retrieved from http://gateway.webofknowledge.com/gateway/Gateway.cgi?GWVersion=2&SrcApp=Summon&SrcAuth=ProQuest&DestApp=WOS&DestLinkType=FullRecord&UT=000322375400011

American Psychological Association. (2010). *Publication manual of the American Psychological Association* (6th ed.). Washington, DC: American Psychological Association.

Brewerton, P. M., & Millward, L. (2001). *Organizational research methods: A guide for students and researchers.* Thousand Oaks, CA: Sage. Retrieved from http://site.ebrary.com/lib/alltitles/docDetail.action?docID=10076726

Carter, S., Kelly, F., & Brailsford, I. (2012). *Structuring your research thesis.* New York, NY: Palgrave Macmillan.

Conrad, L. (2006). Countering isolation – joining the research community. In C. Denholm & T. Evans (Eds.), *Doctorates downunder: Keys to successful doctoral study in Australia and New Zealand* (pp. 34–40). Camberwell, VIC: ACER Press.

Ferguson, T. (2009). The "write" skills and more: A thesis writing group for doctoral students. *Journal of Geography in Higher Education, 33*(2), 285–297. http://doi.org/10.1080/03098260902734968

Hartley, J. (1997). Writing the thesis. In *Working for a Doctorate: A guide for the humanities and social sciences* (p. 96). Retrieved from https://books.google.co.nz/books?hl=en&lr=&id=vPg80Nftks8C&oi=fnd&pg=PA96&dq=writing+a+thesis&ots=4HmU0EO5PM&sig=UOYI-FzcEMtD-Pv3ZNL9oFB_XYY

Holtom, D., & Fisher, E. (1999). *Enjoy writing your science thesis or dissertation: A step by step guide to planning and writing dissertations and theses for undergraduate and graduate science students.* London, UK: Imperial College Press.

Jackson, D. (2013). Completing a PhD by publication: A review of Australian policy and implications for practice. *Higher Education Research and Development, 32*(3), 355–368. http://doi.org/10.1080/07294360.2012.692666

Joyner, R. L., Rouse, W. A., & Glatthorn, A. A. (2013). *Writing the winning thesis or dissertation: A step-by-step guide* (3rd ed.). Thousand Oaks, CA: Corwin Press.

Kumpulainen, K. (2008). *Thesis by publication.* University of Helsinki. Retrieved from https://skrif.hi.is/phd-supervision/files/2008/12/thesis_by_publication.pdf

Kwan, B. S. C. (2009). Reading in preparation for writing a PhD thesis: Case studies of experiences. *Journal of English for Academic Purposes, 8*(3), 180–191. http://doi.org/10.1016/j.jeap.2009.02.001

Massey University. (n.d). *PhD thesis by publication.* Massey University. Retrieved from www.massey.ac.nz/massey/fms/Research/Graduate%20Research%20School/Z_New%20PhD%20Forms/PhD%20Thesis%20by%20Publication%20Dec%202015.pdf?8EBB07C2B2D729878262EEB8B01685CD

McBride, R. S. (2009). Several books to read and thereby delay writing your thesis. *Fisheries, 34*(2), 80–82. Retrieved from http://gateway.webofknowledge.com/gateway/Gateway.cgi?GWVersion=2&SrcApp=Summon&SrcAuth=ProQuest&DestApp=WOS&DestLinkType=FullRecord&UT=000268524600011

Murray, R. (2011). *How to write a thesis* (3rd ed.). London, UK: McGraw-Hill Education.

Oliver, P. (2014). *Writing your thesis* (3rd ed.). Los Angeles, CA: Sage.

Robins, L., & Kanowski, P. (2008). PhD by publication: A student's perspective. *Journal of Research Practice, 4*(2), 1–20. Retrieved from http://search.ebscohost.com/login.aspx?direct=true&db=a9h&AN=37296301&site=ehost-live

Rountree, K., & Laing, P. (1996). *Writing by degrees: A practical guide to writing theses and research papers.* Auckland, NZ: Longman.

The University of Sydney. (2015). *FAQs on theses containing publications.* Retrieved May 15, 2016, from http://sydney.edu.au/stuserv/learning_centre/thesis_pub.shtml

White, B. (2011). *Mapping your thesis: The comprehensive manual of theory and techniques for masters and doctoral research.* Camberwell, VIC: ACER Press.

Index

Note: Page numbers in *italics* indicate figures, and page numbers in **bold** indicate tables on the corresponding pages.